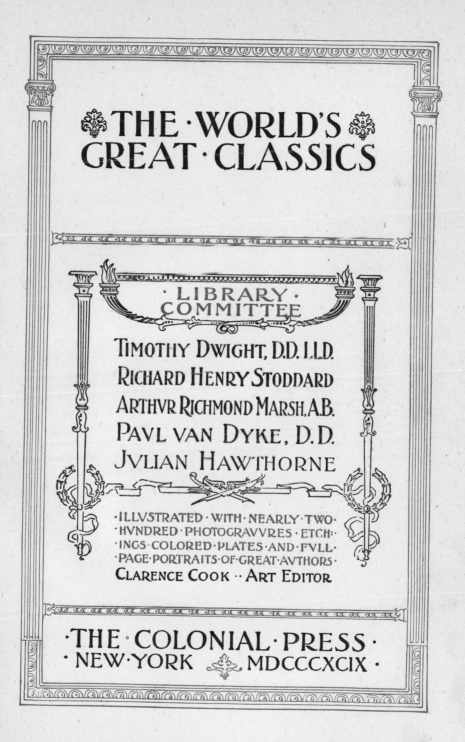

THE · WORLD'S · GREAT · CLASSICS

· LIBRARY · COMMITTEE

TIMOTHY DWIGHT, D.D. LL.D.

RICHARD HENRY STODDARD

ARTHVR RICHMOND MARSH, A.B.

PAVL VAN DYKE, D.D.

JVLIAN HAWTHORNE

· ILLVSTRATED · WITH · NEARLY · TWO ·
· HVNDRED · PHOTOGRAVVRES · ETCH ·
· INGS · COLORED · PLATES · AND · FVLL ·
· PAGE · PORTRAITS · OF · GREAT · AVTHORS ·

CLARENCE COOK ·· ART EDITOR

· THE · COLONIAL · PRESS ·
· NEW · YORK · MDCCCXCIX ·

JOHANN WOLFGANG VON GOETHE.

Photogravure from an oil painting by J. K. Stieler.

In personal appearance Goethe was impressive, rather than handsome. He had the bold, high brow that denotes intellect, and the strong, well-set features that are the outward signs of a firm character. The accompanying picture is the reproduction of a painting made when the author of " Faust " had passed the prime of life, and it is said to be the best likeness of him that is now existing. It is the face of a man who has seen life in all its beauty and ugliness, in all its pathos and sublimity. As in his writings there shines forth, now and then, a ray of the Great Thought that is beyond human ken, so in his countenance there is the reflected sadness of human experience, of human frailties and passions.

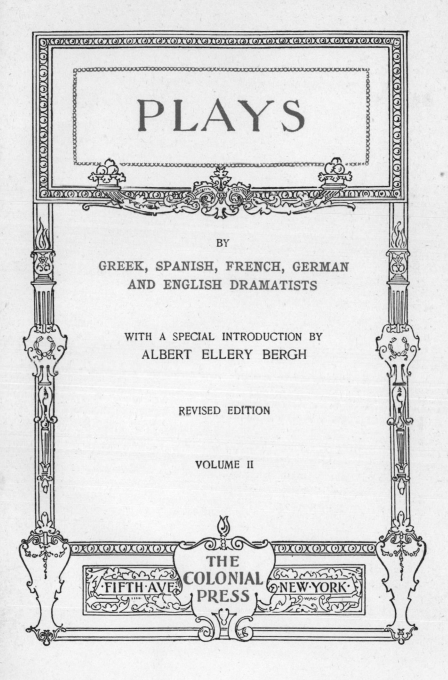

PLAYS

BY

GREEK, SPANISH, FRENCH, GERMAN
AND ENGLISH DRAMATISTS

WITH A SPECIAL INTRODUCTION BY
ALBERT ELLERY BERGH

REVISED EDITION

VOLUME II

THE
COLONIAL
PRESS

FIFTH AVE   NEW YORK

15160

CONTENTS

ILLUSTRATIONS

FAUST

—

BY

JOHANN WOLFGANG VON GOETHE

[Translated into English verse by James Stuart Blackie]

DRAMATIS PERSONÆ

FAUST.

WAGNER.

MEPHISTOPHELES.

FROSCH.

BRANDER.

SIEBEL.

VALENTIN.

ALTMAYER.

MARGARET.

MARTHA.

ELIZA.

Minor speaking characters include Students, Spirits, Women, Angels, Servants, Beggars, Soldiers, Peasants, Cat-Apes, Witches, Director of the Theatre, Leader of the Orchestra, Idealist, Realist, Sceptic, etc.

DEDICATION

Prefixed to the Later Editions of Faust.

Ye hover nigh, dim-floating shapes again,
That erst the misty eye of Fancy knew!
Shall I once more your shadowy flight detain,
And the fond dreamings of my youth pursue?
Ye press around!—resume your ancient reign—
As from the hazy past ye rise to view;
The magic breath that wafts your airy train
Stirs in my breast long-slumbering chords again.

Ye raise the pictured forms of happy days,
And many a dear loved shade comes up with you;
Like the far echo of old-memoried lays,
First love and early friendship ye renew.
Old pangs return; life's labyrinthine maze
Again the plaint of sorrow wanders through,
And names the loved ones who from Fate received
A bitter call, and left my heart bereaved.

They hear no more the sequel of my song,
Who heard my early chant with open ear;
Dispersed forever is the favoring throng,
Dumb the response from friend to friend so dear.
My sorrow floats an unknown crowd among,
Whose very praise comes mingled with strange fear;
And they who once were pleased to hear my lay,
If yet they live, have drifted far away.

And I recall with long-unfelt desire
The realm of spirits, solemn, still, serene;
My faltering lay, like the Æolian lyre,
Gives wavering tones with many a pause between;
The stern heart glows with youth's rekindled fire,
Tear follows tear, where long no tear hath been;
The thing I am fades into distance gray;
And the pale Past stands out a clear to-day.

PRELUDE AT THE THEATRE

MANAGER.—Ye twain, in good and evil day
    So oft my solace and my stay,
    Say, have ye heard sure word, or wandering rumor
    How our new scheme affects the public humor?
    Without the multitude we cannot thrive,
    Their maxim is to live and to let live.
    The posts are up, the planks are fastened, and
    Each man's agog for something gay and grand.
    With arched eyebrows they sit already there,
    Gaping for something new to make them stare.
    I know the public taste, and profit by it;
    But still to-day I've fears of our succeeding:
    'Tis true they're customed to no dainty diet,
    But they've gone through an awful breadth of reading.
    How shall we make our pieces fresh and new,
    And with some meaning in them, pleasing too?
    In sooth, I like to see the people pouring
    Into our booth, like storm and tempest roaring,
    While, as the waving impulse onward heaves them,
    The narrow gate of grace at length receives them,
    When, long ere it be dark, with lusty knocks
    They fight their way on to the money-box,
    And like a starving crowd around a baker's door,
    For tickets as for bread they roar.
    So wonder-working is the poet's sway
    O'er every heart—so may it work to-day!
POET.—O mention not that motley throng to me,
    Which only seen makes frighted genius pause;
    Hide from my view that wild and whirling sea
    That sucks me in, and deep and downward draws.
    No! let some noiseless nook of refuge be

My heaven, remote from boisterous rude applause,
Where Love and Friendship, as a God inspires,
Create and fan the pure heart's chastened fires.
Alas! what there the shaping thought did rear,
And scarce the trembling lip might lisping say,
To Nature's rounded type not always near,
The greedy moment rudely sweeps away.
Ofttimes a work, through many a patient year
Must toil to reach its finished fair display;
The glittering gaud may fix the passing gaze,
But the pure gem gains Time's enduring praise.

MERRYFELLOW.—Pshaw! Time will reap his own; but in our
        power
The moment lies, and we must use the hour.
The Future, no doubt, is the Present's heir,
But we who live must first enjoy our share.
Methinks the present of a goodly boy
Has something that the wisest might enjoy.
Whose ready lips with easy lightness brim,
The people's humor need not trouble him;
He courts a crowd the surer to impart
The quickening word that stirs the kindred heart.
Quit ye like men, be honest bards and true,
Let Fancy with her many-sounding chorus,
Reason, Sense, Feeling, Passion, move before us,
But, mark me well—a spice of folly too!

MANAGER.—Give what you please, so that you give but plenty;
They come to see, and you must feed their eyes;
Scene upon scene, each act may have its twenty,
To keep them gaping still in fresh surprise:
This is the royal road to public favor;
You snatch it thus, and it is yours forever.
A mass of things alone the mass secures;
Each comes at last and culls his own from yours.
Bring much, and every one is sure to find,
In your rich nosegay, something to his mind.
You give a piece, give it at once in pieces;
Such a ragout each taste and temper pleases,
And spares, if only they were wise to know it,
Much fruitless toil to player and to poet.

In vain into an artful whole you glue it;
The public in the long run will undo it.
POET.—What? feel you not the vileness of this trade?
How much the genuine artist ye degrade?
The bungling practice of our hasty school
You raise into a maxim and a rule.
MANAGER.—All very well!—but when a man
Has forged a scheme, and sketched a plan
He must have sense to use the tool
The best that for the job is fit.
Consider what soft wood you have to split,
And who the people are for whom you write.
One comes to kill a few hours o' the night;
Another, with his drowsy wits oppressed,
An over-sated banquet to digest;
And not a few, whom least of all we choose,
Come to the play from reading the " Reviews."
They drift to us as to a masquerade;
Mere curiosity wings their paces;
The ladies show themselves, and show their silks and
laces,
And play their parts well, though they are not paid.
What dream you of, on your poetic height?
A crowded house, forsooth, gives you delight!
Look at your patrons as you should,
You'll find them one-half cold, and one-half crude.
One leaves the play to spend the night
Upon a wench's breast in wild delight;
Another sets him down to cards, or calls
For rattling dice, or clicking billiard balls.
For such like hearers, and for ends like these
Why should a bard the gentle Muses tease?
I tell you, give them more, and ever more, and still
A little more, if you would prove your skill.
And since they can't discern the finer quality,
Confound them with broad sweep of triviality—
But what's the matter?—pain or ravishment?
POET.—If such your service, you must be content
With other servants who will take your pay!
Shall then the bard his noblest right betray?

The right of man, which Nature's gift imparts,
For brainless plaudits basely jest away?
What gives him power to move all hearts,
Each stubborn element to sway,
What but the harmony, his being's inmost tone,
That charms all feelings back into his own?
Where listless Nature, her eternal thread,
The unwilling spindle twists around,
And hostile shocks of things that will not wed
With jarring dissonance resound,
Who guides with living pulse the rhythmic flow
Of powers that make sweet music as they go?
Who consecrates each separate limb and soul
To beat in glorious concert with the whole?
Who makes the surgy-swelling billow
Heave with the wildly heaving breast,
And on the evening's rosy pillow,
Invites the brooding heart to rest?
Who scatters spring's most lovely blooms upon
The path of the belovèd one?
Who plaits the leaves that unregarded grow
Into a crown to deck the honored brow?
Who charms the gods? who makes Olympos yield?
The power of man in poet's art revealed.

MERRYFELLOW.—Then learn such subtle powers to wield,
And on the poet's business enter
As one does on a love-adventure.
They meet by chance, are pleased, and stay
On being pressed, just for a day;
Then hours to hours are sweetly linked in chain,
Till net-caught by degrees, they find retreat is vain.
At first the sky is bright, then darkly lowers;
To-day, fine thrilling rapture wings the hours,
To-morrow, doubts and anguish have their chance,
And, ere one knows, they're deep in a romance.
A play like this both praise and profit brings.
Plunge yourself boldly in the stream of things—
What's lived by all, but known to few—
And bring up something fresh and new,
No matter what; just use your eyes,

And all will praise what all can prize;
Strange motley pictures in a misty mirror,
A spark of truth in a thick cloud of error;
'Tis thus we brew the genuine beverage,
To edify and to refresh the age.
The bloom of youth in eager expectation,
With gaping ears drinks in your revelation;
Each tender sentimental disposition
Sucks from your art sweet woe-be-gone nutrition;
Each hears a part of what his own heart says,
While over all your quickening sceptre sways.
These younglings follow where you bid them go.
Lightly to laughter stirred, or turned to woe,
They love the show, and with an easy swing,
Follow the lordly wafture of your wing;
Your made-up man looks cold on everything,
But growing minds take in what makes them grow.

POET.—Then give me back the years again,
When mine own spirit too was growing,
When my whole being was a vein
Of thronging songs within me flowing!
Then slept the world in misty blue,
Each bud the nascent wonder cherished,
And all for me the flowerets grew,
That on each meadow richly flourished.
Though I had nothing then, I had a treasure,
The thirst for truth, and in illusion pleasure.
Give me the free, unshackled pinion,
The height of joy, the depth of pain,
Strong hate, and stronger love's dominion;
O give me back my youth again!

MERRYFELLOW.—The fire of youth, good friend, you need, of
course,
Into the hostile ranks to break,
Or, when the loveliest damsels hang by force,
With amorous clinging, from your neck,
When swift your wingèd steps advance
To where the racer's prize invites you,
Or, after hours of whirling dance,
The nightly deep carouse invites you.

But to awake the well-known lyre
With graceful touch that tempers fire,
And to a self-appointed goal,
With tuneful rambling on to roll,
Such are your duties, aged sirs; nor we
Less honor pay for this, nor stint your fee;
Old age, not childish, makes the old; but they
Are genuine children of a mellower day.

MANAGER.—Enough of words: 'tis time that we
Were come to deeds; while you are spinning
Fine airy phrases, fancy-free,
We might have made some good beginning.
What stuff you talk of being in the vein!
A lazy man is never in the vein.
If once your names are on the poet's roll,
The Muses should be under your control.
You know our want; a good stiff liquor
To make their creeping blood flow quicker;
Then brew the brews without delay;
What was not done to-day, to-morrow
Will leave undone for greater sorrow.
Don't stand, and stare, and block the way,
But with a firm, set purpose lay
Hold of your bright thoughts as they rise to view,
        And bid them stay;
Once caught, they will not lightly run away,
Till they have done what in them lies to do.

Among the sons of German play,
Each tries his hand at what he may;
Therefore be brilliant in your scenery,
And spare no cost on your machinery.
Let sun and moon be at your call,
And scatter stars on stars around;
Let water, fire, and rocky wall,
And bird and beast and fish abound.
Thus in your narrow booth mete forth
The wide creation's flaming girth,
And wing your progress, pondered well,
From heaven to earth, from earth to hell.

PROLOGUE IN HEAVEN

RAPHAEL.—The Sun doth chime his ancient music
    'Mid brothered spheres' contending song.
    And on his fore-appointed journey
    With pace of thunder rolls along.
    Strength drink the angels from his glory,
    Though none may throughly search his way:
    God's works rehearse their wondrous story
    As bright as on Creation's day.

GABRIEL.—And swift and swift beyond conceiving
    The pomp of earth is wheeled around,
    Alternating Elysian brightness
    With awful gloom of night profound.
    Up foams the sea, a surging river,
    And smites the steep rock's echoing base,
    And rock and sea, unwearied ever,
    Spin their eternal circling race.

MICHAEL.—And storm meets storm with rival greeting,
    From sea to land, from land to sea,
    While from their war a virtue floweth,
    That thrills with life all things that be.
    The lightning darts his fury, blazing
    Before the thunder's sounding way;
    But still thy servants, Lord, are praising
    The gentle going of thy day.

THE THREE.—Strength drink the angels from thy glory,
    Though none may search thy wondrous way;
    Thy works repeat their radiant story,
    As bright as on Creation's day.

MEPHISTOPHELES.—Sith thou, O Lord, approachest near,
    And how we fare wouldst fain have information,
    And thou of old wert glad to see me here,
    I stand to-day amid the courtly nation.

Pardon; no words of fine address I know,
Nor could, though all should hoot me down with sneers;
My pathos would move laughter, and not tears,
Wert thou not weaned from laughter long ago.
Of suns and worlds I've nought to say,
I only see how men must fret their lives away.
The little god o' the world jogs and jogs on, the same
As when from ruddy clay he took his name;
And, sooth to say, remains a riddle, just
As much as when you shaped him from the dust.
Perhaps a little better he had thriven,
Had he not got the show of glimmering light from
    heaven:
He calls it reason, and it makes him free
To be more brutish than a brute can be;
He is, methinks, with reverence of your grace,
Like one of the long-leggèd race
Of grasshoppers that leap in the air, and spring,
And straightway in the grass the same old song they
    sing;
'Twere well that from the grass he never rose,
On every stubble he must break his nose!
THE LORD.—Hast thou then nothing more to say?
And art thou here again to-day
To vent thy grudge in peevish spite
Against the earth, still finding nothing right?
MEPHISTOPHELES.—True, Lord; I find things there no better
    than before;
I must confess I do deplore
Man's hopeless case, and scarce have heart myself
To torture the poor miserable elf.
THE LORD.—Dost thou know Faust?
MEPHISTOPHELES.—   The Doctor?
THE LORD.—   Ay: my servant.
MEPHISTOPHELES.—Indeed! and of his master's will observant,
In fashion quite peculiar to himself;
His food and drink are of no earthly taste,
A restless fever drives him to the waste.
Himself half seems to understand
How his poor wits have run astrand;

From heaven he asks each loveliest star,
Earth's chiefest joy must jump to his demand,
And all that's near, and all that's far,
Soothes not his deep-moved spirit's war.

THE LORD.—Though for a time he blindly grope his way,
Soon will I lead him into open day;
Well knows the gardener, when green shoots appear,
That bloom and fruit await the ripening year.

MEPHISTOPHELES.—What wager you? you yet shall lose that
soul!
Only give me full license, and you'll see
How I shall lead him softly to my goal.

THE LORD.—As long as on the earth he lives
Thou hast my license full and free;
Man still must stumble while he strives.

MEPHISTOPHELES.—My thanks for that! the dead for me
Have little charm; my humor seeks
The bloom of lusty life, with plump and rosy cheeks;
For a vile corpse my tooth is far too nice,
I do just as the cat does with the mice.

THE LORD.—So be it; meanwhile, to tempt him thou are free;
Go, drag this spirit from his native fount,
And lead him on, canst thou his will surmount,
Into perdition down with thee;
But stand ashamed at last, when thou shalt see
An honest man, 'mid all his strivings dark,
Finds the right way, though lit but by a spark.

MEPHISTOPHELES.—Well, well; short time will show; into my
net
I'll draw the fish, and then I've won my bet;
And when I've carried through my measure
Loud blast of trump shall blaze my glory;
Dust shall he eat, and that with pleasure,
Like my cousin the snake in the rare old story.

THE LORD.—And thou mayst show thee here in upper sky
Unhindered, when thou hast a mind;
I never hated much thee or thy kind;
Of all the spirits that deny,
The clever rogue sins least against my mind.
For, in good sooth, the mortal generation,

When a soft pillow they may haply find,
Are far too apt to sink into stagnation;
And therefore man for comrade wisely gets
A devil, who spurs, and stimulates, and whets.
But you, ye sons of heaven's own choice,
In the one living Beautiful rejoice!
The self-evolving Energy divine
Enclasp you round with love's embrace benign,
And on the floating forms of earth and sky
Stamp the fair type of thought that may not die.

MEPHISTOPHELES.—From time to time the ancient gentleman
I see, and keep on the best terms I can.
In a great Lord 'tis surely wondrous civil
So face to face to hold talk with the devil.

FAUST

ACT FIRST

Scene I.—Night

Faust discovered sitting restless at his desk, in a narrow high-vaulted Gothic chamber.

FAUST.—There now, I've toiled my way quite through
Law, Medicine, and Philosophy,
And, to my sorrow, also thee,
Theology, with much ado;
And here I stand, poor human fool,
As wise as when I went to school.
Master, ay, Doctor, titled duly,
An urchin-brood of boys unruly
For ten slow-creeping years and mo,
Up and down, and to and fro,
I lead by the nose: and this I know,
That vain is all our boasted lore—
A thought that burns me to the core!
True, I am wiser than all their tribe,
Doctor, Master, Priest, and Scribe;
No scruples nor doubts in my bosom dwell,
I fear no devil, believe no hell;
But with my fear all joy is gone,
All rare conceit of wisdom won;
All dreams so fond, all faith so fair,
To make men better than they are.
Nor gold have I, nor gear, nor fame,
Station, or rank, or honored name,
Here like a kennelled cur I lie!
Therefore the magic art I'll try,

From spirit's might and mouth to draw,
Mayhap, some key to Nature's law;
That I no more, with solemn show,
May sweat to teach what I do not know;
That I may ken the bond that holds
The world, through all its mystic folds;
The hidden seeds of things explore,
And cheat my thought with words no more.
O might thou shine, thou full moon bright,
For the last time upon my woes,
Thou whom, by this brown desk alone,
So oft my wakeful eyes have known.
Then over books and paper rose
On me thy sad familiar light!
Oh, that beneath thy friendly ray,
On peaky summit I might stray,
Round mountain caves with spirits hover,
And flit the glimmering meadows over,
And from all fevered fumes of thinking free,
Bathe me to health within thy dewy sea.
In vain! still pines my prisoned soul
Within this curst dank dungeon-hole!
Where dimly finds ev'n heaven's blest ray,
Through painted glass, its struggling way.
Shut in by heaps of books up-piled,
All worm-begnawed and dust-besoiled,
With yellowed papers, from the ground
To the smoked ceiling, stuck around;
Caged in with old ancestral lumber,
Cases, boxes, without number,
Broken glass, and crazy chair,
Dust and brittleness everywhere;
This is thy world, a world for a man's soul to breathe in!
And ask I still why in my breast,
My heart beats heavy and oppressed?
And why some secret unknown sorrow
Freezes my blood, and numbs my marrow?
'Stead of the living sphere of Nature,
Where man was placed by his Creator,
Surrounds thee mouldering dust alone,
The grinning skull and skeleton.

Arise! forth to the fields, arise!
And this mysterious magic page,
From Nostradamus' hand so sage,
Should guide thee well. Thy raptured eyes
Shall then behold what force compels
The tuneful spheres to chime together;
When, taught by Nature's mightiest spells,
Thine innate spring of soul upwells,
As speaks one spirit to another.
In vain my thought gropes blindly here,
To make those sacred symbols clear;
Ye unseen Powers that hover near me,
Answer, I charge ye, when ye hear me!

[He opens the book, and sees the sign of the Macrocosm.

Ha! what ecstatic joy this page reveals,
At once through all my thrilling senses flowing!
Young holy zest of life my spirit feels
In every vein, in every nerve, new glowing!
Was it a God whose finger drew these signs,
That, with mild pulse of joy, and breath of rest,
Smooth the tumultuous heaving of my breast,
And with mysterious virtue spread the lines
Of Nature's cipher bare to mortal sight?
Am I a God? so wondrous pure the light
Within me! in these tokens I behold
The powers by which all Nature is besouled.
Now may I reach the sage's words aright;
"The world of spirits is not barred;
Thy sense is shut, thy heart is dead!
Up, scholars, bathe your hearts so hard,
In the fresh dew of morning's red!"

[He scans carefully the sign.

How mingles here in one the soul with soul,
And lives each portion in the living whole!
How heavenly Powers, ascending and descending,
From hand to hand their golden ewers are lending,
And bliss-exhaling swing from pole to pole!
From the high welkin to earth's centre bounding,
Harmonious all through the great All resounding!
What wondrous show! but ah! 'tis but a show!
Where grasp I thee, thou infinite Nature, where?

And you, ye teeming breasts? ye founts whence flow
All living influences fresh and fair?
Whereon the heavens and earth dependent hang,
Where seeks relief the withered bosom's pang?
Your founts still well, and I must pine in vain!

[*He turns the book over impatiently, and beholds the sign of
the Spirit of the Earth.*

What different working hath this sign?
Thou Spirit of the Earth, I feel thee nearer;
Already sees my strengthened spirit clearer;
I glow as I had drunk new wine.
New strength I feel to plunge into the strife,
And bear the woes and share the joys of life,
Buffet the blasts, and where the wild waves dash,
Look calmly on the shipwreck's fearful crash!
Clouds hover o'er me—
The moon is dim!
The lamp's flame wanes!
It smokes!—Red beams dart forth
Around my head—and from the vaulted roof
Falls a cold shudder down,
And grips me!—I feel
Thou hover'st near me, conjured Spirit, now;
Reveal thee!
Ha! how swells with wild delight
My bursting heart!
And feelings, strange and new,
At once through all my ravished senses dart!
I feel my inmost soul made thrall to thee!
Thou must! thou must! and were my life the fee!

[*He seizes the book, and pronounces with a mysterious air the
sign of the Spirit. A red flame darts forth, and the
Spirit appears in the flame.*

SPIRIT.—Who calls me?

FAUST [*turning away*].—Vision of affright!

SPIRIT.—Thou hast with mighty spell invoked me,
And to obey thy call provoked me,
And now——

FAUST.—   Hence from my sight!

SPIRIT.—Thy panting prayer besought my might to view,
To hear my voice, and know my semblance too;

Now bending from my native sphere to please thee,
Here am I!—ha! what pitiful terrors seize thee,
And overman thee quite! where now the call
Of that proud soul, that scorned to own the thrall
Of earth, a world within itself created,
And bore and cherished? that with its fellows sated
Swelled with prophetic joy to leave its sphere,
And live a spirit with spirits, their rightful peer.
Where art thou, Faust? whose invocation rung
Upon mine ear, whose powers all round me clung?
Art thou that Faust? whom melts my breath away,
Trembling even to the life-depths of thy frame,
Like a poor worm that crawls into his clay!

FAUST.—Shall I then yield to thee, thou thing of flame?
I am that Faust, and Spirit is my name!

SPIRIT.—   Where life's floods flow
        And its tempests rave,
        Up and down I wave,
        Flit I to and fro!
        Birth and the grave,
        Life's hidden glow,
        A shifting motion,
        A boundless ocean
        Whose waters heave
          Eternally;
Thus on the sounding loom of Time I weave
    The living·mantle of the Deity.

FAUST.—Thou who round the wide world wendest,
Thou busy Spirit, how near I feel to thee!

SPIRIT.—Thou'rt like the spirit whom thou comprehendest,
Not me!   [*Vanishes.*

FAUST.—Not thee!
Whom, then?
I, image of the Godhead,
Dwarfed by thee!   [*Knocking is heard.*
O death!—'tis Wagner's knock—I know it well,
My famulus; he comes to mar the spell!
Woe's me that such bright vision of the spheres
Must vanish when this pedant-slave appears!

Scene II.

Enter Wagner in night-gown and nightcap; a lamp in his hand.

WAGNER.—Your pardon, sir, I heard your voice declaiming,
　　　No doubt some old Greek drama, and I came in,
　　　To profit by your learned recitation;
　　　For in these days the art of declamation
　　　Is held in highest estimation;
　　　And I have heard asserted that a preacher
　　　Might wisely have an actor for his teacher.
FAUST.—Yes; when our parsons preach to make grimaces,
　　　As here and there a not uncommon case is.
WAGNER.—Alack! when a poor wight is so confined
　　　Amid his books, shut up from all mankind,
　　　And sees the world scarce on a holiday,
　　　As through a telescope and far away,
　　　How may he hope, with nicely tempered skill,
　　　To bend the hearts he knows not to his will?
FAUST.—What you don't feel, you'll hunt to find in vain.
　　　It must gush from the soul, possess the brain,
　　　And with an instinct kindly force compel
　　　All captive hearts to own the grateful spell;
　　　Go to! sit o'er your books, and snip and glue
　　　Your wretched piece-work, dressing your ragout
　　　From others' feasts, your piteous flames still blowing
　　　From sparks beneath dull heaps of ashes glowing;
　　　Vain wonderment of children and of apes,
　　　If with such paltry meed content thou art;
　　　The human heart to heart he only shapes,
　　　Whose words flow warm from human heart to heart.
WAGNER.—   But the delivery is a chief concern
　　　In Rhetoric; and alas! here I have much to learn.
FAUST.—   Be thine to seek the honest gain,
　　　　　No shallow-tinkling fool!
　　　　Sound sense finds utterance for itself,
　　　　　Without the critic's rule.
　　　If clear your thought, and your intention true,
　　　What need to hunt for words with much ado?

The trim orations your fine speaker weaves,
Crisping light shreds of thought for shallow minds,
Are unrefreshing as the foggy winds
That whistle through the sapless autumn leaves.

WAGNER.— Alas! how long is art,
And human life how short!
I feel at times with all my learned pains,
As if a weight of lead were at my heart,
And palsy on my brains.
How high to climb up learning's lofty stair,
How hard to find the helps that guide us there;
And when scarce half the way behind him lies,
His glass is run, and the poor devil dies!

FAUST.—The parchment-roll is that the holy river,
From which one draught shall slake the thirst forever?
The quickening power of science only he
Can know, from whose own soul it gushes free.

WAGNER.— And yet the spirit of a bygone age,
To re-create may well the wise engage;
To know the choicest thoughts of every ancient sage,
And think how far above their best we've mounted high!

FAUST.— O yes, I trow, even to the stars, so high!
My friend, the ages that are past
Are us a book with seven seals made fast;
And what men call the spirit of the age,
Is but the spirit of the gentlemen
Who glass their own thoughts in the pliant page,
And image back themselves. O, then,
What precious stuff they dish, and call't a book,
Your stomach turns at the first look;
A heap of rubbish, and a lumber room,
At best some great state farce with proclamations,
Pragmatic maxims, protocols, orations,
Such as from puppet-mouths do fitly come!

WAGNER.—But then the world!—the human heart and mind!
Somewhat of this to know are all inclined.

FAUST.—Yes! as such knowledge goes! but what man dares
To call the child by the true name it bears?
The noble few that something better knew,
And to the gross reach of the general view,

Their finer feelings bared, and insight true,
From oldest times were burnt and crucified.
I do beseech thee, friend—'tis getting late,
'Twere wise to put an end to our debate.
WAGNER.—Such learned talk to draw through all the night
With Doctor Faust were my supreme delight;
But on the morrow, being Easter, I
Your patience with some questions more may try.
With zeal I've followed Learning's lofty call,
Much I have learned, but fain would master all.

[*Exit.*

Scene III.

FAUST [*alone*].—Strange how his pate alone hope never leaves,
Who still to shallow husks of learning cleaves!
With greedy hand who digs for hidden treasure,
And, when he finds a grub, rejoiceth above measure!
Durst such a mortal voice usurp mine ear
When all the spirit-world was floating near?
Yet, for this once, my thanks are free,
Thou meanest of earth's sons, to thee!
Thy presence drew me back from sheer despair,
And shock too keen for mortal nerve to bear;
Alas! so giant-great the vision came,
That I might feel me dwarf, ev'n as I am.
I, God's own image that already seemed
To gaze where Truth's eternal mirror gleamed,
And, clean divested of this cumbering clay,
Basked in the bliss of heaven's vivific ray;
I, more than cherub, with fresh pulses glowing,
Who well-nigh seemed through Nature's deep veins
    flowing
Like a pure god, creative virtue knowing,
What sharp reproof my hot presumption found!
One word of thunder smote me to the ground.
Alas! 'tis true! not I with thee and thine
May dare to cope! the strength indeed was mine
To make thee own my call, but not
To chain thee to the charmèd spot.

When that blest rapture thrilled my frame,
I felt myself so small, so great;
But thou didst spurn me back with shame,
Into this crazy human state.
Where find I aid? what follow? what eschew?
Shall I that impulse of my soul obey?
Alas! alas! but I must feel it true,
The pains we suffer and the deeds we do,
Are clogs alike in the free spirit's way.
The godlike essence of our heaven-born powers
Must yield to strange and still more strange intrusion;
Soon as the good things of this world are ours,
We deem our nobler self a vain illusion,
And heaven-born instincts—very life of life—
Are strangled in the low terrestrial strife.
Young fancy, that once soared with flight sublime,
On venturous vans, ev'n to th' Eternal's throne,
Now schools her down a little space to own,
When in the dark engulfing stream of time,
Our fair-faced pleasures perish one by one.
Care nestles deep in every heart,
And, cradling there the secret smart,
Rocks to and fro, and peace and joy are gone.
What though new masks she still may wear,
Wealth, house and hall, with acres rich and rare,
As wife or child appear she, water, flame,
Dagger, or poison, she is still the same;
And still we fear the ill which happens never,
And what we lose not are bewailing ever.
Alas! alas! too deep 'tis felt! too deep!
With gods may vie no son of mortal clay;
More am I like to worms that crawl and creep,
And dig, and dig through earth their lightless way,
Which, while they feed on dust in narrow room,
Find from the wanderer's foot their death-blow and their
         tomb.
Is it not dust that this old wall
From all its musty benches shows me?
And dust the trifling trumperies all
That in this world of moths enclose me?

Here is it that I hope to find
Wherewith to sate my craving mind?
Need I spell out page after page,
To know that men in every age
And every clime, have spurred in vain
The jaded muscle and the tortured brain,
And here and there, with centuries between,
One happy man belike hath been?
Thou grinning skull, what wouldst thou say,
Save that thy brain, in chase of truth, like mine,
With patient toil pursued its floundering way
By glimmering lights that through dim twilight shine?
Ye instruments, in sooth, now laugh at me,
With wheel, and cog-wheel, ring, and cylinder;
At Nature's door I stood; ye should have been the key,
But though your ward be good, the bolt ye cannot stir.
Mysterious Nature may not choose
To unveil her secrets to the stare of day,
And what from the mind's eye she stores away,
Thou canst not force from her with levers and with
        screws.
Thou antique gear, why dost thou cumber
My chamber with thy useless lumber?
My father housed thee on this spot,
And I must keep thee, though I need thee not!
Thou parchment roll that hast been smoked upon
Long as around this desk the sorry lamp-light shone;
Much better had I spent my little gear,
Than with this little to sit mouldering here;
Why should a man possess ancestral treasures,
But by possession to enlarge his pleasures?
The thing we use not a dead burden lies,
But what the moment brings the wise man knows to
        prize.
But what is this? there in the corner; why
Does that flask play the magnet to mine eye?
And why within me does this strange light shine,
As the soft nightly moon through groves of sombre pine?
I greet thee, matchless phial; and with devotion
I take thee down, and in thy mellow potion

I reverence human wit and human skill.
Fine essence of the opiate dew of sleep,
Dear extract of all subtle powers that kill,
Be mine the first-fruits of thy strength to reap!
I look on thee, and soothed is my heart's pain;
I grasp thee, straight is lulled my racking brain,
And wave by wave my soul's flood ebbs away.
I see wide ocean's swell invite my wistful eyes,
And at my feet her sparkling mirror lies;
To brighter shores invites a brighter day.
A car of fire comes hovering o'er my head,
With gentle wafture; now let me pursue
New flight adventurous, through the starry blue,
And be my wingèd steps unburdened sped
To spheres of uncramped energy divine!
And may indeed this life of gods be mine,
But now a worm, and cased in mortal clay?
Yes! only let strong will high thought obey,
To turn thy back on the blest light of day,
And open burst the portals which by most
With fear, that fain would pass them by, are crossed.
Now is the time by deeds, not words, to prove
That earth-born man yields not to gods above.
Before that gloomy cavern not to tremble,
Where all those spectral shapes of dread assemble,
Which Fancy, slave of every childish fear,
Bids, to the torment of herself, appear;
Forward to strive unto that passage dire,
Whose narrow mouth seems fenced with hell's collected
    fire;
With glad resolve this leap to make, even though
That thing we call our soul should into nothing flow!
Now come thou forth! thou crystal goblet clear,
From out thy worshipful old case,
Where thou hast lain unused this many a year.
In days of yore right gayly didst thou grace
The festive meetings of my gray-beard sires,
When passed from hand to hand the draught that glee
    inspires.
Thy goodly round, the figures there

Pictured with skill so quaint and rare,
Each lusty drinker's duty to declare
In ready rhyme what meaning they might bear,
And at one draught to drain the brimming cup—
All this recalls full many a youthful night.
Now to no comrade shall I yield thee up,
Nor whet my wit upon thy pictures bright;
Here is a juice intoxicates the soul
Quickly.   With dark brown flood it crowns the bowl.
Let this last draught, my mingling and my choice,
With blithesome heart be quaffed, and joyful voice,
A solemn greeting to the rising morn!
    [*A sound of bells is heard, and distant choir-singing.*

CHOIR OF ANGELS.—Christ is arisen!
        Joy be to mortal man,
        Whom, since the world began,
        Evils inherited,
        By his sins merited,
        Through his veins creeping,
        Sin-bound are keeping.

FAUST.—What sweet soft peals, what notes, so clear and pure,
Draw from my lips the glass perforce away?
Thus early do the bells their homage pay,
Of holy hymning to new Easter day!
Already sing the choirs the soothing song
That erst, round the dark grave, an angel throng
Sang, to proclaim the great salvation sure!

CHOIR OF WOMEN.—With spices and balsams
        All sweetly we bathed Him;
        With cloths of fine linen
        All cleanly we swathed Him;
        In the tomb of the rock, where
        His body was lain,
        We come, and we seek
        Our loved Master, in vain!

CHOIR OF ANGELS.—Christ is arisen!
        Praised be His name!
        Whose love shared with sinners
        Their sorrow and shame;

Who bore the hard trial
Of self-denial,
And, victorious, ascends to the skies whence
He came.

FAUST.—What seek ye here, ye gently-swaying tones,
Sweet seraph-music 'mid a mortal's groans?
Soft-natured men may own that soothing chaunt;
I hear the message, but the faith I want.
For still the child to Faith most dear
Was Miracle: nor I may vaunt
To mount, and mingle with the sphere
Whence such fair news floats down to mortal ear.
And yet, with youthful memories fraught, this strain
Hath power to call me back to life again.
A time there was when Heaven's own kiss,
On solemn Sabbath, seemed to fall on me,
The minister-bell boomed forth no human bliss,
And prayer to God was burning ecstasy.
A dim desire of inarticulate good
Drove me o'er hill and dale, through wold and wood,
And, while hot tears streamed from mine eyes,
I felt a world within me rise.
This hymn proclaimed the sports of youthful days,
And merry-makings when the spring began;
Now Memory's potent spell my spirit sways,
And thoughts of childhood rule the full-grown man.
O! sound thou on, thou sweet celestial strain,
The tear doth gush, Earth claims her truant son again!

CHOIR OF THE DISCIPLES.—By death untimely, though
Laid in the lowly grave,
Soars He sublimely now
Whence He came us to save.
He on His Father's breast,
Fountain of life and light;
We on the earth oppressed,
Groping through cloudy night;
Comfortless left are we,
Toiling through life's annoy,
Weeping to envy thee,
Master, thy joy!

CHOIR OF ANGELS.—Christ is risen
                  From Death's corrupting thrall,
                  Break from your prison
                  And follow His call!
                  Praising by deeds of love
                  Him who now reigns above,
                  Feeding the brethren poor,
                  Preaching salvation sure,
                  Joys that shall aye endure,
                  Knowing nor doubt nor fear,
                  While He is near.

ACT SECOND

Scene I.—Before the Gate of the Town

Motley groups of people crowding out to walk.

SOME JOURNEYMEN.—Brethren, whither bound?

OTHERS.—To the Jægerhaus.

THE FIRST.—   We to the mill.

A JOURNEYMAN.—At Wasserhof best cheer is to be found.

A SECOND.—But then the road is not agreeable.

THE OTHERS.—And what dost thou?

A THIRD.—   I go where others go.

A FOURTH.—Let's go to Burgdorf; there you'll find, I know,
    The best of beer, and maidens to your mind,
    And roaring frolics too, if that's your kind.

A FIFTH.—   Thou over-wanton losel, thou!
    Dost itch again for some new row?
    I loathe the place; and who goes thither,
    He and I don't go together.

A SERVANT GIRL.—No! no! back to the town I'd rather fare.

ANOTHER.—We're sure to find him 'neath the poplars there.

THE FIRST.—No mighty matter that for me,
    Since he will walk with none but thee,
    In every dance, too, he is thine:
    What have thy joys to do with mine?

THE OTHER.—To-day he'll not come single; sure he said
    That he would bring with him the curly-head.

STUDENT.—Blitz, how the buxom wenches do their paces!
    Come, let us make acquaintance with their faces.
    A stiff tobacco, and a good strong beer,
    And a fine girl well-rigged, that's the true Burschen
      cheer!

BURGHERS' DAUGHTERS.—Look only at those spruce young fel-
 lows there!
In sooth, 'tis more than one can bear;
The best society have they, if they please,
And run after such low bred queans as these!

SECOND STUDENT [*to the first*].—Not quite so fast; there
 comes a pair behind,
So smug and trim, so blithe and debonair;
And one is my fair neighbor, I declare;
She is a girl quite to my mind.
They pass along so proper and so shy,
And yet they'll take us with them by and by.

FIRST STUDENT.—No, no! these girls with nice conceits they
 bore you,
Have at the open game that lies before you!
The hand that plies the busy broom on Monday,
Caressed her love the sweetest on the Sunday.

A BURGHER.—No! this new burgomaster don't please me,
Now that he's made, his pride mounts high and higher;
And for the town, say, what does he?
Are we not deep and deeper in the mire?
In strictness day by day he waxes,
And more than ever lays on taxes.

A BEGGAR [*singing*].—Ye gentle sirs, and ladies fair,
With clothes so fine, and cheeks so red,
O pass not by, but from your eye
Be pity's gracious virtue shed!
Let me not harp in vain; for blest
Is he alone who gives away;
And may this merry Easter-feast
Be for the poor no fasting day!

ANOTHER BURGHER.—Upon a Sunday or a holiday,
No better talk I know than war and warlike rumors,
When in Turkey far away,
The nations fight out their ill humors.
We sit i' the window, sip our glass at ease,
And see how down the stream the gay ships gently glide;
Then wend us safely home at even-tide,
Blessing our stars we live in times of peace.

THIRD BURGHER.—Yea, neighbor, there you speak right wisely;
Ev'n so do I opine precisely.

They may split their skulls, they may,
And turn the world upside down,
So long as we, in our good town,
Keep jogging in the good old way.

OLD WOMAN [*to the Burghers' Daughters*].—Hey-day, how
fine! these be of gentle stuff,
The eyes that would not look on you are blind.
Only not quite so high! 'Tis well enough—
And what you wish I think I know to find.

FIRST BURGHER'S DAUGHTER.—Agatha, come! I choose not
to be seen
With such old hags upon the public green;
Though on St. Andrew's night she let me see
My future lover bodily.

SECOND BURGHER'S DAUGHTER.—Mine too, bold, soldier-like,
she made to pass,
With his wild mates, before me in a glass;
I hunt him out from place to place,
But nowhere yet he shows his face.

SOLDIERS.—   Castles and turrets
And battlements high,
Maids with proud spirits,
And looks that defy!
From the red throat of death,
With the spear and the glave,
We pluck the ripe glory
That blooms for the brave.
The trumpet invites him,
With soul-stirring call,
To where joy delights him,
Nor terrors appall.
On storming maintains he
Triumphant the field,
Strong fortresses gains he,
Proud maidens must yield.
Thus carries the soldier
The prize of the day,
And merrily, merrily
Dashes away!

Scene II.

Enter Faust and Wagner.

FAUST.—The ice is now melted from stream and brook
By the Spring's genial life-giving look;
Forth smiles young Hope in the greening vale,
And ancient Winter, feeble and frail,
Creeps cowering back to the mountains gray;
And thence he sends, as he hies him away,
Fitfullest brushes of icy hail,
Sweeping the plain in his harmless flight.
But the sun may brook no white,
Everywhere stirs he the vegetive strife,
Flushing the fields with the glow of life;
But since few flowers yet deck the mead
He takes him gay-dressed folk in their stead.
Now from these heights I turn me back
To view the city's busy track.
Through the dark, deep-throated gate
They are pouring and spreading in motley array.
All sun themselves so blithe to-day.
The Lord's resurrection they celebrate,
For that themselves to life are arisen.
From lowly dwellings' murky prison,
From labor and business' fetters tight,
From the press of gables and roofs that meet
Over the squeezing narrow street,
From the churches' solemn night
Have they all been brought to the light.
Lo! how nimbly the multitude
Through the fields and the gardens hurry
How, in its breadth and length, the flood
Wafts onward many a gleesome wherry,
And this last skiff moves from the brink
So laden that it seems to sink.
Ev'n from the far hills' winding way
I' the sunshine glitter their garments gay.
I hear the hamlet's noisy mirth;
Here is the people's heaven on earth,
And great and small rejoice to-day.

Here may I be a man, here dare
The joys of men with men to share.
WAGNER.—With you, Herr Doctor, one is proud to walk,
Sharing your fame, improving by your talk;
But, for myself, I shun the multitude,
Being a foe to everything that's rude.
I may not brook their senseless howling,
Their fiddling, screaming, ninepin bowling;
Like men possessed, they rave along,
And call it joy, and call it song.

Scene III.

PEASANTS [*beneath a lime-tree*].—The shepherd for the dance
was dressed,
With ribbon, wreath, and spotted vest,
Right sprucely he did show.
And round and round the linden-tree
All danced as mad as mad could be.
Juchhe, juchhe!
Juchheisa, heisa, he!
So went the fiddle bow.

Then with a jerk he wheeled him by,
And on a maiden that stood nigh
He with his elbow came.
Quick turned the wench, and, " Sir," quoth she,
" Such game is rather rough for me."
Juchhe, juchhe!
Juchheisa, heisa, he!
" For shame, I say, for shame!"

Yet merrily went it round and round,
And right and left they swept the ground,
And coat and kirtle flew;
And they grew red, and they grew warm,
And, panting, rested arm in arm;
Juchhe, juchhe!
Juchheisa, heisa, he!
And hips on elbows too.

And " Softly, softly," quoth the quean,
" How many a bride hath cheated been
   By men as fair as you ! "
But he spoke a word in her ear aside,
And from the tree it shouted wide
     Juchhe, juchhe !
    Juchheisa, heisa, he !
   With fife and fiddle too.

AN OLD PEASANT.—Herr Doctor, 'tis most kind in you,
   And all here prize the boon, I'm sure,
   That one so learned should condescend
   To share the pastimes of the poor.
   Here, take this pitcher, filled ev'n now
   With cooling water from the spring.
   May God with grace to slake your thirst,
   Bless the libation that we bring ;
   Be every drop a day to increase
   Your years in happiness and peace !
FAUST.—Your welcome offering I receive ; the draught
   By kind hands given, with grateful heart be quaffed !
           [The people collect round him in a circle.
OLD PEASANT.—Soothly, Herr Doctor, on this tide,
   Your grace and kindness passes praise ;
   Good cause had we whilom to bless
   The name of Faust in evil days.
   Here stand there not a few whose lives
   Your father's pious care attest,
   Saved from fell fever's rage, when he
   Set limits to the deadly pest.
   You were a young man then, and went
   From hospital to hospital ;
   Full many a corpse they bore away,
   But you came scatheless back from all ;
   Full many a test severe you stood
   Helping helped by the Father of Good.
ALL THE PEASANTS.—Long may the man who saved us live,
   His aid in future need to give !
FAUST.—Give thanks to Him above, who made
   The hand that helped you strong to aid.
           [He goes on farther with Wagner.

WAGNER.—How proud must thou not feel, most learnèd man,
 To hear the praises of this multitude;
 Thrice happy he who from his talents can
 Reap such fair harvest of untainted good!
 The father shows you to his son,
 And all in crowds to see you run;
 The dancers cease their giddy round,
 The fiddle stops its gleesome sound;
 They form a ring where'er you go,
 And in the air their caps they throw;
 A little more, and they would bend the knee,
 As if the Holy Host came by in thee!

FAUST.—Yet a few paces, till we reach yon stone,
 And there our wearied strength we may repair.
 Here oft I sat in moody thought alone,
 And vexed my soul with fasting and with prayer.
 Rich then in hope, in faith then strong,
 With tears and sobs my hands I wrung,
 And weened the end of that dire pest,
 From heaven's high-counselled lord to wrest.
 Now their applause with mockery flouts mine ear.
 O couldst thou ope my heart and read it here,
 How little sire and son
 For such huge meed of thanks have done!
 My father was a grave old gentleman,
 Who o'er the holy secrets of creation,
 Sincere, but after his peculiar plan,
 Brooded, with whimsied speculation.
 Who, with adepts in painful gropings spent
 His days, within the smoky kitchen pent,
 And, after recipes unnumbered, made
 The unnatural mixtures of his trade.
 The tender lily and the lion red,
 A suitor bold, in tepid bath were wed,
 With open fiery flame well baked together,
 And squeezed from one bride-chamber to another;
 Then, when the glass the queen discovered,
 Arrayed in youthful glistening pride,
 Here was the medicine, and the patient died,
 But no one questioned who recovered.

Thus in these peaceful vales and hills,
The plague was not the worst of ills,
And Death his ghastly work pursued,
The better for the hellish brews we brewed.
Myself to thousands the curst juice supplied;
They pined away, and I must live to hear
The praise of mercy in the murderer's ear.

WAGNER.—How can you with such whims be grieved?
Surely a good man does his part
With scrupulous care to use the art
Which from his father he received.
When we, in youth, place on our sire reliance,
He opes to us his stores of information;
When we, as men, extend the bounds of science,
Our sons build higher upon our foundation.

FAUST.—O happy he who yet hath hope to float
Above this sea of crude distempered thought!
What we know not is what we need to know,
And what we know, we might as well let go;
But cease; cheat not the moment of its right
By curious care and envious repining;
Behold how fair, in evening's mellow light,
The green-embosomed cottages are shining.
The sun slants down, the day hath lived his date,
But on he hies to tend another sphere.
O that no wing upon my wish may wait
To follow still and still in his career!
Upborne on evening's quenchless beams to greet
The noiseless world illumined at my feet,
Each peaceful vale, each crimson-flaming peak,
Each silver rill whose tinkling waters seek
The golden flood that feeds the fruitful plain.
Then savage crags, and gorges dark, would rein
My proud careering course in vain;
Ev'n now the sea spreads out its shimmering bays,
And charms the sense with ectasy of gaze.
Yet seems the god at length to sink;
But, borne by this new impulse of my mind,
I hasten on, his quenchless ray to drink,
The day before me, and the night behind,

The heavens above me, under me the sea.
A lovely dream! meanwhile the god is gone.
Alas! the soul, in wingèd fancy free,
Seeks for a corporal wing, and findeth none.
Yet in each breast 'tis deeply graven,
Upward and onward still to pant,
When over us, lost in the blue of heaven,
Her quavering song the lark doth chant;
When over piney peaks sublime
The eagle soars with easy strain,
And over lands and seas the crane
Steers homeward to a sunnier clime.

WAGNER.—I too have had my hours of whim,
But feeling here runs over reason's brim.
Forest and field soon tire the eye to scan,
And eagle's wings were never made for man.
How otherwise the mind and its delights!
From book to book, from page to page, we go.
Thus sweeten we the dreary winter nights,
Till every limb with new life is aglow;
And chance we but unroll some rare old parchment scroll,
All heaven stoops down, and finds a lodgment in the soul.

FAUST.—Thou know'st but the one impulse—it is well!
Tempt not the yearning that divides the heart.
Two souls, alas! within my bosom dwell!
This strives from that with adverse strain to part.
The one, bound fast by stubborn might of love,
To this low earth with grappling organs clings;
The other spurns the clod, and soars on wings
To join a nobler ancestry above.
Oh! be there spirits in the air,
'Twixt earth and heaven that float with potent sway,
Drop from your sphere of golden-glowing day,
And waft me hence new varied life to share!
Might I but own a mantle's fold enchanted,
To climes remote to bear me on its wing,
More than the costliest raiment I should vaunt it,
More than the purple robe that clothes a king.

WAGNER.—Invoke not rash the well-known spirit-throng,
That stream unseen the atmosphere along,

And dangers thousandfold prepare,
Weak men from every quarter to ensnare.
From the keen north in troops they float,
With sharpest teeth and arrow-pointed tongues;
From the harsh east they bring a blasting drought,
And feed with wasting greed upon thy lungs.
When from the arid south their sultry powers
They send, hot fires upheaping on thy crown,
The West brings forth his swarms with cooling showers,
To end in floods that sweep thy harvests down.
Quick-ear'd are they, on wanton mischief bent,
And work our will with surer bait to ply us;
They show as fair as heaven's own couriers sent,
And lisp like angels when they most belie us.
But let us hence! the air is chill,
The cold gray mists are creeping down the hill,
Now is the time to seek the bright fireside.
Why standest thou with strange eyes opened wide?
What twilight-spectre may thy fancy trouble?

FAUST.—See'st thou that swarthy dog sweeping through corn
        and stubble?

WAGNER.—I saw him long ago—not strange he seemed to me.

FAUST.—Look at him well—what should the creature be?

WAGNER.—He seems a poodle who employs his snout
        Now here, now there, to snuff his master out.

FAUST.—Dost thou not see how nigher still and nigher
        His spiral circles round us wind?
        And, err I not, he leaves behind
        His track a train of sparkling fire.

WAGNER.—A small black poodle is all I see;
        Surely some strange delusion blinds thee!

FAUST.—Methinks soft magic circles winds he,
        About, about, a snare for thee and me.

WAGNER.—I see him only doubtful springing round,
        Having two strangers for his master found.

FAUST.—He draws him closer—now he comes quite near!

WAGNER.—A dog, be sure, and not a ghost, is here.
        He growls, and looks about in fear,
        And crouches down, and looks to you,
        And wags his tail—what any dog will do.

FAUST.—Come hither, poodle!

WAGNER.—   'Tis a drollish brute;
    When you stand still, then stands he mute,
    But when you speak, he springs as he would speak to
        you;
    He will bring back what you let fall,
    And fetch your stick out of the water.

FAUST.—You are quite right. There's no such matter.
    No trace of ghost—a dog well trained, that's all!

WAGNER.—A well-trained dog may well engage
    The favor of a man most sage;
    This poodle well deserves your recognition;
    Few students learn so much from good tuition.

       [*Exeunt, going in through the gate of the city.*

Scene IV.—Faust's Study

FAUST [*entering with the Poodle*].—Now field and meadow lie
    behind me,
    Hushed 'neath the veil of deepest night,
    And thoughts of solemn seeming find me,
    Too holy for the garish light.
    Calm now the blood that wildly ran,
    Asleep the hand of lawless strife;
    Now wakes to life the love of man,
    The love of God now wakes to life.
Cease, poodle! why snuff'st and snifflest thou so,
Running restless to and fro?
Behind the stove there lie at rest,
And take for bed my cushion the best!
And as without, on our mountain-ramble,
We joyed to see thy freakish gambol,
So here, my hospitable care,
A quiet guest, and welcome share.
    When in our narrow cell confined,
    The friendly lamp begins to burn,
    Then clearer sees the thoughtful mind,
    With searching looks that inward turn.
    Bright Hope again within us beams,
    And Reason's voice again is strong,

   We thirst for life's untroubled streams,
    For the pure fount of life we long.
Quiet thee, poodle! it seems not well
To break, with thy growling, the holy spell
Of my soul's music, that refuses
All fellowship with bestial uses.
Full well we know that the human brood,
What they don't understand condemn,
And murmur in their peevish mood
At things too fair and good for them;
Belike the cur, as curs are they,
Thus growls and snarls his bliss away.
   But, alas! already I feel it well,
No more may peace within this bosom dwell.
Why must the stream so soon dry up,
And I lie panting for the cup
That mocks my lips? so often why
Drink pleasure's shallow fount, when scarce yet tasted,
  dry?
Yet is this evil not without remeid;
We long for heavenly food to feed
Our heaven-born spirit, and the heart, now bent
On things divine, to revelation turns,
Which nowhere worthier or purer burns,
Than here in our New Testament.
I feel strange impulse in my soul
The sacred volume to unroll,
With honest purpose, once for all,
The holy Greek Original
Into my honest German to translate.
     [He opens the Bible and reads.
" In the beginning was the WORD ": thus here
The text stands written; but no clear
Meaning shines here for me, and I must wait,
A beggar at dark mystery's gate,
Lamed in the start of my career.
The naked word I dare not prize so high,
I must translate it differently,
If by the Spirit I am rightly taught.
" In the beginning of all things was THOUGHT."

The first line let me ponder well,
Lest my pen outstrip my sense;
Is it Thought wherein doth dwell
All-creative omnipotence?
I change the phrase, and write—the course
Of the great stream of things was shaped by FORCE.
But even here, before I lift my pen,
A voice of warning bids me try again.
At length, at length, the Spirit helps my need,
I write—" In the beginning was the DEED."
Wilt thou keep thy dainty berth,
Poodle, use a gentler mirth,
Cease thy whimpering and howling,
And keep for other place thy growling.
Such a noisy inmate may
Not my studious leisure cumber;
You or I, without delay,
Restless cur, must leave the chamber!
Not willingly from thee I take
The right of hospitality.
But if thou wilt my quiet break,
Seek other quarters—thou hast exit free.
But what must I see?
What vision strange
Beyond the powers
Of Nature's range?
Am I awake, or bound with a spell?
How wondrously the brute doth swell!
Long and broad
Uprises he,
In a form that no form
Of a dog may be!
What spectre brought I into the house?
He stands already, with glaring eyes,
And teeth in grinning ranks that rise,
Large as a hippopotamus!
O! I have thee now!
For such half-brood of hell as thou
The key of Solomon the wise
Is surest spell to exorcise.

SPIRITS [*in the passage without*].—Brother spirits, have a
    care!
    One within is prisoned there!
    Follow him none!—for he doth quail
    Like a fox, trap-caught by the tail.
    But let us watch!
    Hover here, hover there,
    Up and down amid the air;
    For soon this sly old lynx of hell
    Will tear him free, and all be well.
    If we can by foul or fair,
    We will free him from the snare,
    And repay good service thus,
    Done by him ofttimes for us.
FAUST.—First let the charm of the elements four
    The nature of the brute explore.
    Let the Salamander glow,
    Undene twine her crested wave,
    Silphe into ether flow,
    And Kobold vex him, drudging slave!

Whoso knows not
The elements four,
Their quality,
And hidden power,
In the magic art
Hath he no part.

    Spiring in flames glow
    Salamander!
    Rushing in waves flow
    Undene!
    Shine forth in meteor-beauty
    Silphe!
    Work thy domestic duty
    Incubus Incubus!
    Step forth and finish the spell.
    None of the four
    In the brute doth dwell.
    It lies quite still with elfish grinning there.
    It shall know a stronger charm,

It shall shrink from sharper harm,
When by a mightier name I swear.
Art thou a fugitive
Urchin of hell?
So yield thee at length
To this holiest spell!
Bend thee this sacred
Emblem before,
Which the powers of darkness
Trembling adore.
Already swells he up with bristling hair.
Canst thou read it.
The holy sign,
Reprobate spirit,
The emblem divine?
The unbegotten,
Whom none can name,
Moving and moulding
The wide world's frame,
Yet nailed to the cross
With a death of shame.
Now behind the stove he lies,
And swells him up to an elephant's size,
And fills up all the space.
He'll melt into a cloud; not so!
Down, I say, down, proud imp, and know
Here, at thy master's feet, thy place!
In vain, in vain, thou seekest to turn thee,
With an holy flame I burn thee!
Wait not the charm
Of the triple-glowing light!
Beware the harm
If thou invite
Upon thy head my spell of strongest might!
[*The clouds vanish, and Mephistopheles comes forward from
behind the fireplace, dressed like an itinerant scholar.*

Scene V.

Faust and Mephistopheles.

MEPHISTOPHELES.—What's all the noise about? I'm here at leisure
To work your worship's will and pleasure.
FAUST.—So, so! such kernel cracked from such a shell!
A travelling scholar! the jest likes me well!
MEPHISTOPHELES.—I greet the learned gentleman!
I've got a proper sweating 'neath your ban.
FAUST.—What is thy name?
MEPHISTOPHELES.—What is my power were better,
From one who so despises the mere letter,
Who piercing through the coarse material shell,
With Being's inmost substance loves to dwell.
FAUST.—Yes, but you gentlemen proclaim
Your nature mostly in your name;
Destroyer, God of Flies, the Adversary,*
Such names their own interpretation carry.
But say, who art thou?
MEPHISTOPHELES.—I am a part of that primordial Might,
Which always wills the wrong, and always works the right.
FAUST.—You speak in riddles; the interpretation?
MEPHISTOPHELES.—I am the Spirit of Negation:
And justly so; for all that is created
Deserves to be annihilated.
'Twere better, thus, that there were no creation.
Thus everything that you call evil,
Destruction, ruin, death, the devil,
Is my pure element and sphere.
FAUST.—Thou nam'st thyself a part, yet standest wholly here.
MEPHISTOPHELES.—I speak to thee the truth exact,
The plain, unvarnished, naked fact,
Though man, that microcosm of folly deems
Himself the compact whole he seems.
Part of the part I am that erst was all,
Part of the darkness, from whose primal pall

* Apollyon, Beelzebub, Satan.

Was born the light, the proud rebellious Light,
Which now disputeth with its mother Night,
Her rank and room i' the world by ancient right.
Yet vainly; though it strain and struggle much,
'Tis bound to body with the closer clutch;
From body it streams, on body paints a hue,
And body bends it from its course direct;
Thus in due season I expect,
When bodies perish, Light will perish too.

FAUST.—Hold! now I know thy worthy duties all!
Unable to annihilate wholesale,
Thy mischief now thou workest by retail.

MEPHISTOPHELES.—And even thus, my progress is but small.
This something, the big lumpish world, which stands
Opposed to nothing, still ties my hands,
And spite of all the ground that I seem winning,
Remains as firm as in the beginning;
With storms and tempests, earthquakes and burnings,
Earth still enjoys its evenings and mornings,
And the accursèd fry of brute and human clay,
On them my noblest skill seems worse than thrown away.
How many thousands have I not buried!
Yet still a new fresh blood is hurried
Through fresh young veins, that I must sheer despair.
The earth, the water, and the air,
The moist, the dry, the hot, the cold,
A thousand germs of life unfold;
And had I not of flame made reservation,
I had no portion left in the creation.

FAUST.—And thus thou seekest to oppose
The genial power, from which all life and motion flows,
Against Existence' universal chain,
Clenching thy icy devil's fist in vain!
Try some more profitable feats,
Strange son of Chaos, full of cross conceits.

MEPHISTOPHELES.—The hint is good, and on occasion,
May well deserve consideration;
Meanwhile, with your good leave, I would withdraw.

FAUST.—My leave! do I make devil's law?
The liberty, methinks, is all your own.

I see you here to-day with pleasure,
Go now, and come back at your leisure.
Here is the door, there is the window, and
A chimney if you choose it, is at hand.

MEPHISTOPHELES.—Let me speak plain! there is a small affair,
That, without your assistance, bars my way,
The goblin-foot upon the threshold there——

FAUST.—The pentagram stands in your way!
Ha! tell me then, thou imp of sin,
If this be such a potent spell
To bar thy going out, how cam'st thou in?
What could have cheated such a son of hell?

MEPHISTOPHELES.—Look at it well, the drawing is not true;
One angle, that towards the door, you see,
Left a small opening for me.

FAUST.—So so! for once dame Fortune has been kind,
And I have made a prisoner of you!
Chance is not always blind.

MEPHISTOPHELES.—The cur sprang in before it looked about;
But now the thing puts on a serious air;
The devil is in the house and can't get out.

FAUST.—You have the window, why not jump out there?

MEPHISTOPHELES.—It is a law which binds all ghosts and
sprites;
Wherever they creep in, there too they must creep out;
I came in at the door, by the door I must go out.

FAUST.—So so! then hell too has its laws and rights,
Thus might one profit by the powers of evil,
And make an honest bargain with the devil.

MEPHISTOPHELES.—The devil, sir, makes no undue exaction,
And pays what he has promised to a fraction;
But this affair requires consideration,
We'll leave it for some future conversation.
For this time, I beseech your grace,
Let me be gone; I've work to do.

FAUST.—Stay but one minute, I've scarce seen your face.
Speak; you should know the newest of the new.

MEPHISTOPHELES.—I'll answer thee at length some other day;
At present, I beseech thee, let me loose.

FAUST.—I laid no trap to snare thee in the way,

Thyself didst thrust thy head into the noose;
Whoso hath caught the devil, hold him fast!
Such lucky chance returns not soon again.

MEPHISTOPHELES.—If 'tis your pleasure so, I will remain,
But on condition that the time be passed
In worthy wise, and you consent to see
Some cunning sleights of spirit-craft from me.

FAUST.—Thy fancy jumps with mine. Thou mayst commence,
So that thy dainty tricks but please the sense.

MEPHISTOPHELES.—Thou shalt, in this one hour, my friend,
More for thy noblest senses gain,
Than in the year's dull formal train,
From stale beginning to stale end.
The songs the gentle Spirits sing thee,
The lovely visions that they bring thee,
Are not an empty juggling show.
On thine ear sweet sounds shall fall,
Odorous breezes round thee blow,
Taste, and touch, and senses all
With delicious tingling glow.
No lengthened prelude need we here,
Sing, Spirit-imps that hover near!

SPIRITS.—   Vanish ye murky
Old arches away!
Through the cloud curtain
That blinds heaven's ray
Mild and serenely
Look forth the queenly
Eye of the day!
Star now and starlet
Beam more benign,
And purer suns now
Softlier shine.
In beauty ethereal,
A swift-moving throng,
Of spirits aërial,
Are waving along,
And the soul follows
On wings of desire;
The fluttering garlands

That deck their attire,
Cover the meadows,
Cover the bowers,
Where lovers with lovers
Breathe rapturous hours.
Bower on bower!
The shoots of the vine,
With the leaves of the fig-tree,
Their tendrils entwine!
Clusters of ripe grapes,
Bright-blushing all,
Into the wine-press
Heavily fall;
From fountains divine
Bright rivers of wine
Come foaming and swirling;
O'er gems of the purest,
Sparkling and purling,
They flow and they broaden
In bright vista seen,
To deep-bosomed lakes
Lightly fringed with the green,
Where leafy woods nod
In their tremulous sheen.
On light-oaring pinions
The birds cut the gale,
Through the breezy dominions
As sunward they sail;
They sail on swift wings
To the isles of the blest,
On the soft swelling waves
That are cradled to rest;
Where we hear the glad spirits
In jubilee sing,
As o'er the green meadows
Fleet-bounding they spring:
With light airy footing,
A numberless throng,
Like meteors shooting
The mountains along;

Some there are flinging
Their breasts to the seas,
Others are swinging
In undulant ease,
Lovingly twining
Life's tissue divine,
Where pure stars are shining
In beauty benign!

MEPHISTOPHELES.—He sleeps! well done, ye airy urchins! I
Remain your debtor for this lullaby,
By which so bravely ye have sung asleep
This restless spirit, who, with all his wit,
Is not yet quite the man with cunning cast,
To hook the devil and hold him fast.
Around him let your shapes fantastic flit,
And in a sea of dreams his senses steep.
But now this threshold's charm to disenchant,
The tooth of a rat is all I want;
Nor need I make a lengthened conjuration,
I hear one scraping there in preparation.

The lord of the rats and of the mice,
Of the flies, and frogs, and bugs, and lice,
Commands you with your teeth's good saw,
The threshold of this door to gnaw!
Forth come, and there begin to file,
Where he lets fall this drop of oil.
Ha! there he jumps! that angle there,
With thy sharp teeth I bid thee tear,
Which jutting forward, sad disaster,
Unwilling prisoner keeps thy master.
Briskly let the work go on,
One bite more and it is done!   [Exit.

FAUST [awakening from his trance].—Once more the juggler
Pleasure cheats my lip,
Gone the bright spirit-dream, and left no trace,
That I spake with the devil face to face,
And that a poodle dog gave me the slip!

VOL. II.—4

Scene VI.—Faust's Study

Faust. Mephistopheles.

FAUST.—Who's there to break my peace once more? come in!

MEPHISTOPHELES.—'Tis I!

FAUST.—Come in!

MEPHISTOPHELES.—Thou must repeat it thrice.

FAUST.—Come in.

MEPHISTOPHELES.—Thus with good omen we begin;
 I come to give you good advice,
 And hope we'll understand each other.
 The idle fancies to expel,
 That in your brain make such a pother,
 At your service behold me here,
 Of noble blood, a cavalier,
 A gallant youth rigged out with grace,
 In scarlet coat with golden lace,
 A short silk mantle, and a bonnet,
 With a gay cock's feather on it,
 And at my side a long sharp sword.
 Now listen to a well-meant word;
 Do thou the like, and follow me,
 All unembarrassed thus and free,
 To mingle in the busy scenes
 Of life, and know what living means.

FAUST.—Still must I suffer, clothe me as you may,
 This narrow earthly life's incumbrancy;
 Too old I am to be content with play,
 Too young from every longing to be free.
 What can the world hold forth for me to gain?
 Abstain, it saith, and still it saith, Abstain!
 This is the burden of the song
 That in our ears eternal rings,
 Life's dreary litany lean and long,
 That each dull moment hoarsely sings.
 With terror wake I in the morn from sleep,
 And bitter tears might often weep,
 To see the day, when its dull course is run,
 That brings to fruit not one small wish—not one!

That, with capricious criticising,
Each taste of joy within my bosom rising,
Ere it be born, destroys, and in my breast
Chokes every thought that gives existence zest,
With thousand soulless trifles of an hour.
And when the dark night-shadows lower,
I seek to ease my aching brain
Upon a weary couch in vain.
With throngs of feverish dreams possessed,
Even in the home of sleep I find no rest;
The god, that in my bosom dwells,
Can stir my being's inmost wells;
But he who sways supreme our finer stuff,
Moves not the outward world, hard, obdurate, and tough.
Thus my existence is a load of woes,
Death my best friend, and life my worst of foes.

MEPHISTOPHELES.—And yet methinks this friend you call your
            best,
    Is seldom, when he comes, a welcome guest.

FAUST.—Oh! happy he to whom, in victory's glance,
    Death round his brow the bloody laurel winds!
    Whom, 'mid the circling hurry of the dance,
    Locked in a maiden's close embrace he finds;
    O! would to God that I had sunk that night
    In tranceful death before the Spirit's might!

MEPHISTOPHELES.—Yet, on a certain night, a certain man was
            slow
    To drink a certain brown potation out.

FAUST.—It seems 'tis your delight to play the scout.

MEPHISTOPHELES.—Omniscient am I not; but many things I
            know.

FAUST.—If, in that moment's wild confusion,
    A well-known tone of blithesome youth
    Had power, by memory's dear delusion,
    To cheat me with the guise of truth;
    Then curse I all whate'er the soul
    With luring juggleries entwines,
    And in this gloomy dungeon-hole
    With dazzling flatteries confines!
    Curst be 'fore all the high opinion

The soul has of its own dominion!
Curst all the show of shallow seeming,
Through gates of sense fallacious streaming!
Curst be the hollow dreams of fame,
Of honor, glory, and a name!
Curst be the flattering goods of earth,
Wife, child, and servant, house and hearth!
Accursed be Mammon, when with treasures
To riskful venture he invites us,
Curst when, the slaves of passive pleasures,
On soft-spread cushions he delights us!
Curst be the balsam juice o' the grape!
Accursed be love's deceitful thrall!
Accursed be Hope! accursed be Faith!
Accursed be Patience above all!

CHORUS OF SPIRITS [*invisible*].—Woe! woe!
Thou hast destroyed it!
The beautiful world,
With mightiest hand,
A demigod
In ruin has hurled!
We weep,
And bear its wrecked beauty away,
Whence it may never
Return to the day.
Mightiest one
Of the sons of earth,
Brightest one,
Build it again!
Proudly resurgent with lovelier birth
In thine own bosom build it again!
Life's glad career
Anew commence
With insight clear,
And purgèd sense,
The while new songs around thee play,
To launch thee on more hopeful way!

MEPHISTOPHELES.—These are the tiny
Spirits that wait on me;
Hark how to pleasure

'And action they counsel thee!
Into the world wide
Would they allure thee,
In solitude dull
No more to immure thee,
No more to sit moping
In mouldy mood,
With a film on thy sense,
And a frost in thy blood!
Cease then with thine own peevish whim to play,
That like a vulture makes thy life its prey.
Society, however low,
Still gives thee cause to feel and know
Thyself a man, amid thy fellow-men.
Yet my intent is not to pen
Thee up with the common herd! and though
I cannot boast, or rank, or birth
Of mighty men, the lords of earth,
Yet do I offer, at thy side,
Thy steps through mazy life to guide;
And, wilt thou join in this adventure,
I bind myself by strong indenture,
Here, on the spot, with thee to go.
Call me companion, comrade brave,
Or, if it better please thee so,
I am thy servant, am thy slave!
FAUST.—And in return, say, what the fee
    Thy faithful service claims from me?
MEPHISTOPHELES.—Of that you may consider when you list.
FAUST.—No, no! the devil is an Egotist,
    And seldom gratis sells his labor,
    For love of God, to serve his neighbor.
    Speak boldly out, no private clause conceal;
    With such as you 'tis dangerous to deal.
MEPHISTOPHELES.—I bind myself to be thy servant here,
    And wait with sleepless eyes upon thy pleasure,
    If, when we meet again in yonder sphere,
    Thou wilt repay my service in like measure.
FAUST.—What yonder is I little reck to know,
    Provided I be happy here below;

The future world will soon enough arise,
When the present in ruin lies.
'Tis from this earth my stream of pleasure flows,
This sun it is that shines upon my woes;
And, were I once from this my home away,
Then happen freely what happen may.
Nor hope in me it moves, nor fear,
If then, as now, we hate and love;
Or if in yonder world, as here,
An under be, and an above.

MEPHISTOPHELES.—Well, in this humor, you bid fair
With hope of good result to dare.
Close with my plan, and you will see
Anon such pleasant tricks from me,
As never eyes of man did bliss
From father Adam's time to this.

FAUST.—Poor devil, what hast thou to give,
By which a human soul may live?
By thee or thine was never yet divined
The thought that stirs the deep heart of mankind!
True, thou hast food that sateth never,
And yellow gold that, restless ever,
Like quicksilver between the fingers,
Only to escape us, lingers;
A game where we are sure to lose our labor,
A maiden that, while hanging on my breast,
Flings looks of stolen dalliance on my neighbor;
And honor by which gods are blest,
That, like a meteor, vanishes in air.
Show me the fruit that rots before 'tis broken,
And trees that day by day their green repair!

MEPHISTOPHELES.—A word of mighty meaning thou hast
    spoken,
Yet such commission makes not me despair.
Believe me, friend, we only need to try it,
And we too may enjoy our morsel sweet in quiet.

FAUST.—If ever on a couch of soft repose
My soul shall rock at ease,
If thou canst teach with sweet delusive shows
Myself myself to please,

If thou canst trick me with a toy
To say sincerely I ENJOY,
Then may my latest sand be run!
A wager on it!

MEPHISTOPHELES.—   Done!

FAUST.—   And done, and done!
When to the moment I shall say,
Stay, thou art so lovely, stay!
Then with thy fetters bind me round,
Then perish I with cheerful glee!
Then may the knell of death resound,
Then from thy service art thou free!
The clock may stand,
And the falling hand
Mark the time no more for me!

MEPHISTOPHELES.—Consider well: in things like these
The devil's memory is not apt to slip.

FAUST.—That I know well; may'st keep thy heart at ease,
No random word hath wandered o'er my lip.
Slave I remain, or here, or there,
Thine, or another's, I little care.

MEPHISTOPHELES.—My duty I'll commence without delay,
When with the graduates you dine to-day
One thing remains!—black upon white
A line or two, to make the bargain tight.

FAUST.—A writing, pedant!—hast thou never found
A man whose word was better than his bond?
Is't not enough that by my spoken word,
Of all I am and shall be thou art lord?
The world drives on, wild wave engulfing wave,
And shall a line bind me, if I would be a knave?
Yet 'tis a whim deep-graven in the heart,
And from such fancies who would gladly part?
Happy within whose honest breast concealed
There lives a faith, nor time nor chance can shake;
Yet still a parchment, written, stamped, and sealed,
A spectre is before which all must quake.
Commit but once thy word to the goose-feather,
Then must thou yield the sway to wax and leather.
Say, devil—paper, parchment, stone, or brass?

With me this coin or that will pass;
Style, or chisel, or pen shall it be?
Thou hast thy choice of all the three.

MEPHISTOPHELES.—What need of such a hasty flare
Of words about so paltry an affair?
Paper or parchment, any scrap will do,
Then write in blood your signature thereto.

FAUST.—If this be all, there needs but small delay,
Such trifles shall not stand long in my way.

MEPHISTOPHELES [*while Faust is signing the paper*].—Blood
is a juice of most peculiar virtue.

FAUST.—Only no fear that I shall e'er demur to
The bond as signed; my whole heart swears
Even to the letter that the parchment bears.
Too high hath soared my blown ambition;
I now take rank with thy condition;
The Mighty Spirit of All hath scorned me,
And Nature from her secrets spurned me:
My thread of thought is rent in twain,
All science I loathe with its wranglings vain.
In the depths of sensual joy, let us tame
Our glowing passion's restless flame!
In magic veil, from unseen hand,
Be wonders ever at our command!
Plunge we into the rush of Time!
Into Action's rolling main!
Then let pleasure and pain,
Loss and gain,
Joy and sorrow, alternate chime!
Let bright suns shine, or dark clouds lower,
The man that works is master of the hour.

MEPHISTOPHELES.—To thee I set nor bound nor measure,
Every dainty thou may'st snatch,
Every flying joy may'st catch,
Drink deep, and drain each cup of pleasure;
Only have courage, friend, and be not shy!

FAUST.—Content from thee thy proper wares to buy,
Thou markest well, I do not speak of joy,
Pleasure that smarts, giddy intoxication,
Enamoured hate, and stimulant vexation.

My bosom healed from hungry greed of science
With every human pang shall court alliance;
What all mankind of pain and of enjoyment
May taste, with them to taste be my employment;
Their deepest and their highest I will sound,
Want when they want, be filled when they abound,
My proper self unto their self extend,
And with them too be wrecked, and ruined in the end.

MEPHISTOPHELES.—Believe thou me, who speak from test
   severe,
Chewing the same hard food from year to year,
There lives (were but the naked truth confessed)
No man who, from his cradle to his bier,
The same sour leaven can digest!
Trust one of us—this universe so bright,
He made it only for his own delight;
Supreme He reigns, in endless glory shining,
To utter darkness me and mine consigning,
And grudges ev'n to you the day without the night.

FAUST.—But I will!

MEPHISTOPHELES.— There you are right!
One thing alone gives me concern,
The time is short, and we have much to learn.
There is a way, if you would know it,
Just take into your pay a poet;
Then let the learned gentleman sweep
Through the wide realms of imagination
And every noble qualification,
Upon your honored crown upheap,
The strength of the lion,
The wild deer's agility,
The fire of the south,
With the north's durability.
Then let his invention the secret unfold,
To be crafty and cunning, yet generous and bold;
And teach your youthful blood, as poets can,
To fall in love according to a plan.
Myself have a shrewd notion where we might
Enlist a cunning craftsman of this nature,
And Mr. Microcosmus he is hight.

FAUST.—What am I then, if still I strive in vain
  To reach the crown of manhood's perfect stature,
  The goal for which with all my life of life I strain?
MEPHISTOPHELES.—Thou art, do what thou wilt, just what
    thou art.
  Heap wigs on wigs by millions on thy head,
  And upon yard-high buskins tread,
  Still thou remainest simply what thou art.
FAUST.—I feel it well, in vain have I uphoarded
  All treasures that the mind of man afforded,
  And when I sit me down, I feel no more
  A well of life within me than before;
  Not ev'n one hairbreadth greater is my height,
  Not one inch nearer to the infinite.
MEPHISTOPHELES.—My worthy friend, these things you view,
  Just as they appear to you;
  Some wiser method we must shape us,
  Ere the joys of life escape us.
  Why, what the devil! hands and feet,
  Brain and brawn and blood are thine;
  And what I drink, and what I eat,
  Whose can it be, if 'tis not mine?
  If I can number twice three horses,
  Are not their muscles mine? and when I'm mounted,
  I feel myself a man, and wheel my courses,
  Just as if four-and-twenty legs I counted.
  Quick then! have done with reverie,
  And dash into the world with me!
  I tell thee plain, a speculating fellow
  Is like an ox on heath all brown and yellow,
  Led in a circle by an evil spirit,
  With roods of lush green pasture smiling near it.
FAUST.—But how shall we commence?
MEPHISTOPHELES.—   We start this minute:
  Why, what a place of torture is here,
  And what a life you live within it!
  Yourself and your pack of younkers dear,
  Killing outright with ennui!
  Leave that to honest neighbor Paunch!
  Thrashing of straw is not for thee:

Besides, into the best of all your knowledge,
You know 'tis not permitted you to launch
With chicken-hearted boys at College.
Ev'n now, methinks, I hear one on the stair.
FAUST.—Send him away: I cannot bear——
MEPHISTOPHELES.—Poor boy! he's waited long, nor must
            depart
'Without some friendly word for head and heart;
Come, let me slip into your gown; the mask
Will suit me well; as for the teaching task,
            [*He puts on Faust's scholastic robes.*
Leave that to me! I only ask
A quarter of an hour; and you make speed
And have all ready for our journey's need.   [*Exit.*
MEPHISTOPHELES [*alone*].—Continue thus to hold at nought
Man's highest power, his power of thought;
Thus let the Father of all lies
With shows of magic blind thine eyes,
And thou art mine, a certain prize.
To him hath Fate a spirit given,
With reinless impulse ever forwards driven,
Whose hasty striving overskips
The joys that flow for mortal lips;
Him drag I on through life's wild chase,
Through flat unmeaning emptiness;
He shall cling and cleave to me,
Like a sprawling child in agony,
And food and drink, illusive hovering nigh,
Shall shun his parchèd lips, and cheat his longing eye;
He shall pine and pant and strain
For the thing he may not gain,
And, though he ne'er had sold him to do evil,
He would have damned himself without help from the
            devil.

Scene VII.

Enter a Student.

STUDENT.—I am but fresh arrived to-day,
And come my best respects to pay,
To one whose name, from boor to Kaiser,
None, without veneration, mention.
MEPHISTOPHELES.—I feel obliged by your attention!
You see a man than other men no wiser:
Have you made inquiry elsewhere?
STUDENT.—Beseech you, sir, be my adviser!
I come with money to spend and spare,
With fresh young blood, and a merry heart,
On my college career to start:
My mother sent me, not without a tear,
To get some needful schooling here.
MEPHISTOPHELES.—A better place you could not find.
STUDENT.—To speak the truth, 'tis not much to my mind.
Within these narrow cloister walls,
These antiquated Gothic halls,
I feel myself but ill at ease;
No spot of green I see, no trees,
And 'mid your formal rows of benches,
I almost seem to lose my senses.
MEPHISTOPHELES.—That all depends on custom. Don't you
see
How a young babe at first is slow
To know its mother's breast; but soon
With joy it strains the milky boon;
So you anon will suck nutrition
From Wisdom's breasts with blest fruition.
STUDENT.—I yearn to do so even now;
But, in the first place, tell me how?
MEPHISTOPHELES.—My help is yours, or great or small;
But choose your Faculty, first of all.
STUDENT.—I aim at culture, learning, all
That men call science on the ball
Of earth, or in the starry tent

Of heaven; all Nature high and low,
Broad and deep, I seek to know.
MEPHISTOPHELES.—There you are on the proper scent;
Only beware of too much distraction.
STUDENT.—With soul and body I'm girt for action,
And yet I cannot choose but praise
A little freedom and merriment,
On pleasant summer holidays.
MEPHISTOPHELES.—Redeem the time, for fast it fleets away,
But order rules the hour it cannot stay.
Therefore 'tis plain that you must pass
First of all through the logic class.
There will your mind be postured rightly,
Laced up in Spanish buskins tightly,
That with caution and care, as wisdom ought,
It may creep along the path of thought,
And not with fitful flickering glow
Will o' the wisp it to and fro.
There, too, if you hear the gentleman through
The term, to every lecture true,
You'll learn that a stroke of human thinking,
Which you had practised once as free
And natural as eating and drinking,
Cannot be made without one! two! three!
True, it should seem that the tissue of thought
Is like a web by cunning master wrought,
Where one stroke moves a thousand threads,
The shuttle shoots backwards and forwards between,
The slender threads flow together unseen,
And one with the others thousand-fold weds:
Then steps the philosopher forth to show
How of necessity it must be so:
If the first be so, the second is so,
And therefore the third and the fourth is so;
And unless the first and the second before be,
The third and the fourth can never more be,
So schoolmen teach and scholars believe,
But none of them yet ever learned to weave.
He who strives to know a thing well
Must first the spirit within expel,

Then can he count the parts in his hand,
Only without the spiritual band.
Encheiresis naturæ, 'tis clept in Chemistry,
Thus laughing at herself, albeit she knows not why.
STUDENT.—I must confess I can't quite comprehend you.
MEPHISTOPHELES.—In this respect time by and by will mend
      you,
When you have learned the crude mixed masses
To decompose, and rank them in their classes.
STUDENT.—I feel as stupid to all he has said,
As a mill-wheel were whirling round in my head.
MEPHISTOPHELES.—After logic, first of all,
To the study of metaphysics fall!
There strive to know what ne'er was made
To go into a human head;
For what is within and without its command
A high-sounding word is always at hand.
But chiefly, for the first half year,
Let order in all your studies appear;
Five lectures a day, that no time be lost,
And with the clock be at your post!
Come not, as some, without preparation,
But con his paragraphs o'er and o'er,
To be able to say, when you hear his oration,
That he gives you his book, and nothing more;
Yet not the less take down his words in writing,
As if the Holy Spirit were inditing!
STUDENT.—I shall not quickly give you cause
To repeat so weighty a clause;
For what with black on white is written,
We carry it home, a sure possession.
MEPHISTOPHELES.—But, as I said, you must choose a pro-
      fession.
STUDENT.—With Law, I must confess, I never was much
      smitten.
MEPHISTOPHELES.—I should be loath to force your inclination,
Myself have some small skill in legislation;
For human laws and rights from sire to son,
Like an hereditary ill, flow on;
From generation dragged to generation,

And creeping slow from place to place.
Reason is changed to nonsense, good to evil,
Art thou a grandson, woe betide thy case!
Of Law they prate, most falsely clept the Civil,
But for that right, which from our birth we carry,
'Tis not a word found in their Dictionary.

STUDENT.—Your words have much increased my detestation.
O happy he, to whom such guide points out the way!
And now, I almost feel an inclination
To give Theology the sway.

MEPHISTOPHELES.—I have no wish to lead you astray.
As to this science, 'tis so hard to eschew
The false way, and to hit upon the true,
And so much hidden poison lurks within,
That's scarce distinguished from the medicine.
Methinks that here 'twere safest done
That you should listen but to one,
And *jurare in verba magistri*
Is the best maxim to assist thee.
Upon the whole, I counsel thee
To stick to words as much as may be,
For such will still the surest way be
Into the temple of certainty.

STUDENT.—Yet in a word some sense must surely lurk.

MEPHISTOPHELES.—Yes, but one must not go too curiously to
       work;
For, just when our ideas fail us,
A well-coined word may best avail us.
Words are best weapons in disputing,
In system-building and uprooting,
To words most men will swear, though mean they ne'er
       so little,
From words one cannot filch a single tittle.

STUDENT.—Pardon me, if I trespass on your time,
Though to make wisdom speak seems scarce a crime;
On medicine, too, I am concerned
To hear some pregnant word from one so learned.
Three years, God knows, is a short time,
And we have far to go, and high to climb;

A wise man's fingers pointing to the goal
Will save full many a groan to many a laboring soul.
MEPHISTOPHELES [aside].—I'm weary of this dry pedantic
　　strain,
'Tis time to play the genuine devil again.
[Aloud.] The spirit of Medicine 'tis not hard to seize:
The world, both great and small, you seek to know,
That in the end you may let all things go
As God shall please.
In vain you range around with scientific eyes,
Each one at length learns only what he can;
But he who knows the passing hour to prize,
That is the proper man.
A goodly shape and mien you vaunt,
And confidence, I guess, is not your want,
Trust but yourself, and, without more ado,
All other men will straightway trust you too.
But chiefly be intent to get a hold
O' the women's minds: their endless Oh! and Ah!
So thousandfold,
In all its change, obeys a single law,
And, if with half a modest air you come,
You have them all beneath your thumb.
A title first must purchase their reliance,
That you have skill surpassing vulgar science;
Thus have you hold at once of all the seven ends,
Round which another year of labor spends.
Study to press the pulse right tenderly,
And, with a sly and fiery eye,
To hold her freely round the slender waist,
That you may see how tightly she is laced.
STUDENT.—This seems to promise better; here we see
Where to apply and how to use the knife.
MEPHISTOPHELES.—Gray, my good friend, is every theory,
But green the golden tree of life.
STUDENT.—I vow I feel as in a dream; my brain
Contains much more than it can comprehend;
Some other day may I come back again,
To hear your wisdom to the end?
MEPHISTOPHELES.—What I can teach all men are free to know.

STUDENT.—One little favor grant me ere I go;
    It were my boast to take home on this page
                [*Presenting a leaf from his album.*
    Some sapient maxim from a man so sage.
MEPHISTOPHELES.—Right willingly.
                [*He writes, and gives back the book.*
STUDENT [*reads*].—*Eritis sicut Deus scientes bonum et malum.*
    [*He closes the book reverently, and takes his leave.*
MEPHISTOPHELES.—Follow the ancient saw, and my cousin,
    the famous old Serpent,
    Right soon shalt thou have cause, at thy godlike knowl-
    edge to tremble!

Enter Faust.

FAUST.—Now, whither bound?
MEPHISTOPHELES.—   Where'er it pleases you;
    The world, both great and small, we view.
    O! how it will delight, entrance you,
    The merry reel of life to dance through!
FAUST.—My beard, I am afraid, is rather long;
    And without easy manners, gentle breeding,
    I fear there is small chance of my succeeding;
    I feel so awkward 'mid the busy throng,
    So powerless and so insignificant,
    And what all others have I seem to want.
MEPHISTOPHELES.—Bah! never fear; the simple art of living
    Is just to live right on without misgiving!
FAUST.—But how shall we commence our course?
    I see nor coach, nor groom, nor horse.
MEPHISTOPHELES.—We only need your mantle to unfold,
    And it shall waft us on the wind.
    Who makes with me this journey bold
    No bulky bundle busks behind;
    A single puff of inflammable air,
    And from the ground we nimbly fare.
    Lightly we float. I wish the best of cheer
    To Doctor Faustus on his new career.
    VOL. II.—5

ACT THIRD

Scene I.—Auerbach's Wine-cellar, Leipsic

A Bout of Merry Fellows.

FROSCH.—Will no one sing? none crack a joke?
    I'll teach you to make saucy faces!
    Like old wet straw to-day you smoke,
    While bright as flame your wonted blaze is.
BRANDER.—The blame lies with yourself, for you have given us
    To-day no fun nor frolic to enliven us.
FROSCH [*throwing a glass of wine over his head*].—There
        hast thou both!
BRANDER.—   Double swine!
FROSCH.—You asked a joke—I gave it you in wine!
SIEBEL.—Out at the door with all who dare to quarrel!
    Give all your pipes full play! this is no place to snarl.
    Up! hollo! ho!
ALTMAYER.—Woe's me! the devil and his crew are here!
    Some cotton, ho! he makes my ear-drum crack.
SIEBEL.—Roar on! for, when the vault loud echoes back,
    The deep bass notes come thundering on the ear.
FROSCH.—Right, right! out with each saucy fellow!
    A! tara lara da!
ALTMAYER.—A tara lara da!
FROSCH.—   Our throats are now quite mellow.
    [*Sings.*] The holy Roman empire now,
          How does it hold together?
    A clumsy song!—fie! a political song!
    A scurvy song! thank God, with each to-morrow,
    The Roman empire can give you small sorrow;
    For me, I deem I'm wealthier and wiser
    For being neither Chancellor nor Kaiser.

Yet even we must have a head to rule us;
Let's choose a pope in drinking well to school us,
Come, well you know the qualification
That lifts a man to consideration.

FROSCH [*sings*].—Mount up, lady nightingale,
        Greet my love ten thousand times!

SIEBEL.—No, sir, not once—I'll hear no more of this.

FROSCH.—But you *shall* hear!—A greeting and a kiss!
[*He sings.*]   Ope the door in silent night.
        Ope and let me in, I pray;
        Shut the door, the morn is bright,
        Shut it, love, I must away!

SIEBEL.—Yes! sing and sing! belaud her, and berhyme!
I'll have my laugh at that—all in good time!
She jilted me right rarely; soon
She'll make thee sing to the same tune;
'Twere fit a Kobold with his love should bless her,
On some cross-road to cocker and caress her;
Or that some old he-goat, that tramps away
From merry Blocksberg on the first of May,
Should greet her passing with a lusty baa!
An honest man of genuine flesh and blood
Is for the wench by far too good.
Batter her doors, her windows shiver,
That's all the serenade I'd give her!

BRANDER [*striking the table*].—Gentlemen, hear! only attend
      to me,
You'll see that I know how to live.
If love-sick people here there be,
To honor them, I'm bound to give
A song brimful of the most melting passion.
I'll sing a ditty of the newest fashion!
Give ear! and with full swell sonorous,
Let each and all ring forth the chorus!
[*He sings.*]   In a pantry-hole there lived a rat,
        On bacon and on butter,
        It had a paunch as round and fat
        As Doctor Martin Luther.
        The cook placed poison in its way,
        It felt as straitened all the day,
        As if it had love in its body.

CHORUS [*shouting*].—As if it had love in its body.
BRANDER.—It ran within, it ran without,
  And sipped in every puddle;
  And scratched and gnawed, but bettered not
  The fever of its noddle.
  With many a twinge it tossed and tossed,
  Seemed ready to give up the ghost,
  As if it had love in its body.
CHORUS.— As if it had love in its body.
BRANDER.—It left its hole for very pain,
  Into the kitchen crawling,
  And snuffling there with might and main,
  Upon the earth lay sprawling.
  The cook she laughed when she saw it die;
  " It squeaks," quoth she, " with its latest sigh,
  As if it had love in its body."
CHORUS.— As if it had love in its body.
SIEBEL.— How the hard-hearted boys rejoice!
  As if it were a trade so choice
  To teach the rats and mice to die!
BRANDER.—Rats find great favor in your eyes.
ALTMAYER.—The oily paunch! the bald pate! he
  Has eyes of sorrow for the creature:
  For why? he could not fail to see
  In the swoll'n rat his own best feature!

Scene II.

Enter Faust and Mephistopheles.

MEPHISTOPHELES.—First thing of all I bring you here,
  Into a company of jolly cheer,
  That you may learn how men contrive
  Without much thought or care to live.
  These fellows feast their lives away
  In a continual holiday;
  With little wit and much content
  Their narrow round of life is spent,
  As playful kittens oft are found
  To chase their own tails round and round.

So live they on from day to day,
As long as headache keeps away,
And by no anxious thought are crossed,
While they get credit from the host.

BRANDER.—These gentlemen are strangers; in their face
One reads they lack the breeding of the place;
They're not an hour arrived, I warrant thee.

FROSCH.—There you are right!—Leipsic's the place, I say!
It is a little Paris in its way.

SIEBEL.—What, think you, may the strangers be?

FROSCH.—Leave that to me! I'll soon fish out the truth.
Fill me a bumper till it overflows,
And then I'll draw the worms out of their nose,
As easily as 'twere an infant's tooth.
To me they seem to be of noble blood,
They look so discontented and so proud.

BRANDER.—Quack doctors both!—Altmayer, what think you?

ALTMAYER.—'Tis like.

FROSCH.—   Mark me! I'll make them feel the screw.

MEPHISTOPHELES [to Faust].—They have no nose to smell the
        devil out,
Even when he has them by the snout.

FAUST.—Be greeted, gentlemen!

SIEBEL.—With much respect return we the salute.
        [Softly, eyeing Mephistopheles from the one side.
What! does the fellow limp upon one foot?

MEPHISTOPHELES.—With your permission, we will make so
        free,
As to intrude upon your company.
The host's poor wines may keep us in sobriety,
But we at least enjoy your good society.

ALTMAYER.—Our wine is good; and, for to speak the truth,
Your mother fed you with too nice a tooth.

FROSCH.—When left you Rippach? you must have been
        pressed
For time. Supped you with 'Squire Hans by the way?

MEPHISTOPHELES.—We had no time to stay!
But when I last came by, I was his guest.
He spoke much of his cousins, and he sent
To you and all full many a compliment.
        [He makes a bow to Frosch.

ALTMAYER [*softly*].—You have him there!—he understands
     the jest!

SIEBEL.—He is a knowing one!

FROSCH.—I'll sift him through anon!

MEPHISTOPHELES.—As we came in, a concert struck my ear
     Of skilful voices in a chorus pealing!
     A gleesome song must sound most nobly here,
     Re-echoed freely from the vaulted ceiling.

FROSCH.—Perhaps you have yourself some skill?

MEPHISTOPHELES.—O no! had I the power, I should not want
     the will.

ALTMAYER.—Give us a song!

MEPHISTOPHELES.—   A thousand, willingly!

SIEBEL.—Only brand-new, I say!—no thread bare strain!

MEPHISTOPHELES.—We are but just come from a tour in
     Spain,
     The lovely land of wine and melody.
     [*He sings.*]   There was a king in old times
          That had a huge big flea——

FROSCH.—Ha, ha! a flea!—he seems a man of taste!
     A flea, I wis, is a most dainty guest?

MEPHISTOPHELES [*sings again*].—There was a king in old
     times
     That had a huge big flea,
     As if it were his own son,
     He loved it mightily.
     He sent out for the tailor,
     To get it a suit of clothes;
     He made my lord a dress-coat,
     He made him a pair of hose.

BRANDER.—Be sure that Monsieur le Tailleur be told
     To take his measure most exact and nice,
     And as upon his head he puts a price,
     To make the hose without or crease or fold!

MEPHISTOPHELES.—In velvet and in silk clad
     He strutted proudly then,
     And showed his star and garter
     With titled gentlemen.
     Prime minister they made him,
     With cross and ribbon gay,

And then all his relations
At court had much to say.
This caused no small vexation
At court; I tell you true—
The queen and all her ladies
Were bitten black and blue.
And yet they durst not catch them,
Nor crack them, when they might,
But we are free to catch them,
And crack them when they bite.
CHORUS [*shouting*].—But we are free to catch them
        And crack them when they bite!
FROSCH.—Bravo, bravo!—his voice is quite divine.
SIEBEL.—Such fate may every flea befall!
BRANDER.—Point your nails and crack 'em all!
ALTMAYER.—A glass to liberty!—long live the vine!
MEPHISTOPHELES.—I'd drink to liberty with right good-will,
        If we had only better wine to drink.
SIEBEL.—You might have kept that to yourself, I think!
MEPHISTOPHELES.—I only fear our host might take it ill,
        Else should I give to every honored guest
        From our own cellar of the very best.
SIEBEL.—O never fear!—If you but find the wine,
        Our host shall be content—the risk be mine!
FROSCH.—Give me a flowing glass, and praise you shall not
                want,
        So that your sample, mark me! be not scant;
        I cannot judge of wine, unless I fill
        My mouth and throat too with a goodly swill.
ALTMAYER [*softly*].—I see the gentlemen are from the Rhine.
MEPHISTOPHELES.—Give me a gimlet here!—I'll show you
                wine.
BRANDER.—What would the fellow bore?
        Has he then wine-casks at the door?
ALTMAYER.—There, in the basket, you will find a store
        Of tools, which our good landlord sometimes uses.
MEPHISTOPHELES [*to Frosch*].—Now every man may taste of
                what he chooses.   [*Takes the gimlet.*
FROSCH.—How mean you that? Can you afford?
MEPHISTOPHELES.—No fear of that; my cellar is well stored.

ALTMAYER [*to Frosch*].—Aha! I see you smack your lips
  already.

FROSCH.—I'll have Rhine wine; what fatherland produces
  Is better far than French or Spanish juices.

MEPHISTOPHELES [*boring a hole in the edge of the table where
  Frosch is sitting*].—Fetch me some wax, to make
  the stoppers ready.

ALTMAYER.—He means to put us off with jugglery.

MEPHISTOPHELES [*to Brander*].—And you, sir, what?

BRANDER.—   Champagne for me!
  And brisk and foaming let it be!

[*Mephistopheles bores; meanwhile one of the party has got
  the stoppers ready, and closes the holes.*

BRANDER.—To foreign climes a man must sometimes roam,
  In quest of things he cannot find at home;
  For Frenchmen Germans have no strong affection,
  But to their wines we seldom make objection.

SIEBEL [*while Mephistopheles is coming round to him*].—I
  have no taste for your sour wines to-day,
  I wish to have a swig of good Tokay.

MEPHISTOPHELES [*boring*].—That you shall have, and of the
  very best.

ALTMAYER.—No, gentlemen!—'tis plain you mean to jest;
  If so, in me you much mistake your man.

MEPHISTOPHELES.—Ha! ha!—no little risk, methinks, I ran,
  To venture tricks with noble guests like you.
  Come! make your choice, speak boldly out, and I
  Will do my best your wish to gratify.

ALTMAYER.—Give me what wine you please!—only not much
  ado.

MEPHISTOPHELES [*with strange gestures, after having bored
  and stopped up all the holes*].—Grapes on
  the vine grow!
  Horns on the goat!
  The wine is juicy, the vine is of wood,
  The wooden table can give it as good.
  Look into Nature's depths with me!
  Whoso hath faith shall wonders see!
Now draw the corks, and quaff the wine!

ALL [*drawing the corks, and quaffing the out-streaming liquor
    each as he had desired*].—O blessed stream!—
    O fount divine!

MEPHISTOPHELES.—Drink on! only be cautious in your hurry.
                                    [*They drink freely.*

ALL [*singing*].—No king of cannibals to-day
            More bravely rules the drinking bout,
            Than we, when, like five hundred swine,
            We drain the brimming bumpers out!

MEPHISTOPHELES [*to Faust*].—Look at the fellows now!—
    are they not merry?

FAUST.—I feel inclined to go!—'tis getting late.

MEPHISTOPHELES.—Soon shall we have a glorious revelation
    Of the pure beast in man, if you but wait.

SIEBEL [*drinks carelessly; the wine falls to the ground and
    becomes flame*].—Help! fire! the devil's here!
    death and damnation!

MEPHISTOPHELES [*addressing himself to the flames*].—Peace,
    friendly element! be still!
    [*To the company.*] This time 'twas but a spurt of pur-
    gatorial flame.

SIEBEL.—What's that?—you little know your men; we'll tame
    Your impudence, you juggling knave, we will!

FROSCH.—'Twere dangerous to repeat such gambols here!

ALTMAYER.—Methinks 'twere best to whisper in his ear
    That he had better leave the room.

SIEBEL.—What, sirrah? do you then presume
    To play your hocus-pocus here?

MEPHISTOPHELES.—Peace, old wine-cask!

SIEBEL.—   You broomstick, you!
    Must we then bear your insolence too?

BRANDER.—Wait! wait! it shall rain blows anon!

ALTMAYER [*draws a stopper from the table, and fire rushes out
    on him*].—I burn! I burn!

SIEBEL.—   There's witchcraft in his face!
    The fellow's an outlaw! strike him down!
        [*They draw their knives and attack Mephistopheles.*

MEPHISTOPHELES [*with serious mien*].—False be eye, and false
    be ear!

Change the sense, and change the place!
Now be there, and now be here!
[*They look as thunderstruck, and stare at one another.*
ALTMAYER.—Where am I? in what lovely land?
FROSCH.—Vineyards! can it be so?
SIEBEL.—   And grapes too quite at hand!
BRANDER.—And here beneath this shady tree,
    This noble vine, these blushing clusters see!
[*He seizes Siebel by the nose. The rest seize one another in
    the same manner, and lift up their knives.*
MEPHISTOPHELES [*as above*].—Let Error now their eyes un-
        close,
    The devil's joke to understand!
[*He vanishes with Faust. The fellows start back from one
    another.*
SIEBEL.—What's the matter?
ALTMAYER.—   How now?
FROSCH.—   Was that your nose?
BRANDER [*to Siebel*].—And yours is in my hand!
ALTMAYER.—It was a stroke shot through my every limb!
    Give me a chair!—I faint! My eyes grow dim!
FROSCH.—Now tell me only what has been the matter?
SIEBEL.—Where is the fellow? Could I catch him here,
    His life out of his body I should batter!
ALTMAYER.—I saw him just this instant disappear,
    Riding upon a wine-cask—I declare
    I feel a weight like lead about my feet.
    [*Turning to the table.*] I wonder if his d——d wine
        still be there!
SIEBEL.—There's not a single drop; 'twas all a cheat.
FROSCH.—And yet methinks that I was drinking wine.
BRANDER.—And I could swear I saw a clustered vine.
ALTMAYER.—Let none now say the age of miracles is past!

Scene III.—Witches' Kitchen

[*A caldron is boiling on a low hearth. Strange fantastic figures tumble in the smoke. A Mother-Cat-Ape sits beside the caldron, taking off the scum, and keeping it from boiling over. An Old Cat-Ape beside her warming himself with his young ones. Roof and walls are covered over with the implements used by witches.*

Enter Faust and Mephistopheles.

FAUST.—I cannot brook this brainless bedlam stuff!
    And must it be that I shall cast my slough
    In this hotbed of all unreasoned doing?
    Shall an old beldam give me what I lack?
    And can her pots and pans, with all their brewing,
    Shake off full thirty summers from my back?
    Woe's me, if thou canst boast no better scheme!
    My brightest hopes are vanished as a dream.
    Has Nature then, and has some noble Spirit,
    No balsam for the body to repair it?

MEPHISTOPHELES.—My friend, with your great sense I cannot but be smitten!
    Nature, too, boasts a plan to renovate your age;
    But in a wondrous volume it is written,
    And wondrous is the chapter and the page.

FAUST.—But I must know it.

MEPHISTOPHELES.—   Good! the poorest man may try it,
    Without or witch, or quack, or gold to buy it;
    And yet it works a certain cure.
    Go take thee with the peasant to the moor,
    And straight begin to hew and hack;
    Confine thee there, with patient mood,
    Within the narrow beaten track,
    And nourish thee with simplest food;
    Live with the brute a brute, and count it not too low
    To dung the corn-fields thine own hands shall mow;
    Than this I know on earth no med'cine stronger,
    To make, by fourscore years, both soul and body younger!

FAUST.—I was not trained to this—was never made
    To labor with the pick-axe and the spade;
    Such narrow round of life I may not brook.
MEPHISTOPHELES.—Then you must look into another book,
    And be content to take the witch for cook.
FAUST.—But why this self-same ugly Jezebel?
    Could you not brew the drink yourself as well?
MEPHISTOPHELES.—A precious pastime that indeed! mean-
    while
    I had built bridges many a German mile.
    Not art, and science strict, are here enough,
    But patience too, and perseverance tough.
    A thoughtful soul toils on through many a silent year.
    Time only makes the busy ferment clear,
    Besides that the ingredients all
    Are passing strange and mystical!
    'Tis true the devil taught them how to do it,
    But not the devil with his own hands can brew it.
    [*Looking at the Cat-Apes.*] Lo! what a tiny gay parade!
    Here's the man, and there's the maid!
    [*Addressing them.*] It seems that your good mother
      has gone out?
THE CAT-APES.— Up the chimney,
      Went she out,
      To a drinking bout!
MEPHISTOPHELES.—Is it her wont to gossip long without?
THE ANIMALS.—As long as we sit here and warm our feet.
MEPHISTOPHELES [*to Faust*].—What think you of the brutes?
    are they not neat?
FAUST.—I never saw such tasteless would-be-drolls!
MEPHISTOPHELES.—Pooh! pooh!—I know no greater delecta-
    tion
    On earth, than such a merry conversation.
    [*To the brutes.*] Now let us hear, you pretty dolls,
    What are you stirring there in the pot?
THE ANIMALS.—Soup for beggars, hissing and hot,
    Thin and watery, that's the stew.
MEPHISTOPHELES.—Your customers will not be few.
THE FATHER CAT-APE [*comes up and fawns upon Mephis-
    topheles*].—Come rattle the dice,
      Make me rich in a trice,

Come, come, let me gain!
My case is so bad,
· It scarce could be worse:
Were I right in my purse,
I'd be right in my brain!

MEPHISTOPHELES.—How happy would the apish creature be,
To buy a ticket in the lottery!

[*Meanwhile the young Cat-Apes have been playing with a large globe, and roll it forward.*

THE FATHER CAT-APE.—Such is the world,
So doth it go,
Up and down,
To and fro!
Like glass it tinkles,
Like glass it twinkles,
Breaks in a minute,
Has nothing within it;
Here it sparkles,
There it darkles,
I am alive!
My dear son, I say,
Keep out of the way!
If you don't strive,
You will die, you will die!
It is but of clay,
And in pieces will fly!

MEPHISTOPHELES.—What make you with the sieve?

THE FATHER CAT-APE [*bringing down the sieve*].—When
comes a thief,
On the instant we know him.

[*He runs off to the Mother Cat-Ape, and lets her look through the sieve.*

Look through the sieve!
Seest thou the thief,
And fearest to show him?

MEPHISTOPHELES [*coming near the fire*].—And this pot?

FATHER CAT-APE AND HIS WIFE.—The silly sot!
He knows not the pot!
And he knows not
The kettle, the sot!

MEPHISTOPHELES.—You ill-bred urchin, you!

THE FATHER CAT-APE.—Come, sit thee down,
                        We'll give thee a crown,
                        And a sceptre too!

[*He obliges Mephistopheles to sit down, and gives him a long
brush for a sceptre.*

[*While Mephistopheles was engaged with the animals, Faust
had been standing before a mirror, alternately approaching it and retiring from it.*

FAUST.—What see I here? what heavenly image bright,
        Within this magic mirror, chains my sight?
        O Love, the swiftest of thy pinions lend me,
        That where she is in rapture I may bend me!
        Alas! when I would move one step more near,
        To breathe her balmy atmosphere,
        She seems to melt and disappear,
        And cheats my longing eye.
        Oh she is fair beyond all type of human!
        Is't possible; can this be simple woman?
        There lies she, on that downy couch reposing,
        Within herself the heaven of heavens enclosing!
        Can it then be that earth a thing so fair contains?

MEPHISTOPHELES.—Of course: for when a god has vexed his
                brains
        For six long days, and, when his work is done,
        Says bravo to himself, is it a wonder
        He should make one fair thing without a blunder?
        For this time give thine eyes their pleasure;
        I know how to procure you such an one,
        Whence thou may'st drink delight in brimming measure,
        And blest the man, for whom Fate shall decide,
        To lead home such a treasure as his bride!

[*Faust continues gazing on the mirror. Mephistopheles
stretches himself on the arm-chair, and, playing with
the brush, goes on as follows:*
        Here, from my throne, a monarch, I look down:
        My sceptre this: I wait to get my crown.

[*The Animals, who had in the interval been wheeling about
with strange antic gestures, bring a crown to Mephistopheles, with loud shouts.*

The Animals.—   O be but so good,
        With sweat and with blood,
        Your crown to glue,
        As monarchs do!

[*They use the crown rather roughly, in consequence of which
it falls into two pieces, with which they jump about.*

        O sorrow and shame!
        'Tis broken, no doubt:
        But we'll make a name,
        When our poem comes out!

Faust [*gazing on the mirror*].—Woe's me! her beauty doth
    my wits confound.

Mephistopheles [*pointing to the brutes*].—And even my
    good brain is whirling round and round.

The Animals.—   And if we well speed,
        As speed well we ought,
        We are makers indeed,
        We are moulders of thought.

Faust [*as above*].—I burn, I burn! this rapturous glow
    Consumes me sheer!—come, let us go!

Mephistopheles [*as above*].—One must, at least, confess that
    they
    Are honest poets in their way.

[*The kettle, which had been neglected by the Mother Cat-Ape,
begins to boil over: A great flame arises, and runs up
the chimney. The Witch comes through the flame, down
the chimney, with a terrible noise.*

The Witch.—Ow! ow! ow! ow!
        Thou d——d brute! thou cursèd sow!
        To leave the kettle and singe the frow!
        Thou cursed imp, thou!
                [*Turning to Faust and Mephistopheles.*
        What's this here now?
        Who are you? who are you?
        What's here ado?
        Ye are scouts! ye are scouts!
        Out with the louts!
        A fiery arrow
        Consume your marrow!

[*She plunges the ladle into the kettle, and spurts out flame on
    Faust, Mephistopheles, and the brutes.   These last
    whine.*

[*Mephistopheles, who in the meantime, had turned round the
    butt-end of the brush, now dashes in amongst the pots
    and glasses.*

MEPHISTOPHELES.—In two! in two!
                    There lies the broth!
                    The glass and the kettle,
                    Shiver them both!
                    'Tis a jest, thou must know,
                    Thou carrion crow!
                    'Tis a tune to keep time,
                    To thy senseless rhyme.
        [*The Witch, foaming with rage and fury, draws back.*
    What! know'st me not? thou scrag! thou Jezebel!
    Thy lord and master? thou shouldst know me well.
    What hinders me, in all my strength to come
    And crush you and your cat-imps 'neath my thumb?
    Know'st not the scarlet-doublet, mole-eyed mother?
    Bow'st not the knee before the famed cock's feather?
    Use your old eyes; behind a mask
    Did I conceal my honest face?
    And when I come here must I ask
    A special introduction to your Grace?
THE WITCH.—O my liege lord! forgive the rough salute!
    I did not see the horse's foot:
    And where too have you left your pair of ravens?
MEPHISTOPHELES.—For this time you may thank the heavens
    That you have made so cheap an escape;
    'Tis some time since I saw your face,
    And things since then have moved apace.
    The march of modern cultivation,
    That licks the whole world into shape,
    Has reached the Devil. In this wise generation
    The Northern phantom is no longer seen,
    And horns and tail and claws have been.
    And for my hoof, with which I can't dispense,
    In good society 'twould give great offence;

Therefore, like many a smart sprig of nobility,
I use false calves to trick out my gentility.

THE WITCH [*dancing*].—Heyday! it almost turns my brain
To see 'Squire Satan here again!

MEPHISTOPHELES.—Woman, you must not call me by that
name!

THE WITCH.—And wherefore not? I see no cause for shame.

MEPHISTOPHELES.—That name has had its station long as-
signed
With Mother Bunch; and yet I cannot see
Men are much better for the want of me.
The wicked one is gone, the wicked stay behind.
Call me now Baron, less than that were rude—
I am a cavalier like other cavaliers;
My line is noble, and my blood is good;
Here is a coat of arms that all the world reveres.
[*He makes an indecent gesture.*

THE WITCH [*laughing immoderately*].—Ha! ha! now I perceive Old Nick is here!
You are a rogue still, as you always were.

MEPHISTOPHELES [*aside to Faust*].—My friend, I give you
here, your wit to whet,
A little lesson in witch-etiquette.

THE WITCH.—Now say, good sirs, what would you have with
me?

MEPHISTOPHELES.—A glass of your restoring liquor,
That makes an old man's blood run quicker:
And bring the best out from your bins;
With years the juice in virtue wins.

THE WITCH.—Most willingly. Here I have got a phial
Of which myself at times make trial:
'Tis now a pleasant mellow potion;
You shall not meet with a denial.
[*Softly.*] Yet if this worthy man drinks it without pre-
caution,
His life can't stand an hour against its strong infection.

MEPHISTOPHELES.—Leave that to me; he's under my protection,
Ripe for the draught; no harm will come to him.

[*The Witch, with strange gestures, draws a circle and places
    many curious things within it; meanwhile the glasses
    begin to tinkle, and the kettle to sound and make music.
    She brings a large book, puts the Cat-Apes into the
    circle, and makes them serve as a desk to lay the book
    on, and hold the torches.   She motions to Faust to come
    near.*

FAUST [*to Mephistopheles*].—Now say, what would she with
            this flummery?
These antic gestures, this wild bedlam-stuff,
This most insipid of all mummery,
I know it well, I hate it well enough.

MEPHISTOPHELES.—Pshaw, nonsense! come, give up your
            sermonizing,
And learn to understand what a good joke is!
Like other quacks, she plays her hocus-pocus;
It gives the juice a virtue most surprising!
                    [*He obliges Faust to enter the circle.*

THE WITCH [*declaiming from the book with great emphasis*].—
            Now be exact!
            Of one make ten,
            Then two subtract,
            And add three then,
            This makes thee rich.
            Four shalt thou bate,
            Of five and six,
            So says the Witch,
            Make seven and eight,
            And all is done.
            And nine is one,
            And ten is none;
            Here take and spell, if you are able,
            The Witches' multiplication table.

FAUST.—This is a jargon worse than Babel;
            Say, is she fevered? is she mad?

MEPHISTOPHELES.—O never fear! the rest is quite as bad;
            I know the book, and oft have vexed my brains
            With bootless labor on its rhymes and rules;
            A downright contradiction still remains,
            Mysterious alike for wise men and for fools.

My friend, the art is old and new;
Ancient and modern schools agree
With three and one, and one and three
Plain to perplex, and false inweave with true.
So they expound, discourse, dispute, debate;
What man of sense would plague him with their prate?
Men pin their faith to words, in sounds high sapience
    weening,
Though words were surely made to have a meaning.

THE WITCH [*reading from the book*].—The soul to know
        Beneath the show,
        And view it without blinking;
        The simple mind
        The craft will find,
        Without the toil of thinking.

FAUST.—What flood of nonsense now she's pouring o'er us?
She'll split my skull with her insensate chatter.
I feel as if I heard the ceaseless clatter
Of thirty thousand idiots in a chorus.

MEPHISTOPHELES.—Enough, kind Sibyl; thanks for thy good-
    will!
Now bring your jug here, and the goblet fill
With this prime juice, till it be brimming o'er.
My friend here is a man of high degrees,
And will digest the draught with ease.
He has swilled many a goodly glass before.

[*The Witch, with many ceremonies, pours the beverage into
a cup. While Faust brings it to his mouth a light flame
arises.*

MEPHISTOPHELES.—Come, quaff it boldly, without thinking!
The draught will make thy heart to burn with love.
Art with the Devil hand and glove,
And from a fire-spurt wouldst be shrinking?

        [*The Witch looses the circle. Faust steps out.*

MEPHISTOPHELES.—Come quickly out; you must not rest.

THE WITCH.—I hope the swig will wonders work on thee!

MEPHISTOPHELES.—And you, if you have aught to beg of me,
Upon Walpurgis' night make your request.

THE WITCH.—Here is a song! at times sung, you will find
It hath a wondrous working on your mind.

MEPHISTOPHELES [*to Faust*].—Come, yield thee now to my
    desire;
  Be meek for once, and own the bridle.
  You must keep quiet, and let yourself perspire,
  That through your inmost frame the potent juice may
    pierce.
  When we have time to spare, I will rehearse
  Some lessons on the art of being nobly idle;
  And soon thy heart with ecstasy shall know,
  How Cupid 'gins to stir, and boundeth to and fro.
FAUST [*turning again towards the mirror*].—Indulge me with
    one glance!—one moment spare!
  It was a virgin-form surpassing fair!
MEPHISTOPHELES.—No! No! with my good aid thou soon
    shalt see
  The paragon of women bodily.
  [*Aside.*] Anon, if this good potion does its duty,
  He'll see in every wench the Trojan beauty.

Scene IV.—A Street

Faust. Margaret passes over.

FAUST.—My fair young lady, may I dare
  To offer you my escort home?
MARGARET.—Nor lady I, good sir, nor fair,
  And need no guide to show me home.   [*Exit.*
FAUST.—By heaven, this child is passing fair!
  A fairer never crossed my view;
  Of such a modest gentle air,
  Yet with a dash of pertness too,
  And girlish innocent conceit;
  Her lips so red, her cheeks so bright,
  Forget I could not, if I might.
  How she casts down her lovely eyes
  Deep graven in my heart it lies,
  And how so smartly she replied,
  And with a sharp turn stepped aside,
  It was most ravishingly sweet!

Enter Mephistopheles.

FAUST.—Hark! you must get the girl for me!

MEPHISTOPHELES.—Which one?

FAUST.—   She's just gone by.

MEPHISTOPHELES.—   What! she?
    She's only now come from confession,
    Where she received a full remission.
    I slinked close by the box, and heard
    The simple damsel's every word;
    'Tis a most guileless thing, that goes
    For very nothing to the priest.
    My power does not extend to those.

FAUST.—Yet she is fourteen years of age at least.

MEPHISTOPHELES.—You speak like Jack the debauchee,
    Who thinks each sweet flow'r grows for me;
    As if his wish sufficed alone
    To make each priceless pearl his own:
    But 'tis not so; and cannot be.

FAUST.—My good Sir Knight of pedantry,
    Lay not thou down the law to me!
    And this, for good and all, be told,
    Unless, this very night, I hold
    The sweet young maid in my embrace,
    'Tis the last time that you shall see my face.

MEPHISTOPHELES.—Bethink thee!—what with here, and what
        with there,
    The thing requires no little care.
    Full fourteen days must first be spent,
    To come upon the proper scent.

FAUST.—Had I but seven good hours of rest,
    The devil's aid I'd ne'er request,
    To mould this fair young creature to my bent.

MEPHISTOPHELES.—You speak as if you were a Frenchman
        born;
    But though the end be good, we must not scorn
    The means; what boots the mere gratification?
    It is the best half of the recreation,
    When, up and down, and to and fro,
    The pretty doll, through every kind

Of fiddle-faddle sweet flirtation,
You knead out first, and dress up to your mind—
As many an Italian tale can show.

FAUST.—I need no tricks to whet my zest.

MEPHISTOPHELES.—I tell thee plainly without jest,
As things stand here, we cannot win
The fort by hotly rushing in;
To gain fair lady's favor, you
Must boldly scheme, and gently do.

FAUST.—Fetch me something that breathed her air!
Her home, her chamber, plant me there!
A kerchief of her chaste attire!
A garter of my heart's desire!

MEPHISTOPHELES.—That you may see how I would fain
Do all I can to ease your pain,
We shall not lose a single minute;
I know her room—thou shalt enjoy thee in it.

FAUST.—And I shall see her?—have her?

MEPHISTOPHELES.—   No!
She'll be with a neighbor—better so.
Meanwhile, unhindered thou may'st go,
And on the hope of joys that wait thee,
Within her atmosphere may'st sate thee.

FAUST.—Can we go now?

MEPHISTOPHELES.—   No; we must wait till night.

FAUST.—Go fetch a present for my heart's delight.   [*Exit.*

MEPHISTOPHELES.—Presents already! good!—a lover should
not loiter!
I know some dainty spots of ground,
Where hidden treasures can be found;
I will go straight and reconnoitre.   [*Exit.*

Scene V.—A Small, Neat Chamber

MARGARET [*plaiting and putting up her hair*].—I wonder who
the gentleman could be,
That on the street accosted me to-day!
He looked a gallant cavalier and gay,
And must be of a noble family;
That I could read upon his brow—
Else had he never been so free.   [*Exit.*

Enter Faust and Mephistopheles.

MEPHISTOPHELES.—Come in—but softly—we are landed now!
FAUST [*after a pause*].—Leave me alone a minute, I entreat!
MEPHISTOPHELES [*looking round about*].—Not every maiden
    keeps her room so neat.   [*Exit.*
FAUST [*looking round*].—Be greeted, thou sweet twilight-
    shine!
Through this chaste sanctuary shed!
Oh seize my heart, sweet pains of love divine,
That on the languid dew of hope are fed!
What sacred stillness holds the air!
What order, what contentment rare!
[*He throws himself on the old leathern arm-chair beside the
    bed.*
Receive thou me! thou, who, in ages gone,
In joy and grief hast welcomed sire and son.
How often round this old paternal throne,
A clambering host of playful children hung!
Belike that here my loved one too hath clung
To her hoar grandsire's neck, with childish joy
Thankful received the yearly Christmas toy,
And with the full red cheeks of childhood pressed
Upon his withered hand a pious kiss.
I feel, sweet maid, mine inmost soul possessed
By thy calm spirit of order and of bliss,
That motherly doth teach thee day by day:
That bids thee deck the table clean and neat,
And crisps the very sand strewn at thy feet.
Sweet hand! sweet, lovely hand! where thou dost sway,
The meanest hut is decked in heaven's array.
And here!   [*He lifts up the bed-curtain.*
O Heaven, what strange o'ermastering might
Thrills every sense with fine delight!
Here might I gaze unwearied day and night.
Nature! in airy dreams here didst thou build
The mortal hull of the angelic child;
Here she reposed! her tender bosom teeming
With warmest life, in buoyant fulness streaming,
And here, with pulse of gently gracious power,

The heaven-born bud was nursed into a flower!
And thou! what brought thee here? why now back-
    shrinks
Thy courage from the prize it sought before?
What wouldst thou have? Thy heart within thee sinks;
Poor wretched Faust! thou know'st thyself no more.
Do I then breathe a magic atmosphere?
I sought immediate enjoyment here,
And into viewless dreams my passion flows!
Are we the sport of every breath that blows?
If now she came, and found me gazing here,
How for this boldfaced presence must I pay!
The mighty man, how small would he appear,
And at her feet, a suppliant, sink away!

MEPHISTOPHELES [*coming back*].—Quick! quick! I see her
    —she'll be here anon.

FAUST.—Yes, let's be gone! for once and all be gone!

MEPHISTOPHELES.—Here is a casket, of a goodly weight;
Its former lord, I ween, bewails its fate.
Come, put it in the press. I swear
She'll lose her senses when she sees it there.
The trinkets that I stowed within it
Were bait meant for a nobler prey:
But child is child, and play is play!

FAUST.—I know not—shall I?

MEPHISTOPHELES.—   Can you doubt a minute?
Would you then keep the dainty pelf,
Like an old miser, to yourself?
If so, I would advise you, sir,
To spare your squire the bitter toil,
And with some choicer sport the hour beguile
Than looking lustfully at her.
I scratch my head and rub my hands that you—

[*He puts the casket into the cupboard, and locks the door again.*
Come, let's away!—
With this sweet piece of womanhood may do,
As will may sway;
And you stand there,
And gape and stare,
As if you looked into a lecture-room,

And there with awe
The twin gray spectres bodily saw,
Physics and Metaphysics! Come!   *[Exeunt.*

Enter Margaret, with a lamp.

MARGARET.—It is so sultry here, so hot!
                                        [She opens the window.
And yet so warm without 'tis not.
I feel—I know not how—oppressed;
Would to God that my mother came!
A shivering cold runs o'er my frame—
I'm but a silly timid girl at best!
                        [While taking off her clothes, she sings.

There was a king in Thule,
True-hearted to his grave:
To him his dying lady
A golden goblet gave.

He prized it more than rubies;
At every drinking-bout
His eyes they swam in glory,
When he would drain it out.

On his death-bed he counted
His cities one by one;
Unto his heirs he left them;
The bowl he gave to none.

He sat amid his barons,
And feasted merrily,
Within his father's castle,
That beetles o'er the sea.

There stood the old carouser,
And drank his life's last glow;
Then flung the goblet over
Into the sea below.

He saw it fall, and gurgling
Sink deep into the sea;
His eyes they sank in darkness;
No bumper more drank he.

[*She opens the cupboard to put in her clothes, and sees the casket.*

How came the pretty casket here? no doubt
I locked the press when I went out.
'Tis really strange!—Belike that it was sent
A pledge for money that my mother lent.
Here hangs the key; sure there can be no sin
In only looking what may be within.
What have we here? good heavens! see!
What a display of finery!
Here is a dress in which a queen
Might on a gala-day be seen.
I wonder how the necklace would suit me!
Who may the lord of all this splendor be?
[*She puts on the necklace, and looks at herself in the glass.*
Were but the ear-rings mine to wear!
It gives one such a different air.
What boots the beauty of the poor?
'Tis very beautiful to be sure,
But without riches little weighs;
They praise you, but half pity while they praise.
Gold is the pole,
To which all point: the whole
Big world hangs on gold. Alas we poor!

Scene VI.—A Walk

Faust going up and down, thoughtfully. Enter Mephistopheles.

MEPHISTOPHELES.—By all the keen pangs of love! by all the
hot blasts of hell!
By all the fellest of curses, if curse there be any more
fell!
FAUST.—How now, Mephisto? what the devil's wrong?
I ne'er beheld a face one half so long!
MEPHISTOPHELES.—But that I am a devil myself, I'd sell
Both soul and body on the spot to hell!
FAUST.—I verily believe you've got a craze!
Beseems it you with such outrageous phrase,
To rage like any bedlamite?

MEPHISTOPHELES.—Only conceive! the box of rare gewgaws
    For Margaret got, is in a parson's claws!
    The thing came to the mother's sight,
    Who soon suspected all was not right:
    The woman has got a most delicate nose,
    That snuffling through the prayer-book goes,
    And seldom scents a thing in vain,
    If it be holy or profane.
    Your jewels, she was not long in guessing,
    Were not like to bring a blessing.
    " My child," quoth she, " ill-gotten gear
    Ensnares the soul, consumes the blood;
    We'll give it to Mary-mother dear,
    And she will feed us with heavenly food!"
    Margaret looked blank—" 'tis hard," thought she,
    " To put a gift-horse away from me;
    And surely godless was he never
    Who lodged it here, a gracious giver."
    The mother then brought in the priest;
    He quickly understood the jest,
    And his eyes watered at the sight.
    " Good dame," quoth he, " you have done right!
    He conquers all the world who wins
    A victory o'er his darling sins.
    The Church is a most sharp-set lady,
    And her stomach holds good store,
    Has swallowed lands on lands already,
    And, still unglutted, craves for more;
    The Church alone, my ladies dear,
    Can digest ill-gotten gear."
FAUST.—That is a general fashion—Jew,
    And King, and Kaiser have it too.
MEPHISTOPHELES.—Then ring and ear-ring, and necklace, and
        casket,
    Like a bundle of toad-stools away he bore;
    Thanked her no less, and thanked her no more,
    Than had it been so many nuts in a basket;
    On heavenly treasures then held an oration,
    Much, of course, to their edification.
FAUST.—And Margaret?

MEPHISTOPHELES.— Sits now in restless mood,
Knows neither what she would, nor what she should;
Broods o'er the trinkets night and day,
And on him who sent them, more.

FAUST.—Sweet love! her grief doth vex me sore.
Mephisto, mark well what I say!
Get her another set straightway!
The first were not so very fine.

MEPHISTOPHELES.—O yes! with you all things are mere child's
play.

FAUST.—Quick hence! and match your will with mine!
Throw thee oft in her neighbor's way.
Be not a devil of milk and water,
And for another gift go cater.

MEPHISTOPHELES.—Yes, gracious sir! most humbly I obey.

[*Exit Faust.*

MEPHISTOPHELES.—Such love-sick fools as these would blow
Sun, moon, and stars, like vilest stuff,
To nothing with a single puff,
To make their lady-love a show!

Scene VII.—Martha's House

MARTHA [*alone*].—In honest truth, it was not nobly done,
In my good spouse to leave me here alone!
May God forgive him! while he roams at large,
O'er the wide world, I live at my own charge.
Sure he could have no reason to complain!
So good a wife he'll not find soon again.

[*She weeps.*

He may be dead!—Ah me!—could I but know,
By a certificate, that 'tis really so!

Enter Margaret.

MARGARET.—Martha!
MARTHA.— What wouldst thou, dear?
MARGARET.—My knees can scarcely bear me!—only hear!
I found a second box to-day
Of ebon-wood, just where the first one lay,

MEPHISTOPHELES.—   Sweet guileless heart!
   Ladies, farewell!
MARGARET.—   Farewell!
MARTHA.—   One word before we part!
   I fain would have it solemnly averred,
   How my dear husband died, and where he was interred.
   Order was aye my special virtue; and
   'Tis right both where and when he died should stand
   In the newspapers.
MEPHISTOPHELES.—   Yes, when two attest,
   As Scripture saith, the truth is manifest.
   I have a friend, who, at your requisition,
   Before the judge will make a deposition.
   I'll bring him here
MARTHA.—   Yes, bring him with you, do!
MEPHISTOPHELES.—And we shall meet your fair young lady
     too?
   [*To Margaret.*]   A gallant youth!—has been abroad,
     and seen
   The world—a perfect cavalier, I trow.
MARGARET.—'Twould make me blush, should he bestow
   A single look on one so mean.
MEPHISTOPHELES.—You have no cause to be ashamed before
   The proudest king that ever sceptre bore.
MARTHA.—This evening, in the garden then, behind
   The house, you'll find warm hearts and welcome kind!

Scene VIII.—A Street

Faust and Mephistopheles, meeting

FAUST.—How now? what news? how speed your labors?
MEPHISTOPHELES.—Bravo! 'tis well you are on fire;
   Soon shall you have your heart's desire.
   This evening you shall meet her at her neighbor's.
   A dame 'tis to a nicety made
   For the bawd and gypsy trade.
FAUST.—'Tis well.
MEPHISTOPHELES.—But you must lend a hand, and so must I.
   VOL. II.—7

FAUST.—One good turn deserves another.

MEPHISTOPHELES.—We must appear before a judge together,
　　And solemnly there testify
　　That stiff and stark her worthy spouse doth lie,
　　Beside the shrine of holy Antony.

FAUST.—Most wise! we must first make a goodly travel!

MEPHISTOPHELES.—*Sancta simplicitas!* what stuff you drivel!
　　We may make oath, and not know much about it.

FAUST.—If that's your best, your best is bad. I scout it.

MEPHISTOPHELES.—O holy man that would outwit the devil!
　　Is it the first time in your life that you
　　Have sworn to what you knew could not be true?
　　Of God, the world, and all that it contains,
　　Of man, and all that circles in his veins,
　　Or dwells within the compass of his brains,
　　Have you not pompous definitions given,
　　With swelling breast and dogmatizing brow,
　　As if you were an oracle from heaven?
　　And yet, if the plain truth you will avow,
　　You knew as much of all these things, in faith,
　　As now you know of Master Schwerdtlein's death!

FAUST.—Thou art, and wert, a sophist and a liar.

MEPHISTOPHELES.—Yes, unless one could mount a little higher.
　　To-morrow I shall hear you pour
　　False vows that silly girl before,
　　Swear to do everything to serve her,
　　And love her with a quenchless fervor.

FAUST.—And from my heart too.

MEPHISTOPHELES.—　　　　　　　　Oh! of course, of course!
　　Then will you speak, till you are hoarse,
　　Of love, and constancy, and truth,
　　And feelings of eternal youth—
　　Will that too be the simple sooth?

FAUST.—It will! it will!—for, when I feel,
　　And for the feeling, the confusion
　　Of feelings, that absorbs my mind,
　　Seek for names, and none can find,
　　Sweep through the universe's girth
　　For every highest word to give it birth;
　　And then this soul-pervading flame,

Infinite, endless, endless name,
Call you this nought but devilish delusion?
MEPHISTOPHELES.—Still I am right!
FAUST.—   Hold! mark me, you
Are right indeed! for this is true,
Who will be right, and only has a tongue,
Is never wrong.
Come, I confess thee master in debating,
That I may be delivered from thy prating.

ACT FOURTH

Scene I.—Martha's Garden

*Margaret on Faust's arm; Martha with Mephistopheles,
walking up and down.*

MARGARET.—I feel it well, 'tis from pure condescension
You pay to one like me so much attention.
With travellers 'tis a thing of course,
To be contented with the best they find;
For sure a man of cultivated mind
Can have small pleasure in my poor discourse.

FAUST.—One look from thee, one word, delights me more
Than all the world's high-vaunted lore.
                                        [*He kisses her hand.*

MARGARET.—O trouble not yourself! how could you kiss it so?
It is so coarse, so rough! for I must go
Through all the work above stairs and below,
Mother will have it so.   [*They pass on.*

MARTHA.—   And you, sir, will it still
Be your delight from place to place to roam?

MEPHISTOPHELES.—In this our duty guides us, not our will.
With what sad hearts from many a place we go,
Where we had almost learned to be at home!

MARTHA.—When one is young it seems a harmless gambol,
Thus round and round through the wide world to
    ramble:
But soon the evil day comes on,
And as a stiff old bachelor to die
Has never yet done good to any one.

MEPHISTOPHELES.—I see ahead, and fear such wretched fate.

MARTHA.—Then, sir, take warning ere it be too late!
                                        [*They pass on.*

MARGARET.—Yes, out of sight, and out of mind!
     You see me now, and are so kind:
     But you have friends at home of station high,
     With far more wit and far more sense than I.
FAUST.—Their sense, dear girl, is often nothing more
     Than vain conceit of vain short-sighted lore.
MARGARET.—How mean you that?
FAUST.—   Oh that the innocent heart
     And sweet simplicity, unspoiled by art,
     So seldom knows its own rare quality!
     That fair humility, the comeliest grace
     Which bounteous Nature sheds on blooming face——
MARGARET.—Do thou bestow a moment's thought on me,
     I shall have time enough to think of thee.
FAUST.—You are then much alone?
MARGARET.—Our household is but small, I own,
     And yet must be attended to.
     We keep no maid; I have the whole to do,
     Must wash and brush, and sew and knit,
     And cook, and early run and late;
     And then my mother is, in every whit,
     So accurate!
     Not that she needs to pinch her household; we
     Might do much more than many others do:
     My father left a goodly sum, quite free
     From debt, with a neat house and garden too,
     Close by the town, just as you pass the gate;
     But we have lived retired enough of late.
     My brother is a soldier: he
     Is at the wars: my little sister's dead:
     Poor thing! it caused me many an hour of pain
     To see it pine, and droop its little head,
     But gladly would I suffer all again,
     So much I loved the child!
FAUST.—   An angel, if like thee!
MARGARET.—I nursed it, and it loved me heartily.
     My father died before it saw the light,
     My mother was despaired of quite,
     So miserably weak she lay.
     Yet she recovered slowly, day by day;

And as she had not strength herself
To suckle the poor helpless elf,
She gave it in charge to me, and I
With milk and water nursed it carefully.
Thus in my arm, and on my lap, it grew,
And smiled and crowed, and flung its legs about,
And called me mother too.

FAUST.—To thy pure heart the purest joy, no doubt.

MARGARET.—Ay! but full many an hour
Heavy with sorrow, and with labor sour.
The infant's cradle stood beside
My bed, and when it stirred or cried,
I must awake;
Sometimes to give it drink, sometimes to take
It with me to my bed, and fondle it:
And when all this its fretting might not stay,
I rose, and danced about, and dandled it;
And after that I must away
To wash the clothes by break of day.
I make the markets too, and keep house for my mother,
One weary day just like another;
Thus drudging on, the day might lack delights,
But food went lightly down, and sleep was sweet o'
     nights.   [*They pass on.*

MARTHA.—A woman's case is not much to be vaunted;
A hardened bachelor is hard to mend.

MEPHISTOPHELES.—A few apostles such as you were wanted,
From evil ways their vagrant steps to bend.

MARTHA.—Speak plainly, sir, have you found nothing yet?
Are you quite disentangled from the net?

MEPHISTOPHELES.—A house and hearth, we have been often
          told,
With a good wife, is worth its weight in gold.

MARTHA.—I mean, sir, have you never felt the want?

MEPHISTOPHELES.—A good reception I have always found.

MARTHA.—I mean to say, did your heart never pant?

MEPHISTOPHELES.—For ladies my respect is too profound
     To jest on such a serious theme as this.

MARTHA.—My meaning still you strangely miss!

MEPHISTOPHELES.—Alas, that I should be so blind!
  One thing I plainly see, that you are very kind!
             [They pass on.

FAUST.—You knew me, then, you little angel! straight,
  When you beheld me at the garden-gate?

MARGARET.—Marked you it not?—You saw my downward
   look.

FAUST.—And you forgive the liberty I took,
  When from the minster you came out that day,
  And I, with forward boldness more than meet,
  Then ventured to address you on the street?

MARGARET.—I was surprised, I knew not what to say;
  No one could speak an evil word of me.
  Did he, perchance, in my comportment see
  Aught careless or improper on that day,
  That he should take me for a worthless girl,
  Whom round his little finger he might twirl?
  Not yet the favorable thoughts I knew,
  That even then were rising here for you;
  One thing I know, myself I sharply chid,
  That I could treat you then no harshlier than I did.

FAUST.—Sweet love!

MARGARET.—   Let go!

*[She plucks a star-flower, and pulls the petals off, one after
  another.*

FAUST.—   What's that? a nosegay? let me see!

MARGARET.—'Tis but a game.

FAUST.—   How so?

MARGARET.—   Go! you would laugh at me.

[She continues pulling the petals, and murmuring to herself.

FAUST.—What are you murmuring now, so sweetly low?

MARGARET *[half aloud]*.—He loves me, yes!—he loves me, no!

FAUST.—Thou sweet angelic face!

MARGARET *[murmuring as before]*.—He loves me, yes!—he
  loves me, no!

   [Pulling out the last petal with manifest delight.

  He loves me, yes!

FAUST.—Yes, child! the fair flower-star hath answered YES!
  In this the judgment of the gods approves thee;
  He loves thee! know'st thou what it means?—He loves
   thee!   *[He seizes her by both hands.*

MARGARET.—I scarce can speak for joy!

FAUST.—Fear thee not, love! But let this look proclaim,
This pressure of my hand declare
What words can never name:
To yield us to an ecstacy of joy,
And feel this tranceful bliss must be
Eternal! yes! its end would be despair!
It hath no end! no end for thee and me!

[*Margaret presses his hands, makes herself free, and runs away.
He stands still for a moment, thoughtfully, then follows
her.*

MARTHA [*coming up*].—'Tis getting late.

MEPHISTOPHELES.—   Yes, and we must away.

MARTHA.—I fain would have you stay;
But 'tis an evil neighborhood,
Where idle gossips find their only good,
Their pleasure and their business too,
In spying out all that their neighbors do.
And thus, the whole town in a moment knows
The veriest trifle. But where is our young pair?

MEPHISTOPHELES.—Like wanton birds of summer, through the
air
I saw them dart away.

MARTHA.—   He seems well pleased with her.

MEPHISTOPHELES.—And she with him. 'Tis thus the world
goes.

Scene II.—A Summer-house in the Garden

*Margaret comes in, and hides herself behind the door. She
places her finger on her lips, and looks through a rent.*

MARGARET.—He comes!

FAUST [*coming up*].— Ha! ha! thou cunning soul, and thou
Wouldst trick me thus; but I have caught thee now!
[*He kisses her.*

MARGARET [*clasping him and returning the kiss*].—Thou best
of men, with my whole heart I love thee!
[*Mephistopheles heard knocking.*

FAUST [*stamping*].—Who's there?

MEPHISTOPHELES.—   A friend!
FAUST.—   A beast!
MEPHISTOPHELES.—   'Tis time now to remove thee.
MARTHA [*coming up*].—Yes, sir, 'tis getting late.
FAUST.—   May I not take you home?
MARGARET.—My mother would—farewell!
FAUST.—   And must I leave you then?
      Farewell!
MARTHA.—   Adieu!
MARGARET.—   Right soon to meet again!
                    [*Exeunt Faust and Mephistopheles.*
MARGARET [*alone*].—Dear God! what such a man as this
      Can think on all and everything!
      I stand ashamed, and simple *yes*
      Is the one answer I can bring.
      I wonder what a man, so learned as he,
      Can find in a poor simple girl like me.   [*Exit.*

Scene III.—Wood and Cavern

FAUST [*alone*].—Spirit Supreme! thou gav'st me—gav'st me
            all,
      For which I asked thee. Not in vain hast thou
      Turned toward me thy countenance in fire.
      Thou gavest me wide Nature for my kingdom,
      And power to feel it, to enjoy it. Not
      Cold gaze of wonder gav'st thou me alone,
      But even into her bosom's depth to look,
      As it might be the bosom of a friend.
      The grand array of living things thou mad'st
      To pass before me, mad'st me know my brothers
      In silent bush, in water, and in air.
      And when the straining storm loud roars, and raves
      Through the dark forest, and the giant pine,
      Root-wrenched, tears all the neighboring branches down
      And neighboring stems, and strews the ground with
            wreck,
      And to their fall the hollow mountain thunders;
      Then dost thou guide me to the cave, where safe

I learn to know myself, and from my breast
Deep and mysterious wonders are unfolded.
Then mounts the pure white moon before mine eye
With mellow ray, and in her softening light,
From rocky wall, from humid brake, upfloat
The silvery shapes of times by-gone, and soothe
The painful pleasure of deep-brooding thought.
Alas! that man enjoys no perfect bliss,
I feel it now. Thou gav'st me with this joy,
Which brings me near and nearer to the gods,
A fellow, whom I cannot do without.
All cold and heartless, he debases me
Before myself, and, with a single breath,
Blows all the bounties of thy love to nought;
And fans within my breast a raging fire
For that fair image, busy to do ill.
Thus reel I from desire on to enjoyment,
And in enjoyment languish for desire.

Enter Mephistopheles.

MEPHISTOPHELES.—What! not yet tired of meditation?
Methinks this is a sorry recreation.
To try it once or twice might do;
But then, again to something new.
FAUST.—You might employ your time some better way
Than thus to plague me on a happy day.
MEPHISTOPHELES.—Well, well! I do not grudge you quiet,
You need my aid, and you cannot deny it.
There is not much to lose, I trow,
With one so harsh, and gruff, and mad as thou.
Toil! moil! from morn to ev'n, so on it goes!
And what one should, and what one should not do,
One cannot always read it on your nose.
FAUST.—This is the proper tone for you!
Annoy me first, and then my thanks are due.
MEPHISTOPHELES.—Poor son of Earth! without my timed as-
sistance,
How had you ever dragged on your existence?
From freakish fancy's fevered effervescence,

I have worked long ago your convalescence,
And, but for me, you would have marched away,
In your best youth, from the blest light of day.
What have you here, in caves and clefts, to do,
Like an old owl, screeching to-whit, to-whoo?
Or like a torpid toad, that sits alone
Sipping the oozing moss and dripping stone?
A precious condition to be in!
I see the Doctor sticks yet in your skin.

FAUST.—Couldst thou but know what reborn vigor springs
From this lone wandering in the wilderness,
Couldst thou conceive what heavenly joy it brings,
Then wert thou fiend enough to envy me my bliss.

MEPHISTOPHELES.—A supermundane bliss!
In night and dew to lie upon the height,
And clasp the heaven and earth in wild delight,
To swell up to the godhead's stature,
And pierce with clear miraculous sight
The inmost pith of central Nature,
To carry in your breast with strange elation,
The ferment of the whole six days' creation,
With proud anticipation of—I know
Not what—to glow in rapturous overflow,
And melt into the universal mind,
Casting the paltry son of earth behind;
And then, the heaven-sprung intuition
[*With a gesture.*] To end—I shall not say in what—
    fruition.

FAUST.—Shame on thee!

MEPHISTOPHELES.—   Yes! that's not quite to your mind.
You have a privilege to cry out shame,
When things are mentioned by their proper name.
Before chaste ears one may not dare to spout
What chastest hearts yet cannot do without.
I do not envy you the pleasure
Of palming lies upon yourself at leisure;
But long it cannot last, I warrant thee.
You are returned to your old whims, I see,
And, at this rate, you soon will wear
Your strength away, in madness and despair.

Of this enough! thy love sits waiting thee,
In doubt and darkness, cabined and confined.
By day, by night, she has thee in her mind;
I trow she loves thee in no common kind.
Thy raging passion 'gan to flow,
Like a torrent in spring from melted snow;
Into her heart thy tide gushed high,
Now is thy shallow streamlet dry.
Instead of standing here to overbrim
With fine ecstatic rapture to the trees,
Methinks the mighty gentleman might please
To drop some words of fond regard, to ease
The sweet young chick who droops and pines for him.
Poor thing, she is half dead of ennui,
And at the window stands whole hours, to see
The clouds pass by the old town-wall along.
Were I a little bird! so goes her song
The live-long day, and half the night to boot.
Sometimes she will be merry, mostly sad,
Now, like a child, weeping her sorrows out,
Now calm again to look at, never glad;
Always in love.

FAUST.—   Thou snake! thou snake!

MEPHISTOPHELES [*to himself*].—So be it! that my guile thy
        stubborn will may break!

FAUST.—Hence and begone, thou son of filth and fire!
        Name not the lovely maid again!
        Bring not that overmastering desire
        Once more to tempt my poor bewildered brain!

MEPHISTOPHELES.—What then? she deems that you are gone
        forever;
        And half and half methinks you are.

FAUST.—No! I am nigh, and were I ne'er so far,
        I could forget her, I could lose her never;
        I envy ev'n the body of the Lord,
        When on the sacred cake her lips she closes.

MEPHISTOPHELES.—Yes! to be honest, and confess my sins,
        I oft have envied thee the lovely twins
        That have their fragrant pasture among roses.

FAUST.—Avaunt, thou pimp!

MEPHISTOPHELES.—   Rail you, and I will laugh;
    The God who made the human stuff
    Both male and female, if the book don't lie,
    Himself the noblest trade knew well enough,
    How to carve out an opportunity.
    But come, why peak and pine you here?
    I lead you to the chamber of your dear,
    Not to the gallows.
FAUST.—Ah! what were Heaven's supremest blessedness
    Within her arms, upon her breast, to me!
    Must I not still be wrung with agony,
    That I should plunge her into such distress?
    I, the poor fugitive! outlaw from my kind,
    Without a friend, without a home,
    With restless heart, and aimless mind,
    Unblest, unblessing, ever doomed to roam;
    Who, like a waterfall, from rock to rock came roaring,
    With greedy rage into the caldron pouring;
    While she, a heedless infant, rears
    Sidewards her hut upon the Alpine field,
    With all her hopes, and all her fears,
    Within this little world concealed.
    And I—the God-detested—not content
    To seize the rocks, and in my headlong bent
    To shatter them to dust, with ruthless tide
    Her little shielding on the mountain side
    Bore down, and wrecked her life's sweet peace with mine.
    And such an offering, Hell, must it be thine?
    Help, Devil, to cut short the hour of ill!
    What happen must, may happen when it will!
    May her sad fate my crashing fall attend,
    And she with me be ruined in the end!
MEPHISTOPHELES.—Lo! how it boils again and blows
    Like furnace, wherefore no man knows.
    Go in, thou fool, and let her borrow
    From thee, sweet solace to her sorrow!
    When such a brain-sick dreamer sees
    No road, where he to walk may please,
    He stands and stares like Balaam's ass,
    As if a god did block the pass.

A man's a man who does and dares!
In other points you're spiced not scantly with the devil;
Nothing more silly moves on earth's wide level,
Than is a devil who despairs.

Scene IV.—Margaret's Room

Margaret alone, at a Spinning-wheel.

MARGARET.—
My rest is gone,
My heart is sore;
Peace find I never,
And nevermore.

Where he is not
Life is the tomb,
The world is bitterness
And gloom.

Crazed is my poor
Distracted brain,
My thread of thought
Is rent in twain.

My rest is gone,
My heart is sore;
Peace find I never,
And nevermore.

I look from the window
For none but him,
I go abroad
For only him.

His noble air,
His bearing high,
The smile of his mouth,
The might of his eye,

And, when he speaks,
What flow of bliss!

The clasp of his hand,
And ah! his kiss!

My rest is gone,
My heart is sore;
Peace find I never,
And nevermore.

My bosom swells,
And pants for him.
O that I might clasp him,
And cling to him!
And kiss him, and kiss him
The live-long day,
And on his kisses
Melt away!

Scene V.—Martha's Garden

Margaret and Faust.

MARGARET.—Promise me, Henry!
FAUST.—   What I can.
MARGARET.—Of your religion I am fain to hear;
    I know thou art a most kind-hearted man,
    But as to thy belief I fear——
FAUST.—Fear not! thou know'st I love thee well: and know
    For whom I love my life's last drop shall flow!
    For other men, I have nor wish nor need
    To rob them of their church, or of their creed.
MARGARET.—That's not enough; you must believe it too!
FAUST.—Must I?
MARGARET.— Alas! that I might work some change on you!
    Not even the holy mass do you revere.
FAUST.—I do revere 't.
MARGARET.—   Yes, but without desire.
    At mass and at confession, too, I fear,
    Thou hast not shown thyself this many a year.
    Dost thou believe in God?
FAUST.—   My love, who dares aspire

To say he doth believe in God?
May'st ask thy priests and sages all,
Their answer seems like mockery to fall
Upon the asker's ear.

MARGARET.—   Then thou dost not believe?

FAUST.—Misunderstand me not, thou sweet, angelic face!
Who dares pronounce His name?
And who proclaim—
I do believe in Him?
And who dares presume
To utter—I believe Him not?
The All-embracer,
The All-upholder,
Grasps and upholds He not
Thee, me, Himself?
Vaults not the Heaven his vasty dome above thee?
Stand not the earth's foundations firm beneath thee?
And climb not, with benignant beaming,
Up heaven's slope the eternal stars?
Looks not mine eye now into thine?
And feel'st thou not an innate force propelling
Thy tide of life to head and heart,
A power that, in eternal mystery dwelling,
Invisible visible moves beside thee?
Go, fill thy heart therewith, in all its greatness,
And when thy heart brims with this feeling,
Then call it what thou wilt,
Heart! Happiness! Love! God!
I have no name for that which passes all revealing!
Feeling is all in all;
Name is but smoke and sound,
Enshrouding heaven's pure glow.

MARGARET.—All that appears most pious and profound;
Much of the same our parson says,
Only he clothes it in a different phrase.

FAUST.—All places speak it forth;
All hearts, from farthest South to farthest North,
Proclaim the tale divine,
Each in its proper speech;
Wherefore not I in mine?

MARGARET.—When thus you speak it does not seem so bad,
    And yet is your condition still most sad:
    Unless you are a Christian, all is vain.
FAUST.—Sweet love!
MARGARET.—   Henry, it gives me pain,
    More than my lips can speak, to see
    Thee joined to such strange company.
FAUST.—How so?
MARGARET.—   The man whom thou hast made thy mate,
    Deep in my inmost soul I hate;
    Nothing in all my life hath made me smart
    So much as his disgusting leer.
    His face stabs like a dagger through my heart!
FAUST.—Sweet doll! thou hast no cause to fear.
MARGARET.—It makes my blood to freeze when he comes near.
    To other men I have no lack
    Of kindly thoughts; but as I long
    To see thy face, I shudder back
    From him. That he's a knave I make no doubt;
    May God forgive me, if I do him wrong!
FAUST.—Such grim old owls must be; without
    Their help the world could not get on, I fear.
MARGARET.—With men like him I would have nought to do!
    As often as he shows him here,
    He looks in at the door with such a scornful leer,
    Half angry too;
    Whate'er is done, he takes no kindly part;
    And one can see it written on his face,
    He never loved a son of Adam's race.
    Henry, within thy loving arm
    I feel so free, so trustful-warm;
    But when his foot comes near, I start,
    And feel a freezing grip tie up my heart.
FAUST.—O thou prophetic angel, thou!
MARGARET.—This overpowers me so
    That, when his icy foot may cross the door,
    I feel as if I could not love thee more.
    When he is here, too, I could never pray;
    This eats my very heart. Now say,
    Henry, is't not the same with thee?
    VOL. II.—8

FAUST.—Nay now, this is mere blind antipathy!

MARGARET.—I must be gone.

FAUST.—   Oh! may it never be
     That I shall spend one quiet hour with thee,
     One single little hour, and breast on breast,
     And soul on soul, with panting love, be pressed?

MARGARET.—Alas! did I but sleep alone, this night
     The door unbarred thy coming should invite;
     But my good mother has but broken sleep;
     And, if her ears an inkling got,
     Then were I dead upon the spot!

FAUST.—Sweet angel! that's an easy fence to leap.
     Here is a juice, whose grateful power can steep
     Her senses in a slumber soft and deep;
     Three drops mixed with her evening draught will do.

MARGARET.—I would adventure this and more for you.
     Of course, there's nothing hurtful in the phial?

FAUST.—If so, would I advise the trial?

MARGARET.—Thou best of men, if I but look on thee,
     All will deserts me to thy wish untrue;
     So much already have I done for thee
     That now scarce aught remains for me to do.   [*Exit.*

Enter Mephistopheles.

MEPHISTOPHELES.—Well, is the monkey gone?

FAUST.—   And you—must I
     Submit again to see you play the spy?

MEPHISTOPHELES.—I have been duly advertised
     How Doctor Faust was catechised:
     I hope it will agree with you.
     The girls are wont—they have their reasons too—
     To see that one, in every point, believes
     The faith, that from his fathers he receives.
     They think, if little mettle here he shows,
     We too may lead him by the nose.

FAUST.—Thou monster! dost not know how this fond soul,
     Who yields her being's whole
     To God, and feels and knows
     That from such faith alone her own salvation flows,

With many an anxious holy fear is tossed,
Lest he, whom best she loves, should be forever lost?
MEPHISTOPHELES.—Thou super-sensual sensual fool,
A silly girl takes thee to school!
FAUST.—Thou son of filth and fire, thou monster, thou!
MEPHISTOPHELES.—And then her skill in reading faces
Is not the least of all her graces!
When I come near, she feels, she knows not how,
And through my mask can read it on my brow
That I must be, if not the very Devil,
A genius far above the common level.
And now to-night——
FAUST.—   What's that to thee?
MEPHISTOPHELES.—What brings my master joy, brings joy
to me.

Scene VI.—At the Well

Margaret and Eliza, with water-pitchers.

ELIZA.—Have you heard nought of Barbara?
MARGARET.—Nothing at all. I seldom stray
From home, to hear of other folk's affairs.
ELIZA.—You may believe me every whit;
Sibylla told it me to-day.
She too has been befooled: that comes of it,
When people give themselves such airs!
MARGARET.—   How so?
ELIZA.—   'Tis rank!
She eats and drinks for two, not now for one.
MARGARET.—Poor girl!
ELIZA.—   Well, well! she has herself to thank.
How long did she not hang upon
The fellow!—Yes! that was a parading,
A dancing and a promenading!
Must always be before the rest!
And to wines and pasties be pressed;
Began then to be proud of her beauty,
And was so reckless of her duty
As to take presents from him too.

That was a cooing and a caressing!
No wonder if the flower too be a-missing!
MARGARET.—I pity her.
ELIZA.—   Methinks you have not much to do.
When we were not allowed to venture o'er
The threshold, night and day kept close at spinning,
There stood she, with her paramour,
Upon the bench, before the door,
Or in the lane, and hour for hour
Scarce knew the end from the beginning.
'Tis time that she should go to school
And learn—on the repentance-stool!
MARGARET.—But he will take her for his wife.
ELIZA.—He marry her! not for his life!
An active youth like him can find,
Where'er he pleases, quarters to his mind.
Besides, he's gone!
MARGARET.—   That was not fair.
ELIZA.—And if he should come back, she'll not enjoy him more.
Her marriage wreath the boys will tear,
And we will strew chopped straw before the door.
                                        [Exit.

MARGARET [going homewards].—How could I once so boldly
    chide
When a poor maiden stepped aside,
And scarce found words enough to name
The measure of a sister's shame!
If it was black, I blackened it yet more,
And with that blackness not content,
More thickly still laid on the paint,
And blessed my stars, as cased in mail,
Against all frailties of the frail;
And now myself am what I chid before!—
Yet was each step that lured my slippery feet
So good, so lovely, so enticing sweet!

Scene VII.—An Enclosed Area

In a niche of the wall an image of the Mater dolorosa, with flower-jugs before it.

MARGARET [*placing fresh flowers in the jugs*].—O mother rich
      in sorrows,
    Bend down to hear my cry!
    O bend thee, gracious mother,
    To my sore agony!

    Thy heart with swords is piercèd,
    And tears are in thine eye,
    Because they made thy dear Son
    A cruel death to die.

    Thou lookest up to heaven,
    And deeply thou dost sigh;
    His God and thine beholds thee,
    And heals thine agony.

    Oh! who can know
    What bitter woe
    Doth pierce me through and through?
    The fear, the anguish of my heart,
    Its every pang, its every smart,
    Know'st thou, and only thou.

    And wheresoe'er I wend me,
    What woes, what woes attend me,
    And how my bosom quakes!
    And in my chamber lonely,
    With weeping, weeping only,
    My heart for sorrow breaks.

    These flower-pots on the window
    I wet with tears, ah me!
    When with the early morning,
    I plucked these flowers for thee.

And when the morn's first sunbeam
Into my room was shed,
I sat, in deepest anguish,
And watched it on my bed.

O save me, Mother of Sorrows!
Unto my prayer give heed,
By all the swords that pierced thee,
O save me in my need!

Scene VIII.—Night

Street before Margaret's door.   Enter Valentin.

VALENTIN.—When I sat with our merry men,
At a carousal, now and then,
Where one may be allowed a boast,
And my messmates gave toast for toast
To the girl they prized the most,
And with a bumper then swilled o'er
Their praise, when they could praise no more;
I'd sit at ease, and lean upon
My elbow, while they prated on,
Till all the swaggerers had done,
And smile and stroke my beard, and fill
The goodly rummer to my hand,
And say, All that is very well!
But is there one, in all the land,
That with my Margaret may compare,
Or even tie the shoe to her?
Rap, rap! cling, clang! so went it round!
From man to man, with gleesome sound,
And one cried out with lusty breath,
" Yes, Gretchen! Gretchen! she's the girl,
Of womanhood the perfect pearl!"
And all the braggarts were dumb as death.
And now—the devil's in the matter!
It is enough to make one clatter,
Like a rat, along the walls!

Shall every boor, with gibe and jeer,
Turn up his nose when I appear?
And every pettiest word that falls
Me, like a purseless debtor, torture?
And though I bruised them in a mortar,
I could not say that they were wrong.
What comes apace?—what creeps along?
A pair of them comes slinking by.
If 'tis the man I look for, I
Will dust his coat so well he'll not,
By Jove! go living from the spot!   [*Retires.*

Enter Faust and Mephistopheles.

FAUST.—As from the window of the vestry there,
　The light of the undying lamp doth glare,
　And sidewards gleameth, dimmer still and dimmer,
　Till darkness closes round its fitful glimmer,
　So murky is it in my soul.
MEPHISTOPHELES.—And I've a qualmish sort of feeling,
　Like a cat on a rainy day,
　Creeping round the wall, and stealing
　Near the fireplace, if it may.
　Yet am I in most virtuous trim
　For a small turn at stealing, or at lechery;
　So jumps already through my every limb
　Walpurgis-Night, with all its glorious witchery.
　The day after to-morrow brings again
　The Feast, with fun and frolic in its train.
FAUST.—Is it not time that you were raising
　The treasure there in the distance blazing?
MEPHISTOPHELES.—Soon shall you sate your eyes with gazing,
　And lift up from the urn yourself
　A little mine of precious pelf.
　I gave it a side-glance before—
　Saw lion-dollars by the score.
FAUST.—Is there no gaud?—no jewel at all?
　To deck my sweet little mistress withal.
MEPHISTOPHELES.—O yes! I saw some trinkets for the girls—
　A sort of necklace strung with pearls.

FAUST.—'Tis well that we have this to give her,
    For empty-handed go I never.
MEPHISTOPHELES.—And yet a wise man ought to learn
    To enjoy gratis, as well as to earn.
    Now, that the stars are bright and clear the sky,
    I'll give you a touch of choicest melody;
    A moral song—that, while we seem to school her,
    With the more certainty we may befool her.
                    [*Sings to the guitar.*

    Why stands before
    Her lover's door,
    Young Catherine here,
    At early break of day?
    Beware, beware!
    He lets thee in,
    A maiden in,
    A maiden not away!
    When full it blows,
    He breaks the rose,
    And leaves thee then,
    A wretched outcast thing!
    Take warning, then,
    And yield to none
    But who hath shown,
    And changed with thee the ring.

VALENTIN [*advancing*].—Ho, serenaders! by the Element!
    You wretched rascals! you rat-catchers, you!
    First, to the devil with the instrument,
    And, after it, the harper too!
MEPHISTOPHELES.—Donner and blitz! my good guitar is
    broken!
VALENTIN.—And your skull, too, anon: by this sure token!
MEPHISTOPHELES.—Quick, Doctor! here's no time to tarry!
    Keep close, as I shall lead the way.
    Out with your goosewing!* out, I say!
    Make you the thrusts, and I will parry.
VALENTIN.—Then parry that!
MEPHISTOPHELES.—   Why not?
VALENTIN.—   And that!

             * A cant word for a sword.

MEPHISTOPHELES.—   Of course!
VALENTIN.—I deem the devil is here, or something worse.
  Good God! what's this?—my arm is lamed!
MEPHISTOPHELES [*to Faust*].—Have at him there!
VALENTIN [*falls*].—   O woe!
MEPHISTOPHELES.—   Now is the lubber tamed!
  But let's be gone! why stand you gaping there?
  They'll raise a cry of murder! I can play
  A game with the policeman, any day;
  But blood spilt is a dangerous affair.
                    [*Exeunt Mephistopheles and Faust.*
MARTHA [*at the window*].—Ho! murder, ho!
MARGARET [*at the window*].—   A light! a light!
MARTHA [*as above*].—They bawl, they bawl, they strike, they
      fight.
THE PEOPLE.—And here lies one already dead!
MARTHA [*appearing below*].—Where are the murderers? are
      they fled?
GRETCHEN [*below*].—Who's this lies here?
THE PEOPLE.—   Thy mother's son.
MARGARET.—Almighty God! my brother dead!
VALENTIN.—I die! I die!—'tis quickly said,
  And yet more quickly done.
  Why stand you, women, and weep and wail?
  Draw near, and listen to my tale!
                    [*They all come round him.*
  My Margaret, mark me, you are young,
  And in sense not overstrong;
  You manage matters ill.
  I tell thee in thine ear, that thou
  Art, once for all, a strumpet—now
  May'st go and take thy fill.
MARGARET.—My brother! God! what do you mean?
VALENTIN.—Leave the Lord God out of the jest;
  Said is said, and done is done;
  Now you may manage, as you best
  Know how to help the matter on.
  You commenced the trade with one,
  We shall have two, three, four, anon,
  Next a dozen, and next a score,

And then the whole town at your door.
When sin is born it shuns the light
(For conscience guilt may not abide it),
And they draw the veil of night
Over head and ears, to hide it;
Yea, they would murder it, if they might.
But anon it waxes bolder,
And walks about in broad daylight,
And, uglier still as it grows older,
The less it offers to invite,
The more it courts the public sight.
Even now, methinks, I see the day,
When every honest citizen,
As from a corpse of tainted clay,
From thee, thou wretch! will turn away.
Thy very heart shall fail thee then,
When they shall look thee in the face!
No more shall golden chain thee grace!
The Church shall spurn thee from its door!
The altar shall not own thee more!
Nor longer, with thy spruce lace-tippet,
Where the dance wheels, shalt thou trip it!
In some vile den of want and woe,
With beggars and cripples thou shalt bed;
And, if from Heaven forgiveness flow,
Earth shall rain curses on thy head!

MARTHA.—Speak softly, and prepare thy soul for death,
    Nor mingle slander with thy parting breath!

VALENTIN.—Could I but reach thy withered skin,
    Thou hag, thou bawd, so vile and shameless!
    For such fair deed I might pass blameless,
    To score the black mark from my blackest sin.

MARGARET.—Brother, thou mak'st me feel a hell of pain!

VALENTIN.—I tell thee, all thy tears are vain!
    When with thy honor thou didst part,
    Thou dealt the blow that pierced my heart.
    I go through death, with fearless mood,
    To meet my God, as a soldier should.   [*Dies.*

Scene IX.—A Cathedral

*Mass, Organ, and Song. Margaret amid a crowd of people,
Evil Spirit behind her.*

EVIL SPIRIT.—How different, Margaret, was thy case,
    When, in thine innocence, thou didst kneel
    Before the altar,
    And from the well-worn book
    Didst lisp thy prayers,
    Half childish play,
    Half God in thy heart!
    Margaret!
    Where is thy head?
    Within thy heart
    What dire misdeed?
    Prayest thou for thy mother's soul, whom thou
    Didst make to sleep a long, long sleep of sorrow?
    Whose blood is on thy threshold?
    —And, underneath thy heart,
    Moves not the swelling germ•of life already,
    And, with its boding presence
    Thee tortures, and itself?
MARGARET.—Woe, woe!
    That I might shake away the thoughts,
    That hither flit and thither,
    Against me!
CHOIR.—   *Dies iræ, dies illa,*
           Solvet saeclum in favilla.
                    [The organ sounds.

EVIL SPIRIT.—Terror doth seize thee!
    The trumpet sounds!
    The graves quake!
    And thy heart,
    From its rest of ashes,
    To fiery pain
    Created again,
    Quivers to life!
MARGARET.—Would I were hence!

I feel as if the organ stopped
My breath,
And, at the hymn,
My inmost heart
Melted away!

CHOIR.—   *Judex ergo cum sedebit,*
                 Quidquid latet adparebit,
                 Nil inultum remanebit.

MARGARET.—I feel so straitened!
The pillar shafts
Enclasp me round!
The vault
Is closing o'er me!—Air!

EVIL SPIRIT.—Yea! let them hide thee! but thy sin and shame
No vault can hide!
Air? Light? No!
Woe on thee! woe!

CHOIR.—   *Quid sum miser tunc dicturus?*
                 Quem patronum rogaturus?
                 Cum vix justus sit securus.

EVIL SPIRIT.—The blessèd turn
Their looks away,
And the pure shudder
From touch of thee!
Woe!

MARGARET.—Neighbor, help! help! I faint!
                               [She falls down in a swoon.

FAUST AND MARGARET.

Photogravure from a painting by Carl Becker.

This picture is a representation of Faust's first meeting with Margaret. Though the innocent maiden appears to shrink from the advances of the handsome stranger, her eyes are returning his intent gaze with an expression of fascinated interest. In the background Mephistopheles is seen looking on with an expression of mocking insight that suggests a knowledge of the tragic outcome of the meeting.

ACT FIFTH

Scene I.—Walpurgis-Night

*The Hartz Mountains. Neighborhood of Schirke and Elend.
Faust and Mephistopheles.*

MEPHISTOPHELES.—Would you not like a broomstick to be-
        stride?
    Would God I had a stout old goat to ride!
    The way is long; and I would rather spare me
    This uphill work.
FAUST.—   While my good legs can bear me,
    This knotted stick will serve my end.
    What boots it to cut short the way?
    Through the long labyrinth of vales to wend,
    These rugged mountain-steeps to climb,
    And hear the gushing waters' ceaseless chime,
    No better seasoning on my wish to-day
    Could wait, to make the Brocken banquet prime!
    The Spring is waving in the birchen bower,
    And ev'n the pine begins to feel its power;
    Shall we alone be strangers to its sway?
MEPHISTOPHELES.—No whiff I feel that hath a smell of May;
    I am most wintry cold in every limb;
    I'd sooner track my road o'er frost and snow.
    How sadly mounts the imperfect moon!—so dim
    Shines forth its red disc, with belated glow,
    We run the risk, at every step, on stones
    Or stumps of crazy trees, to break our bones.
    You must allow me to request the aid
    Of a Will-o-the-Wisp;—I see one right ahead,
    And in the bog it blazes merrily.
    Holla! my good friend! dare I be so free?
    Two travellers here stand much in need of thee;

Why shouldst thou waste thy flickering flame in vain?
Pray be so good as light us up the hill!

WILL-O-THE-WISP.—Out of respect to you, I will restrain,
If possible, my ever-shifting will;
But all our natural genius, and our skill
Is zigzag; straight lines go against the grain.

MEPHISTOPHELES.—Ha! ha! hast learned from men how to
declaim?
March on, I tell thee, in the Devil's name!
Else will I blow thy flickering life-spark out.

WILL-O-THE-WISP.—You are the master of the house, no doubt,
And therefore I obey you cheerfully.
Only remember! 'tis the first of May,
The Brocken is as mad as mad can be;
And when an *ignis fatuus* leads the way,
You have yourselves to blame, if you should stray.

FAUST, MEPHISTOPHELES, AND WILL-O-THE-WISP [*in recipro-
cal song*].—Through the realms of fairy dream-
ing,
Through the air with magic teeming,
Guide us forward, guide us fairly,
Thanks to thee be rendered rarely;
Guide us quick, and guide us sure,
O'er the wide waste Brocken moor.
Trees on trees thick massed before us
Flit, and fling dark shadows o'er us,
Cliffs on cliffs in rugged masses
Nod above the narrow passes,
And each rock from jagged nose,
How it snorts, and how it blows!
Over turf and stones are pouring
Stream and streamlet, wildly roaring;
Is it rustling? is it singing?
Love's sweet plaint with gentle winging!
Voices of those days, the dearest,
When our light of hope was clearest!
And the echo, like the sounds
Of ancient story, back rebounds.
Oohoo! Shoohoo! what a riot!
Owl and pewit, jay and piet!

Will no bird to-night be quiet?
What is this? red salamanders,
With long legs and swoll'n paunches,
Weaving wreathy fire-meanders
Through the thicket's bristling branches!
And the trees, their roots outspreading
From the sand and rocky bedding,
Winding, stretching, twisting grimly,
Through the dun air darting dimly
Seek to seize us, seek to grasp us,
And with snaky coils enclasp us!
And the mice in motley muster,
Red and white, and blue and gray,
Thick as bees that hang in cluster,
Crowd along the heathy way.
And the fire-flies shooting lightly
Through the weirdly winding glade,
With bewildering escort, brightly
Lead the streaming cavalcade!
But tell me, in this strange confusion,
What is real, what delusion?
Do we walk with forward faces,
Or stand and halt with baffled paces?
All things seem to change their places,
Rocks and trees to make grimaces,
And the lights in witchy row,
Twinkle more and more they blow!

MEPHISTOPHELES.—Hold me tightly by the cue!
From this hillock, we may view,
At leisure, with admiring gaze,
How Mammon in the mount doth blaze!

FAUST.—How strangely through the glooming glens
Dim sheen, like morning redness, glimmers!
Ev'n to the darkest, deepest dens
With its long streaky rays it shimmers.
Here mounts the smoke, there rolls the steam,
There flames through the white vapors gleam,
Here like a thread along the mountain
It creeps; there gushes in a fountain!
Here stretching out, in many a rood,

Along the vale, its veinèd flood,
And here at once it checks its flight,
And bursts in globes of studded light.
There sparks are showering on the ground,
Like golden sand besprinkled round,
And lo! where all the rocky height,
From head to foot is bathed in light!

MEPHISTOPHELES.—Hath not old Mammon lit with goodly
   flame
His palace for the jubilee?
Thou art in luck to see the game;
Even now I scent the lusty company.

FAUST.—How the mad storm doth howl and hiss
And beats my neck with angry buffeting!

MEPHISTOPHELES.—To the old mountain's hard ribs cling,
Or the strong blast will hurl thee down the abyss;
The night with clouds is overcast;
Hear in the woods the grinding of the blast!
How the frightened owlets flit!
How the massive pillars split
Of the dark pine-palaces!
How the branches creak and break!
How the riven stems are groaning!
How the gaping roots are moaning!
In terrible confusion all,
One on another clashing, they fall,
And through the clefts, where their wrecks are buried,
Hissing and howling the winds are hurried.
Sounds of voices dost thou hear?
Voices far, and voices near?
And, all the mountain-side along,
Streams a raving wizard song.

WITCHES [in chorus].—The witches to the Brocken ride,
The stubble is yellow, the corn is green;
A merry crew to a merry scene,
And good Sir Urian is the guide.
Over stock and stone we float,
Wrinkled hag and rank old goat.

A VOICE.—Old mother Baubo comes up now,
Alone, and riding on a sow.

Chorus.—Honor to him to whom honor is due!
    Lady Baubo heads the crew!
    On the back of a sow, with the wings of the wind,
    And all the host of witches behind.
A Voice.—Sister, which way came you?
A Voice.—By Ilsenstein! and I looked into
    An owlet's nest, as on I fared,
    That with its two eyes broadly stared!
A Voice.—The deuce! at what a devil's pace
    You go; this march is not a race.
A Voice.—It tore me, it flayed me!
    These red wounds it made me!
Witches [*in chorus*].—The road is broad, the road is long,
    Why crowd you so on one another?
    Scrapes the besom, pricks the prong,
    Chokes the child, and bursts the mother.
Wizards [*semi-chorus*].—We trail us on, like very snails,
    The women fly with flaunting sails;
    For, when we run 'Squire Satan's races,
    They always win by a thousand paces.
Semi-Chorus.—Not quite so bad: the women need
    A thousand paces to help their speed;
    But let them speed what most they can,
    With one spring comes up the man.
Voice [*from above*].—Come up! come up from the lake with
    me.
Voices [*from below*].—Right gladly would we mount with
    thee;
    We wash, and wash, and cease from washing never;
    Our skins are as white as white can be,
    But we are as dry and barren as ever.
Both Choruses.—The wind is hushed, the stars take flight,
    The sullen moon hath veiled her light,
    The magic choir from whizzing wings,
    Long lines of sparkling glory flings.
Voice [*from below*].—Stop, stop!
Voice [*from above*].—Who bawls so loud from the cleft?
Voice [*from below*].—Let me go with you! let me not be left!
    Three hundred years I grope and grope
    Round the base and up the slope,
    Vol. II.—9

But still the summit cheats my hope.
I fain would be a merry guest
At Satan's banquet with the rest.

BOTH CHORUSES.—On broomstick, and on lusty goat,
On pitchfork, and on stick, we float;
And he, to-day who cannot soar,
Is a lost man for evermore.

HALF-WITCH [below].—I hobble on behind them all,
The others scarcely hear my call!
I find no rest at home: and here,
I limp on lamely in the rear.

CHORUS OF WITCHES.—The ointment gives our sinews might,
For us each rag is sail enough,
We find a ship in every trough;
Whoso will fly must fly to-night.

BOTH CHORUSES.—While we upon the summit ride,
Be yours to sweep along the side;
Up and down, and far and wide,
On the left, and on the right,
Witch and wizard massed together,
Scour the moor and sweep the heather,
Bravely on Walpurgis-night!   [They alight.

MEPHISTOPHELES.—What a thronging, and jolting, and rolling,
and rattling!
What a whizzing, and whirling, and jostling, and bat-
tling!
What a sparkling, and blazing, and stinking, and
burning!
And witches that all topsy-turvy are turning!—
Hold fast by me, or I shall lose you quite,
Where are you?

FAUST [at a distance].—Here!

MEPHISTOPHELES.—   What! so far in the rear!
Why then 'tis time that I should use my right,
As master of the house to-night.
Make way! 'Squire Voland comes, sweet mob, make
way!
Here, Doctor, hold by me!—and now, I say,
                    We must cut clear
Of this wild hubbub, while we may;

Even my cloth is puzzled here.
See'st thou that light on yonder mound quite near,
It hath a most peculiar glare,
    We'll slip in there,
And watch behind the bush the humors of the Fair.

FAUST.—Strange son of contradiction!—may'st even guide us!
A rare conceit! of course you must be right;
This weary way we march on famed Walpurgis-night,
Like hermits in a corner here to hide us!

MEPHISTOPHELES.—Lo! where the flames mount up with
            bickering glee;
In sooth it is a goodly company.
In such a place one cannot be alone.

FAUST.—And yet a place I'd rather own
Upon the top, where whirling smoke I see;
There thousands to the evil Spirit hie,
And many a riddle there he will untie.

MEPHISTOPHELES.—Yes: and for every knot he disentangles,
He'll make another to produce new wrangles.
Let the great world rant and riot,
We'll know to house us here in quiet;
In the great world 'tis a sanctioned plan,
Each makes a little world the best he can.
Look there; you see young witches without cover,
And old ones prudently veiled over;
Yield but to me, and I can promise thee,
With little labor, mickle glee.
I hear their noisy instruments begin!
Confound their scraping!—one must bear the din.
Come, come! what must be must be—let's go in!
With my good introduction on this night,
Thou shalt have laughter to thy heart's delight.
What say'st thou, friend? this is no common show,
A hundred lights are burning in a row,
You scarce may see the end;
They dance, they talk, they cook, they drink, they court;
Now tell me, saw you ever better sport?

FAUST.—Say, in what character do you intend
To appear here, and introduce your friend?
Devil or conjurer?

MEPHISTOPHELES.—   I love incognito,
Yet on a gala-day my order I may show;
And, though a garter here is but of small avail,
The famous horse's foot I ne'er yet knew to fail.
See even now that cautious creeping snail!
With her long feeling visage, she
Has smelt out something of hell in me.
Do what I can, they have a snout,
In this keen air to scent me out;
Come! come; from fire to fire we roam; the game
Be mine to start, and yours to woo the dame.
[*To some who are sitting round a glimmering coal-
      fire.*] Why mope you here, old sirs, toasting
      your toes?
Methinks your Brocken hours were better spent
Amid the youthful roar and merriment;
One is enough alone at home, God knows.

GENERAL.—Who would rely upon the faith of nations!
They leave you thankless, when their work is done;
The people, like the women, pour libations
Only in honor of the rising sun.

MINISTER.—The liberties these modern changes bring,
I must confess I cannot praise;
The good old times, when we were everything,
These were the truly golden days.

PARVENU.—We, too, pushed forward with the pushing crew,
'And for the need could stretch a point or two;
But now all's changed; and with the whirling bucket,
We lose the fruit, just when our hand would pluck it.

AUTHOR.—No solid work now suits the reading nation,
And year by year the world more shallow grows;
And, for the glib-tongued rising generation,
They hang their wisdom on their up-turned nose!

MEPHISTOPHELES [*who all at once appears very old*].—The
      people here seem ripe for Doom's day; I
Suspect the world is now on its last legs;
And, since mine own good cask is running dry,
Men and their ways, I guess, are near the dregs!

PEDDLER-WITCH.—Good sirs, I pray you pass not by,
Cast on my wares a friendly eye!

One cannot see such rich display
Of curious trinkets every day.
Yet is there nothing in my store
(Which far all other stores excels),
That hath not done some mischief sore
To earth, and all on earth that dwells;
No dagger by which blood hath not been shed,
No cup from which, through sound and healthy life,
Corroding fiery juice hath not been spread,
No gaud but hath seduced some lovely wife,
No sword that hath not made a truce miscarry,
Or stabbed behind the back its adversary.

MEPHISTOPHELES.—Good lady cousin! you come rather late.
Your wares, believe me, are quite out of date;
Deal in the new and newest; that
Our palate smacks; all else is flat.

FAUST.—This is a fair that beats the Leipsic hollow!
My head is so confused, I scarce can follow.

MEPHISTOPHELES.—To the top the stream is rushing,
And we are pushed, when we think we are pushing.

FAUST.—Who, then, is that?

MEPHISTOPHELES.— Look at her well.
'Tis Lilith.

FAUST.— Who?

MEPHISTOPHELES.— Adam's first wife. Beware,
Art thou a wise man, of her glossy hair!
'Tis fair to look on, but its look is fell.
Those locks with which she outshines all the train,
When she hath bound a young man with that chain,
She'll hold him fast; he'll scarce come back again.

FAUST.—There sit an old and young one on the sward;
They seem to have been dancing somewhat hard.

MEPHISTOPHELES.—O! once begun, they'll go on like the devil.
Come, come! they rise again—let's join the revel.

[*Faust and Mephistopheles join the dance; the former with
the Young Witch as his partner; the latter with the
Old one.*

FAUST [*dancing with the young Witch*].—A lovely dream once
came to me,
I saw in my sleep an apple-tree;

Two lovely apples on it did shine;
I clomb the pole to make them mine.

THE YOUNG WITCH.—For apples your sire in Paradise
And primal dame had longing eyes:
And, if your eyes are wise to see,
You'll find such apples on my tree.

MEPHISTOPHELES [*dancing with the old Witch*].—An ugly
dream once came to me,
I dreamed I saw a cloven tree;
In the tree there sat an ugly owl;
I called it fair, though it was foul.

THE OLD WITCH.—My best salute this night shall be,
Thou knight of the cloven foot, to thee;
A cloven tree with an ugly owl,
And I for thee, or fair, or foul.

PROCTOPHANTASMIST [*to the dancers*].—Listen to order, you
presumptuous brood!
Have we not proved beyond disputing,
That ghosts on terra firma have no footing?
And yet you dance like any flesh and blood?

THE YOUNG WITCH [*dancing*].—What wants he here, that
rude-like fellow there?

FAUST [*dancing*].—O, he is everywhere!
What others dance 'tis his to prize;
Each step he cannot criticise
Had as well not been made. But in the dance
It grieves him most when we advance.
If we would wheel still round and round in a ring,
As he is fond to do in his old mill,
He would not take it half so ill;
Especially if you take care to bring
Your praiseful offering to his master skill.

PROCTOPHANTASMIST.—What! still there, phantoms? this is
past endurance!
In this enlightened age you have the assurance
To show your face and play your tricks undaunted;
We are so wise, and yet a man's own house is haunted.
How long have I not swept the cobwebs of delusion,
And still the world remains in the same wild confusion!

THE YOUNG WITCH.—Be quiet then, and seek some other place!

PROCTOPHANTASMIST.—I tell you, Spirits, in your face,
    This intellectual thrall I cannot bear it;
    I love to have a free unshackled spirit.

                          [The dance goes on.
    To-day I see that all my strength is spent in vain;
    I've had a tour, at least, to compensate my evils,
    And hope, before I come to Blocksberg back again,
    To crush, with one good stroke, the poets and the devils.
MEPHISTOPHELES.—He will now go, and, bare of breeches,
    Sit in a pool with solemn patience;
    And, when his buttocks are well sucked by leeches,
    Be cured of ghosts and ghostly inspirations.

              [To Faust, who has just left the dance.
    Why do you let the lovely damsel go,
    That in the dance with sweet song pleased you so?
FAUST.—Alas! while she so passing sweet was singing,
    I saw a red mouse from her mouth outspringing.
MEPHISTOPHELES.—Pooh! on the Brocken that's a thing of
       course;
    Let not such trifles mar your sweet discourse.
    Go, join the crew, and dance away;
    Enough, the red mouse was not gray.
FAUST.—Then saw I——
MEPHISTOPHELES.—   What?
FAUST.—   Mephisto, see'st thou there
    A pale yet lovely girl, in lonely distance fare?
    From place to place she moveth slow;
    With shackled feet she seems to go;
    I must confess, she has a cast
    Of Margaret, when I saw her last.
MEPHISTOPHELES.—Let that alone! it brings thee certain harm;
    It is bewitched, a bloodless, breathless form,
    For men to look upon it is not good.
    Its fixèd gaze hath power to freeze the blood,
    And petrify thee stark and stiff.
    Of course I need not ask you if
    You've heard of the Medusa's head.
FAUST.—In truth I see the eyes of one that's dead,
    On which no closing hand of love was laid.
    That is my Margaret's kindly breast,
    That the sweet body I caressed.

MEPHISTOPHELES.—There lies the witchcraft o't, thou fool!
  A phantom takes thy wit to school:
  She is the love of every lover's brain.

FAUST.—What ecstasy! and yet what pain!
  I cannot leave it for my life.
  How strangely this most lovely neck
  A single streak of red doth deck,
  No broader than the back o' a knife!

MEPHISTOPHELES.—Quite right! I see it, just as well as you.
  Sometimes her head beneath her elbow too
  She wears; for Perseus cut it off, you know.
  What! will you still a-dreaming go?
  Come, let us mount the hillock—there
  We shall have noble sport, believe me;
  For, unless mine eyes deceive me,
  They have got up a theatre.
  What make you here?

A SERVANT.—   You are just come in time.
  'Tis a new piece, the last of all the seven,
  For such the number that with us is given.
  A dilettante 'twas that wrote the rhyme,
  And dilettanti are the actors too.
  Excuse me, sirs—no disrespect to you,
  If I seem curt: I am the dilettante
  To draw the curtain; and our time is scanty.

MEPHISTOPHELES.—Just so; I only wish you were so clever
  To know your home;
  Then from the Blocksberg you would never
  Have lust to roam!

WALPURGIS-NIGHT'S DREAM

INTERMEZZO

Scene II.

DIRECTOR OF THE THEATRE.—We players here may take our
     ease;
    For all we need for scenery
    Is mount and mead, and trees, and seas
    Of Nature's leafy greenery.
HERALD.—The golden high-tide is it then,
    When fifty years pass over;
    But doubly golden is it when
    All brawls and strifes they cover.
OBERON.—Ye spirits, who obey my law,
    Are to this feast invited,
    When Oberon and Titania
    In love are reunited.
PUCK.—Puck comes in first, and turns athwart,
    His merry circles wheeling;
    And hundreds more behind him dart,
    Loud shouts of laughter pealing.
ARIEL.—I fill the air with thrilling song
    Of virtue quite enchanting;
    Though ugly imps I lure along,
    The fair are never wanting!
OBERON.—When man and wife begin to strive,
    Just give them length of tether!
    They will learn in peace to live,
    When not too much together.
TITANIA.—When pouts the wife, and frets the man,
    This cure is best in Nature,

Him to the Arctic circle ban,
And her to the Equator.
ORCHESTRA [*fortissimo*].—Snout of fly, and nose of gnat,
Lead on the band before us!
Frog and cricket, cat and bat,
Join merry in the chorus!
SOLO.—A soap-bell for a doodle-sack,*
The merry waters troubling!
Hear the snecke-snicke-snack,
From its snub-nose bubbling!
EMBRYO-SPIRIT.—Legs of spider, paunch of toad,
And wings, if you would know it;
Nor fish, nor fowl, but on the road
Perhaps to be a poet!
A PAIR OF DANCERS.—With many a nimble pace and spring,
Through honey-dew and vapor,
Trips o'er the ground the little thing,
But higher cannot caper.
INQUISITIVE TRAVELLER.—Do I see a real thing,
Or is it all delusion?
Oberon, the fairy king,
Amid this wild confusion.
ORTHODOX.—Though neither tail nor claws are his,
'Tis true beyond all cavil,
As devils were the gods of Greece,
He too must be a devil.
NORTHERN ARTIST.—'Tis but a sketch, I must admit;
But what I can't unravel
To-night, I'll know, with larger wit,
From my Italian travel.
PURIST.—Alas! that I should see it too!
Here we a riot rare have!
Of all the crew, there are but two
That powder on their hair have.
YOUNG WITCH.—Powder and petticoat for gray
And wrinkled hags are fitting;
But I my lusty limbs display,
Upon a he-goat sitting.
MATRON.—To speak with such a shameless pack

* Dudelsack. A bagpipe.

We have nor will nor leisure;
Soon may your flesh rot on your back,
And we look on with pleasure!

LEADER OF THE ORCHESTRA.—Snout of fly, and nose of gnat,
Sting not the naked beauty!
Frog and cricket, cat and bat,
Attend ye to your duty!

WEATHERCOCK [*to the one side*].—A goodly company! as sure
As I stand on the steeple;
With brides and bridegrooms swarms the moor,
The hopefulest of people!

WEATHERCOCK [*to the other side*].—And opes not suddenly the
ground,
To swallow one and all up,
Then, with a jerk, I'll veer me round,
And straight to hell I'll gallop.

XENIEN.—We insects keep them all in awe,
With sharpest scissors shear we!
Old Nick, our worthy 'Squire Papa,
Here to salute appear we.

HENNINGS.—See! how in merry circles they
Sit gossiping together;
The graceless crew have hearts, they say,
As good as any other.

MUSAGETES.—This witch and wizard crew to lead,
My willing fancy chooses;
More hopeful field is here indeed,
Than when I lead the Muses.

CI-DEVANT GENIUS OF THE AGE.—The Brocken has a good
broad back,
Like the High-Dutch Parnassus;
The Jury here no man can pack,
Or with proud silence pass us.

INQUISITIVE TRAVELLER.—Say, who is he so stiff that goes,
That stately-stalking stranger?
He snuffs for Jesuits with sharp nose,
And cries—the Church in danger!

CRANE.—In muddy waters do I fish
As well as where it clear is,
And only for such cause as this
The pious man too here is.

WORLDLING.—Yes! though the saints declare that sin
    And Blocksberg are identical,
    Yet here, amid this demon din,
    They'll set up their conventicle.
DANCER.—A sound of drums! a sound of men!
    That wafted on the wind came!—
    The weary bitterns in the fen
    Are booming—never mind 'em!
DANCING-MASTER.—Lo! how they kick, and how they jump!
    How well each figure shown is!
    Springs the crooked, hops the plump!
    Each thinks him an Adonis!
A GOOD FELLOW.—A sorry lot! What muffled ire
    Their swelling breasts inflames here!
    The beasts were tamed by Orpheus' lyre,
    And them the bagpipe tames here!
PROFESSOR OF SYSTEMATIC THEOLOGY.—I let no one bamboozle
        me
    With doubts and critic cavils;
    The devil sure must something be,
    Else whence so many devils?
IDEALIST.—Imagination travels free
    Without or rein or rule here;
    If I am all that now I see,
    Myself must be a fool here.
REALIST.—That on the Brocken ghosts appear
    Now scarce admits disputing;
    Amid this hurly-burly here
    I've fairly lost my footing.
SUPERNATURALIST.—Into this swarming hellish brood
    I come, without intrusion;
    From evil spirits to the good,
    It is a just conclusion.
SCEPTIC.—They chase the flame that flits about,
    And deem them near their treasure;
    Best rhymes with doubt this demon-rout,
    And I look on with pleasure.
LEADER OF THE ORCHESTRA.—Snout of fly, and nose of gnat,
    Ye stupid Dilettanti!
    Frog and cricket, cat and bat,
    Keep better time, why can't ye?

CLEVER SPIRITS.—*Sans-souci* is hight the crew
    On limber limbs that ply it;
    When on our feet it will not do,
    Then on our heads we try it.
AWKWARD SPIRITS.—With once or twice a lucky throw
    We tramped the road together;
    But now we flounder on, and show
    Our toes outside the leather!
IGNES FATUI.—Though born but with the sultry ray
    This morn, in the morass all,
    Yet now, amid the gallants gay,
    We shine here and surpass all.
FALLING STAR.—Last night I shot from starry sky
    And fell upon my nose here;
    Will no one come where flat I lie,
    And plant me on my toes here?
STOUT SPIRITS.—Make way, make way! and brush the dew
    Right bravely from the lawn here;
    Spirits we are, but Spirits too
    Can show both pith and brawn here!
PUCK.—Why tramp ye so majestical
    As cub of river-horse is?
    The plumpest spirit of you all
    Stout Puck himself of course is.
ARIEL.—If loving Nature's bounteous care
    Hath fitted you with pinions,
    Then cleave with me the yielding air
    To rosy bright dominions.
ORCHESTRA.—The mist draws off, and overhead
    All clear and bright the air is,
    And with the rustling breeze are fled
    The devils and the fairies!

End of the Interlude.

Scene III.—A Cloudy Day.   The Fields

Faust and Mephistopheles.

FAUST.—In misery! in despair! Wandering in hopeless wretchedness over the wide earth, and at last made prisoner!
Shut up like a malefactor in a dungeon, victim of the
most horrible woes—poor miserable girl! Must it then
come to this? Thou treacherous and worthless Spirit!
this hast thou concealed from me!—Stand thou there!
stand!—Roll round thy fiendish eyes, infuriate in thy
head! Stand and confront me with thy insupportable
presence. A prisoner! in irredeemable misery! given
over to evil Spirits, and to the condemning voice of the
unfeeling world! and me, meanwhile, thou cradlest to
sleep amid a host of the most vapid dissipations, conceal-
ing from my knowledge her aggravated woes!—while
she—she is left in hopeless wretchedness to die!

MEPHISTOPHELES.—She's not the first.

FAUST.—Dog! abominable monster!—Change him, O thou
infinite Spirit! change the reptile back again into his
original form—the poodle that ran before me in the twilight, now cowering at the feet of the harmless wanderer,
now springing on his shoulders!—Change him again
into his favorite shape, that he may crouch on his belly in
the sand before me, and I may tramp him underneath my
feet, the reprobate!—Not the first! Misery, misery! by
no human soul to be conceived! that more than one creature of God should ever have been plunged into the depth
of this woe! that the first, in the writhing agony of her
death, should not have atoned for the guilt of all the rest
before the eyes of the All-merciful! It digs even
into the marrow of my life, the misery of this *one;*
and thou—thou grinnest in cold composure over the
wretchedness of thousands!

MEPHISTOPHELES.—Here we are arrived once more at the limit
of our wits, where the thread of human reason snaps in
sunder. Wherefore seekest thou communion with us,
unless thou wouldst carry it through? Wouldst fly,

and yet art not proof against giddiness? Did we thrust ourselves on you, or you on us?

FAUST.—Whet not thy rows of voracious teeth at me! I loathe it!—Great and glorious Spirit, who didst condescend to reveal thyself to me, who knowest my heart and my soul, wherefore didst thou yoke me to this vilest of complices, who feeds on mischief and banquets on destruction?

MEPHISTOPHELES.—Art done?

FAUST.—Deliver her! or woe thee!—the direst of curses lie on thee forever!

MEPHISTOPHELES.—I cannot loose the bonds of the avenger, nor open his bars.—Deliver her! Who was it that plunged her into ruin? I or thou?

[*Faust looks wildly round.*

MEPHISTOPHELES [*continues*].—Wouldst grasp the thunder? 'Tis well that you, poor mortals, have it not to wield! To smash the innocent in pieces is the proper tyrant's fashion of venting one's spleen in a dilemma.

FAUST.—Bring me to her! She shall be free!

MEPHISTOPHELES.—And the danger to which thou exposest thyself! Know that the guilt of blood from thy hand still lies upon the town. Above the spot where the slain fell, avenging Spirits hover and lie in wait for the returning murderer.

FAUST.—That too from thee? Murder and death of a world on thee, thou monster! Bring me to her, I say, and deliver her!

MEPHISTOPHELES.—I'll lead thee thither, and what I can do that I will do. Mark me! Have I all power in heaven and on earth? I will cloud the wits of the warder, and thou may'st seize the keys, and bring her out with the hand of a man. I wait for you with the magic horses to insure your escape. This I can do.

FAUST.—Up and away!

Scene IV.—Night. The Open Field

Faust and Mephistopheles.   Galloping past on black horses.

FAUST.—What are they about there, bustling round the Raven-
stone? *

MEPHISTOPHELES.—Can't say what they are cooking and
kitchening.

FAUST.—They hover up, they hover down, bending and bowing.

MEPHISTOPHELES.—A corporation of Witches.

FAUST.—They seem to be sprinkling and blessing something.

MEPHISTOPHELES.—On! on!

Scene V.—A Prison

*Faust, with a bundle of keys in his hand and a lamp, before
an iron door.*

FAUST.—A strange cold shuddering dread comes o'er me, all
The up-heaped wretchedness of time.
Here dwells she now behind this damp cold wall,
And dear delusion was her only crime!
Fear'st thou to go to her?
Tremblest to meet her eye?
Quick! thy delay but brings her death more nigh.
[*He seizes the lock.   Singing heard from within.*
My mother, the wanton,
That choked my breath!
My father, the villain,
That dined on my death!
My sister dear,
In the cool green shade
My bones she laid;
Then was I a glad little bird in the May;
Fly away! fly away!

FAUST [*opening the door*].—She dreams not that her loved one
is so near,
The clinking chains and rustling straw to hear.

MARGARET [*hiding herself on the bed*].—Woe, woe! they
come.—To bitter death they call.

* Rabenstein.   Place of execution.

FAUST [*softly*].—Hush! hush! I come to free thee from their
        thrall!

MARGARET [*throwing herself at his feet*].—Art thou a man? feel
        for my hapless plight.

FAUST.—Thy cries will wake the watchers of the night!
             [*He takes hold of the chains to unloose them.*

MARGARET [*on her knees*].—Who gave thee, hangman, such a
        power
    To drag me from my cell at midnight hour?
    Have pity on me! Be not so harsh!—so rough!
    Surely to-morrow morn is soon enough.
                   [*She stands up.*
    So young, so very young, am I,
    And must already die!
    Once I was lovely too—'twas this that caused my fall.
    Near was the friend, but far from me to-day;
    Torn lies the wreath, the flowers are scattered all.
    Oh tear me not so forcibly away!
    Spare me! what have I done to injure thee?
    Oh hear my prayer! for once compassion show!—
    'Tis the first time I ever looked on thee.

FAUST.—That I should live to see such depth of woe!

MARGARET.—Thou hast me now completely in thy might.
    Only first give me time to suckle my sweet child.
    I hugged it the whole weary night;
    They took 't from me in very spite;
    And now they say I murdered the sweet child,
    And never more shall I be glad again.
    They sing songs on me, too!
    A wicked thing to do!
    'Tis the refrain
    Of a grim old melody:
    Who taught them that its words were meant for me?

FAUST [*throwing himself down*].—Here, at thy feet, behold
        who loves thee fall,
    To strike thy shackles, and to break thy thrall!

MARGARET [*falling beside him on her knees*].—Yes! let us kneel
        and call upon the Saints!
    Beneath these steps,
    I hear it well!
    VOL. II.—10

Beneath the threshold,
Boileth Hell!
The evil One
His fury vents,
With fearful yell!

FAUST [*loud*].—Gretchen! Gretchen!

MARGARET [*attentive*].—That was the loved one's voice!

[*She springs up; the chains fall away.*

Where is he? where? I heard him call on me,
Now I am free! and none shall hinder me!
To his neck will I fly!
On his bosom lie!
He called me his Gretchen! he stood at the door.
Through the wild howling and hissing of Hell,
Through the loud-laughing scorn and the fiendish up-
    roar,
Came the sweet voice of love that I know so well.

FAUST.—'Tis I!

MARGARET.—'Tis thou! O say it yet again!   [*Clasping him.*
'Tis he! 'tis he! Where now is all my pain?
Where all my prison's woe? my fetters where?
'Tis he! he comes to lift me from this lair
Of wretchedness! I'm free, I'm free!
Already the well-known street I see,
Where the first time I spake to thee,
And the pleasant garden, where
Martha and I did wait for thee.

FAUST [*striving forward*].—Come, come!

MARGARET.—O stay, stay!
Thou know'st how pleased I stay where thou dost stay.
[*Caressing him.*

FAUST.—Away, away!
Unless we haste,
Dearly we'll pay for these few moments' waste.

MARGARET.—How! giv'st thou me no kiss?
My friend, so very short a space away,
And hast forgot to kiss?
Why feel I now so straitened when I hold
Thee in my arms? It was not so of old,
When from thy words and looks, a heaven of bliss

Came down; and thou didst kiss
As thou wouldst smother me. Come, kiss me! kiss!
Else kiss I thee!   *[She embraces him.*
O woe! thy lips are cold,
Are dumb;
Where is the love thy swelling bosom bore
Whilome for me? why are thy lips so cold?

               [She turns away from him.

FAUST.—Come with me, sweet love, come!
    I'll hug thee ten times closer than before,
    Only come with me now! Come, I implore!

MARGARET [*turning to him*].—Art thou then *he?* Art thou
    then truly *he?*

FAUST.—'Tis I, in truth. Come, love, and follow me.

MARGARET.—And these vile chains thou breakest,
    And me again unto thy bosom takest?
    How canst thou dare to turn fond eyes on me?
    Know'st thou then, Henry, whom thou com'st to free?

FAUST.—Come, come! the night sinks fast; come, follow me!

MARGARET.—My mother slept a sleep profound!
    I drugged her to't;
    My little babe I drowned!
    Was it not heaven's boon to me and thee?
    Thee, too!—'tis thou! I scarce may deem
    My sense speaks true. Give me thy hand!
    It is no dream!
    Thy dear, dear hand!
    Alas! but it is wet!
    Wipe it; for it is wet
    With blood! O God! what hast thou done?
    Put up thy sword;
    I pray thee put it up.

FAUST.—Let gone be gone!
    Thou stabbest me with daggers, every word.

MARGARET.—No! thou shalt survive our sorrow!
    I will describe the graves to thee,
    Where thou shalt bury them and me
    To-morrow.
    The best place thou shalt give my mother;
    Close beside her lay my brother;

Me a little to the side,
But at distance not too wide!
And my child at my right breast.—
These, and none else with us shall rest!
Me on thy loving side to press,
That was a heaven of blessedness!
But now, I cannot do it more;
I feel as I must force my love to thee,
And thou didst coldly fling me back from thee;
And yet 'tis thou!—as good, as loving as before.

FAUST.—'Tis I, even I, come, sweet love, come!

MARGARET.—Out there?

FAUST.—Into the open air.

MARGARET.—   If the grave be there,
And death there waits, then come!
Hence to my eternal home,
Not a step more.——
Thou leav'st me now?—would I might go with thee?

FAUST.—Thou canst, if thou but wilt. I have unbarred the
            door.

MARGARET.—I may not go; no hope for me remains;
They watch me close—my home is with my chains.
It is so sad to beg from door to door;
A guilty thing from human loves outcast,
A homeless earth to wander o'er;
And they are sure to find me out at last.

FAUST.—I will protect thee.

MARGARET.—Quick! Quick!
            Save thy poor child!
            Away, away!
            Keep the path
            Up the stream,
            Across the bridge,
            To the left hand,
            Where the plank stands,
            In the pond,
            Seize it, quick!
            It rises up,
            It kicks! it lives!
            O save it, save it!

FAUST.—Only bethink thee!
    One step more, and thou art free.
MARGARET.—Would we were past that mountain gray!
    There sits my mother on a stone—
    I feel a hand that pulls me back
    As cold as clay!
    There sits my mother on a stone;
    Her head sways heavily;
    She winks not, she nods not, her head she may not raise.
    She slept so long, she never more may wake.
    She slept that we might our enjoyment take.
    O these were happy days!
FAUST.—Here words and prayers will only make things worse;
    Come! come; or I must hale thee hence by force.
MARGARET.—Let me alone! lay no rough hands on me!
    Nor with such murderous clutches seize me!
FAUST.—Thou know'st I have done everything to please thee.
    The day dawns. Come, my Gretchen, follow me!
MARGARET.—Day! yes, it is day! the Judgment-day breaks in!
    My marriage-day it should have been!
    Let no one know thou wert before with Margaret.
    Woe to my wreath!
    'Tis done! oh, pain!
    We will meet again;
    But not at the dance.
    The thronging crowds advance
    With bated breath;
    No word is spoken;
    The squares, the streets,
    Cannot contain them all.
    The bell doth call,
    The staff is broken,
    They bind me with cords, they drag me away,
    And on the bloody block me lay;
    And every trembling eye doth quake
    At the blade that is brandished o'er my neck.
    Mute lies the world as the grave!
FAUST.—O had I ne'er been born!
MEPHISTOPHELES [*appearing from without*].—Up! or no help
        can save!

Profitless whining, whimpering, and prating!
Meanwhile my eager steeds are waiting,
Snuffing the scent of the morning air.

MARGARET.—What's that from the floor uprising there?
'Tis he! 'Tis he! O send his hateful face
Away! What seeks he in this holy place?
He comes for me!

FAUST.—No! thou shalt live.

MARGARET.—Judgment of God! to thee my soul I give.

MEPHISTOPHELES [*to Faust*].—Come, come! else will I leave
you to your fate!

MARGARET.—Thine am I, Father! O shut not the gate
Of mercy on me!
Ye angels! ye most holy Spirits! now
Encamp around me! and protect me now!
Henry, I tremble when I think on thee.

MEPHISTOPHELES.—She is judged!

VOICE [*from above*].—Is saved!

MEPHISTOPHELES [*to Faust*].—Hither to me!

VOICE [*from within, dying away*].—Henry! Henry!

THE RIVALS

—

BY

RICHARD BRINSLEY SHERIDAN

DRAMATIS PERSONÆ

SIR ANTHONY ABSOLUTE.

CAPTAIN ABSOLUTE.

FAULKLAND.

ACRES.

SIR LUCIUS O'TRIGGER.

FAG.

DAVID.

THOMAS.

MRS. MALAPROP.

LYDIA LANGUISH.

JULIA.

LUCY.

Maid, Boy, Servants.

The scene is at Bath, England.

THE RIVALS

Prologue.—By the Author *

Enter Serjeant-at-law and Attorney following and giving a paper.

SERJEANT.—What's here!—a vile cramp hand! I cannot see
 Without my spectacles.
ATTORNEY.—   He means his fee.
 Nay, Mr. Serjeant, good sir, try again. [*Gives money.*
SERJEANT.—The scrawl improves! [*more*] O come, 'tis pretty
 plain.
 Hey! how's this? Dibble!—sure it cannot be!
 A poet's brief! a poet and a fee!
ATTORNEY.—Yes, sir! though you without reward, I know,
 Would gladly plead the Muse's cause.
SERJEANT.—   So!—so!
ATTORNEY.—And if the fee offends, your wrath should fall
 On me.
SERJEANT.—Dear Dibble, no offence at all.
ATTORNEY.—Some sons of Phœbos in the courts we meet—
SERJEANT.—And fifty sons of Phœbos in the Fleet!
ATTORNEY.—Nor pleads he worse, who with a decent sprig
 Of bays adorns his legal waste of wig.
SERJEANT.—Full-bottomed heroes thus, on signs, unfurl
 A leaf of laurel in a grove of curl!
 Yet tell your client, that, in adverse days,
 This wig is warmer than a bush of bays.
ATTORNEY.—Do you, then, sir, my client's place supply,
 Profuse of robe, and prodigal of tie——
 Do you, with all those blushing powers of face,
 And wonted bashful hesitating grace,
 Rise in the court, and flourish on the case. [*Exit.*

* This Prologue was spoken at the original production by Mr. Woodward and Mr. Quick.

Serjeant.—For practice then suppose—this brief will show
          it—
    Me, Serjeant Woodward—counsel for the poet.
    Used to the ground, I know 'tis hard to deal
    With this dread court, from whence there's no appeal;
    No tricking here, to blunt the edge of law,
    Or, damned in equity, escape by flaw:
    But judgment given, your sentence must remain;
    No writ of error lies—to Drury-lane:
    Yet when so kind you seem, 'tis past dispute
    We gain some favor, if not costs of suit.
    No spleen is here! I see no hoarded fury;—
    I think I never faced a milder jury!
    Sad else our plight! where frowns are transportation,
    A hiss the gallows, and a groan damnation!
    But such the public candor, without fear
    My client waives all right of challenge here.
    No newsman from our session is dismissed,
    Nor wit nor critic we scratch off the list;
    His faults can never hurt another's ease,
    His crime, at worst, a bad attempt to please:
    Thus, all respecting, he appeals to all,
    And by the general voice will stand or fall.

Prologue.—By the Author *

    Granted our cause, our suit and trial o'er,
    The worthy serjeant need appear no more:
    In pleasing I a different client choose,
    He served the Poet—I would serve the Muse:
    Like him, I'll try to merit your applause,
    A female counsel in a female's cause.
        Look on this form†—where humor, quaint and sly,
    Dimples the cheek, and points the beaming eye;
    Where gay invention seems to boast its wiles
    In amorous hint, and half-triumphant smiles;
    While her light mask or covers satire's strokes,
    Or hides the conscious blush her wit provokes.

* This Prologue was spoken by Mrs. Bulkley on the night of the tenth performance.
† Pointing to the figure of Comedy.

Look on her well—does she seem formed to teach?
Should you expect to hear this lady preach?
Is gray experience suited to her youth?
Do solemn sentiments become that mouth?
Bid her be grave, those lips should rebel prove
To every theme that slanders mirth or love.

Yet, thus adorned with every graceful art
To charm the fancy and yet reach the heart,
Must we displace her? And instead advance
The goddess of the woful countenance—
The sentimental Muse!—Her emblems view,
The Pilgrim's Progress, and a sprig of rue!
View her—too chaste to look like flesh and blood—
Primly portrayed on emblematic wood!
There, fixed in usurpation, should she stand,
She'll snatch the dagger from her sister's hand:
And having made her votaries weep a flood,
Good heaven! she'll end her comedies in blood—
Bid Harry Woodward break poor Dunstal's crown!
Imprison Quick, and knock Ned Shuter down;
While sad Barsanti, weeping o'er the scene,
Shall stab herself—or poison Mrs. Green.

Such dire encroachments to prevent in time,
Demands the critic's voice—the poet's rhyme.
Can our light scenes add strength to holy laws!
Such puny patronage but hurts the cause:
Fair virtue scorns our feeble aid to ask;
And moral truth disdains the trickster's mask.
For here their favorite stands,* whose brow severe
And sad, claims youth's respect, and pity's tear;
Who, when oppress'd by foes her worth creates,
Can point a poniard at the guilt she hates.†

* Pointing to Tragedy.
[† The lines of this Prologue may be spoken by any of the female characters presenting the Comedy. As given here, they were spoken by a member of the stock
company at the Author's London theatre, and the lines—

"Bid Harry Woodward break poor Dunstal's crown!
Imprison Quick, and knock Ned Shuter down;
While sad Barsanti, weeping o'er the scene,
Shall stab herself—or poison Mrs. Green "—

Are intended as humorous references to the persons named, who were members
of the same company. In like manner these lines may be used, by the person
speaking them, for humorous or satirical references to any one.—EDITOR'S NOTE.]

ACT FIRST

Scene I.—A Street

Enter Thomas; he crosses the stage; Fag follows, looking after him.

FAG.—What! Thomas! sure 'tis he?—What! Thomas! Thomas!

THOMAS.—Hey!—Odd's life! Mr. Fag!—give us your hand, my old fellow-servant.

FAG.—Excuse my glove, Thomas:—I'm devilish glad to see you, my lad. Why, my prince of charioteers, you look as hearty—but who the deuce thought of seeing you in Bath?

THOMAS.—Sure, master, Madam Julia, Harry, Mrs. Kate, and the postilion, be all come.

FAG.—Indeed!

THOMAS.—Ay, master thought another fit of the gout was coming to make him a visit;—so he'd a mind to gi 't the slip, and whip! we were all off at an hour's warning.

FAG.—Ay, ay, hasty in everything, or it would not be Sir Anthony Absolute!

THOMAS.—But tell us, Mr. Fag, how does young master? Odd! Sir Anthony will stare to see the Captain here!

FAG.—I do not serve Captain Absolute now.

THOMAS.—Why sure!

FAG.—At present I am employed by Ensign Beverley.

THOMAS.—I doubt, Mr. Fag, you ha'n't changed for the better.

FAG.—I have not changed, Thomas.

THOMAS.—No! Why, didn't you say you had left young master?

FAG.—No.—Well, honest Thomas, I must puzzle you no farther:—briefly then—Captain Absolute and Ensign Beverley are one and the same person.

THOMAS.—The devil they are!

FAG.—So it is indeed, Thomas; and the ensign half of my master being on guard at present—the captain has nothing to do with me.

THOMAS.—So, so!—What, this is some freak, I warrant!—Do tell us, Mr. Fag, the meaning o't—you know I ha' trusted you.

FAG.—You'll be secret, Thomas?

THOMAS.—As a coach-horse.

FAG.—Why then the cause of all this is—Love—Love, Thomas, who, (as you may get read to you,) has been a masquerader ever since the days of Jupiter.

THOMAS.—Ay, ay;—I guessed there was a lady in the case:—But pray, why does your master pass only for ensign?—Now if he had shammed general indeed——

FAG.—Ah! Thomas, there lies the mystery o' the matter. Hark 'ee, Thomas, my master is in love with a lady of a very singular taste: a lady who likes him better as a half pay ensign than if she knew he was son and heir to Sir Anthony Absolute, a baronet of three thousand a year.

THOMAS.—That is an odd taste indeed!—But has she got the stuff, Mr. Fag? Is she rich, hey?

FAG.—Rich!—Why, I believe she owns half the stocks! Zounds! Thomas, she could pay the national debt as easily as I could my washerwoman! She has a lapdog that eats out of gold—she feeds her parrot with small pearls—and all her thread-papers are made of banknotes.

THOMAS.—Bravo, faith!—Odd! I warrant she has a set of thousands at least:—but does she draw kindly with the captain?

FAG.—As fond as pigeons.

THOMAS.—May one hear her name?

FAG.—Miss Lydia Languish. But there is an old tough aunt in the way; though, by the by, she has never seen my master—for we got acquainted with miss while on a visit in Gloucestershire.

THOMAS.—Well—I wish they were once harnessed together in matrimony.—But pray, Mr. Fag, what kind of a place is this Bath?—I ha' heard a deal of it—here's a mort * o' merry-making, hey?

* A Devonshire word for " a quantity."

FAG.—Pretty well, Thomas, pretty well—'tis a good lounge; in the morning we go to the pump-room (though neither my master nor I drink the waters); after breakfast we saunter on the parades, or play a game at billiards; at night we dance; but d—n the place, I'm tired of it: their regular hours stupefy me—not a fiddle nor a card after eleven!—However, Mr. Faulkland's gentleman and I keep it up a little in private parties;—I'll introduce you there, Thomas—you'll like him much.

THOMAS.—Sure I know Mr. Du-Peigne—you know his master is to marry Madam Julia.

FAG.—I had forgot. But, Thomas, you must polish a little—indeed you must. Here now—this wig! What the devil do you do with a wig, Thomas? None of the London whips of any degree of *ton* wear wigs now.

THOMAS.—More's the pity! more's the pity, I say. Odd's 'life! when I heard how the lawyers and doctors had took to their own hair, I thought how 'twould go next—odd rabbit it! when the fashion had got foot on the bar, I guessed 'twould mount to the box!—but 'tis all out of character, believe me, Mr. Fag: and look'ee, I'll never gi' up mine—the lawyers and doctors may do as they will.

FAG.—Well, Thomas, we'll not quarrel about that.

THOMAS.—Why, bless you, the gentlemen of the professions ben't all of a mind—for in our village now, tho' Jack Gauge, the exciseman, has ta'en to his carrots, there's little Dick the farrier swears he'll never forsake his bob, though all the college should appear with their own heads!

FAG.—Indeed! well said, Dick!—But hold—mark! mark! Thomas.

THOMAS.—Zooks! 'tis the captain. Is that the lady with him?

FAG.—No, no, that is Madam Lucy, my master's mistress's maid. They lodge at that house—but I must after him to tell him the news.

THOMAS.—Odd! he's giving her money!—Well, Mr. Fag——

FAG.—Good-by, Thomas. I have an appointment in Gyde's Porch this evening at eight; meet me there, and we'll make a little party. [*Exeunt severally.*

Scene II.—Dressing-room, Mrs. Malaprop's Lodgings

Lydia sitting on a sofa, with a book in her hand. Lucy, as just returned from a message.

LUCY.—Indeed, ma'am, I traversed half the town in search of it: I don't believe there's a circulating library in Bath I ha'n't been at.

LYDIA.—And could not you get " The Reward of Constancy "?

LUCY.—No, indeed, ma'am.

LYDIA.—Nor " The Fatal Connexion "?

LUCY.—No, indeed, ma'am.

LYDIA.—Nor " The Mistakes of the Heart "?

LUCY.—Ma'am, as ill luck would have it, Mr. Bull said Miss Sukey Saunter had just fetched it away.

LYDIA.—Heigh-ho!—Did you inquire for " The Delicate Distress "?

LUCY.—Or, " The Memoirs of Lady Woodford "? Yes, indeed, ma'am. I asked everywhere for it; and I might have brought it from Mr. Frederick's, but Lady Slattern Lounger, who had just sent it home, had so soiled and dog's-eared it, it wa'n't fit for a Christian to read.

LYDIA.—Heigh-ho!—Yes, I always know when Lady Slattern has been before me. She has a most observing thumb; and, I believe, cherishes her nails for the convenience of making marginal notes. Well, child, what have you brought me?

LUCY.—Oh! here, ma'am. [*Taking books from under her cloak, and from her pockets.*] This is " The Gordian Knot "—and this " Peregrine Pickle." Here are " The Tears of Sensibility," and " Humphrey Clinker." This is " The Memoirs of a Lady of Quality—written by herself," and here the second volume of " The Sentimental Journey."

LYDIA.—Heigh-ho!—What are those books by the glass?

LUCY.—The great one is only " The Whole Duty of Man."

LYDIA.—Very well—give me the sal volatile.

LUCY.—Is it in a blue cover, ma'am?

LYDIA.—My smelling-bottle, you simpleton!

Lucy.—Oh, the drops!—here, ma'am.

Lydia.—Hold!—here's some one coming—quick, see who it is. [*Exit Lucy.*] Surely I heard my cousin Julia's voice.

Re-enter Lucy.

Lucy.—Lud! ma'am, here is Miss Melville.

Lydia.—Is it possible!— [*Exit Lucy.*

Enter Julia.

Lydia.—My dearest Julia, how delighted am I!—[*Embrace.*] How unexpected was this happiness!

Julia.—True, Lydia—and our pleasure is the greater. But what has been the matter?—you were denied to me at first!

Lydia.—Ah, Julia, I have a thousand things to tell you!— But first inform me what has conjured you to Bath? Is Sir Anthony here?

Julia.—He is—we are arrived within this hour!—and I suppose he will be here to wait on Mrs. Malaprop as soon as he is dressed.

Lydia.—Then before we are interrupted, let me impart to you some of my distress!—I know your gentle nature will sympathize with me, though your prudence may condemn me! My letters have informed you of my whole connection with Beverley; but I have lost him, Julia! My aunt has discovered our intercourse by a note she intercepted, and has confined me ever since! Yet would you believe it? She has absolutely fallen in love with a tall Irish baronet she met one night since we have been here, at Lady Macshuffle's rout.

Julia.—You jest, Lydia!

Lydia.—No, upon my word.—She really carries on a kind of correspondence with him, under a feigned name though, till she chooses to be known to him—but it is a Delia or a Celia, I assure you.

Julia.—Then, surely, she is now more indulgent to her niece.

Lydia.—Quite the contrary. Since she has discovered her own frailty, she is become more suspicious of mine. Then I must inform you of another plague!—That odious

Acres is to be in Bath to-day; so that I protest I shall
be teased out of all spirits!

JULIA.—Come, come, Lydia, hope for the best—Sir Anthony
shall use his interest with Mrs. Malaprop.

LYDIA.—But you have not heard the worst. Unfortunately I
had quarrelled with my poor Beverley, just before my
aunt made the discovery, and I have not seen him since,
to make it up.

JULIA.—What was his offence?

LYDIA.—Nothing at all! But, I don't know how it was, as often
as we had been together, we had never had a quarrel,
and, somehow, I was afraid he would never give me an
opportunity. So, last Thursday, I wrote a letter to myself, to inform myself that Beverley was at that time
paying his addresses to another woman. I signed it
your friend unknown, showed it to Beverley, charged
him with his falsehood, put myself in a violent passion,
and vowed I'd never see him more.

JULIA.—And you let him depart so, and have not seen him since?

LYDIA.—'Twas the next day my aunt found the matter out. I
intended only to have teased him three days and a half,
and now I've lost him forever.

JULIA.—If he is as deserving and sincere as you have repre-
sented him to me, he will never give you up so. Yet
consider, Lydia, you tell me he is but an ensign, and you
have thirty thousand pounds.

LYDIA.—But you know I lose most of my fortune if I marry
without my aunt's consent, till of age; and that is what
I have determined to do, ever since I knew the penalty.
Nor could I love the man who would wish to wait a day
for the alternative.

JULIA.—Nay, this is caprice!

LYDIA.—What, does Julia tax me with caprice?—I thought her
lover Faulkland had inured her to it.

JULIA.—I do not love even his faults.

LYDIA.—But apropos—you have sent to him, I suppose?

JULIA.—Not yet, upon my word—nor has he the least idea of
my being in Bath. Sir Anthony's resolution was so sudden, I could not inform him of it.

LYDIA.—Well, Julia, you are your own mistress, (though under the protection of Sir Anthony,) yet have you, for this long year, been a slave to the caprice, the whim, the jealousy of this ungrateful Faulkland, who will ever delay assuming the right of a husband while you suffer him to be equally imperious as a lover.

JULIA.—Nay, you are wrong entirely. We were contracted before my father's death. That, and some consequent embarrassments, have delayed what I know to be my Faulkland's most ardent wish. He is too generous to trifle on such a point:—and for his character, you wrong him there too. No, Lydia, he is too proud, too noble to be jealous; if he is captious, 'tis without dissembling; if fretful, without rudeness. Unused to the fopperies of love, he is negligent of the little duties expected from a lover—but being unhackneyed in the passion, his affection is ardent and sincere; and as it engrosses his whole soul, he expects every thought and emotion of his mistress to move in unison with his. Yet, though his pride calls for this full return, his humility makes him undervalue those qualities in him which would entitle him to it; and not feeling why he should be loved to the degree he wishes, he still suspects that he is not loved enough. This temper, I must own, has cost me many unhappy hours; but I have learned to think myself his debtor, for those imperfections which arise from the ardor of his attachment.

LYDIA.—Well, I cannot blame you for defending him. But tell me candidly, Julia, had he never saved your life, do you think you should have been attached to him as you are? Believe me, the rude blast that overset your boat was a prosperous gale of love to him.

JULIA.—Gratitude may have strengthened my attachment to Mr. Faulkland, but I loved him before he had preserved me; yet surely that alone were an obligation sufficient.

LYDIA.—Obligation! why a water-spaniel would have done as much! Well, I should never think of giving my heart to a man because he could swim.

JULIA.—Come, Lydia, you are too inconsiderate.

LYDIA.—Nay, I do but jest. What's here?

Re-enter Lucy in a hurry.

LUCY.—O ma'am, here is Sir Anthony Absolute just come home with your aunt.

LYDIA.—They'll not come here. Lucy, do you watch.

[*Exit Lucy.*

JULIA.—Yet I must go. Sir Anthony does not know I am here, and if we meet, he'll detain me, to show me the town. I'll take another opportunity of paying my respects to Mrs. Malaprop, when she shall treat me, as long as she chooses, with her select words so ingeniously misapplied, without being mispronounced.

Re-enter Lucy.

LUCY.—O Lud! ma'am, they are both coming up-stairs.

LYDIA.—Well, I'll not detain you, coz. Adieu, my dear Julia, I'm sure you are in haste to send to Faulkland. There— through my room you'll find another staircase.

JULIA.—Adieu! [*Embraces Lydia and exit.*

LYDIA.—Here, my dear Lucy, hide these books. Quick, quick. Fling " Peregrine Pickle " under the toilet—throw " Roderick Random " into the closet—put " The Innocent Adultery " into " The Whole Duty of Man "— thrust " Lord Aimworth " under the sofa—cram " Ovid " behind the bolster—there—put " The Man of Feeling " into your pocket—so, so—now lay " Mrs. Chapone " in sight, and leave " Fordyce's Sermons " open on the table.

LUCY.—O burn it, ma'am! the hairdresser has torn away as far as " Proper Pride."

LYDIA.—Never mind—open at " Sobriety." Fling me " Lord Chesterfield's Letters." Now for 'em. [*Exit Lucy.*

Enter Mrs. Malaprop, and Sir Anthony Absolute.

MRS. MALAPROP.—There, Sir Anthony, there sits the deliberate simpleton who wants to disgrace her family, and lavish herself on a fellow not worth a shilling.

LYDIA.—Madam, I thought you once——

MRS. MALAPROP.—You thought, miss! I don't know any business you have to think at all—thought does not become a young woman. But the point we would request of you is, that you will promise to forget this fellow—to illiterate him, I say; quite from your memory.

LYDIA.—Ah, madam! our memories are independent of our wills. It is not so easy to forget.

MRS. MALAPROP.—But I say it is, miss; there is nothing on earth so easy as to forget, if a person chooses to set about it. I'm sure I have as much forgot your poor dear uncle as if he had never existed—and I thought it my duty so to do; and let me tell you, Lydia, these violent memories don't become a young woman.

SIR ANTHONY.—Why sure she won't pretend to remember what she's ordered not!—ay, this comes of her reading!

LYDIA.—What crime, madam, have I committed, to be treated thus?

MRS. MALAPROP.—Now don't attempt to extirpate yourself from the matter; you know I have proof controvertible of it. But tell me, will you promise to do as you're bid? Will you take a husband of your friends' choosing?

LYDIA.—Madam, I must tell you plainly, that had I no preference for anyone else, the choice you have made would be my aversion.

MRS. MALAPROP.—What business have you, miss, with preference and aversion? They don't become a young woman; and you ought to know, that as both always wear off, 'tis safest in matrimony to begin with a little aversion. I am sure I hated your poor dear uncle before marriage as if he had been a blackamoor—and yet, miss, you are sensible what a wife I made!—and when it pleased Heaven to release me from him, 'tis unknown what tears I shed! But suppose we were going to give you another choice, will you promise us to give up this Beverley?

LYDIA.—Could I belie my thoughts so far as to give that promise, my actions would certainly as far belie my words.

MRS. MALAPROP.—Take yourself to your room. You are fit company for nothing but your own ill-humors.

LYDIA.—Willingly, ma'am—I cannot change for the worse.

[*Exit.*

MRS. MALAPROP.—There's a little intricate hussy for you!

SIR ANTHONY.—It is not to be wondered at, ma'am—all this is the natural consequence of teaching girls to read. Had I a thousand daughters, by Heaven! I'd as soon have them taught the black art as their alphabet!

MRS. MALAPROP.—Nay, nay, Sir Anthony, you are an absolute misanthropy.

SIR ANTHONY.—In my way hither, Mrs. Malaprop, I observed your niece's maid coming forth from a circulating library! She had a book in each hand—they were half-bound volumes, with marble covers! From that moment I guessed how full of duty I should see her mistress!

MRS. MALAPROP.—Those are vile places, indeed!

SIR ANTHONY.—Madam, a circulating library in a town is as an evergreen tree of diabolical knowledge! It blossoms through the year! And depend on it, Mrs. Malaprop, that they who are so fond of handling the leaves, will long for the fruit at last.

MRS. MALAPROP.—Fy, fy, Sir Anthony! you surely speak laconically.

SIR ANTHONY.—Why, Mrs. Malaprop, in moderation now, what would you have a woman know?

MRS. MALAPROP.—Observe me, Sir Anthony. I would by no means wish a daughter of mine to be a progeny of learning; I don't think so much learning becomes a young woman; for instance, I would never let her meddle with Greek, or Hebrew, or algebra, or simony, or fluxions, or paradoxes or such inflammatory branches of learning—neither would it be necessary for her to handle any of your mathematical, astronomical, diabolical instruments. But, Sir Anthony, I would send her, at nine years old, to a boarding-school in order to learn a little ingenuity and artifice. Then, sir, she should have a supercilious knowledge in accounts;—and as she grew up, I would have her instructed in geometry, that she might know something of the contagious countries;—but above all, Sir Anthony, she should be mistress of orthodoxy, that she might not mis-spell, and mispronounce words so shamefully as girls usually do; and likewise that she might

reprehend the true meaning of what she is saying.
This, Sir Anthony, is what I would have a woman know;
—and I don't think there is a superstitious article in it.

SIR ANTHONY.—Well, well, Mrs. Malaprop, I will dispute the
point no further with you; though I must confess, that
you are a truly moderate and polite arguer, for almost
every word you say is on my side of the question. But,
Mrs. Malaprop, to the more important point in debate—
you say you have no objection to my proposal?

MRS. MALAPROP.—None, I assure you. I am under no positive
engagement with Mr. Acres, and as Lydia is so obstinate
against him, perhaps your son may have better success.

SIR ANTHONY.—Well, madam, I will write for the boy directly.
He knows not a syllable of this yet, though I have for
some time had the proposal in my head. He is at present
with his regiment.

MRS. MALAPROP.—We have never seen your son, Sir Anthony;
but I hope no objection on his side.

SIR ANTHONY.—Objection!—let him object if he dare! No,
no, Mrs. Malaprop, Jack knows that the least demur
puts me in a frenzy directly. My process was always very
simple—in their younger days, 'twas " Jack, do this ";—
if he demurred, I knocked him down—and if he grum-
bled at that, I always sent him out of the room.

MRS. MALAPROP.—Ay, and the properest way, o' my conscience!
nothing is so conciliating to young people as severity.
Well, Sir Anthony, I shall give Mr. Acres his discharge,
and prepare Lydia to receive your son's invocations;—
and I hope you will represent her to the captain as an
object not altogether illegible.

SIR ANTHONY.—Madam, I will handle the subject prudently.
Well, I must leave you; and let me beg you, Mrs. Malaprop, to enforce this matter roundly to the girl. Take
my advice—keep a tight hand: if she rejects this proposal, clap her under lock and key; and if you were just
to let the servants forget to bring her dinner for three or
four days, you can't conceive how she'd come about.

[*Exit.*

MRS. MALAPROP.—Well, at any rate I shall be glad to get her
from under my intuition. She has somehow discovered

my partiality for Sir Lucius O'Trigger—sure, Lucy can't have betrayed me! No, the girl is such a simpleton. I should have made her confess it. Lucy! Lucy! [*Calls.*] Had she been one of your artificial ones, I should never have trusted her.

Re-enter Lucy.

LUCY.—Did you call, ma'am?

MRS. MALAPROP.—Yes, girl. Did you see Sir Lucius while you was out?

LUCY.—No, indeed, ma'am, not a glimpse of him.

MRS. MALAPROP.—You are sure, Lucy, that you never mentioned—

LUCY.—Oh gemini! I'd sooner cut my tongue out.

MRS. MALAPROP.—Well, don't let your simplicity be imposed on.

LUCY.—No, ma'am.

MRS. MALAPROP.—So, come to me presently, and I'll give you another letter to Sir Lucius; but mind, Lucy—if ever you betray what you are entrusted with (unless it be other people's secrets to me), you forfeit my malevolence forever; and your being a simpleton shall be no excuse for your locality. [*Exit.*

LUCY.—Ha! ha! ha! So, my dear Simplicity, let me give you a little respite. [*Altering her manner.*] Let girls in my station be as fond as they please of appearing expert and knowing in their trusts; commend me to a mask of silliness, and a pair of sharp eyes for my own interest under it! Let me see to what account have I turned my simplicity lately. [*Looks at a paper.*] "For abetting Miss Lydia Languish in a design of running away with an ensign!—in money, sundry times, twelve pound twelve; gowns, five; hats, ruffles, caps, etc., etc., numberless! From the said ensign, within this last month, six guineas and a half."—About a quarter's pay! Item, "from Mrs. Malaprop, for betraying the young people to her"—when I found matters were likely to be discovered—"two guineas, and a black paduasoy." * Item, "from

---

* A silk stuff, named from Padua, and the French *soie*.

Mr. Acres, for carrying divers letters "—which I never
delivered—" two guineas and a pair of buckles." Item,
"from Sir Lucius O'Trigger, three crowns, two gold
pocket-pieces and a silver snuff-box!" Well done, Simplicity! Yet I was forced to make my Hibernian believe,
that he was corresponding, not with the aunt, but with
the niece: for though not over rich, I found he had too
much pride and delicacy to sacrifice the feelings of a
gentleman to the necessities of his fortune.   [*Exit.*

ACT SECOND

Scene I.—Captain Absolute's Lodgings

Captain Absolute and Fag.

FAG.—Sir, while I was there Sir Anthony came in: I told him,
you had sent me to inquire after his health, and to know
if he was at leisure to see you.

ABSOLUTE.—And what did he say, on hearing I was at Bath?

FAG.—Sir, in my life I never saw an elderly gentleman more astonished! He started back two or three paces, rapped
out a dozen interjectural oaths, and asked, what the
devil had brought you here.

ABSOLUTE.—Well, sir, and what did you say?

FAG.—Oh, I lied, sir—I forget the precise lie; but you may
depend on't, he got no truth from me. Yet, with submission, for fear of blunders in future, I should be glad
to fix what has brought us to Bath; in order that we may
lie a little consistently. Sir Anthony's servants were
curious, sir, very curious indeed.

ABSOLUTE.—You have said nothing to them?

FAG.—Oh, not a word, sir—not a word! Mr. Thomas, indeed,
the coachman (whom I take to be the discreetest of
whips)——

ABSOLUTE.—'Sdeath!—you rascal! you have not trusted him!

FAG.—Oh, no, sir—no—no—not a syllable, upon my veracity!
He was, indeed, a little inquisitive; but I was sly, sir—
devilish sly! My master (said I), honest Thomas (you

know, sir, one says honest to one's inferiors,) is come to
Bath to recruit—Yes, sir, I said to recruit—and whether
for men, money, or constitution, you know, sir, is nothing to him, nor anyone else.

ABSOLUTE.—Well, recruit will do—let it be so.

FAG.—Oh, sir, recruit will do surprisingly—indeed, to give the
thing an air, I told Thomas, that your honor had already
enlisted five disbanded chairmen, seven minority waiters,
and thirteen billiard-markers.

ABSOLUTE.—You blockhead, never say more than is necessary.

FAG.—I beg pardon, sir—I beg pardon—but, with submission,
a lie is nothing unless one supports it. Sir, whenever I
draw on my invention for a good current lie, I always
forge indorsements as well as the bill.

ABSOLUTE.—Well, take care you don't hurt your credit, by offering too much security. Is Mr. Faulkland returned?

FAG.—He is above, sir, changing his dress.

ABSOLUTE.—Can you tell whether he has been informed of Sir
Anthony and Miss Melville's arrival?

FAG.—I fancy, not, sir; he has seen no one since he came in but
his gentleman, who was with him at Bristol. I think,
sir, I hear Mr. Faulkland coming down——

ABSOLUTE.—Go, tell him I am here.

FAG.—Yes, sir.—[*Going.*] I beg pardon, sir, but should Sir
Anthony call, you will do me the favor to remember that
we are recruiting, if you please.

ABSOLUTE.—Well, well.

FAG.—And, in tenderness to my character, if your honor could
bring in the chairmen and waiters, I should esteem it as
an obligation; for though I never scruple a lie to serve
my master, yet it hurts one's conscience to be found out.

[*Exit.*

ABSOLUTE.—Now for my whimsical friend—if he does not
know that his mistress is here, I'll tease him a little before
I tell him—

Enter Faulkland.

Faulkland, you're welcome to Bath again; you are punctual in your return.

FAULKLAND.—Yes; I had nothing to detain me, when I had

finished the business I went on. Well, what news since
I left you? How stand matters between you and Lydia?

ABSOLUTE.—Faith, much as they were; I have not seen her
since our quarrel; however, I expect to be recalled every
hour.

FAULKLAND.—Why don't you persuade her to go off with you
at once?

ABSOLUTE.—What, and lose two-thirds of her fortune? you forget that, my friend. No, no, I could have brought her
to that long ago.

FAULKLAND.—Nay then, you trifle too long—if you are sure of
her, propose to the aunt in your own character, and write
to Sir Anthony for his consent.

ABSOLUTE.—Softly, softly; for though I am convinced my little Lydia would elope with me as Ensign Beverley, yet
am I by no means certain that she would take me with
the impediment of our friend's consent, a regular hum-
drum wedding, and the reversion of a good fortune on
my side: no, no; I must prepare her gradually for the
discovery, and make myself necessary to her, before I
risk it. Well, but, Faulkland, you'll dine with us to-day
at the hotel?

FAULKLAND.—Indeed I cannot; I am not in spirits to be of
such a party.

ABSOLUTE.—By heavens! I shall forswear your company. You
are the most teasing, captious, incorrigible lover! Do
love like a man.

FAULKLAND.—I own I am unfit for company.

ABSOLUTE.—Am not I a lover; ay, and a romantic one too?
Yet do I carry everywhere with me such a confounded
farrago of doubts, fears, hopes, wishes, and all the flimsy
furniture of a country miss's brain?

FAULKLAND.—Ah! Jack, your heart and soul are not, like mine,
fixed immutably on one only object. You throw for a
large stake, but losing, you could stake and throw again:
—but I have set my sum of happiness on this cast, and
not to succeed, were to be stripped of all.

ABSOLUTE.—But, for Heaven's sake! what grounds for apprehension can your whimsical brain conjure up at present?

FAULKLAND.—What grounds for apprehension, did you say?

Heavens! are there not a thousand! I fear for her spirits
—her health—her life. My absence may fret her; her
anxiety for my return, her fears for me may oppress her
gentle temper; and for her health, does not every hour
bring me cause to be alarmed? If it rains, some shower
may even then have chilled her delicate frame! If the
wind be keen, some rude blast may have affected her!
The heat of noon, the dews of the evening, may endanger
the life of her, for whom only I value mine. O Jack!
when delicate and feeling souls are separated, there is
not a feature in the sky, not a movement of the elements,
not an aspiration of the breeze, but hints some cause for
a lover's apprehension!

ABSOLUTE.—Ay, but we may choose whether we will take the
hint or not. So, then, Faulkland, if you were convinced
that Julia were well and in spirits, you would be entirely
content?

FAULKLAND.—I should be happy beyond measure—I am
anxious only for that.

ABSOLUTE.—Then to cure your anxiety at once—Miss Melville
is in perfect health, and is at this moment in Bath.

FAULKLAND.—Nay, Jack—don't trifle with me.

ABSOLUTE.—She is arrived here with my father within this
hour.

FAULKLAND.—Can you be serious?

ABSOLUTE.—I thought you knew Sir Anthony better than to be
surprised at a sudden whim of this kind. Seriously, then,
it is as I tell you—upon my honor.

FAULKLAND.—My dear friend! Hollo, Du Peigne! my hat.
My dear Jack—now nothing on earth can give me a
moment's uneasiness.

Re-enter Fag.

FAG.—Sir, Mr. Acres, just arrived, is below.

ABSOLUTE.—Stay, Faulkland, this Acres lives within a mile of
Sir Anthony, and he shall tell you how your mistress has
been ever since you left her. Fag, show the gentleman
up.   [*Exit Fag.*

FAULKLAND.—What, is he much acquainted in the family?

ABSOLUTE.—Oh, very intimate : I insist on your not going : besides, his character will divert you.

FAULKLAND.—Well, I should like to ask him a few questions.

ABSOLUTE.—He is likewise a rival of mine—that is, of my other self's, for he does not think his friend Captain Absolute ever saw the lady in question ; and it is ridiculous enough to hear him complain to me of one Beverley, a concealed skulking rival, who——

FAULKLAND.—Hush !—he's here.

Enter Acres.

ACRES.—Ha ! my dear friend, noble captain, and honest Jack, how do'st thou ? just arrived, faith, as you see. Sir, your humble servant. Warm work on the roads, Jack ! Odds whips and wheels ! I've travelled like a comet, with a tail of dust all the way as long as the Mall.

ABSOLUTE.—Ah ! Bob, you are indeed an eccentric planet, but we know your attraction hither. Give me leave to introduce Mr. Faulkland to you ; Mr. Faulkland, Mr. Acres.

ACRES.—Sir, I am most heartily glad to see you : sir, I solicit your connections. Hey, Jack—what, this is Mr. Faulkland, who——

ABSOLUTE.—Ay, Bob, Miss Melville's Mr. Faulkland.

ACRES.—Odso ! she and your father can be but just arrived before me :—I suppose you have seen them. Ah ! Mr. Faulkland, you are indeed a happy man.

FAULKLAND.—I have not seen Miss Melville yet, sir ;—I hope she enjoyed full health and spirits in Devonshire ?

ACRES.—Never knew her better in my life, sir—never better. Odds blushes and blooms ! she has been as healthy as the German Spa.

FAULKLAND.—Indeed ! I did hear that she had been a little indisposed.

ACRES.—False, false, sir—only said to vex you : quite the reverse, I assure you.

FAULKLAND.—There, Jack, you see she has the advantage of me ; I had almost fretted myself ill.

ABSOLUTE.—Now are you angry with your mistress for not having been sick ?

FAULKLAND.—No, no, you misunderstand me: yet surely a little trifling indisposition is not an unnatural consequence of absence from those we love. Now confess—isn't there something unkind in this violent, robust, unfeeling health?

ABSOLUTE.—Oh, it was very unkind of her to be well in your absence, to be sure!

ACRES.—Good apartments, Jack.

FAULKLAND.—Well, sir, but you was saying that Miss Melville has been so exceedingly well—what, then, she has been merry and gay, I suppose? Always in spirits—hey?

ACRES.—Merry, odds crickets! she has been the belle and spirit of the company wherever she has been—so lively and entertaining! so full of wit and humor!

FAULKLAND.—There, Jack, there. Oh, by my soul! there is an innate levity in woman, that nothing can overcome. What! happy, and I away!

ABSOLUTE.—Have done. How foolish this is! just now you were only apprehensive for your mistress' spirits.

FAULKLAND.—Why, Jack, have I been the joy and spirit of the company.

ABSOLUTE.—No indeed, you have not.

FAULKLAND.—Have I been lively and entertaining?

ABSOLUTE.—Oh, upon my word, I acquit you.

FAULKLAND.—Have I been full of wit and humor?

ABSOLUTE.—No, faith, to do you justice, you have been confoundedly stupid indeed.

ACRES.—What's the matter with the gentleman?

ABSOLUTE.—He is only expressing his great satisfaction at hearing that Julia has been so well and happy—that's all hey, Faulkland?

FAULKLAND.—Oh! I am rejoiced to hear it—yes, yes, she has a happy disposition!

ACRES.—That she has indeed. Then she is so accomplished—so sweet a voice—so expert at her harpsichord—such a mistress of flat and sharp, squallante, rumblante, and quiverante! There was this time month—odds minims and crochets! how she did chirrup at Mrs. Piano's concert!

FAULKLAND.—There again, what say you to this? you see she has been all mirth and song—not a thought of me!

ABSOLUTE.—Pho! man, is not music the food of love?

FAULKLAND.—Well, well, it may be so. Pray, Mr. ——, what's his d——d name? Do you remember what songs Miss Melville sung?

ACRES.—Not I indeed.

ABSOLUTE.—Stay, now, they were some pretty melancholy purling-stream airs, I warrant; perhaps you may recollect;—did she sing, " When absent from my soul's delight "?

ACRES.—No, that wa'n't it.

ABSOLUTE.—Or, " Go, gentle gales "?　　　　　　[Sings.

ACRES.—Oh, no! nothing like it. Odds! now I recollect one of them—" My heart's my own, my will is free." [Sings.

FAULKLAND.—Fool! fool that I am! to fix all my happiness on such a trifler! 'Sdeath! to make herself the pipe and ballad-monger of a circle! to soothe her light heart with catches and glees! What can you say to this, sir?

ABSOLUTE.—Why, that I should be glad to hear my mistress had been so merry, sir.

FAULKLAND.—Nay, nay, nay—I'm not sorry that she has been happy—no, no, I am glad of that—I would not have had her sad or sick—yet surely a sympathetic heart would have shown itself even in the choice of a song—she might have been temperately healthy, and somehow, plaintively gay;—but she has been dancing too, I doubt not!

ACRES.—What does the gentleman say about dancing?

ABSOLUTE.—He says the lady we speak of dances as well as she sings.

ACRES.—Ay, truly, does she—there was at our last race ball——

FAULKLAND.—Hell and the devil! There!—there—I told you so! I told you so! Oh! she thrives in my absence!— Dancing! but her whole feelings have been in opposition with mine;—I have been anxious, silent, pensive, sedentary—my days have been hours of care, my nights of watchfulness. She has been all health! spirit! laugh! song! dance!—Oh! d——d, d——d levity!

ABSOLUTE.—For Heaven's sake, Faulkland, don't expose yourself so!—Suppose she has danced, what then?—does not the ceremony of society often oblige——

FAULKLAND.—Well, well, I'll contain myself—perhaps as you say—for form sake. What, Mr. Acres, you were praising Miss Melville's manner of dancing a minuet—hey?

ACRES.—Oh, I dare insure her for that—but what I was going to speak of was her country-dancing. Odds swimmings! she has such an air with her!

FAULKLAND.—Now disappointment on her!—Defend this, Absolute; why don't you defend this?—Country-dances! jigs and reels! am I to blame now? A minuet I could have forgiven—I should not have minded that—I say I should not have regarded a minuet—but country-dances!—Zounds! had she made one in a cotillon—I believe I could have forgiven even that—but to be monkey-led for a night!—to run the gauntlet through a string of amorous palming puppies!—to show paces like a managed filly!—Oh, Jack, there never can be but one man in the world whom a truly modest and delicate woman ought to pair with in a country-dance; and, even then, the rest of the couples should be her great-uncles and aunts!

ABSOLUTE.—Ay, to be sure!—grandfathers and grandmothers!

FAULKLAND.—If there be but one vicious mind in the set, 'twill spread like a contagion—the action of their pulse beats to the lascivious movement of the jig—their quivering, warm-breathed sighs impregnate the very air—the atmosphere becomes electrical to love, and each amorous spark darts through every link of the chain!—I must leave you—I own I am somewhat flurried—and that confounded looby has perceived it.   [Going.

ABSOLUTE.—Nay, but stay, Faulkland, and thank Mr. Acres for his good news.

FAULKLAND.—D——n his news!   [Exit.

ABSOLUTE.—Ha! ha! ha! poor Faulkland five minutes since —"nothing on earth could give him a moment's uneasiness!"

ACRES.—The gentleman wa'n't angry at my praising his mistress, was he?

ABSOLUTE.—A little jealous, I believe, Bob.

ACRES.—You don't say so? Ha! ha! jealous of me—that's a good joke.

ABSOLUTE.—There's nothing strange in that, Bob; let me tell you, that sprightly grace and insinuating manner of yours will do some mischief among the girls here.

ACRES.—Ah! you joke—ha! ha! mischief—ha! ha! but you know I am not my own property, my dear Lydia has forestalled me. She could never abide me in the country, because I used to dress so badly—but odds frogs and tambours! I shan't take matters so here, now ancient madam has no voice in it, I'll make my old clothes know who's master. I shall straightway cashier the hunting-frock, and render my leather breeches incapable. My hair has been in training some time.

ABSOLUTE.—Indeed!

ACRES.—Ay—and tho' the side curls are a little restive, my hind-part takes it very kindly.

ABSOLUTE.—Oh, you'll polish, I doubt not.

ACRES.—Absolutely I propose so—then if I can find out this Ensign Beverley, odds triggers and flints! I'll make him know the difference o't.

ABSOLUTE.—Spoke like a man! But pray, Bob, I observe you have got an odd kind of a new method of swearing——

ACRES.—Ha! ha! you've taken notice of it—'tis genteel, isn't it!—I didn't invent it myself though; but a commander in our militia, a great scholar, I assure you, says that there is no meaning in the common oaths, and that nothing but their antiquity makes them respectable;—because, he says, the ancients would never stick to an oath or two, but would say, by Jove! or by Bacchus! or by Mars! or by Venus! or by Pallas, according to the sentiment: so that to swear with propriety, says my little major, the oath should be an echo to the sense; and this we call the oath referential or sentimental swearing—ha! ha! 'tis genteel, isn't it?

ABSOLUTE.—Very genteel, and very new, indeed!—and I dare say will supplant all other figures of imprecation.

ACRES.—Ay, ay, the best terms will grow obsolete—Damns have had their day.

Re-enter Fag.

FAG.—Sir, there is a gentleman below desires to see you.—
Shall I show him into the parlor?

ABSOLUTE.—Ay, you may.

ACRES.—Well, I must be gone——

ABSOLUTE.—Stay; who is it, Fag?

FAG.—Your father, sir.

ABSOLUTE.—You puppy, why didn't you show him up directly?

[*Exit Fag.*

ACRES.—You have business with Sir Anthony. I expect a
message from Mrs. Malaprop at my lodgings. I have
sent also to my dear friend Sir Lucius O"Trigger.
Adieu, Jack! we must meet at night, when you shall
give me a dozen bumpers to little Lydia.

ABSOLUTE.—That I will with all my heart.—[*Exit Acres.*]
Now for a parental lecture—I hope he has heard nothing
of the business that has brought me here—I wish the
gout had held him fast in Devonshire, with all my
soul!

Enter Sir Anthony Absolute.

Sir, I am delighted to see you here, looking so well! your
sudden arrival at Bath made me apprehensive for your
health.

SIR ANTHONY.—Very apprehensive, I dare say, Jack.—What,
you are recruiting here, hey?

ABSOLUTE.—Yes, sir, I am on duty.

SIR ANTHONY.—Well, Jack, I am glad to see you, though I
did not expect it, for I was going to write to you on a
little matter of business.—Jack, I have been considering
that I grow old and infirm, and shall probably not trouble
you long.

ABSOLUTE.—Pardon me, sir, I never saw you look more strong
and hearty; and I pray frequently that you may continue so.

SIR ANTHONY.—I hope your prayers may be heard, with all
my heart. Well then, Jack, I have been considering that
I am so strong and hearty I may continue to plague you
a long time. Now, Jack, I am sensible that the income

VOL. II.—12

of your commission, and what I have hitherto allowed you, is but a small pittance for a lad of your spirit.

ABSOLUTE.—Sir, you are very good.

SIR ANTHONY.—And it is my wish, while yet I live, to have my boy make some figure in the world. I have resolved, therefore, to fix you at once in a noble independence.

ABSOLUTE.—Sir, your kindness overpowers me—such generosity makes the gratitude of reason more lively than the sensations even of filial affection.

SIR ANTHONY.—I am glad you are so sensible of my attention —and you shall be master of a large estate in a few weeks.

ABSOLUTE.—Let my future life, sir, speak my gratitude; I cannot express the sense I have of your munificence.—Yet, sir, I presume you would not wish me to quit the army?

SIR ANTHONY.—Oh, that shall be as your wife chooses.

ABSOLUTE.—My wife, sir!

SIR ANTHONY.—Ay, ay, settle that between you—settle that between you.

ABSOLUTE.—A wife, sir, did you say?

SIR ANTHONY.—Ay, a wife—why, did not I mention her before?

ABSOLUTE.—Not a word of her, sir.

SIR ANTHONY.—Odd so!—I mustn't forget her though.—Yes, Jack, the independence I was talking of is by a marriage —the fortune is saddled with a wife—but I suppose that makes no difference.

ABSOLUTE.—Sir! sir!—you amaze me!

SIR ANTHONY.—Why, what the devil's the matter with the fool? Just now you were all gratitude and duty.

ABSOLUTE.—I was, sir—you talked to me of independence and a fortune, but not a word of a wife.

SIR ANTHONY.—Why—what difference does that make? Odds life, sir! if you have the estate, you must take it with the live stock on it, as it stands.

ABSOLUTE.—If my happiness is to be the price, I must beg leave to decline the purchase.—Pray, sir, who is the lady?

SIR ANTHONY.—What's that to you, sir?—Come, give me your promise to love, and to marry her directly.

ABSOLUTE.—Sure, sir, this is not very reasonable, to summon my affections for a lady I know nothing of!

SIR ANTHONY.—I am sure, sir, 'tis more unreasonable in you to object to a lady you know nothing of.

ABSOLUTE.—Then, sir, I must tell you plainly that my inclinations are fixed on another—my heart is engaged to an angel.

SIR ANTHONY.—Then pray let it send an excuse. It is very sorry—but business prevents its waiting on her.

ABSOLUTE.—But my vows are pledged to her.

SIR ANTHONY.—Let her foreclose, Jack; let her foreclose; they are not worth redeeming; besides, you have the angel's vows in exchange, I suppose; so there can be no loss there.

ABSOLUTE.—You must excuse me, sir, if I tell you, once for all, that in this point I cannot obey you.

SIR ANTHONY.—Hark'ee, Jack; I have heard you for some time with patience—I have been cool—quite cool; but take care—you know I am compliance itself—when I am not thwarted;—no one more easily led—when I have my own way;—but don't put me in a frenzy.

ABSOLUTE.—Sir, I must repeat it—in this I cannot obey you.

SIR ANTHONY.—Now d—n me! if ever I call you Jack again while I live!

ABSOLUTE.—Nay, sir, but hear me.

SIR ANTHONY.—Sir, I won't hear a word—not a word! not one word! so give me your promise by a nod—and I'll tell you what, Jack—I mean, you dog—if you don't, by——

ABSOLUTE.—What, sir, promise to link myself to some mass of ugliness! to——

SIR ANTHONY.—Zounds! sirrah! the lady shall be as ugly as I choose: she shall have a lump on each shoulder; she shall be as crooked as the crescent; her one eye shall roll like the bull's in Cox's Museum; she shall have a skin like a mummy, and the beard of a Jew—she shall be all this, sirrah!—yet I will make you ogle her all day, and sit up all night to write sonnets on her beauty.

ABSOLUTE.—This is reason and moderation indeed!

SIR ANTHONY.—None of your sneering, puppy! no grinning, jackanapes!

ABSOLUTE.—Indeed, sir, I never was in a worse humor for mirth in my life.

SIR ANTHONY.—'Tis false, sir, I know you are laughing in your sleeve; I know you'll grin when I am gone, sirrah!

ABSOLUTE.—Sir, I hope I know my duty better.

SIR ANTHONY.—None of your passion, sir! none of your violence, if you please!—It won't do with me, I promise you.

ABSOLUTE.—Indeed, sir, I never was cooler in my life.

SIR ANTHONY.—'Tis a confounded lie!—I know you are in a passion in your heart; I know you are, you hypocritical young dog! but it won't do.

ABSOLUTE.—Nay, sir, upon my word——

SIR ANTHONY.—So you will fly out! can't you be cool like me? What the devil good can passion do?—Passion is of no service, you impudent, insolent, overbearing reprobate!—There, you sneer again! don't provoke me!— but you rely upon the mildness of my temper—you do, you dog! you play upon the meekness of my disposition! —Yet take care—the patience of a saint may be overcome at last!—but mark! I give you six hours and a half to consider of this: if you then agree, without any condition, to do everything on earth that I choose, why—confound you! I may in time forgive you.—If not, zounds! don't enter the same hemisphere with me! don't dare to breathe the same air, or use the same light with me; but get an atmosphere and a sun of your own! I'll strip you of your commission; I'll lodge a five-and-threepence in the hands of trustees, and you shall live on the interest.— I'll disown you, I'll disinherit you, I'll unget you! and d—n me! if ever I call you Jack again! [Exit.

ABSOLUTE.—Mild, gentle, considerate father—I kiss your hands! What a tender method of giving his opinion in these matters Sir Anthony has! I dare not trust him with the truth. I wonder what old wealthy hag it is that he wants to bestow on me!—Yet he married himself for love! and was in his youth a bold intriguer, and a gay companion!

Re-enter Fag.

FAG.—Assuredly, sir, your father is wrath to a degree; he comes downstairs eight or ten steps at a time—muttering, growling, and thumping the banisters all the way: I and the cook's dog stand bowing at the door—rap! he gives me a stroke on the head with his cane; bids me carry that to my master; then kicking the poor turnspit into the area, d—ns us all, for a puppy triumvirate!—Upon my credit, sir, were I in your place, and found my father such very bad company, I should certainly drop his acquaintance.

ABSOLUTE.—Cease your impertinence, sir, at present.—Did you come in for nothing more?—Stand out of the way!

[*Pushes him aside and exit.*

FAG.—So! Sir Anthony trims my master: he is afraid to reply to his father—then vents his spleen on poor Fag! When one is vexed by one person, to revenge one's self on another, who happens to come in the way, is the vilest injustice! Ah! it shows the worst temper—the basest——

Enter Boy.

BOY.—Mr. Fag; Mr. Fag! your master calls you.

FAG.—Well, you little dirty puppy, you need not bawl so!—The meanest disposition! the——

BOY.—Quick, quick, Mr. Fag!

FAG.—Quick! quick! you impudent jackanapes! am I to be commanded by you too? you little impertinent, insolent, kitchen-bred——   [*Exit, kicking and beating him.*

Scene II.—The North Parade

Enter Lucy.

LUCY.—So—I shall have another rival to add to my mistress's list—Captain Absolute. However, I shall not enter his name till my purse has received notice in form. Poor Acres is dismissed!—Well, I have done him a last friendly office; in letting him know that Beverley was here be-

fore him. Sir Lucius is generally more punctual, when
he expects to hear from his *dear Dalia,* as he calls her:
I wonder he's not here!—I have a little scruple of conscience from this deceit; though I should not be paid
so well, if my hero knew that Delia was near fifty, and
her own mistress.

Enter Sir Lucius O'Trigger.

Sir Lucius.—Ha! my little ambassadress—upon my conscience, I have been looking for you; I have been on
the South Parade this half hour.

Lucy [*speaking simply*].—O gemini! and I have been waiting for your worship here on the North.

Sir Lucius.—Faith!—may be that was the reason we did not
meet; and it is very comical too, how you could go out
and I not see you—for I was only taking a nap at the
Parade Coffee-house, and I chose the window on purpose that I might not miss you.

Lucy.—My stars! Now I'd wager a sixpence I went by while
you were asleep.

Sir Lucius.—Sure enough it must have been so—and I never
dreamt it was so late, till I waked. Well, but my little
girl, have you got nothing for me?

Lucy.—Yes, but I have—I've got a letter for you in my pocket.

Sir Lucius.—O faith! I guessed you weren't come empty-
handed.—Well—let me see what the dear creature
says.

Lucy.—There, Sir Lucius.   [*Gives him a letter.*

Sir Lucius.—[*Reads.*] "Sir—there is often a sudden incen-
tive impulse in love, that has a greater induction than
years of domestic combination: such was the commotion
I felt at the first superfluous view of Sir Lucius O'Trigger.—[*Very pretty, upon my word.*]—Female punctua-
tion forbids me to say more, yet let me add, that it will
give me joy infallible to find Sir Lucius worthy the last
criterion of my affections.   Delia."—
Upon my conscience! Lucy, your lady is a great mistress of language. Faith, she's quite the queen of the
dictionary!—for the devil a word dare refuse coming

at her call—though one would think it was quite out of hearing.

LUCY.—Ay, sir, a lady of her experience——

SIR LUCIUS.—Experience! what, at seventeen?

LUCY.—O true, sir—but then she reads so—my stars! how she will read off-hand!

SIR LUCIUS.—Faith, she must be very deep read to write this way—though she is rather an arbitrary writer too— for here are a great many poor words pressed into the service of this note, that would get their *habeas corpus* from any court in Christendom.

LUCY.—Ah! Sir Lucius, if you were to hear how she talks of you!

SIR LUCIUS.—Oh, tell her I'll make her the best husband in the world, and Lady O'Trigger into the bargain.—But we must get the old gentlewoman's consent—and do everything fairly.

LUCY.—Nay, Sir Lucius, I thought you wa'n't rich enough to be so nice!

SIR LUCIUS.—Upon my word, young woman, you have hit it: —I am so poor, that I can't afford to do a dirty action. If I did not want money, I'd steal your mistress and her fortune with a great deal of pleasure. However, my pretty girl, [*Gives her money,*] here's a little something to buy you a ribbon; and meet me in the evening, and I'll give you an answer to this. So, hussy, take a kiss beforehand to put you in mind. [*Kisses her.*

LUCY.—O Lud! Sir Lucius—I never seed such a gemman! My lady won't like you if you're so impudent.

SIR LUCIUS.—Faith she will, Lucy!—That same—pho! what's the name of it?—modesty—is a quality in a lover more praised by the women than liked; so, if your mistress asks you whether Sir Lucius ever gave you a kiss, tell her fifty—my dear.

LUCY.—What, would you have me tell her a lie?

SIR LUCIUS.—Ah, then, you baggage! I'll make it a truth presently.

LUCY.—For shame now! here is some one coming.

SIR LUCIUS.—Oh, faith, I'll quiet your conscience!

[*Exit, humming a tune.*

Enter Fag.

FAG.—So, so, ma'am! I humbly beg pardon.

LUCY.—O Lud! now, Mr. Fag—you flurry one so.

FAG.—Come, come, Lucy, here's no one by—so a little less simplicity, with a grain or two more sincerity, if you please. —You play false with us, madam—I saw you give the baronet a letter. My master shall know this—and if he don't call him out, I will.

LUCY.—Ha! ha! ha! you gentlemen's gentlemen are so hasty. —That letter was from Mrs. Malaprop, simpleton.— She is taken with Sir Lucius's address.

FAG.—How! what tastes some people have!—Why, I suppose I have walked by her window a hundred times.—But what says our young lady? any message to my master?

LUCY.—Sad news, Mr. Fag.—A worse rival than Acres! Sir Anthony Absolute has proposed his son.

FAG.—What, Captain Absolute?

LUCY.—Even so—I overheard it all.

FAG.—Ha! ha! ha! very good faith. Good-by, Lucy, I must away with this news.

LUCY.—Well, you may laugh—but it is true, I assure you.— [*Going.*] But, Mr. Fag, tell your master not to be cast down by this.

FAG.—Oh, he'll be so disconsolate!

LUCY.—And charge him not to think of quarrelling with young Absolute.

FAG.—Never fear! never fear!

LUCY.—Be sure—bid him keep up his spirits.

FAG.—We will—we will. [*Exeunt severally.*

ACT THIRD

Scene I.—The North Parade

Enter Captain Absolute.

ABSOLUTE.—'Tis just as Fag told me, indeed. Whimsical enough, faith! My father wants to force me to marry the very girl I am plotting to run away with! He must not know of my connection with her yet awhile. He has too summary a method of proceeding in these matters. However, I'll read my recantation instantly. My conversion is something sudden, indeed—but I can assure him it is very sincere. So, so—here he comes. He looks plaguey gruff. [*Steps aside.*

Enter Sir Anthony Absolute.

SIR ANTHONY.—No—I'll die sooner than forgive him. Die, did I say? I'll live these fifty years to plague him. At our last meeting, his impudence had almost put me out of temper. An obstinate, passionate, self-willed boy! Who can he take after? This is my return for getting him before all his brothers and sisters!—for putting him, at twelve years old, into a marching regiment, and allowing him fifty pounds a year, besides his pay, ever since! But I have done with him; he's anybody's son for me. I never will see him more, never—never—never.

ABSOLUTE [*aside, coming forward*].—Now for a penitential face.

SIR ANTHONY.—Fellow, get out of my way!

ABSOLUTE.—Sir, you see a penitent before you.

SIR ANTHONY.—I see an impudent scoundrel before me.

ABSOLUTE.—A sincere penitent. I am come, sir, to acknowledge my error, and to submit entirely to your will.

185

Sir Anthony.—What's that?

Absolute.—I have been revolving, and reflecting, and considering on your past goodness, and kindness, and condescension to me.

Sir Anthony.—Well, sir?

Absolute.—I have been likewise weighing and balancing what you were pleased to mention concerning duty, and obedience, and authority.

Sir Anthony.—Well, puppy?

Absolute.—Why then, sir, the result of my reflections is—a resolution to sacrifice every inclination of my own to your satisfaction.

Sir Anthony.—Why now you talk sense—absolute sense—I never heard anything more sensible in my life. Confound you! you shall be Jack again.

Absolute.—I am happy in the appellation.

Sir Anthony.—Why then, Jack, my dear Jack, I will now inform you who the lady really is. Nothing but your passion and violence, you silly fellow, prevented my telling you at first. Prepare, Jack, for wonder and rapture—prepare. What think you of Miss Lydia Languish?

Absolute.—Languish! What, the Languishes of Worcestershire?

Sir Anthony.—Worcestershire! no. Did you never meet Mrs. Malaprop and her niece, Miss Languish, who came into our country just before you were last ordered to your regiment!

Absolute.—Malaprop! Languish! I don't remember ever to have heard the names before. Yet, stay—I think I do recollect something. Languish! Languish! She squints, don't she? A little red-haired girl?

Sir Anthony.—Squints! A red-haired girl! Zounds! no.

Absolute.—Then I must have forgot; it can't be the same person.

Sir Anthony.—Jack! Jack! what think you of blooming, love-breathing seventeen?

Absolute.—As to that, sir, I am quite indifferent. If I can please you in the matter, 'tis all I desire.

Sir Anthony.—Nay, but Jack, such eyes! such eyes! so innocently wild! so bashfully irresolute! not a glance but

speaks and kindles some thought of love! Then, Jack,
her cheeks! her cheeks, Jack! so deeply blushing at the
insinuations of her tell-tale eyes! Then, Jack, her lips!
O Jack, lips smiling at their own discretion; and if not
smiling, more sweetly pouting; more lovely in sullen-
ness!

ABSOLUTE [*aside*].—That's she indeed. Well done, old gentleman.   [*Aside.*

SIR ANTHONY.—Then, Jack, her neck! O Jack! Jack!

ABSOLUTE.—And which is to be mine, sir, the niece, or the
aunt?

SIR ANTHONY.—Why, you unfeeling, insensible puppy, I despise you! When I was of your age, such a description
would have made me fly like a rocket! The aunt indeed! Odds life! when I ran away with your mother,
I would not have touched anything old or ugly to gain
an empire.

ABSOLUTE.—Not to please your father, sir?

SIR ANTHONY.—To please my father! zounds! not to please—
Oh, my father—odd so!—yes—yes; if my father indeed
had desired—that's quite another matter. Though he
wa'n't the indulgent father that I am, Jack.

ABSOLUTE.—I dare say not, sir.

SIR ANTHONY.—But, Jack, you are not sorry to find your mistress is so beautiful?

ABSOLUTE.—Sir, I repeat it—if I please you in this affair, 'tis
all I desire. Not that I think a woman the worse for
being handsome; but, sir, if you please to recollect, you
before hinted something about a hump or two, one eye,
and a few more graces of that kind—now, without being
very nice, I own I should rather choose a wife of mine
to have the usual number of limbs, and a limited quantity of back: and though one eye may be very agreeable,
yet as the prejudice has always run in favor of two, I
would not wish to affect a singularity in that article.

SIR ANTHONY.—What a phlegmatic sot it is! Why, sirrah,
you're an anchorite!—a vile, insensible stock. You a
soldier!—you're a walking block, fit only to dust the
company's regimentals on! Odds life! I have a great
mind to marry the girl myself.

ABSOLUTE.—I am entirely at your disposal, sir: if you should think of addressing Miss Languish yourself, I suppose you would have me marry the aunt; or if you should change your mind, and take the old lady—'tis the same to me—I'll marry the niece.

SIR ANTHONY.—Upon my word, Jack, thou'rt either a very great hypocrite, or—but, come, I know your indifference on such a subject must be all a lie—I'm sure it must—come, now—d—n your demure face!—come, confess Jack—you have been lying—ha'n't you? You have been playing the hypocrite, hey!—I'll never forgive you, if you ha'n't been lying and playing the hypocrite.

ABSOLUTE.—I'm sorry, sir, that the respect and duty which I bear to you should be so mistaken.

SIR ANTHONY.—Hang your respect and duty! But come along with me, I'll write a note to Mrs. Malaprop, and you shall visit the lady directly. Her eyes shall be the Promethean torch to you—come along, I'll never forgive you, if you don't come back stark mad with rapture and impatience—if you don't, egad, I will marry the girl myself!   [*Exeunt.*

Scene II.—Julia's Dressing-room

Faulkland discovered alone.

FAULKLAND.—They told me Julia would return directly; I wonder she is not yet come! How mean does this captious, unsatisfied temper of mine appear to my cooler judgment! Yet I know not that I indulge it in any other point: but on this one subject, and to this one subject, whom I think I love beyond my life, I am ever ungenerously fretful and madly capricious! I am conscious of it—yet I cannot correct myself! What tender honest joy sparkled in her eyes when we met! how delicate was the warmth of her expressions! I was ashamed to appear less happy—though I had come resolved to wear a face of coolness and upbraiding. Sir Anthony's presence prevented my proposed expostulations: Yet I must be satisfied that she has not been so very happy in

my absence. She is coming! Yes!—I know the nimble-
ness of her tread, when she thinks her impatient Faulkland counts the moments of her stay.

Enter Julia.

JULIA.—I had not hoped to see you again so soon.

FAULKLAND.—Could I, Julia, be contented with my first welcome—restrained as we were by the presence of a third
person?

JULIA.—O Faulkland, when your kindness can make me thus
happy, let me not think that I discovered something of
coldness in your first salutation.

FAULKLAND.—'Twas but your fancy, Julia. I was rejoiced
to see you—to see you in such health. Sure I had no
cause for coldness?

JULIA.—Nay then, I see you have taken something ill. You
must not conceal from me what it is.

FAULKLAND.—Well, then—shall I own to you that my joy at
hearing of your health and arrival here, by your neighbor Acres, was somewhat damped by his dwelling much
on the high spirits you had enjoyed in Devonshire—on
your mirth—your singing—dancing—and I know not
what! For such is my temper, Julia, that I should regard every mirthful moment in your absence as a treason
to constancy. The mutual tear that steals down the
cheek of parting lovers is a compact, that no smile shall
live there till they meet again.

JULIA.—Must I never cease to tax my Faulkland with this
teasing minute caprice? Can the idle reports of a silly
boor weigh in your breast against my tried affection?

FAULKLAND.—They have no weight with me, Julia: No, no—I
am happy if you have been so—yet only say, that you did
not sing with mirth—say that you thought of Faulkland
in the dance.

JULIA.—I never can be happy in your absence. If I wear a
countenance of content, it is to show that my mind holds
no doubt of my Faulkland's truth. If I seemed sad, it
were to make malice triumph; and say, that I had fixed
my heart on one, who left me to lament his roving, and

my own credulity. Believe me, Faulkland, I mean not to upbraid you, when I say, that I have often dressed sorrow in smiles, lest my friends should guess whose unkindness had caused my tears.

FAULKLAND.—You were ever all goodness to me. Oh, I am a brute, when I but admit a doubt of your true constancy!

JULIA.—If ever without such cause from you, as I will not suppose possible, you find my affections veering but a point, may I become a proverbial scoff for levity and base ingratitude.

FAULKLAND.—Ah! Julia, that last word is grating to me. I would I had no title to your gratitude! Search your heart, Julia; perhaps what you have mistaken for love, is but the warm effusion of a too thankful heart.

JULIA.—For what quality must I love you?

FAULKLAND.—For no quality! To regard me for any quality of mind or understanding, were only to esteem me. And for person—I have often wished myself deformed, to be convinced that I owed no obligation there for any part of your affection.

JULIA.—Where nature has bestowed a show of nice attention in the features of a man, he should laugh at it as misplaced. I have seen men, who in this vain article, perhaps, might rank above you; but my heart has never asked my eyes if it were so or not.

FAULKLAND.—Now this is not well from you, Julia—I despise person in a man—yet if you loved me as I wish, though I were an Æthiop, you'd think none so fair.

JULIA.—I see you are determined to be unkind! The contract which my poor father bound us in gives you more than a lover's privilege.

FAULKLAND.—Again, Julia, you raise ideas that feed and justify my doubts. I would not have been more free—no— I am proud of my restraint. Yet—yet—perhaps your high respect alone for this solemn compact has fettered your inclinations, which else had made a worthier choice. How shall I be sure, had you remained unbound in thought and promise, that I should still have been the object of your persevering love?

JULIA.—Then try me now. Let us be free as strangers as to what is past: my heart will not feel more liberty!

FAULKLAND.—There now! so hasty, Julia! so anxious to be free! If your love for me were fixed and ardent, you would not lose your hold, even though I wished it!

JULIA.—Oh! you torture me to the heart! I cannot bear it.

FAULKLAND.—I do not mean to distress you. If I loved you less I should never give you an uneasy moment. But hear me. All my fretful doubts arise from this. Women are not used to weigh and separate the motives of their affections: the cold dictates of prudence, gratitude, or filial duty, may sometimes be mistaken for the pleadings of the heart. I would not boast—yet let me say, that I have neither age, person, nor character, to found dislike on; my fortune such as few ladies could be charged with indiscretion in the match. O Julia! when love receives such countenance from prudence, nice minds will be suspicious of its birth.

JULIA.—I know not whither your insinuations would tend:— but as they seem pressing to insult me, I will spare you the regret of having done so.—I have given you no cause for this! [*Exit in tears.*

FAULKLAND.—In tears! Stay, Julia: stay but for a moment. —The door is fastened!—Julia!—my soul—but for one moment!—I hear her sobbing!—'Sdeath! what a brute am I to use her thus! Yet stay.—Ay—she is coming now:—how little resolution there is in woman!—How a few soft words can turn them!—No, faith!—she is not coming either.—Why, Julia—my love—say but that you forgive me come but to tell me that—now this is being too resentful. Stay! she is coming too—I thought she would—no steadiness in anything: her going away must have been a mere trick then—she sha'n't see that I was hurt by it.—I'll affect indifference— [*Hums a tune: then listens.*] No—zounds! she's not coming!—nor don't intend it, I suppose.—This is not steadiness, but obstinacy! Yet I deserve it.—What, after so long an absence to quarrel with her tenderness!— 'twas barbarous and unmanly!—I should be ashamed to see her now.—I'll wait till her just resentment is abated —and when I distress her so again, may I lose her forever, and be linked instead to some antique virago, whose

gnawing passions, and long hoarded spleen, shall make
me curse my folly half the day and all the night! [*Exit.*

Scene III.—Mrs. Malaprop's Lodgings

Mrs. Malaprop, with a letter in her hand, and Captain Absolute.

MRS. MALAPROP.—Your being Sir Anthony's son, captain,
would itself be a sufficient accommodation; but from
the ingenuity of your appearance, I am convinced you
deserve the character here given of you.

ABSOLUTE.—Permit me to say, madam, that as I never yet have
had the pleasure of seeing Miss Languish, my principal
inducement in this affair at present is the honor of being
allied to Mrs. Malaprop; of whose intellectual accom-
plishments, elegant manners, and unaffected learning,
no tongue is silent.

MRS. MALAPROP.—Sir, you do me infinite honor! I beg, captain, you'll be seated.—[*They sit.*] Ah! few gentlemen, nowadays, know how to value the ineffectual qualities in a woman! few think how a little knowledge
becomes a gentlewoman!—Men have no sense now but
for the worthless flower of beauty!

ABSOLUTE.—It is but too true, indeed, ma'am;—yet I fear our
ladies should share the blame—they think our admiration of beauty so great, that knowledge in them would be
superfluous. Thus, like garden-trees, they seldom show
fruit, till time has robbed them of the more specious
blossom.—Few, like Mrs. Malaprop and the orange-
tree, are rich in both at once.

MRS. MALAPROP.—Sir, you overpower me with good-breeding.
—He is the very pine-apple of politeness!—You are not
ignorant, captain, that this giddy girl has somehow con-
trived to fix her affections on a beggarly, strolling, eaves-
dropping ensign, whom none of us have seen, and nobody knows anything of.

ABSOLUTE.—Oh, I have heard the silly affair before.—I'm not
at all prejudiced against her on that account.

MRS. MALAPROP.—You are very good and very considerate,
captain. I am sure I have done everything in my power

since I exploded the affair; long ago I laid my positive
conjunctions on her, never to think on the fellow again;
—I have since laid Sir Anthony's preposition before her;
but, I am sorry to say, she seems resolved to decline every
particle that I enjoin her.

ABSOLUTE.—It must be very distressing, indeed, ma'am.

MRS. MALAPROP.—Oh! it gives me the hydrostatics to such a
degree!—I thought she had persisted from corresponding with him; but, behold, this very day, I have inter-
ceded another letter from the fellow; I believe I have it
in my pocket.

ABSOLUTE.—Oh, the devil! my last note.   [Aside.

MRS. MALAPROP.—Ay, here it is.

ABSOLUTE.—Ay, my note indeed! O the little traitress Lucy.
                                                         [Aside.

MRS. MALAPROP.—There, perhaps you may know the writing.
                                          [Gives him the letter.

ABSOLUTE.—I think I have seen the hand before—yes, I certainly must have seen this hand before——

MRS. MALAPROP.—Nay, but read it, captain.

ABSOLUTE.—[Reads.] "My soul's idol, my adored Lydia!"
Very tender indeed!

MRS. MALAPROP.—Tender! ay, and profane too, o' my conscience.

ABSOLUTE.—[Reads.] "I am excessively alarmed at the intelligence you send me, the more so as my new
rival "——

MRS. MALAPROP.—That's you, sir.

ABSOLUTE.—[Reads.] "Has universally the character of being an accomplished gentleman and a man of honor."
Well, that's handsome enough.

MRS. MALAPROP.—Oh, the fellow has some design in writing so.

ABSOLUTE.—That he had, I'll answer for him, ma'am.

MRS. MALAPROP.—But go on, sir—you'll see presently.

ABSOLUTE.—[Reads.] "As for the old weather-beaten she-
dragon who guards you "—Who can he mean by that?

MRS. MALAPROP.—Me, sir!—me!—he means me!—There—
what do you think now?—but go on a little further.

ABSOLUTE.—Impudent scoundrel!—[Reads.] "it shall go hard
but I will elude her vigilance, as I am told that the same

ridiculous vanity, which makes her dress up her coarse features, and deck her dull chat with hard words which she don't understand "——

MRS. MALAPROP.—There, sir, an attack upon my language! what do you think of that?—an aspersion upon my parts of speech! was ever such a brute! Sure, if I reprehend anything in this world, it is the use of my oracular tongue, and a nice derangement of epitaphs!

ABSOLUTE.—He deserves to be hanged and quartered! let me see—[*Reads.*] " same ridiculous vanity "——

MRS. MALAPROP.—You need not read it again, sir.

ABSOLUTE.—I beg pardon, ma'am.—[*Reads.*] " does also lay her open to the grossest deceptions from flattery and pretended admiration "—an impudent coxcomb!—" so that I have a scheme to see you shortly with the old harridan's consent, and even to make her a go-between in our interview."—Was ever such assurance!

MRS. MALAPROP.—Did you ever hear anything like it?—he'll elude my vigilance, will he—yes, yes! ha! ha! he's very likely to enter these doors; we'll try who can plot best!

ABSOLUTE.—So we will, ma'am—so we will! Ha! ha! ha! a conceited puppy, ha! ha! ha!—Well, but, Mrs. Malaprop, as the girl seems so infatuated by this fellow, suppose you were to wink at her corresponding with him for a little time—let her even plot an elopement with him—then do you connive at her escape—while I, just in the nick, will have the fellow laid by the heels, and fairly contrive to carry her off in his stead.

MRS. MALAPROP.—I am delighted with the scheme; never was anything better perpetrated!

ABSOLUTE.—But, pray, could not I see the lady for a few minutes now?—I should like to try her temper a little.

MRS. MALAPROP.—Why, I don't know—I doubt she is not prepared for a visit of this kind. There is a decorum in these matters.

ABSOLUTE.—O Lord! she won't mind me—only tell her Beverley——

MRS. MALAPROP.—Sir!

ABSOLUTE.—Gently, good tongue.   [*Aside.*

MRS. MALAPROP.—What did you say of Beverley?

ABSOLUTE.—Oh, I was going to propose that you should tell her, by way of jest, that it was Beverley who was below; she'd come down fast enough then—ha! ha! ha!

MRS. MALAPROP.—'Twould be a trick she well deserves; besides, you know the fellow tells her he'll get my consent to see her—ha! ha! Let him if he can, I say again. Lydia, come down here!—[*Calling.*] He'll make me a go-between in their interviews!—ha! ha! ha! Come down, I say, Lydia! I don't wonder at your laughing, ha! ha! ha! his impudence is truly ridiculous.

ABSOLUTE.—'Tis very ridiculous, upon my soul, ma'am, ha! ha! ha!

MRS. MALAPROP.—The little hussy won't hear. Well, I'll go and tell her at once who it is—she shall know that Captain Absolute is come to wait on her. And I'll make her behave as becomes a young woman.

ABSOLUTE.—As you please, ma'am.

MRS. MALAPROP.—For the present, captain, your servant. Ah! you've not done laughing yet, I see—elude my vigilance; yes, yes; ha! ha! ha!
                                                            [*Exit.*

ABSOLUTE.—Ha! ha! ha! one would think now that I might throw off all disguise at once, and seize my prize with security; but such is Lydia's caprice, that to undeceive were probably to lose her. I'll see whether she knows me.

[*Walks aside, and seems engaged in looking at the pictures.*

Enter Lydia.

LYDIA.—What a scene am I now to go through! surely nothing can be more dreadful than to be obliged to listen to the loathsome addresses of a stranger to one's heart. I have heard of girls persecuted as I am, who have appealed in behalf of their favored lover to the generosity of his rival; suppose I were to try it—there stands the hated rival—an officer too!—but oh, how unlike my Beverley! I wonder he don't begin—truly he seems a very negligent wooer!—quite at his ease, upon my word!—I'll speak first—Mr. Absolute.

ABSOLUTE.—Ma'am.
                                                    [*Turns round.*

Lydia.—O heavens! Beverley!

Absolute.—Hush!—hush, my life! softly! be not surprised!

Lydia.—I am so astonished! and so terrified! and so over-
joyed!—for Heaven's sake! how came you here?

Absolute.—Briefly, I have deceived your aunt—I was informed that my new rival was to visit here this evening,
and contriving to have him kept away, have passed myself on her for Captain Absolute.

Lydia.—O charming! And she really takes you for young Absolute!

Absolute.—Oh, she's convinced of it.

Lydia.—Ha! ha! ha! I can't forbear laughing to think how
her sagacity is overreached!

Absolute.—But we trifle with our precious moments—such
another opportunity may not occur; then let me now
conjure my kind, my condescending angel, to fix the time
when I may rescue her from undeserving persecution,
and with a licensed warmth plead for my reward.

Lydia.—Will you then, Beverley, consent to forfeit that portion
of my paltry wealth?—that burden on the wings of love?

Absolute.—Oh, come to me—rich only thus—in loveliness!
Bring no portion to me but thy love—'twill be generous
in you, Lydia—for well you know, it is the only dower
your poor Beverley can repay.

Lydia.—How persuasive are his words!—how charming will
poverty be with him!   [Aside.

Absolute.—Ah! my soul, what a life will we then live! Love
shall be our idol and support! we will worship him with
a monastic strictness; abjuring all worldly toys, to centre
every thought and action there. Proud of calamity, we
will enjoy the wreck of wealth; while the surrounding
gloom of adversity shall make the flame of our pure love
show doubly bright. By Heavens! I would fling all
goods of fortune from me with a prodigal hand, to enjoy
the scene where I might clasp my Lydia to my bosom,
and say, the world affords no smile to me but here—
[Embracing her.] If she holds out now, the devil is in
it!   [Aside.

Lydia.—Now could I fly with him to the antipodes! but my
persecution is not yet come to a crisis.   [Aside.

Re-enter Mrs. Malaprop, listening.

MRS. MALAPROP.—I am impatient to know how the little hussy deports herself. [*Aside.*

ABSOLUTE.—So pensive, Lydia!—is then your warmth abated?

MRS. MALAPROP.—Warmth abated!—so!—she has been in a passion, I suppose. [*Aside.*

LYDIA.—No—nor ever can while I have life.

MRS. MALAPROP.—An ill-tempered little devil! She'll be in a passion all her life—will she? [*Aside.*

LYDIA.—Think not the idle threats of my ridiculous aunt can ever have any weight with me.

MRS. MALAPROP.—Very dutiful, upon my word! [*Aside.*

LYDIA.—Let her choice be Captain Absolute, but Beverley is mine.

MRS. MALAPROP.—I am astonished at her assurance!—to his face—this is to his face! [*Aside.*

ABSOLUTE.—Thus then let me enforce my suit. [*Kneeling.*

MRS. MALAPROP [*aside*].—Ay, poor young man!—down on his knees entreating for pity!—I can contain no longer. —[*Coming forward.*] Why, thou vixen! I have overheard you.

ABSOLUTE..—Oh, confound her vigilance!

MRS. MALAPROP.—Captain Absolute, I know not how to apologize for her shocking rudeness.

ABSOLUTE [*aside*].— So all's safe, I find.—[*Aloud.*] I have hopes, madam, that time will bring the young lady——

MRS. MALAPROP.—Oh, there's nothing to be hoped for from her! she's as headstrong as an allegory on the banks of Nile.

LYDIA.—Nay, madam, what do you charge me with now?

MRS. MALAPROP.—Why, thou unblushing rebel—didn't you tell this gentleman to his face that you loved another better? —didn't you say you never would be his?

LYDIA.—No, madam—I did not.

MRS. MALAPROP.—Good Heavens! What assurance!—Lydia, Lydia, you ought to know that lying don't become a young woman!—Didn't you boast that Beverley, that stroller Beverley, possessed your heart?—Tell me that, I say.

LYDIA.—'Tis true, ma'am, and none but Beverley——

MRS. MALAPROP.—Hold!—hold, Assurance!—you shall not be so rude.

ABSOLUTE.—Nay, pray, Mrs. Malaprop, don't stop the young lady's speech: she's very welcome to talk thus—it does not hurt me in the least, I assure you.

MRS. MALAPROP.—You are too good, captain—too amiably patient—but come with me, miss.—Let us see you again soon, captain—remember what we have fixed.

ABSOLUTE.—I shall, ma'am.

MRS. MALAPROP.—Come, take a graceful leave of the gentleman.

LYDIA.—May every blessing wait on my Beverley, my loved Bev——

MRS. MALAPROP.—Hussy! I'll choke the word in your throat! —come along—come along.

[*Exeunt severally; Captain Absolute kissing his hand to Lydia —Mrs. Malaprop stopping her from speaking.*

Scene IV.—Acres' Lodgings

Acres, as just dressed, and David.

ACRES.—Indeed, David—do you think I become it so?

DAVID.—You are quite another creature, believe me, master, by the mass! an we've any luck we shall see the Devon monkerony * in all the print shops in Bath!

ACRES.—Dress does make a difference, David.

DAVID.—'Tis all in all, I think.—Difference! why, an you were to go now to Clod-hall, I am certain the old lady wouldn't know you: master Butler wouldn't believe his own eyes, and Mrs. Pickle would cry, Lard presarve me! Our dairy-maid would come giggling to the door, and I warrant Dolly Tester, your honor's favorite, would blush like my waistcoat.—Oons! I'll hold a gallon, there an't a dog in the house but would bark, and I question whether Phillis would wag a hair of her tail!

ACRES.—Ay, David, there's nothing like polishing.

* Macaroni, or dandy.

DAVID.—So I says of your honor's boots; but the boy never heeds me!

ACRES.—But, David, has Mr. De-la-grace been here? I must rub up my balancing, and chasing, and boring.

DAVID.—I'll call again, sir.

ACRES.—Do—and see if there are any letters for me at the post-office.

DAVID.—I will.—By the mass, I can't help looking at your head!—if I hadn't been at the cooking, I wish I may die if I should have known the dish again myself! [*Exit.*

ACRES [*practising a dancing-step*].—Sink, slide—coupee.— Confound the first inventors of cotillions! say I—they are as bad as algebra to us country gentlemen—I can walk a minuet easy enough when I am forced!—and I have been accounted a good stick in a country-dance. —Odds jigs and tabors! I never valued your cross-over to couple—figure in—right and left—and I'd foot it with e'er a captain in the county!—but these outlandish heathen allemandes and cotillions are quite beyond me! —I shall never prosper at 'em, that's sure—mine are true-born English legs—they don't understand their curst French lingo!—their *pas* this, and *pas* that, and *pas* t'other!—d—n me! my feet don't like to be called paws! no, 'tis certain I have most Antigallican toes!

Enter servant.

SERVANT.—Here is Sir Lucius O'Trigger to wait on you, sir.

ACRES.—Show him in. [*Exit servant.*

Enter Sir Lucius O'Trigger.

SIR LUCIUS.—Mr. Acres, I am delighted to embrace you.

ACRES.—My dear Sir Lucius, I kiss your hands.

SIR LUCIUS.—Pray, my friend, what has brought you so suddenly to Bath?

ACRES.—Faith! I have followed Cupid's Jack-a-lantern, and find myself in a quagmire at last.—In short, I have been very ill-used, Sir Lucius.—I don't choose to mention names, but look on me as on a very ill-used gentleman.

SIR LUCIUS.—Pray what is the case?—I ask no names.

ACRES.—Mark me, Sir Lucius, I fall as deep as need be in love
with a young lady—her friends take my part—I follow
her to Bath—send word of my arrival; and receive answer, that the lady is to be otherwise disposed of.—This,
Sir Lucius, I call being ill-used.

SIR LUCIUS.—Very ill, upon my conscience.—Pray, can you
divine the cause of it?

ACRES.—Why, there's the matter; she has another lover, one
Beverley, who, I am told, is now in Bath.—Odds slanders
and lies! he must be at the bottom of it.

SIR LUCIUS.—A rival in the case, is there?—and you think he
has supplanted you unfairly?

ACRES.—Unfairly! to be sure he has. He never could have
done it fairly.

SIR LUCIUS.—Then sure you know what is to be done!

ACRES.—Not I, upon my soul!

SIR LUCIUS.—We wear no swords here, but you understand
me.

ACRES.—What! fight him!

SIR LUCIUS.—Ay, to be sure: what can I mean else?

ACRES.—But he has given me no provocation.

SIR LUCIUS.—Now, I think he has given you the greatest provocation in the world. Can a man commit a more heinous
offence against another than to fall in love with the
same woman? Oh, by my soul! it is the most unpardon-
able breach of friendship.

ACRES.—Breach of friendship! ay, ay; but I have no acquaintance with this man. I never saw him in my life.

SIR LUCIUS.—That's no argument at all—he has the less right
then to take such a liberty.

ACRES.—Gad, that's true—I grow full of anger, Sir Lucius!—
I fire apace! Odds hilts and blades! I find a man may
have a deal of valor in him, and not know it! But
couldn't I contrive to have a little right of my side?

SIR LUCIUS.—What the devil signifies right, when your honor
is concerned? Do you think Achilles, or my little Alex-
ander the Great, ever inquired where the right lay? No,
by my soul, they drew their broadswords, and left the
lazy sons of peace to settle the justice of it.

ACRES.—Your words are a grenadier's march to my heart! I

believe courage must be catching! I certainly do feel a kind of valor rising as it were—a kind of courage, as I may say.—Odds flints, pans, and triggers! I'll challenge him directly.

SIR LUCIUS.—Ah, my little friend, if I had Blunderbuss Hall here, I could show you a range of ancestry, in the O'Trigger line, that would furnish the new room; every one of whom had killed his man!—For though the mansion-house and dirty acres have slipped through my fingers, I thank Heaven our honor and the family-pictures are as fresh as ever.

ACRES.—O, Sir Lucius! I have had ancestors too!—every man of 'em colonel or captain in the militia!—Odds balls and barrels! say no more—I'm braced for it. The thunder of your words has soured the milk of human kindness in my breast;—Zounds! as the man in the play says, " I could do such deeds! "

SIR LUCIUS.—Come, come, there must be no passion at all in the case—these things should always be done civilly.

ACRES.—I must be in a passion, Sir Lucius—I must be in a rage. —Dear Sir Lucius, let me be in a rage, if you love me. Come, here's pen and paper.—[*Sits down to write.*] I would the ink were red!—Indite, I say indite!—How shall I begin? Odds bullets and blades! I'll write a good bold hand, however.

SIR LUCIUS.—Pray compose yourself.

ACRES.—Come—now, shall I begin with an oath? Do, Sir Lucius, let me begin with a damme.

SIR LUCIUS.—Pho! pho! do the thing decently, and like a Christian. Begin now—Sir——

ACRES.—That's too civil by half.

SIR LUCIUS.—To prevent the confusion that might arise——

ACRES.—Well——

SIR LUCIUS.—From our both addressing the same lady——

ACRES.—Ay, there's the reason—same lady—well——

SIR LUCIUS.—I shall expect the honor of your company——

ACRES.—Zounds! I'm not asking him to dinner.

SIR LUCIUS.—Pray be easy.

ACRES.—Well then, " honor of your company "——

SIR LUCIUS.—To settle our pretensions——

ACRES.—Well.

SIR LUCIUS.—Let me see, ay, King's-Mead-Fields will do—in King's-Mead-Fields.

ACRES.—So, that's done—Well, I'll fold it up presently; my own crest—a hand and dagger shall be the seal.

SIR LUCIUS.—You see now this little explanation will put a stop at once to all confusion or misunderstanding that might arise between you.

ACRES.—Ay, we fight to prevent any misunderstanding.

SIR LUCIUS.—Now, I'll leave you to fix your own time. Take my advice, and you'll decide it this evening if you can; then let the worst come of it, 'twill be off your mind to-morrow.

ACRES.—Very true.

SIR LUCIUS.—So I shall see nothing more of you, unless it be by letter, till the evening.—I would do myself the honor to carry your message; but, to tell you a secret, I believe I shall have just such another affair on my own hands. There is a gay captain here, who put a jest on me lately, at the expense of my country, and I only want to fall in with the gentleman, to call him out.

ACRES.—By my valor, I should like to see you fight first! Odds life! I should like to see you kill him if it was only to get a little lesson.

SIR LUCIUS.—I shall be very proud of instructing you.—Well, for the present—but remember now, when you meet your antagonist, do everything in a mild and agreeable man-ner.—Let your courage be as keen, but at the same time as polished, as your sword.   [*Exeunt severally.*

ACT FOURTH

Scene I.—Acres' Lodgings

Acres and David.

DAVID.—Then, by the mass, sir! I would do no such thing— ne'er a Sir Lucius O'Trigger in the kingdom should make me fight, when I wa'n't so minded. Oons! what will the old lady say when she hears o't?

ACRES.—Ah! David, if you had heard Sir Lucius!—Odds sparks and flames! he would have roused your valor.

DAVID.—Not he, indeed. I hate such bloodthirsty cormorants. Look'ee, master, if you'd wanted a bout at boxing, quarter-staff, or short-staff, I should never be the man to bid you cry off: but for your curst sharps and snaps, I never knew any good come of 'em.

ACRES.—But my honor, David, my honor! I must be very careful of my honor.

DAVID.—Ay, by the mass! and I would be very careful of it; and I think in return my honor couldn't do less than to be very careful of me.

ACRES.—Odds blades! David, no gentleman will ever risk the loss of his honor.

DAVID.—I say then, it would be but civil in honor never to risk the loss of a gentleman.— Look'ee, master, this honor seems to me to be a marvellous false friend: ay, truly, a very courtier-like servant.—Put the case, I was a gentleman (which, thank God, no one can say of me;) well —my honor makes me quarrel with another gentleman of my acquaintance.—So—we fight. (Pleasant enough that!) Boh! I kill him—(the more's my luck!) now, pray who gets the profit of it?—Why, my honor. But put the case that he kills me!—by the mass! I go to the worms, and my honor whips over to my enemy.

ACRES.—No, David—in that case—Odds crowns and laurels!
—your honor follows you to the grave.

DAVID.—Now, that's just the place where I could make a shift
to do without it.

ACRES.—Zounds! David, you are a coward!—It doesn't become my valor to listen to you.—What, shall I disgrace
my ancestors?—Think of that, David—think what it
would be to disgrace my ancestors!

DAVID.—Under favor, the surest way of not disgracing them,
is to keep as long as you can out of their company.
Look'ee now, master, to go to them in such haste—with
an ounce of lead in your brains—I should think might
as well be let alone. Our ancestors are very good kind
of folks; but they are the last people I should choose
to have a visiting acquaintance with.

ACRES.—But, David, now, you don't think there is such very,
very, very great danger, hey?—Odds life! people often
fight without any mischief done!

DAVID.—By the mass, I think 'tis ten to one against you!—
Oons! here to meet some lion-headed fellow, I warrant, with his d——d double-barrelled swords, and
cut-and-thrust pistols!—Lord bless us! it makes me
tremble to think o't—Those be such desperate bloody-
minded weapons! Well, I never could abide 'em—from
a child I never could fancy 'em!—I suppose there a'nt
been so merciless a beast in the world as your loaded
pistol!

ACRES.—Zounds! I won't be afraid!—Odds fire and fury!
you shan't make me afraid.—Here is the challenge, and
I have sent for my dear friend Jack Absolute to carry it
for me.

DAVID.—Ay, i' the name of mischief, let him be the messenger.
—For my part, I wouldn't lend a hand to it for the best
horse in your stable. By the mass! it don't look like
another letter. It is, as I may say, a designing and
malicious-looking letter; and I warrant smells of gun-
powder like a soldier's pouch!—Oons! I wouldn't
swear it mayn't go off!

ACRES.—Out, you poltroon! you ha'nt the valor of a grass-
hopper.

Scene II.—Mrs. Malaprop's Lodgings

Mrs. Malaprop and Lydia.

MRS. MALAPROP.—Why, thou perverse one!—tell me why you can object to him? Isn't he a handsome man?—tell me that. A genteel man? a pretty figure of a man?

LYDIA [*aside*].—She little thinks whom she is praising!—[*Aloud.*] So is Beverley, ma'am.

MRS. MALAPROP.—No caparisons, miss, if you please. Caparisons don't become a young woman.* No! Captain Absolute is indeed a fine gentleman!

LYDIA.—Ay, the Captain Absolute you have seen.   [*Aside.*

MRS. MALAPROP.—Then he's so well bred;—so full of alacrity, and adulation!—and has so much to say for himself:—in such good language too! His physiognomy so grammatical! Then his presence is so noble! I protest, when I saw him, I thought of what Hamlet says in the play:—

> "Hesperian curls—the front of Job himself!—
> An eye, like March, to threaten at command!—
> A station, like Harry Mercury, new——"

Something about kissing—on a hill—however, the similitude struck me directly.

LYDIA.—How enraged she'll be presently, when she discovers her mistake!   [*Aside.*

Enter servant.

SERVANT.—Sir Anthony and Captain Absolute are below, ma'am.

MRS. MALAPROP.—Show them up here.—[*Exit servant.*] Now, Lydia, I insist on your behaving as becomes a young woman. Show your good breeding, at least, though you have forgot your duty.

LYDIA.—Madam, I have told you my resolution!—I shall not only give him no encouragement, but I won't even speak to, or look at him.

[*Flings herself into a chair, with her face from the door.*

* In "Much Ado About Nothing" Dogberry had said: "Comparisons are odorous."

Enter Sir Anthony Absolute and Captain Absolute.

SIR ANTHONY.—Here we are, Mrs. Malaprop; come to miti-
gate the frowns of unrelenting beauty—and difficulty
enough I had to bring this fellow. I don't know what's
the matter; but if I had not held him by force, he'd
have given me the slip.

MRS. MALAPROP.—You have infinite trouble, Sir Anthony, in
the affair. I am ashamed for the cause!—[*Aside to
Lydia.*] Lydia, Lydia, rise, I beseech you!—pay your
respects!

SIR ANTHONY.—I hope, madam, that Miss Languish has reflected on the worth of this gentleman, and the regard
due to her aunt's choice, and my alliance.—[*Aside to
Captain Absolute.*] Now, Jack, speak to her.

ABSOLUTE [*aside*].—What the devil shall I do!—[*Aside to
Sir Anthony.*] You see, sir, she won't even look at me
whilst you are here. I knew she wouldn't! I told you
so. Let me entreat you, sir, to leave us together!
                    [*Seems to expostulate with his father.*

LYDIA [*aside*].—I wonder I ha'n't heard my aunt exclaim yet!
sure she can't have looked at him!—perhaps their regimentals are alike, and she is something blind.

SIR ANTHONY.—I say, sir, I won't stir a foot yet!

MRS. MALAPROP.—I am sorry to say, Sir Anthony, that my
affluence over my niece is very small.—[*Aside to Lydia.*]
Turn round, Lydia: I blush for you!

SIR ANTHONY.—May I not flatter myself, that Miss Languish
will assign what cause of dislike she can have to my
son! [*Aside to Captain Absolute.*] Why don't you
begin, Jack?—Speak, you puppy—speak!

MRS. MALAPROP.—It is impossible, Sir Anthony, she can have
any. She will not say she has. [*Aside to Lydia.*] Answer, hussy! why don't you answer?

SIR ANTHONY.—Then, madam, I trust that a childish and hasty
predilection will be no bar to Jack's happiness. [*Aside
to Captain Absolute.*]—Zounds! sirrah! why don't you
speak!

LYDIA [*aside*].—I think my lover seems as little inclined to
conversation as myself.—How strangely blind my aunt
must be!

ABSOLUTE.—Hem! hem! madam—hem!—[*Attempts to speak, then returns to Sir Anthony.*] Faith! sir, I am so confounded!—and—so—so—confused!—I told you I should be so, sir—I knew it.—The—the—tremor of my passion entirely takes away my presence of mind.

SIR ANTHONY.—But it don't take away your voice, fool, does it?—Go up, and speak to her directly!

[*Captain Absolute makes signs to Mrs. Malaprop to leave them together.*

MRS. MALAPROP.—Sir Anthony, shall we leave them together? —[*Aside to Lydia.*] Ah! you stubborn little vixen!

SIR ANTHONY.—Not yet, ma'am, not yet!—[*Aside to Captain Absolute.*] What the devil are you at? unlock your jaws, sirrah, or——

ABSOLUTE [*aside*].—Now Heaven send she may be too sullen to look round!—I must disguise my voice.—[*Draws near Lydia, and speaks in a low hoarse tone.*] Will not Miss Languish lend an ear to the mild accents of true love? Will not——

SIR ANTHONY.—What the devil ails the fellow? Why don't you speak out?—not stand croaking like a frog in a quinsy!

ABSOLUTE.—The—the—excess of my awe, and my my my modesty, quite choke me!

SIR ANTHONY.—Ah! your modesty again!—I'll tell you what, Jack; if you don't speak out directly, and glibly too, I shall be in such a rage!—Mrs. Malaprop, I wish the lady would favor us with something more than a side-front. [*Mrs. Malaprop seems to chide Lydia.*

ABSOLUTE [*Aside*].—So all will out, I see!—[*Goes up to Lydia, speaks softly.*] Be not surprised, my Lydia, suppress all surprise at present.

LYDIA [*aside*].—Heavens! 'tis Beverley's voice! Sure he can't have imposed on Sir Anthony too!—[*Looks round by degrees, then starts up.*] Is this possible!—my Beverley!—how can this be?—my Beverley?

ABSOLUTE.—Ah! 'tis all over. [*Aside.*

SIR ANTHONY.—Beverley!—the devil—Beverley!—What can the girl mean?—This is my son, Jack Absolute.

MRS. MALAPROP.—For shame, hussy! for shame! your head runs so on that fellow, that you have him always in your eyes!—beg Captain Absolute's pardon directly.

LYDIA.—I see no Captain Absolute, but my loved Beverley!

SIR ANTHONY.—Zounds! the girl's mad!—her brain's turned by reading.

MRS. MALAPROP.—O' my conscience, I believe so!—What do you mean by Beverley, hussy?—You saw Captain Absolute before to-day; there he is—your husband that shall be.

LYDIA.—With all my soul, ma'am—when I refuse my Beverley——

SIR ANTHONY.—Oh! she's as mad as Bedlam!—or has this fellow been playing us a rogue's trick!—Come here, sirrah, who the devil are you?

ABSOLUTE.—Faith, sir, I am not quite clear myself; but I'll endeavor to recollect.

SIR ANTHONY.—Are you my son or not?—answer for your mother, you dog, if you won't for me.

MRS. MALAPROP.—Ay, sir, who are you? O mercy! I begin to suspect!—

ABSOLUTE [*aside*].—Ye powers of impudence, befriend me! —[*Aloud.*] Sir Anthony, most assuredly I am your wife's son and that I sincerely believe myself to be yours also, I hope my duty has always shown.—Mrs. Malaprop, I am your most respectful admirer, and shall be proud to add affectionate nephew.—I need not tell my Lydia, that she sees her faithful Beverley, who, knowing the singular generosity of her temper, assumed that name and station, which has proved a test of the most disinterested love, which he now hopes to enjoy in a more elevated character.

LYDIA.—So!—there will be no elopement after all! [*Sullenly.*

SIR ANTHONY.—Upon my soul, Jack, thou art a very impudent fellow! to do you justice, I think I never saw a piece of more consummate assurance!

ABSOLUTE.—Oh, you flatter me, sir—you compliment—'tis my modesty you know, sir—my modesty that has stood in my way.

SIR ANTHONY.—Well, I am glad you are not the dull insensible varlet you pretended to be, however!—I'm glad you have made a fool of your father, you dog—I am. So this was your penitence, your duty and obedience!—I thought it was d——d sudden!—You never heard their names before, not you!—what, the Languishes of Worcestershire, hey?—if you could please me in the affair it was all you desired!—Ah! you dissembling villain!—What! [*Pointing to Lydia*] she squints, don't she?—a little red-haired girl!—hey?—Why, you hypocritical young rascal!—I wonder you an't ashamed to hold up your head!

ABSOLUTE.—'Tis with difficulty, sir.—I am confused—very much confused, as you must perceive.

MRS. MALAPROP.—O Lud! Sir Anthony!—a new light breaks in upon me!—hey!—how! what! captain, did you write the letters then?—What—am I to thank you for the elegant compilation of an old weather-beaten she-dragon —hey!—O mercy!—was it you that reflected on my parts of speech?

ABSOLUTE. Dear sir! my modesty will be overpowered at last, if you don't assist me—I shall certainly not be able to stand it!

SIR ANTHONY.—Come, come, Mrs. Malaprop, we must forget and forgive;—odds life! matters have taken so clever a turn all of a sudden, that I could find in my heart to be so good-humored! and so gallant! hey! Mrs. Malaprop!

MRS. MALAPROP.—Well, Sir Anthony, since you desire it, we will not anticipate the past!—so mind, young people— our retrospection will be all to the future.

SIR ANTHONY.—Come, we must leave them together; Mrs. Malaprop, they long to fly into each other's arms, I warrant!—Jack—isn't the cheek as I said, hey?—and the eye, you rogue!—and the lip—hey? Come, Mrs. Malaprop, we'll not disturb their tenderness—theirs is the time of life for happiness!—" Youth's the season made for joy "—[*Sings*]—hey!—Odds life! I'm in such spirits—I don't know what I could not do!—Permit me, ma'am—[*Gives his hand to Mrs. Malaprop.*] Tol-de-

rol—'gad, I should like to have a little fooling myself
—Tol-de-rol! de-rol.

[*Exit, singing and handing Mrs. Malaprop.—Lydia sits sullenly in her chair.*

ABSOLUTE [*aside*].—So much thought bodes me no good.—
[*Aloud.*] So grave, Lydia!

LYDIA.—Sir!

ABSOLUTE [*aside*].—So!—egad! I thought as much!—that
d——d monosyllable has froze me!—[*Aloud.*] What,
Lydia, now that we are as happy in our friends' consent, as in our mutual vows——

LYDIA.—Friends' consent indeed!   [*Peevishly.*

ABSOLUTE.—Come, come, we must lay aside some of our romance—a little wealth and comfort may be endured
after all. And for your fortune, the lawyers shall make
such settlements as——

LYDIA.—Lawyers! I hate lawyers!

ABSOLUTE.—Nay, then, we will not wait for their lingering
forms, but instantly procure the license, and——

LYDIA.—The license!—I hate license!

ABSOLUTE.—Oh my love! be not so unkind!—thus let me entreat——   [*Kneeling.*

LYDIA.—Psha!—what signifies kneeling, when you know I
must have you?

ABSOLUTE [*rising*].—Nay, madam, there shall be no constraint upon your inclinations, I promise you.—If I have
lost your heart, I resign the rest.—[*Aside.*] 'Gad, I must
try what a little spirit will do.

LYDIA [*rising*].—Then, sir, let me tell you, the interest you
had there was acquired by a mean, unmanly imposition,
and deserves the punishment of fraud.—What, you
have been treating me like a child!—humoring my romance! and laughing, I suppose, at your success!

ABSOLUTE.—You wrong me, Lydia, you wrong me—only
hear——

LYDIA.—So, while I fondly imagined we were deceiving my
relations, and flattered myself that I should outwit and
incense them all—behold my hopes are to be crushed at
once, by my aunt's consent and approbation—and I am
myself the only dupe at last!—[*Walking about in a*

heat.] But here, sir, here is the picture—Beverley's
picture! [*taking a miniature from her bosom*] which
I have worn, night and day, in spite of threats and entreaties!—There, sir; [*flings it to him*] and be assured
I throw the original from my heart as easily.

ABSOLUTE.—Nay, nay, ma'am, we will not differ as to that.
—Here [*taking out a picture*] here is Miss Lydia Languish.—What a difference!—ay, there is the heavenly
assenting smile that first gave soul and spirit to my
hopes!—those are the lips which sealed a vow, as yet
scarce dry in Cupid's calendar! and there the half-re-
sentful blush, that would have checked the ardor of my
thanks!—Well, all that's past!—all over indeed!—
There, madam—in beauty, that copy is not equal to
you, but in my mind its merit over the original, in being
still the same, is such—that—I cannot find in my heart
to part with it.   [*Puts it up again.*

LYDIA [*Softening*].—'Tis your own doing, sir—I—I—I suppose you are perfectly satisfied.

ABSOLUTE.—O, most certainly—sure, now, this is much better
than being in love!—ha! ha! ha!—there's some spirit
in this!—What signifies breaking some scores of solemn
promises:—all that's of no consequence, you know.—
To be sure people will say, that miss don't know her own
mind—but never mind that! Or, perhaps, they may be
ill-natured enough to hint, that the gentleman grew tired
of the lady and forsook her—but don't let that fret you.

LYDIA.—There is no bearing his insolence.   [*Bursts into tears.*

Re-enter Mrs. Malaprop and Sir Anthony Absolute.

MRS. MALAPROP.—Come, we must interrupt your billing and
cooing awhile.

LYDIA.—This is worse than your treachery and deceit, you base
ingrate!   [*Sobbing.*

SIR ANTHONY.—What the devil's the matter now—Zounds!
Mrs. Malaprop, this is the oddest billing and cooing I
ever heard!—but what the deuce is the meaning of it?
—I am quite astonished!

ABSOLUTE.—Ask the lady, sir.

Mrs. Malaprop.—Oh mercy!—I'm quite analyzed, for my
    part!—Why, Lydia, what is the reason of this?

Lydia.—Ask the gentleman, ma'am.

Sir Anthony.—Zounds! I shall be in a frenzy!—Why, Jack,
    you are not come out to be anyone else, are you?

Mrs. Malaprop.—Ay, sir, there's no more trick, is there?—
    you are not like Cerberus, three gentlemen at once, are
    you?

Absolute.—You'll not let me speak—I say the lady can ac-
    count for this much better than I can.

Lydia.—Ma'am, you once commanded me never to think of
    Beverley again—there is the man—I now obey you: for,
    from this moment, I renounce him forever.   [Exit.

Mrs. Malaprop.—O mercy! and miracles! what a turn here
    is—why sure, captain, you haven't behaved disrespect-
    fully to my niece.

Sir Anthony.—Ha! ha! ha!—ha! ha! ha!—now I see it.
    Ha! ha! ha!—now I see it—you have been too lively,
    Jack.

Absolute.—Nay, sir, upon my word——

Sir Anthony.—Come, no lying, Jack—I'm sure 'twas so.

Mrs. Malaprop.—O Lud! Sir Anthony!—O fy, captain!

Absolute.—Upon my soul, ma'am——

Sir Anthony.—Come, no excuses, Jack; why, your father,
    you rogue, was so before you:—the blood of the Ab-
    solutes was always impatient.—Ha! ha! ha! poor little
    Lydia! why, you've frightened her, you dog, you have.

Absolute.—By all that's good, sir——

Sir Anthony.—Zounds! say no more, I tell you—Mrs. Mala-
    prop shall make your peace.—You must make his peace,
    Mrs. Malaprop:—you must tell her 'tis Jack's way—
    tell her 'tis all our ways—it runs in the blood of our
    family!—Come away, Jack—Ha! ha! ha! Mrs. Mala-
    prop—a young villain!   [Pushing him out.

Mrs. Malaprop.—O! Sir Anthony!—O fy, captain!
                                      [Exeunt severally.

Scene III.—The North Parade

Enter Sir Lucius O'Trigger.

SIR LUCIUS.—I wonder where this Captain Absolute hides himself! Upon my conscience! these officers are always in one's way in love affairs:—I remember I might have married lady Dorothy Carmine, if it had not been for a little rogue of a major, who ran away with her before she could get a sight of me! And I wonder too what it is the ladies can see in them to be so fond of them—unless it be a touch of the old serpent in 'em, that makes the little creatures be caught, like vipers, with a bit of red cloth. Ha! isn't this the captain coming?—faith it is!—There is a probability of succeeding about that fellow, that is mighty provoking! Who the devil is he talking to?   [*Steps aside.*

Enter Captain Absolute.

ABSOLUTE [*aside*].—To what fine purpose I have been plotting! a noble reward for all my schemes, upon my soul! —a little gipsy!—I did not think her romance could have made her so d——d absurd either. 'Sdeath, I never was in a worse humor in my life!—I could cut my own throat, or any other person's, with the greatest pleasure in the world!

SIR LUCIUS.—Oh, faith! I'm in the luck of it. I never could have found him in a sweeter temper for my purpose— to be sure I'm just come in the nick! Now to enter into conversation with him, and so quarrel genteelly.—[*Goes up to Captain Absolute.*] With regard to that matter, captain, I must beg leave to differ in opinion with you.

ABSOLUTE.—Upon my word, then, you must be a very subtle disputant:—because, sir, I happened just then to be giving no opinion at all.

SIR LUCIUS.—That's no reason. For, give me leave to tell you, a man may think an untruth as well as speak one.

ABSOLUTE.—Very true, sir; but if a man never utters his thoughts I should think they might stand a chance of escaping controversy.

Sir Lucius.—Then, sir, you differ in opinion with me, which
amounts to the same thing.

Absolute.—Hark'ee, Sir Lucius; if I had not before known
you to be a gentleman, upon my soul, I should not have
discovered it at this interview: for what you can drive
at, unless you mean to quarrel with me, I cannot conceive!

Sir Lucius.—I humbly thank you, sir, for the quickness of
your apprehension.—[*Bowing.*] You have named the
very thing I would be at.

Absolute.—Very well, sir; I shall certainly not balk your inclinations.—But I should·be glad you would please to
explain your motives.

Sir Lucius.—Pray sir, be easy, the quarrel is a very pretty
quarrel as it stands; we should only spoil it by trying
to explain it. However, your memory is very short, or
you could not have forgot an affront you passed on me
within this week. So, no more, but name your time and
place.

Absolute.—Well, sir, since you are so bent on it, the sooner
the better; let it be this evening—here, by the Spring
Gardens. We shall scarcely be interrupted.

Sir Lucius.—Faith! that same interruption in affairs of this
nature shows very great ill-breeding. I don't know
what's the reason, but in England, if a thing of this kind
gets wind, people make such a pother, that a gentleman
can never fight in peace and quietness. However, if it's
the same to you, captain, I should take it as a particular
kindness if you'd let us meet in King's-Mead-Fields, as
a little business will call me there about six o'clock, and
I may despatch both matters at once.

Absolute.—'Tis the same to me exactly. A little after six,
then, we will discuss this matter more seriously.

Sir Lucius.—If you please, sir; there will be very pretty
small-sword light, though it won't do for a long shot.
So that matter's settled, and my mind's at ease! [*Exit.*

Enter Faulkland.

Absolute.—Well met! I was going to look for you. O
Faulkland! all the demons of spite and disappointment

have conspired against me! I'm so vexed, that if I had not the prospect of a resource in being knocked o' the head by-and-by, I should scarce have spirits to tell you the cause.

FAULKLAND.—What can you mean?—Has Lydia changed her mind?—I should have thought her duty and inclination would now have pointed to the same object.

ABSOLUTE.—Ay, just as the eyes do of a person who squints: when her love-eye was fixed on me, t'other, her eye of duty, was finely obliqued: but when duty bid her point that the same way, off t'other turned on a swivel, and secured its retreat with a frown!

FAULKLAND.—But what's the resource you——

ABSOLUTE.—Oh, to wind up the whole, a good-natured Irish-man here has—[*mimicking Sir Lucius*]—begged leave to have the pleasure of cutting my throat; and I mean to indulge him—that's all.

FAULKLAND.—Prithee, be serious!

ABSOLUTE.—'Tis fact, upon my soul! Sir Lucius O'Trigger —you know him by sight—for some affront, which I am sure I never intended, has obliged me to meet him this evening at six o'clock: 'tis on that account I wished to see you; you must go with me.

FAULKLAND.—Nay, there must be some mistake, sure. Sir Lucius shall explain himself, and I dare say matters may be accommodated. But this evening did you say? I wish it had been any other time.

ABSOLUTE.—Why? there will be light enough: there will (as Sir Lucius says) be very pretty small-sword light, though it will not do for a long shot. Confound his long shots!

FAULKLAND.—But I am myself a good deal ruffled by a dif-ference I have had with Julia. My vile tormenting temper has made me treat her so cruelly, that I shall not be myself till we are reconciled.

ABSOLUTE.—By heavens! Faulkland, you don't deserve her!

Enter servant, gives Faulkland a letter, and exit.

FAULKLAND.—Oh, Jack! this is from Julia. I dread to open it! I fear it may be to take a last leave!—perhaps to

bid me return her letters, and restore——Oh, how I suffer for my folly!

ABSOLUTE.—Here, let me see.—[*Takes the letter and opens
it.*] Ay, a final sentence, indeed!—'tis all over with
you, faith!

FAULKLAND.—Nay, Jack, don't keep me in suspense!

ABSOLUTE.—Hear then.—[*Reads.*] " As I am convinced that
my dear Faulkland's own reflections have already up-
braided him for his last unkindness to me, I will not add
a word on the subject. I wish to speak with you as
soon as possible. Yours ever and truly, JULIA."
There's stubbornness and resentment for you!—[*Gives
him the letter.*] Why, man, you don't seem one whit
the happier at this!

FAULKLAND.—O yes, I am; but—but——

ABSOLUTE.—Confound your buts! you never hear anything
that would make another man bless himself, but you
immediately d—n it with a but!

FAULKLAND.—Now, Jack, as you are my friend, own honestly
—don't you think there is something forward, something indelicate, in this haste to forgive? Women
should never sue for reconciliation: that should always
come from us. They should retain their coldness till
wooed to kindness; and their pardon, like their love,
should " not unsought be won."

ABSOLUTE.—I have not patience to listen to you! thou'rt incorrigible! so say no more on the subject. I must go
to settle a few matters. Let me see you before six, remember, at my lodgings. A poor industrious devil like
me, who have toiled, and drudged, and plotted to gain
my ends, and am at last disappointed by other people's
folly, may in pity be allowed to swear and grumble a
little; but a captious sceptic in love, a slave to fretful-
ness and whim, who has no difficulties but of his own
creating, is a subject more fit for ridicule than compassion!   [*Exit.*

FAULKLAND.—I feel his reproaches; yet I would not change
this too exquisite nicety for the gross content with which
he tramples on the thorns of love! His engaging me in
this duel has started an idea in my head, which I will

instantly pursue. I'll use it as the touchstone of Julia's sincerity and disinterestedness. If her love prove pure and sterling ore, my name will rest on it with honor; and once I've stamped it there, I lay aside my doubts forever! But if the dross of selfishness, the alloy of pride, predominate, 'twill be best to leave her as a toy for some less cautious fool to sigh for! [*Exit.*

ACT FIFTH

Scene I.—Julia's Dressing-room

Julia discovered alone.

JULIA.—How this message has alarmed me! what dreadful accident can he mean? why such charge to be alone?— O Faulkland!—how many unhappy moments—how many tears have you cost me.

Enter Faulkland.

JULIA.—What means this?—why this caution, Faulkland?
FAULKLAND.—Alas! Julia, I am come to take a long farewell.
JULIA.—Heavens! what do you mean?
FAULKLAND.—You see before you a wretch, whose life is forfeited. Nay, start not!— the infirmity of my temper has drawn all this misery on me. I left you fretful and passionate—an untoward accident drew me into a quarrel — the event is, that I must fly this kingdom instantly. O Julia, had I been so fortunate as to have called you mine entirely, before this mischance had fallen on me, I should not so deeply dread my banishment!

JULIA.—My soul is oppressed with sorrow at the nature of your misfortune: had these adverse circumstances arisen from a less fatal cause, I should have felt strong comfort in the thought that I could now chase from your bosom every doubt of the warm sincerity of my love. My heart has long known no other guardian—I now entrust my person to your honor—we will fly together.

When safe from pursuit, my father's will may be ful-
filled—and I receive a legal claim to be the partner of
your sorrows, and tenderest comforter. Then on the
bosom of your wedded Julia, you may lull your keen regret to slumbering; while virtuous love, with a cherub's
hand, shall smooth the brow of upbraiding thought, and
pluck the thorn from compunction.

FAULKLAND.—O Julia! I am bankrupt in gratitude! but the
time is so pressing, it calls on you for so hasty a resolution!—Would you not wish some hours to weigh the
advantages you forego, and what little compensation
poor Faulkland can make you beside his solitary love?

JULIA.—I ask not a moment. No, Faulkland, I have loved you
for yourself: and if I now, more than ever, prize the
solemn engagement which so long has pledged us to
each other, it is because it leaves no room for hard as-
persions on my fame, and puts the seal of duty to an
act of love. But let us not linger. Perhaps this
delay——

FAULKLAND.—'Twill be better I should not venture out again
till dark. Yet am I grieved to think what numberless
distresses will press heavy on your gentle disposition!

JULIA.—Perhaps your fortune may be forfeited by this unhappy act. I know not whether 'tis so; but sure that
alone can never make us unhappy. The little I have will
be sufficient to support us; and exile never should be
splendid.

FAULKLAND.—Ay, but in such an abject state of life, my
wounded pride perhaps may increase the natural fret-
fulness of my temper, till I become a rude, morose companion, beyond your patience to endure. Perhaps the
recollection of a deed my conscience cannot justify may
haunt me in such gloomy and unsocial fits, that I shall
hate the tenderness that would relieve me, break from
your arms, and quarrel with your fondness!

JULIA.—If your thoughts should assume so unhappy a bent,
you will the more want some mild and affectionate spirit
to watch over and console you: one who, by bearing
your infirmities with gentleness and resignation, may
teach you so to bear the evils of your fortune.

FAULKLAND.—Julia, I have proved you to the quick! and with this useless device I throw away all my doubts. How shall I plead to be forgiven this last unworthy effect of my restless, unsatisfied disposition?

JULIA.—Has no such disaster happened as you related?

FAULKLAND.—I am ashamed to own that it was pretended; yet in pity, Julia, do not kill me with resenting a fault which never can be repeated: but sealing, this once, my pardon, let me to-morrow, in the face of Heaven, receive my future guide and monitress, and expiate my past folly by years of tender adoration.

JULIA.—Hold, Faulkland!—that you are free from a crime, which I before feared to name, Heaven knows how sincerely I rejoice! These are tears of thankfulness for that! But that your cruel doubts should have urged you to an imposition that has wrung my heart, gives me now a pang more keen than I can express!

FAULKLAND.—By Heavens! Julia——

JULIA.—Yet hear me.—My father loved you, Faulkland! and you preserved the life that tender parent gave me; in his presence I pledged my hand—joyfully pledged it— where before I had given my heart. When, soon after, I lost that parent, it seemed to me that Providence had, in Faulkland, shown me whither to transfer without a pause, my grateful duty, as well as my affection: hence I have been content to bear from you what pride and delicacy would have forbid me from another. I will not upbraid you, by repeating how you have trifled with my sincerity——

FAULKLAND.—I confess it all! yet hear——

JULIA.—After such a year of trial, I might have flattered myself that I should not have been insulted with a new probation of my sincerity, as cruel as unnecessary! I now see it is not in your nature to be content or confident in love. With this conviction—I never will be yours. While I had hopes that my persevering attention, and unreproaching kindness, might in time reform your temper, I should have been happy to have gained a dearer influence over you; but I will not furnish you with a licensed power to keep alive an incorrigible fault,

at the expense of one who never would contend with
you.

FAULKLAND.—Nay, but, Julia, by my soul and honor, if after
this——

JULIA.—But one word more.—As my faith has once been given
to you, I never will barter it with another. I shall pray
for your happiness with the truest sincerity; and the
dearest blessing I can ask of Heaven to send you will
be to charm you from that unhappy temper, which alone
has prevented the performance of our solemn engagement. All I request of you is, that you will yourself
reflect upon this infirmity, and when you number up the
many true delights it has deprived you of, let it not be
your least regret, that it lost you the love of one who
would have followed you in beggary through the world!
[Exit.

FAULKLAND.—She's gone—forever!—There was an awful
resolution in her manner, that riveted me to my place.
—O fool!—dolt!—barbarian! Cursed as I am, with
more imperfections than my fellow wretches, kind Fortune sent a heaven-gifted cherub to my aid, and, like a
ruffian, I have driven her from my side!—I must now
haste to my appointment. Well, my mind is tuned for
such a scene. I shall wish only to become a principal in
it, and reverse the tale my cursed folly put me upon
forging here.—O Love!—tormentor!—fiend!—whose
influence, like the moon's, acting on men of dull souls,
makes idiots of them, but meeting subtler spirits, betrays their course, and urges sensibility to madness!
[Exit.

Enter Lydia and Maid.

MAID.—My mistress, ma'am, I know, was here just now—
perhaps she is only in the next room.   [Exit.

LYDIA.—Heigh-ho! Though he has used me so, this fellow
runs strangely in my head. I believe one lecture from
my grave cousin will make me recall him. [*Re-enter
Julia.*] O Julia, I am come to you with such an appetite for consolation.—Lud! child, what's the matter with
you? You have been crying!—I'll be hanged if that
Faulkland has not been tormenting you!

JULIA.—You mistake the cause of my uneasiness!—Something has flurried me a little. Nothing that you can guess at. —[*Aside.*] I would not accuse Faulkland to a sister!

LYDIA.—Ah! whatever vexations you may have, I can assure you mine surpass them. You know who Beverley proves to be?

JULIA.—I will now own to you, Lydia, that Mr. Faulkland had before informed me of the whole affair. Had young Absolute been the person you took him for, I should not have accepted your confidence on the subject, without a serious endeavor to counteract your caprice.

LYDIA.—So, then, I see I have been deceived by every one! But I don't care—I'll never have him.

JULIA.—Nay, Lydia——

LYDIA.—Why, is it not provoking? when I thought we were coming to the prettiest distress imaginable, to find myself made a mere Smithfield bargain of at last! There had I projected one of the most sentimental elopements! —so becoming a disguise!—so amiable a ladder of ropes!—conscious moon—four horses—Scotch parson —with such surprise to Mrs. Malaprop—and such paragraphs in the newspapers!—Oh, I shall die with disappointment!

JULIA.—I don't wonder at it!

LYDIA.—Now—sad reverse!—what have I to expect, but, after a deal of flimsy preparation with a bishop's license, and my aunt's blessing, to go simpering up to the altar; or perhaps be cried three times in a country church, and have an unmannerly fat clerk ask the consent of every butcher in the parish to join John Absolute and Lydia Languish, spinster! Oh that I should live to hear myself called spinster!

JULIA.—Melancholy indeed!

LYDIA.—How mortifying, to remember the dear delicious shifts I used to be put to, to gain half a minute's conversation with this fellow! How often have I stole forth, in the coldest night in January, and found him in the garden, stuck like a dripping statue! There would he kneel to me in the snow, and sneeze and cough so pathetically! he shivering with cold and I with apprehension! and

while the freezing blast numbed our joints, how warmly
would he press me to pity his flame, and glow with
mutual ardor!—Ah, Julia, that was something like being
in love.

JULIA.—If I were in spirits, Lydia, I should chide you only
by laughing heartily at you; but it suits more the situation of my mind, at present, earnestly to entreat you not
to let a man, who loves you with sincerity, suffer that
unhappiness from your caprice, which I know too well
caprice can inflict.

LYDIA.—O Lud! what has brought my aunt here?

Enter Mrs. Malaprop, Fag, and David.

MRS. MALAPROP.—So! so! here's fine work!—here's fine sui-
cide, parricide, and simulation, going on in the fields!
and Sir Anthony not to be found to prevent the anti-
strophe!

JULIA.—For Heaven's sake, madam, what's the meaning of
this?

MRS. MALAPROP.—That gentleman can tell you—'twas he en-
veloped the affair to me.

LYDIA.—Do, sir, will you, inform us?   [*To Fag.*

FAG.—Ma'am, I should hold myself very deficient in every req-
uisite that forms the man of breeding, if I delayed a
moment to give all the information in my power to a
lady so deeply interested in the affair as you are.

LYDIA.—But quick! quick, sir!

FAG.—True, ma'am, as you say, one should be quick in divulg-
ing matters of this nature; for should we be tedious,
perhaps while we are flourishing on the subject, two or
three lives may be lost!

LYDIA.—O patience!—Do, ma'am, for Heaven's sake! tell us
what is the matter?

MRS. MALAPROP.—Why, murder's the matter! slaughter's the
matter! killing's the matter!—but he can tell you the
perpendiculars.

LYDIA.—Then, prithee, sir, be brief.

FAG.—Why then, ma'am, as to murder—I cannot take upon
me to say—and as to slaughter, or manslaughter, that
will be as the jury finds it.

Lydia.—But who, sir—who are engaged in this?

Fag.—Faith, ma'am, one is a young gentleman whom I should be very sorry anything was to happen to—a very pretty behaved gentleman! We have lived much together, and always on terms.

Lydia.—But who is this? who! who! who?

Fag.—My master, ma'am—my master—I speak of my master.

Lydia.—Heavens! What, Captain Absolute!

Mrs. Malaprop.—Oh, to be sure, you are frightened now!

Julia.—But who are with him, sir?

Fag.—As to the rest, ma'am, this gentleman can inform you better than I.

Julia.—Do speak, friend. [*To David.*

David.—Look'ee, my lady—by the mass! there's mischief going on. Folks don't use to meet for amusement with firearms, firelocks, fire-engines, fire-screens, fire-office, and the devil knows what other crackers beside!—This, my lady, I say, has an angry flavor.

Julia.—But who is there beside Captain Absolute, friend?

David.—My poor master—under favor for mentioning him first. You know me, my lady—I am David—and my master of course is, or was, 'Squire Acres. Then comes 'Squire Faulkland.

Julia.—Do, ma'am, let us instantly endeavor to prevent mischief.

Mrs. Malaprop.—O fy!—it would be very inelegant in us:—we should only participate things.

David.—Ah! do, Mrs. Aunt, save a few lives—they are desperately given, believe me.—Above all, there is that bloodthirsty Philistine, Sir Lucius O'Trigger.

Mrs. Malaprop.—Sir Lucius O'Trigger? O mercy! have they drawn poor little dear Sir Lucius into the scrape?—Why, how you stand, girl! you have no more feeling than one of the Derbyshire petrifactions!

Lydia.—What are we to do, madam?

Mrs. Malaprop.—Why fly with the utmost felicity, to be sure, to prevent mischief!—Here, friend, you can show us the place?

Fag.—If you please, ma'am, I will conduct you.—David, do you look for Sir Anthony. [*Exit David.*

Mrs. Malaprop.—Come, girls! this gentleman will exhort us.
—Come, sir, you're our envoy—lead the way, and we'll
precede.

Fag.—Not a step before the ladies for the world!

Mrs. Malaprop.—You're sure you know the spot?

Fag.—I think I can find it, ma'am; and one good thing is, we
shall hear the report of the pistols as we draw near, so
we can't well miss them;—never fear, ma'am, never fear.
[*Exeunt, he talking.*

Scene II.—The South Parade

Enter Captain Absolute, putting his sword under his great-coat.

Absolute.—A sword seen in the streets of Bath would raise
as great an alarm as a mad dog.—How provoking this
is in Faulkland!—never punctual! I shall be obliged to
go without him at last.—Oh, the devil! here's Sir Anthony! how shall I escape him?
[*Muffles up his face, and takes a circle to go off.*

Enter Sir Anthony Absolute.

Sir Anthony.—How one may be deceived at a little distance!
only that I see he don't know me, I could have sworn
that was Jack!—Hey! Gad's life! it is.—Why, Jack,
what are you afraid of? hey!—sure I'm right.—Why
Jack, Jack Absolute!   [*Goes up to him.*

Absolute.—Really, sir, you have the advantage of me:—I
don't remember ever to have had the honor—my name
is Saunderson, at your service.

Sir Anthony.—Sir, I beg your pardon—I took you—hey?—
why, zounds! it is—Stay—[*Looks up to his face.*] So,
so—your humble servant, Mr. Saunderson! Why, you
scoundrel, what tricks are you after now?

Absolute.—Oh, a joke, sir, a joke! I came here on purpose
to look for you, sir.

Sir Anthony.—You did! well, I am glad you were so lucky:
—but what are you muffled up so for?—what's this for?
—hey!

ABSOLUTE.—'Tis cool, sir; isn't it?—rather chilly somehow;—but I shall be late—I have a particular engagement.

SIR ANTHONY.—Stay!—Why, I thought you were looking for me?—Pray, Jack, where is't you are going?

ABSOLUTE.—Going, sir!

SIR ANTHONY.—Ay, where are you going?

ABSOLUTE.—Where am I going?

SIR ANTHONY.—You unmannerly puppy!

ABSOLUTE.—I was going, sir, to—to—to—to Lydia—sir, to Lydia—to make matters up if I could;—and I was looking for you, sir, to—to—

SIR ANTHONY.—To go with you, I suppose.—Well, come along.

ABSOLUTE.—Oh! zounds! no, sir, not for the world!—I wished to meet with you, sir—to—to—to—You find it cool, I'm sure, sir—you'd better not stay out.

SIR ANTHONY.—Cool!—not at all.—Well, Jack—and what will you say to Lydia?

ABSOLUTE.—Oh, sir, beg her pardon, humor her—promise and vow: but I detain you, sir—consider the cold air on your gout.

SIR ANTHONY.—Oh, not at all!—not at all! I'm in no hurry. —Ah! Jack, you youngsters, when once you are wounded here [*Putting his hand to Captain Absolute's breast.*] Hey! what the deuce have you got here?

ABSOLUTE.—Nothing, sir—nothing.

SIR ANTHONY.—What's this?—here's something d——d hard.

ABSOLUTE.—Oh, trinkets, sir! trinkets!—a bauble for Lydia!

SIR ANTHONY.—Nay, let me see your taste.—[*Pulls his coat open, the sword falls.*] Trinkets!—a bauble for Lydia! —Zounds! sirrah, you are not going to cut her throat, are you?

ABSOLUTE.—Ha! ha! ha!—I thought it would divert you, sir, though I didn't mean to tell you till afterwards.

SIR ANTHONY.—You didn't?—Yes, this is a very diverting trinket, truly!

ABSOLUTE.—Sir, I'll explain to you.—You know, sir, Lydia is romantic, devilish romantic, and very absurd of course: now, sir, I intend, if she refuses to forgive me, to unsheath this sword, and swear I'll fall upon its point, and expire at her feet!

SIR ANTHONY.—Fall upon a fiddlestick's end!—why, I suppose it is the very thing that would please her.—Get along, you fool!

ABSOLUTE.—Well, sir, you shall hear of my success—you shall hear.—O Lydia!—forgive me, or this pointed steel—says I.

SIR ANTHONY.—O, booby! stab away and welcome—says she.—Get along! and d—n your trinkets!

[*Exit Captain Absolute.*

Enter David, running.

DAVID.—Stop him! stop him! Murder! Thief! Fire!—Stop fire! Stop fire!—O Sir Anthony—call! call! bid 'm stop! Murder! Fire!

SIR ANTHONY.—Fire! Murder!—Where?

DAVID.—Oons! he's out of sight! and I'm out of breath, for my part! O Sir Anthony, why didn't you stop him? why didn't you stop him?

SIR ANTHONY.—Zounds! the fellow's mad!—Stop whom? stop Jack?

DAVID.—Ay, the captain, sir!—there's murder and slaughter——

SIR ANTHONY.—Murder!

DAVID.—Ay, please you, Sir Anthony, there's all kinds of murder, all sorts of slaughter to be seen in the fields: there's fighting going on, sir—bloody sword-and-gun fighting!

SIR ANTHONY.—Who are going to fight, dunce?

DAVID.—Everybody that I know of, Sir Anthony:—everybody is going to fight, my poor master, Sir Lucius O'Trigger, your son, the captain——

SIR ANTHONY.—Oh, the dog! I see his tricks.—Do you know the place?

SIR ANTHONY.—King's-Mead-Fields.

SIR ANTHONY.—You know the way?

DAVID.—Not an inch; but I'll call the mayor—aldermen—constables—churchwardens—and beadles—we can't be too many to part them.

SIR ANTHONY.—Come along—give me your shoulder! we'll get assistance as we go—the lying villain!—Well, I shall be in such a frenzy!—So—this was the history of his trinkets! I'll bauble him!   [*Exeunt.*

Scene III.—King's-Mead-Fields

Enter Sir Lucius O'Trigger and Acres, with pistols.

ACRES.—By my valor! then, Sir Lucius, forty yards is a good distance. Odds levels and aims!—I say it is a good distance.

SIR LUCIUS.—Is it for muskets or small field-pieces? Upon my conscience, Mr. Acres, you must leave those things to me.—Stay now—I'll show you.—[*Measures paces along the stage.*] There now, that is a very pretty distance—a pretty gentleman's distance.

ACRES.—Zounds! we might as well fight in a sentry-box! I tell you, Sir Lucius, the farther he is off, the cooler I shall take my aim.

SIR LUCIUS.—Faith! then I suppose you would aim at him best of all if he was out of sight!

ACRES.—No, Sir Lucius; but I should think forty or eight-and-thirty yards——

SIR LUCIUS.—Pho! pho! nonsense! three or four feet between the mouths of your pistols is as good as a mile.

ACRES.—Odds bullets, no!—by my valor! there is no merit in killing him so near: do, my dear Sir Lucius, let me bring him down at a long shot:—a long shot, Sir Lucius, if you love me!

SIR LUCIUS.—Well, the gentleman's friend and I must settle that.—But tell me now, Mr. Acres, in case of an accident, is there any little will or commission I could execute for you?

ACRES.—I am much obliged to you, Sir Lucius—but I don't understand——

SIR LUCIUS.—Why, you may think there's no being shot at without a little risk—and if an unlucky bullet should carry a quietus with it—I say it will be no time then to be bothering you about family matters.

ACRES.—A quietus!

SIR LUCIUS.—For instance, now—if that should be the case—

would you choose to be pickled and sent home?—or
would it be the same to you to lie here in the Abbey?—
I'm told there is very snug lying in the Abbey.

Acres.—Pickled!—Snug lying in the Abbey!—Odds tremors!
Sir Lucius, don't talk so!

Sir Lucius.—I suppose, Mr. Acres, you never were engaged
in an affair of this kind before?

Acres.—No, Sir Lucius, never before.

Sir Lucius.—Ah! that's a pity!—there's nothing like being
used to a thing.—Pray now, how would you receive the
gentleman's shot?

Acres.—Odds files!—I've practised that—there, Sir Lucius—
there.—[*Puts himself in an attitude.*] A side-front,
hey? Odds! I'll make myself small enough: I'll stand
edgeways.

Sir Lucius.—Now—you're quite out—for if you stand so
when I take my aim——   [*Levelling at him.*

Acres.—Zounds! Sir Lucius—are you sure it is not cocked?

Sir Lucius.—Never fear.

Acres.—But—but—you don't know—it may go off of its own
head!

Sir Lucius.—Pho! be easy.—Well, now if I hit you in the
body, my bullet has a double chance—for if it misses a
vital part of your right side—'twill be very hard if it
don't succeed on the left!

Acres.—A vital part?

Sir Lucius.—But, there—fix yourself so—[*Placing him*]—
let him see the broad-side of your full front—there—
now a ball or two may pass clean through your body,
and never do any harm at all.

Acres.—Clean through me!—a ball or two clean through me!

Sir Lucius.—Ay, may they—and it is much the genteelest attitude into the bargain.

Acres.—Look'ee! Sir Lucius—I'd just as lieve be shot in an
awkward posture as a genteel one; so, by my valor! I
will stand edgeways.

Sir Lucius [*looking at his watch*].—Sure they don't mean
to disappoint us—Hah!—no, faith—I think I see them
coming.

Acres.—Hey!—what!—coming!——

SIR LUCIUS.—Ay.—Who are those yonder getting over the stile?

ACRES.—There are two of them indeed!—well—let them come —hey, Sir Lucius!—we—we—we—we—won't run.

SIR LUCIUS.—Run!

ACRES.—No—I say—we won't run, by my valor!

SIR LUCIUS.—What the devil's the matter with you?

ACRES.—Nothing—nothing—my dear friend—my dear Sir Lucius—but I—I—I don't feel quite so bold, somehow, as I did.

SIR LUCIUS.—O fy!—consider your honor.

ACRES.—Ay—true—my honor. Do, Sir Lucius, edge in a word or two every now and then about my honor.

SIR LUCIUS.—Well, here they're coming. [*Looking.*

ACRES.—Sir Lucius—if I wa'n't with you, I should almost think I was afraid.—If my valor should leave me!— Valor will come and go.

SIR LUCIUS.—Then pray keep it fast, while you have it.

ACRES.—Sir Lucius—I doubt it is going—yes—my valor is certainly going!—it is sneaking off!—I feel it oozing out as it were at the palms of my hands!

SIR LUCIUS.—Your honor—your honor!—Here they are.

ACRES.—O mercy!—now—that I was safe at Clod-Hall! or could be shot before I was aware!

Enter Faulkland and Captain Absolute.

SIR LUCIUS.—Gentlemen, your most obedient.—Hah!—what, Captain Absolute!—So, I suppose, sir, you are come here, just like myself—to do a kind office, first for your friend— then to proceed to business on your own account.

ACRES.—What, Jack!—my dear Jack!—my dear friend!

ABSOLUTE.—Hark'ee, Bob, Beverley's at hand.

SIR LUCIUS.—Well, Mr. Acres—I don't blame your saluting the gentleman civilly.—[*To Faulkland.*] So, Mr. Beverley, if you'll choose your weapons, the captain and I will measure the ground.

FAULKLAND.—My weapons, sir!

ACRES.—Odds life! Sir Lucius, I'm not going to fight Mr. Faulkland; these are my particular friends.

SIR LUCIUS.—What, sir, did you not come here to fight Mr. Acres?

FAULKLAND.—Not I, upon my word, sir.

SIR LUCIUS.—Well, now, that's mighty provoking! But I hope, Mr. Faulkland, as there are three of us come on purpose for the game, you won't be so cantankerous as to spoil the party by sitting out.

ABSOLUTE.—O pray, Faulkland, fight to oblige Sir Lucius.

FAULKLAND.—Nay, if Mr. Acres is so bent on the matter——

ACRES.—No, no, Mr. Faulkland;—I'll bear my disappointment like a Christian.—Look'ee, Sir Lucius, there's no occasion at all for me to fight; and if it is the same to you, I'd as lieve let it alone.

SIR LUCIUS.—Observe me, Mr. Acres—I must not be trifled with. You have certainly challenged somebody—and you came here to fight him. Now, if that gentleman is willing to represent him, I can't see, for my soul, why it isn't just the same thing.

ACRES.—Why no—Sir Lucius—I tell you, 'tis one Beverley I've challenged—a fellow, you see, that dare not show his face!—If he were here, I'd make him give up his pretensions directly!

ABSOLUTE.—Hold, Bob—let me set you right—there is no such man as Beverley in the case.—The person who assumed that name is before you; and as his pretensions are the same in both characters, he is ready to support them in whatever way you please.

SIR LUCIUS.—Well, this is lucky.—Now you have an opportunity——

ACRES.—What, quarrel with my dear friend Jack Absolute?—not if he were fifty Beverleys! Zounds! Sir Lucius, you would not have me so unnatural.

SIR LUCIUS.—Upon my conscience, Mr. Acres, your valor has oozed away with a vengeance!

ACRES.—Not in the least! Odds backs and abettors! I'll be your second with all my heart—and if you should get a quietus, you may command me entirely. I'll get you snug lying in the Abbey here; or pickle you, and send you over to Blunderbuss-hall, or anything of the kind, with the greatest pleasure.

SIR LUCIUS.—Pho! pho! you are little better than a coward.

ACRES.—Mind, gentlemen, he calls me a coward; coward was the word, by my valor!

SIR LUCIUS.—Well, sir?

ACRES.—Look'ee, Sir Lucius, 'tisn't that I mind the word coward—coward may be said in joke—but if you had called me a poltroon, odds daggers and balls——

SIR LUCIUS.—Well, sir?

ACRES.—I should have thought you a very ill-bred man.

SIR LUCIUS.—Pho! you are beneath my notice.

ABSOLUTE.—Nay, Sir Lucius, you can't have a better second than my friend Acres.—He is a most determined dog— called in the country, Fighting Bob.—He generally kills a man a week—don't you, Bob?

ACRES.—Ay—at home!

SIR LUCIUS.—Well, then, captain, 'tis we must begin—so come out, my little counsellor—[*Draws his sword.*]—and ask the gentleman, whether he will resign the lady, without forcing you to proceed against him?

ABSOLUTE.—Come on then, sir—[*draws*]; since you won't let it be an amicable suit, here's my reply.

Enter Sir Anthony Absolute, David, Mrs. Malaprop, Lydia, and Julia.

DAVID.—Knock 'em all down, sweet Sir Anthony; knock down my master in particular; and bind his hands over to their good behavior!

SIR ANTHONY.—Put up, Jack, put up, or I shall be in a frenzy —how came you in a duel, sir?

ABSOLUTE.—Faith, sir, that gentleman can tell you better than I; 'twas he called on me, and you know, sir, I serve his majesty.

SIR ANTHONY.—Here's a pretty fellow; I catch him going to cut a man's throat, and he tells me, he serves his majesty!—Zounds! sirrah, then how durst you draw the king's sword against one of his subjects?

ABSOLUTE.—Sir, I tell you! that gentleman called me out, without explaining his reasons.

SIR ANTHONY.—Gad! sir, how came you to call my son out, without explaining your reasons?

SIR LUCIUS.—Your son, sir, insulted me in a manner which my
    honor could not brook.

SIR ANTHONY.—Zounds! Jack, how durst you insult the gen-
    tleman in a manner which his honor could not brook?

MRS. MALAPROP.—Come, come, let's have no honor before
    ladies.—Captain Absolute, come here—How could you
    intimidate us so?—Here's Lydia has been terrified to
    death for you.

ABSOLUTE.—For fear I should be killed, or escape, ma'am?

MRS. MALAPROP.—Nay, no delusions to the past—Lydia is con-
    vinced; speak, child.

SIR LUCIUS.—With your leave, ma'am, I must put in a word
    here: I believe I could interpret the young lady's si-
    lence. Now mark——

LYDIA.—What is it you mean, sir?

SIR LUCIUS.—Come, come, Delia, we must be serious now—
    this is no time for trifling.

LYDIA.—'Tis true, sir; and your reproof bids me offer this
    gentleman my hand, and solicit the return of his affec-
    tions.

ABSOLUTE.—O! my little angel, say you so!—Sir Lucius—I
    perceive there must be some mistake here, with regard
    to the affront which you affirm I have given you. I can
    only say, that it could not have been intentional. And
    as you must be convinced, that I should not fear to sup-
    port a real injury, you shall now see that I am not
    ashamed to atone for an inadvertency—I ask your par-
    don.—But for this lady, while honored with her appro-
    bation, I will support my claim against any man what-
    ever.

SIR ANTHONY.—Well said, Jack, and I'll stand by you, my
    boy.

ACRES.—Mind, I give up all my claim—I make no pretensions
    to anything in the world; and if I can't get a wife with-
    out fighting for her, by my valor! I'll live a bachelor.

SIR LUCIUS.—Captain, give me your hand: an affront hand-
    somely acknowledged becomes an obligation; and as for
    the lady, if she chooses to deny her own hand-writing,
    here——   [Takes out letters.

MRS. MALAPROP.—O, he will dissolve my mystery!—Sir Lucius, perhaps there's some mistake—perhaps I can illuminate——

SIR LUCIUS.—Pray, old gentlewoman, don't interfere where you have no business.—Miss Languish, are you my Delia, or not?

LYDIA.—Indeed, Sir Lucius, I am not.

[Walks aside with Captain Absolute.

MRS. MALAPROP.—Sir Lucius O'Trigger—ungrateful as you are—I own the soft impeachment—pardon my blushes, I am Delia.

SIR LUCIUS.—You Delia—pho! pho! be easy.

MRS. MALAPROP.—Why, thou barbarous Vandyke—those letters are mine—When you are more sensible of my benignity—perhaps I may be brought to encourage your addresses.

SIR LUCIUS.—Mrs. Malaprop, I am extremely sensible of your condescension; and whether you or Lucy have put this trick on me, I am equally beholden to you.—And, to show you I am not ungrateful, Captain Absolute, since you have taken that lady from me, I'll give you my Delia into the bargain.

ABSOLUTE. I am much obliged to you, Sir Lucius; but here's my friend, Fighting Bob, unprovided for.

SIR LUCIUS.—Hah! little Valor—here, will you make your fortune?

ACRES.—Odds wrinkles! No.—But give me your hand, Sir Lucius, forget and forgive; but if ever I give you a chance of pickling me again, say Bob Acres is a dunce, that's all.

SIR ANTHONY.— Come, Mrs. Malaprop, don't be cast down— you are in your bloom yet.

MRS. MALAPROP.—O Sir Anthony—men are all barbarians.

[All retire but Julia and Faulkland.

JULIA [*aside*].—He seems dejected and unhappy—not sullen; there was some foundation, however, for the tale he told me—O woman! how true should be your judgment, when your resolution is so weak!

FAULKLAND.—Julia!—how can I sue for what I so little deserve? I dare not presume—yet Hope is the child of Penitence.

JULIA.—O! Faulkland, you have not been more faulty in your unkind treatment of me, than I am now in wanting inclination to resent it. As my heart honestly bids me place my weakness to the account of love, I should be ungenerous not to admit the same plea for yours.

FAULKLAND.—Now I shall be blest indeed!

SIR ANTHONY [*coming forward*].—What's going on here?—So you have been quarrelling too, I warrant! Come, Julia, I never interfered before; but let me have a hand in the matter at last.—All the faults I have ever seen in my friend Faulkland seemed to proceed from what he calls the delicacy and warmth of his affection for you—There, marry him directly, Julia; you'll find he'll mend surprisingly! [*The rest come forward.*

SIR LUCIUS.—Come, now, I hope there is no dissatisfied person, but what is content; for as I have been disappointed myself, it will be very hard if I have not the satisfaction of seeing other people succeed better.

ACRES.—You are right, Sir Lucius.—So Jack, I wish you joy—Mr. Faulkland the same.—Ladies—come now, to show you I'm neither vexed nor angry, odds tabors and pipes! I'll order the fiddles in half an hour to the New Rooms—and I insist on your all meeting me there.

SIR ANTHONY.—'Gad! sir, I like your spirit; and at night we single lads will drink a health to the young couples, and a husband to Mrs. Malaprop.

FAULKLAND.—Our partners are stolen from us, Jack—I hope to be congratulated by each other—yours for having checked in time the errors of an ill-directed imagination, which might have betrayed an innocent heart; and mine, for having, by her gentleness and candor, reformed the unhappy temper of one, who by it made wretched whom he loved most, and tortured the heart he ought to have adored.

ABSOLUTE.—Well, Jack, we have both tasted the bitters, as well as the sweets of love; with this difference only, that you always prepared the bitter cup for yourself, while I——

LYDIA.—Was always obliged to me for it, hey! Mr. Modesty?——But, come, no more of that—our happiness is now as unalloyed as general.

Julia.—Then let us study to preserve it so: and while Hope pictures to us a flattering scene of future bliss, let us deny its pencil those colors which are too bright to be lasting.—When hearts deserving happiness would unite their fortunes, Virtue would crown them with an unfading garland of modest hurtless flowers; but ill-judging Passion will force the gaudier rose into the wreath, whose thorn offends them when its leaves are dropped!

[*Exeunt omnes.*

EPILOGUE

By the Author

Ladies, for you—I heard our poet say—
He'd try to coax some moral from his play:
" One moral's plain," cried I, " without more fuss;
Man's social happiness all rests on us:
Through all the drama—whether d——d or not—
Love gilds the scene, and women guide the plot.
From every rank obedience is our due—
D'ye doubt?—The world's great stage shall prove it
    true.

The cit, well skilled to shun domestic strife,
Will sup abroad; but first he'll ask his wife:
John Trot, his friend, for once will do the same,
But then—he'll just step home to tell his dame.

The surly 'Squire at noon resolves to rule,
And half the day—Zounds! madam is a fool!
Convinced at night, the vanquished victor says,
Ah, Kate! you women have such coaxing ways.

The jolly toper chides each tardy blade,
Till reeling Bacchus calls on Love for aid:
Then with each toast he sees fair bumpers swim,
And kisses Chloe on the sparkling brim!

Nay, I have heard that statesmen—great and wise—
Will sometimes counsel with a lady's eyes!
The servile suitors watch her various face,

She smiles preferment, or she frowns disgrace,
Curtsies a pension here—there nods a place.
　Nor with less awe, in scenes of humbler life,
Is viewed the mistress, or is heard the wife.
The poorest peasant of the poorest soil,
The child of poverty, and heir to toil,
Early from radiant Love's impartial light
Steals one small spark to cheer this world of night:
Dear spark! that oft through winter's chilling woes
Is all the warmth his little cottage knows!
　The wandering tar, who not for years has pressed
The widowed partner of his day of rest,
On the cold deck, far from her arms removed,
Still hums the ditty which his Susan loved;
And while around the cadence rude is blown,
The boatswain whistles in a softer tone.
　The soldier, fairly proud of wounds and toil,
Pants for the triumph of his Nancy's smile;
But ere the battle should he list her cries,
The lover trembles—and the hero dies!
That heart, by war and honor steeled to fear,
Droops on a sigh, and sickens at a tear!
　But ye more cautious, ye nice-judging few,
Who give to beauty only beauty's due,
Though friends to love—ye view with deep regret
Our conquests marred, our triumphs incomplete,
Till polished wit more lasting charms disclose,
And judgment fix the darts which beauty throws!
In female breasts did sense and merit rule,
The lover's mind would ask no other school;
Shamed into sense, the scholars of our eyes,
Our beaux from gallantry would soon be wise;
Would gladly light, their homage to improve,
The lamp of knowledge at the torch of love!

CHOICE EXAMPLES OF EARLY PRINTING AND ENGRAVING.

Fac-similes from Rare and Curious Books.

DIALOGUE OF THE SUN AND MOON.

The present plate is from a book called "The Dialogus Creaturarum," in which conversations between the Sun and Moon and various animals are related and illustrated. The work was first printed by Gerard Leew at Gouda, Holland, in 1480. Each dialogue is set off with cuts in the style of the present one, and the work is by no means the least interesting amongst Dutch examples.

Dyalogus creaturarū optime mozaliʒatus·omni materie mozali foꝛ
tudo mo applicabik⁏ ad laudē dei z edificacionē hoīm Incipit feliciter

De fole z luna Dyalogus pꝛimus

Ol eſt ſecundum philoſophum oculꝰ
mundi·iocūditas diei·pulchꝛitudo
celi·menſura tempoꝛum·virtus et
oꝛigo omnium naſcencium·dominꝰ
planetarum·ductoꝛ et perfectoꝛ om̄
nium ſtellarum   luna vero vt dicit
Ambꝛoſius iu exameron eſt decoꝛ noc
tis·mater totius humoꝛis et miniſt
tra·menſura tempoꝛum·domina
trix maris·immutatrix aeris et emu

MARY STUART

—

BY

FRIEDRICH VON SCHILLER

[Metrical Translation by J. Mellish]

DRAMATIS PERSONÆ

ELIZABETH, Queen of England.

MARY STUART, Queen of Scots, a Prisoner in England.

ROBERT DUDLEY, Earl of Leicester.

GEORGE TALBOT, Earl of Shrewsbury.

WILLIAM CECIL, Lord Burleigh, Lord High Treasurer.

EARL OF KENT.

SIR WILLIAM DAVISON, Secretary of State.

SIR AMIAS PAULET, Keeper of Mary.

SIR EDWARD MORTIMER, his Nephew.

COUNT L'AUBESPINE, the French Ambassador.

COUNT BELLIEVRE, Envoy Extraordinary from France.

O'KELLY, Mortimer's friend.

SIR DRUE DRURY, another Keeper of Mary.

SIR ANDREW MELVIL, her House-Steward.

BURGOYNE, her Physician.

HANNAH KENNEDY, her Nurse.

MARGARET CURL, her Attendant.

Sheriff of the County.

Officer of the Guard.

French and English Lords.

Soldiers.

Servants of State, belonging to Elizabeth.

Servants and Female Attendants of the Queen of Scots.

MARY STUART

ACT FIRST

Scene I.—Apartment in Castle of Fotheringay

[*Hannah Kennedy contending violently with Paulet, who is
about to break open a closet; Drury with an iron crow.*

KENNEDY.—How now, Sir? What fresh outrage have we
    here?
    Back from that cabinet!
PAULET.—   Whence came the jewel?
    I know 'twas from an upper chamber thrown;
    And you would bribe the gard'ner with your trinkets.
    A curse on woman's wiles! In spite of all
    My strict precaution and my active search,
    Still treasures here, still costly gems concealed!
    And doubtless there are more where this lay hid.
                    [*Advancing towards the cabinet.*
KENNEDY.—Intruder, back! here lie my lady's secrets.
PAULET.—Exactly what I seek.   [*Drawing forth papers.*
KENNEDY.—   Mere trifling papers;
    The amusements only of an idle pen,
    To cheat the dreary tedium of a dungeon.
PAULET.—In idle hours the evil mind is busy.
KENNEDY.—Those writings are in French.
PAULET.—   So much the worse!
    That tongue betokens England's enemy.
KENNEDY.—Sketches of letters to the Queen of England.
PAULET.—I'll be their bearer. Ha! what glitters here?
[*He touches a secret spring, and draws out jewels from a pri-
vate drawer.*
    A royal diadem enriched with stones,

And studded with the fleur-de-lis of France!
                         [*He hands it to his assistant.*
Here, take it, Drury, lay it with the rest.
                              [*Exit Drury.*
(And ye have found the means to hide from us
Such costly things, and screen them, until now,
From our inquiring eyes?)
KENNEDY.—   O insolent
And tyrant power, to which we must submit!
PAULET.—She can work ill as long as she hath treasures;
For all things turn to weapons in her hands.
KENNEDY [*supplicating*].—O Sir! be merciful; deprive us not
Of the last jewel that adorns our life!
'Tis my poor Lady's only joy to view
This symbol of her former majesty
Your hands long since have robbed us of the rest.
PAULET.—'Tis in safe custody; in proper time
'Twill be restored to you with scrupulous care.
KENNEDY.—Who that beholds these naked walls could say
That Majesty dwelt here? Where is the throne?
Where the imperial canopy of state?
Must she not set her tender foot, still used
To softest treading, on the rugged ground?
With common pewter, which the lowliest dame
Would scorn, they furnish forth her homely table.
PAULET.—Thus did she treat her spouse at Stirling once;
And pledged, the while, her paramour in gold.
KENNEDY.—Even the mirror's trifling aid withheld.
PAULET.—The contemplation of her own vain image
Incites to hope, and prompts to daring deeds.
KENNEDY.—Books are denied her to divert her mind.
PAULET.—The Bible still is left, to mend her heart.
KENNEDY.—Even of her very lute she is deprived!
PAULET.—Because she tuned it to her wanton airs.
KENNEDY.—Is this a fate for her, the gentle born,
Who in her very cradle was a Queen;
Who, rear'd in Catherine's luxurious court,
Enjoyed the fulness of each earthly pleasure?
Was 't not enough to rob her of her power,
Must ye then envy her its paltry tinsel?

A noble heart in time resigns itself
To great calamities with fortitude;
But yet it cuts one to the soul, to part
At once with all life's little outward trappings!

PAULET.—These are the things that turn the human heart
To vanity, which should collect itself
In penitence;—for a lewd, vicious life,
Want and abasement are the only penance.

KENNEDY.—If youthful blood has led her into error,
With her own heart and God she must account:—
There is no judge in England over her.

PAULET.—She shall have judgment where she hath trans-
          gress'd.

KENNEDY.—Her narrow bonds restrain her from transgression.

PAULET.—And yet she found the means to stretch her arm
Into the world, from out these narrow bonds,
And, with the torch of civil war, inflame
This realm against our Queen, (whom God preserve,)
And arm assassin bands. Did she not rouse
From out these walls the malefactor Parry,
And Babington, to the detested crime
Of regicide? And did this iron grate
Prevent her from decoying to her toils
The virtuous heart of Norfolk? Saw we not
The first, best head, in all this island fall
A sacrifice for her upon the block?
(The noble house of Howard fell with him.)
And did this sad example terrify
These mad adventurers, whose rival zeal
Plunges for her into this deep abyss?
The bloody scaffold bends beneath the weight
Of her new daily victims; and we ne'er
Shall see an end till she herself, of all
The guiltiest, be offer'd up upon it.
O! curses on the day when England took
This Helen to its hospitable arms.

KENNEDY.—Did England then receive her hospitably?
O hapless Queen! who, since that fatal day
When first she set her foot within this realm,
And, as a suppliant—a fugitive—

Came to implore protection from her sister,
Has been condemned, despite the law of nations,
And royal privilege, to weep away
The fairest years of youth in prison walls.
And now, when she hath suffer'd everything
Which in imprisonment is hard and bitter,
Is like a felon summoned to the bar,
Foully accused, and though herself a queen
Constrained to plead for honor and for life.

PAULET.—She came amongst us as a murderess,
Chased by her very subjects from a throne
Which she had oft by vilest deeds disgrac'd.
Sworn against England's welfare came she hither
To call the times of bloody Mary back,
Betray our Church to Romish tyranny,
And sell our dear-bought liberties to France.
Say, why disdain'd she to subscribe the treaty
Of Edinborough—to resign her claim
To England's crown—and with one single word,
Trac'd by her pen, throw wide her prison gates?
No:—she had rather live in vile confinement,
And see herself ill-treated, than renounce
The empty honors of her barren title.
Why acts she thus? Because she trusts to wiles,
And treacherous arts of base conspiracy;
And, hourly plotting schemes of mischief, hopes
To conquer, from her prison, all this isle.

KENNEDY.—You mock us, Sir, and edge your cruelty
With words of bitter scorn:—that *she* should form
Such projects; *she,* who's here immured alive,
To whom no sound of comfort, not a voice
Of friendship comes from her beloved home;
Who hath so long no human face beheld,
Save her stern jailer's unrelenting brows;
Till now, of late, in your uncourteous cousin
She sees a second keeper, and beholds
Fresh bolts and bars around her multiplied.

PAULET.—No iron-grate is proof against her wiles.
How do I know these bars are not fil'd through?
How that this floor, these walls, that seem so strong

Without, may not be hollow from within,
And let in felon treach'ry when I sleep?
Accursed office, that's intrusted to me,
To guard this cunning mother of all ill!
Fear scares me from my sleep; and in the night
I, like a troubled spirit, roam and try
The strength of every bolt, and put to proof
Each guard's fidelity:—I see, with fear,
The dawning of each morn, which may confirm
My apprehensions:—yet, thank God, there's hope
That all my fears will soon be at an end;
For rather would I at the gates of hell
Stand sentinel, and guard the dev'lish host
Of damned souls, than this deceitful Queen.

KENNEDY.—Here comes the Queen.

PAULET.—   Christ's image in her hand,
Pride, and all worldly lusts within her heart.

Scene II.—The Same

Enter Mary veiled, a crucifix in her hand.

KENNEDY [*hastening towards her*].—O gracious Queen! they
        tread us under foot;
No end of tyranny and base oppression;
Each coming day heaps fresh indignities,
New sufferings on thy royal head.

MARY.—   Be calm—
Say, what has happened?

KENNEDY.—   See! thy cabinet
Is forc'd,—thy papers—and thy only treasure,
Which with such pains we had secur'd, the last
Poor remnant of thy bridal ornaments
From France, is in his hands:—nought now remains
Of royal state—thou art indeed bereft!

MARY.—Compose yourself, my Hannah! and believe me,
'Tis not these baubles which can make a queen:—
Basely indeed they may behave to us,
But they cannot debase us. I have learnt
To use myself to many a change in England;

I can support this too. Sir, you have ta'en
By force, what I this very day designed
To have deliver'd to you.   There's a letter
Amongst these papers, for my royal sister
Of England—Pledge me, Sir, your word of honor,
To give it to her majesty's own hands,
And not to the deceitful care of Burleigh.

PAULET.—I shall consider what is best to do.

MARY.—Sir, you shall know its import. In this letter
I beg a favor, a great favor of her—
That she herself will give me audience—she!
Whom I have never seen. I have been summon'd
Before a court of men, whom I can ne'er
Acknowledge as my peers—of men to whom
My heart denies its confidence. The Queen
Is of my family, my rank, my sex;
To her alone—a sister, queen, and woman—
Can I unfold my heart.

PAULET.—   Too oft, my Lady,
Have you intrusted both your fate and honor
To men less worthy your esteem than these.

MARY.—I, in the letter, beg another favor,
And surely nought but inhumanity
Can here reject my prayer. These many years
Have I, in prison, miss'd the church's comfort,
The blessing of the sacraments:—and she
Who robs me of my freedom and my crown,
Who seeks my very life, can never wish
To shut the gates of heaven upon my soul.

PAULET.—Whene'er you wish, the Dean shall wait upon
     you——

MARY [*interrupting him sharply*].—Talk to me not of Deans.
          I ask the aid
     Of one of my own church—a Catholic priest.

PAULET.—That is against the published laws of England.

MARY.—The laws of England are no rule for me.
I am not England's subject; I have ne'er
Consented to its laws, and will not bow
Before their cruel and despotic sway.
If 'tis your will, to the unheard-of rigor

Which I have borne, to add this new oppression,
I must submit to what your power ordains;—
Yet will I raise my voice in loud complaints.
I also wish a public notary,
And secretaries, to prepare my will—
My sorrows, and my prison's wretchedness
Prey on my life—my days, I fear, are number'd—
I feel that I am near the gates of death.

PAULET.—These serious contemplations well become you.

MARY.—And know I then, that some too ready hand
May not abridge this tedious work of sorrow?
I would indite my will, and make disposal
Of what belongs to me.

PAULET.—   This liberty
May be allow'd to you, for England's Queen
Will not enrich herself by plundering you.

MARY.—I have been parted from my faithful women,
And from my servants;—tell me, where are they?
What is their fate? I can indeed dispense
At present with their service, but my heart
Will feel rejoiced to know these faithful ones
Are not exposed to suff'ring and to want!

PAULET.—Your servants have been cared for; and again
You shall behold whate'er is taken from you:
And all shall be restored in proper season.   [Going.

MARY.—And will you leave my presence thus again,
And not relieve my fearful anxious heart
From the fell torments of uncertainty?
Thanks to the vigilance of your hateful spies,
I am divided from the world;—no voice
Can reach me through these prison-walls;—my fate
Lies in the hands of those who wish my ruin.
A month of dread suspense is pass'd already,
Since when the forty high commissioners
Surprised me in this castle, and erected,
With most unseemly haste, their dread tribunal;
They forced me, stunn'd, amaz'd, and unprepar'd,
Without an advocate, from memory,
Before their unexampled court, to answer
Their weighty charges artfully arranged.

—They came like ghosts—like ghosts they disappeared,
And since that day all mouths are clos'd to me.
In vain I seek to construe from your looks
Which hath prevail'd—my cause's innocence
And my friends' zeal—or my foes' cursed counsel.
O! break this silence—let me know the worst—
What I have still to fear, and what to hope.

PAULET.—Close your accounts with heaven.

MARY.—   From heaven I hope
For mercy, Sir;—and from my earthly judges
I hope, and still expect, the strictest justice.

PAULET.—Justice, depend upon it, will be done you.

MARY.—Is the suit ended, Sir?

PAULET.—   I cannot tell.

MARY.—Am I condemn'd?

PAULET.—   I cannot answer, Lady.

MARY.—Sir, a good work fears not the light of day.

PAULET.—The day will shine upon it, doubt it not.

MARY.—Despatch is here the fashion. Is it meant
The murderer shall surprise me, like the judges?

PAULET.—Still entertain that thought, and he will find you
Better prepared to meet your fate than they did.

MARY [*after a pause*].—Sir, nothing can surprise me, which
            a court,
Inspired by Burleigh's hate and Hatton's zeal,
Howe'er unjust, may venture to pronounce:—
But I have yet to learn, how far the Queen
Will dare in execution of the sentence.

PAULET.—The sovereigns of England have no fear
But for their conscience, and their parliament.
What justice hath decreed, her fearless hand
Will execute before th' assembled world.

Scene III.—The Same

*Mortimer enters, and without paying attention to the Queen,
                addresses Paulet.*

MORTIMER.—Uncle, you're sought for.
[*He retires in the same manner. The Queen remarks it, and
    turns towards Paulet, who is about to follow him.*

MARY.— Sir, one favor more:—
    If you have aught to say to me—from you
    I can bear much—I rev'rence your gray hairs—
    But cannot bear that young man's insolence;—
    Spare me in future his unmanner'd rudeness.
PAULET.—I prize him most for that which makes you hate
        him:—
    He is not, truly, one of those poor fools
    Who melt before a woman's treacherous tears.
    He has seen much—has been to Rheims and Paris,
    And brings us back his true old English heart.
    Lady, your cunning arts are lost on him.   [*Exit.*

Scene IV. —The Same

Mary, Kennedy.

KENNEDY.—And dares the ruffian venture to your face
    Such language!—O, 'tis hard—'tis past endurance.
MARY [*lost in reflection*].—In the fair moments of our former
        splendor
    We lent to flatt'rers a too willing ear;—
    It is but just, good Hannah, we should now
    Be forced to hear the bitter voice of censure.
KENNEDY.—So downcast, so depressed, my dearest Lady!
    You, who before so gay, so full of hope,
    Were used to comfort me in my distress?
    More gracious were the task to check your mirth
    Than chide your heavy sadness.
MARY.— Well I know him—
    It is the bleeding Darnley's royal shade,
    Rising in anger from his darksome grave:
    And never will he make his peace with me
    Until the measure of my woes be full.
KENNEDY.—What thoughts are these—
MARY.— Thou may'st forget it, Hannah:
    But I've a faithful mem'ry—'tis this day
    Another wretched anniversary
    Of that regretted, that unhappy deed—
    Which I must celebrate with fast and penance.

KENNEDY.—Dismiss at length in peace this evil spirit.
　　The penitence of many a heavy year,
　　Of many a suffering, has atoned the deed:
　　The church, which holds the key of absolution,
　　Pardons the crime, and heav'n itself 's appeas'd.
MARY.—This long atoned crime arises fresh
　　And bleeding from its lightly cover'd grave—
　　My husband's restless spirit seeks revenge—
　　No sacred bell can exorcise, no host
　　In priestly hands dismiss it to his tomb.
KENNEDY.—You did not murder him—'twas done by others.
MARY.—But it was known to me;—I suffer'd it,
　　And lured him with my smiles to death's embrace.
KENNEDY.—Your youth extenuates your guilt. You were
　　Of tender years.
MARY.—　　　　　　　So tender, yet I drew
　　This heavy guilt upon my youthful head.
KENNEDY.—You were provok'd by direst injuries,
　　And by the rude presumption of the man,
　　Whom out of darkness, like the hand of heav'n,
　　Your love drew forth, and raised above all others;
　　Whom through your bridal chamber you conducted
　　Up to your throne, and with your lovely self,
　　And your hereditary crown, distinguish'd:—
　　Your work was his existence, and your grace
　　Bedew'd him like the gentle rains of heav'n.
　　Could he forget, that his so splendid lot
　　Was the creation of your gen'rous love?
　　Yet did he, worthless as he was, forget it.
　　With base suspicions, and with brutal manners,
　　He wearied your affections, and became
　　An object to you of deserv'd disgust:—
　　Th' illusion, which till now had overcast
　　Your judgment, vanish'd; angrily you fled
　　His foul embrace, and gave him up to scorn.
　　And did he seek again to win your love?
　　Your favor? Did he e'er implore your pardon?
　　Or fall in deep repentance at your feet?
　　No; the base wretch defied you:—he, who was
　　Your bounty's creature, wish'd to play your king,

'(And strove, through fear, to force your inclination.)
Before your eyes he had your fav'rite singer,
Poor Rizzio, murder'd: you did but avenge
With blood, the bloody deed——

MARY.—   And bloodily,
I fear, too soon 'twill be aveng'd on me:—
You seek to comfort me, and you condemn me.

KENNEDY.—You were, when you consented to this deed,
No more yourself—belong'd not to yourself—
The madness of a frantic love possess'd you,
And bound you to a terrible seducer,
The wretched Bothwell. That despotic man
Rul'd you with shameful, overbearing will,
And with his philters and his hellish arts
Inflamed your passions.

MARY.—   All the arts he used
Were man's superior strength, and woman's weakness.

KENNEDY.—No, no, I say. The most pernicious spirits
Of hell he must have summoned to his aid,
To cast this mist before your waking senses.
Your ear no more was open to the voice
Of friendly warning, and your eyes were shut
To decency; soft female bashfulness
Deserted you; those cheeks, which were before
The seat of virtuous blushing modesty,
Glow'd with the flames of unrestrain'd desire;
You cast away the veil of secrecy,
And the flagitious daring of the man
O'ercame your natural coyness: you expos'd
Your shame, unblushingly, to public gaze:
You let the murd'rer, whom the people follow'd
With curses, through the streets of Edinburgh,
Before you bear the royal sword of Scotland
In triumph. You begirt your parliament
With armed bands; and by this shameless farce,
There, in the very temple of great Justice,
You forc'd the judges of the land to clear
The murderer of his guilt. You went still farther—
O God!

MARY.—   Conclude—nay, pause not—say for this
I gave my hand in marriage at the altar.

KENNEDY.—O let an everlasting silence veil
    That dreadful deed: the heart revolts at it,
    A crime to stain the darkest criminal!
    Yet you are no such lost one, that I know.
    I nurs'd your youth myself—your heart is fram'd
    For tender softness: 'tis alive to shame,
    And all your fault is thoughtless levity.
    Yes, I repeat it, there are evil spirits,
    Who sudden fix in man's unguarded breast
    Their fatal residence, and there delight
    To act their dev'lish deeds; then hurry back
    Unto their native hell, and leave behind
    Remorse and horror in the poison'd bosom.
    Since this misdeed, which blackens thus your life,
    You have done nothing ill; your conduct has
    Been pure; myself can witness your amendment.
    Take courage, then; with your own heart make peace.
    Whatever cause you have for penitence,
    You are not guilty here. Nor England's Queen,
    Nor England's parliament can be your judge.
    Here might oppresses you: you may present
    Yourself before this self-created court
    With all the fortitude of innocence.
MARY.—I hear a step.
KENNEDY.—   It is the nephew—In.

Scene V.—The Same

Enter Mortimer, approaching cautiously.

MORTIMER [*to Kennedy*].—Step to the door, and keep a care-
    ful watch,
I have important business with the Queen.
MARY [*with dignity*].—I charge thee, Hannah, go not hence—
    remain.
MORTIMER.—Fear not, my gracious Lady—learn to know me.
                     [*He gives her a card.*
MARY [*she examines it and starts back astonished*].—Heav'ns!
    What is this?
MORTIMER [*to Kennedy*].—Retire, good Kennedy;
    See that my uncle comes not unawares.

MARY [*to Kennedy, who hesitates, and looks at the Queen inquiringly*].—Go in; do as he bids you.
> [*Kennedy retires with signs of wonder.*

Scene VI.—The Same

Mary, Mortimer.

MARY.—   From my uncle
   In France—the worthy Card'nal of Lorrain?
> [*She reads.*

" Confide in Mortimer, who brings you this;
  You have no truer, firmer friend in England."
> [*Looking at him with astonishment.*

Can I believe it? Is there no delusion
To cheat my senses? Do I find a friend
So near, when I conceiv'd myself abandon'd
By the whole world? And find that friend in you,
The nephew of my jailer, whom I thought
My most invet'rate enemy?

MORTIMER [*kneeling*].—   O pardon,
My gracious Liege, for the detested mask,
Which it has cost me pain enough to wear;
Yet through such means alone have I the pow'r
To see you, and to bring you help and rescue.

MARY.—Arise, Sir; you astonish me; I cannot
So suddenly emerge from the abyss
Of wretchedness to hope: let me conceive
This happiness, that I may credit it.

MORTIMER.—Our time is brief: each moment I expect
My uncle, whom a hated man attends:
Hear, then, before his terrible commission
Surprises you, how Heav'n prepares your rescue.

MARY.—You come, in token of its wondrous pow'r.

MORTIMER.—Allow me of myself to speak.

MARY.—   Say on.

MORTIMER.—I scarce, my Liege, had numbered twenty years,
Train'd in the path of strictest discipline,
And nurs'd in deadliest hate to Papacy,
When led by irresistible desire

For foreign travel, I resolv'd to leave
My country and its puritanic faith
Far, far behind me: soon with rapid speed
I flew through France, and bent my eager course
On to the plains of far-famed Italy.
'Twas then the time of the great Jubilee:—
And crowds of palmers fill'd the public roads;
Each image was adorn'd with garlands; 'twas
As if all human-kind were wand'ring forth
In pilgrimage towards the heav'nly kingdom.
The tide of the believing multitude
Bore me too onward with resistless force,
Into the streets of Rome. What was my wonder,
As the magnificence of stately columns
Rush'd on my sight! the vast triumphal arches,
The Colosseum's grandeur, with amazement
Struck my admiring senses; the sublime
Creative spirit held my soul a prisoner
In the fair world of wonders it had fram'd.
I ne'er had felt the power of art till now.
The Church that rear'd me hates the charms of sense;
It tolerates no image, it adores
But the unseen, the incorporeal word.
What were my feelings, then, as I approach'd
The threshold of the churches, and within,
Heard heav'nly music floating in the air:
While from the walls and high-wrought roofs there
    stream'd
Crowds of celestial forms in endless train—
When the Most High, Most Glorious, pervaded
My captivated sense in real presence!
And when I saw the great and godlike visions,
The Salutation, the Nativity,
The Holy Mother, and the Trinity's
Descent, the luminous Transfiguration:
And last the holy Pontiff, clad in all
The glory of his office, bless the people!
O! what is all the pomp of gold and jewels
With which the kings of earth adorn themselves?
He is alone surrounded by the Godhead;

His mansion is in truth an heav'nly kingdom,
For not of earthly moulding are these forms!
MARY.—O spare me, Sir! No further. Spread no more
Life's verdant carpet out before my eyes,
Remember I am wretched, and a prisoner.
MORTIMER.—I was a prisoner too, my Queen; but swift
My prison-gates flew open, when at once
My spirit felt its liberty, and hail'd
The smiling dawn of life. I learn'd to burst
Each narrow prejudice of education,
To crown my brows with never-fading wreaths,
And mix my joy with the rejoicing crowd.
Full many noble Scots, who saw my zeal,
Encourag'd me, and with the gallant French
They kindly led me to your princely uncle,
The Cardinal of Guise. O what a man!
How firm, how clear, how manly, and how great!
Born to control the human mind at will!
The very model of a royal priest;
A ruler of the Church without an equal!
MARY.—You've seen him then—the much lov'd, honor'd man,
Who was the guardian of my tender years
O speak of him! Does he remember me?
Does fortune favor him? And prospers still
His life? And does he still majestic stand,
A very rock and pillar of the Church?
MORTIMER.—The holy man descended from his height,
And deign'd to teach me the important creed
Of the true Church, and dissipate my doubts.
He show'd me, how the glimm'ring light of reason
Serves but to lead us to eternal error:
That what the heart is call'd on to believe,
The eye must see: that he who rules the Church
Must needs be visible; and that the Spirit
Of truth inspir'd the Councils of the Fathers.
How vanish'd, then, the fond imaginings
And weak conceptions of my childish soul
Before his conquering judgment, and the soft
Persuasion of his tongue! So I return'd
Back to the bosom of the holy Church,
And at his feet abjur'd my heresies.

MARY.—Then of those happy thousands, you are one,
    Whom he, with his celestial eloquence,
    Like the immortal preacher of the mount,
    Has turn'd, and led to everlasting joy!

MORTIMER.—The duties of his office call'd him soon
    To France, and I was sent by him to Rheims,
    Where, by the Jesuits' anxious labor, priests
    Are train'd to preach our holy faith in England.
    There, 'mongst the Scots, I found the noble Morgan,
    And your true Lesley, Ross's learned bishop,
    Who pass in France their joyless days of exile.
    I join'd with heartfelt zeal these worthy men,
    And fortified my faith. As I one day
    Roam'd through the Bishop's dwelling, I was struck
    With a fair female portrait; it was full
    Of touching, wond'rous charms; with magic might
    It mov'd my inmost soul, and there I stood
    Speechless, and overmaster'd by my feeling.
    "Well," cried the Bishop, "may you linger thus
    In deep emotion near this lovely face!
    For the most beautiful of womankind,
    Is also matchless in calamity.
    She is a prisoner for our holy faith,
    And in your native land, alas! she suffers."
            [Mary is in great agitation.—He pauses.

MARY.—Excellent man! All is not lost, indeed,
    While such a friend remains in my misfortunes!

MORTIMER.—Then he began, with moving eloquence,
    To paint the suff'rings of your martyrdom;
    He showed me, then, your lofty pedigree,
    And your descent from Tudor's royal House.
    He prov'd to me that you alone have right
    To reign in England, not this upstart Queen,
    The base-born fruit of an adult'rous bed,
    Whom Henry's self rejected as a bastard.
    He from my eyes remov'd delusion's mist,
    And taught me to lament you as a victim,
    To honor you as my true Queen, whom I,
    Deceiv'd, like thousands of my noble fellows,
    Had ever hated as my country's foe.

I would not trust his evidence alone;
I question'd learned doctors; I consulted
The most authentic books of heraldry;
And every man of knowledge, whom I ask'd,
Confirm'd to me your claim's validity.
And now I know that your undoubted right
To England's throne has been your only wrong.
This realm is justly yours by heritage,
In which you innocently pine as pris'ner.
MARY.—O this unhappy right!—'tis this alone
    Which is the source of all my sufferings.
MORTIMER.—Just at this time the tidings reached my ears,
    Of your removal from old Talbot's charge,
And your committal to my uncle's care.
It seem'd to me that this disposal mark'd
The wondrous, outstretch'd hand of fav'ring Heaven:
It seem'd to be a loud decree of fate,
That it had chosen me to rescue you.
My friends concur with me; the Cardinal
Bestows on me his counsel and his blessing,
And tutors me in the hard task of feigning.
The plan in haste digested, I commenced
My journey homewards, and ten days ago
On England's shores I landed.—Oh, my Queen,
                        [He pauses.
I saw then, not your picture, but yourself—
Oh what a treasure do these walls enclose!
No prison this, but the abode of gods,
More splendid far than England's royal Court.
Happy, thrice happy he, whose envied lot
Permits to breathe the self-same air with you!
It is a prudent policy in her
To bury you so deep! All England's youth
Would rise at once in general mutiny,
And not a sword lie quiet in its sheath:
Rebellion would uprear its giant head,
Through all this peaceful isle, if Britons once
Beheld their captive Queen.
MARY.—   'Twere well with her
    If ev'ry Briton saw her with your eyes!
      VOL. II.—17

MORTIMER.—Were each, like me, a witness of your wrongs,
    Your meekness, and the noble fortitude
    With which you suffer these indignities—
    Would you not then emerge from all these trials
    Like a true Queen? Your prison's infamy,
    Hath it despoil'd your beauty of its charms?
    You are depriv'd of all that graces life,
    Yet round you life and light eternal beam.
    Ne'er on this threshold can I set my foot,
    That my poor heart with anguish is not torn,
    Not ravish'd with delight at gazing on you.
    Yet fearfully the fatal time draws near,
    And danger hourly growing presses on.
    I can delay no longer—can no more
    Conceal the dreadful news.—

MARY.—   My sentence then!
    Is it pronounc'd? Speak freely—I can bear it.

MORTIMER.—It is pronounc'd! The two-and-forty judges
    Have giv'n the verdict, " guilty "; and the Houses
    Of Lords and Commons, with the citizens
    Of London, eagerly and urgently
    Demand the execution of the sentence:—
    The Queen alone still craftily delays,
    That she may be constrain'd to yield, but not
    From feelings of humanity or mercy.

MARY [*collected*].—Sir, I am not surpris'd, nor terrified;
    I have been long prepar'd for such a message.
    Too well I know my judges. After all
    Their cruel treatment I can well conceive
    They dare not now restore my liberty.
    I know their aim: they mean to keep me here
    In everlasting bondage, and to bury,
    In the sepulchral darkness of my prison,
    My vengeance with me, and my rightful claims.

MORTIMER.—O! no, my gracious Queen;—they stop not there:
    Oppression will not be content to do
    Its work by halves:—as long as e'er you live,
    Distrust and fear will haunt the English Queen.
    No dungeon can inter you deep enough;
    Your death alone can make her throne secure.

MARY.—Will she then dare, regardless of the shame,
    Lay my crown'd head upon the fatal block?
MORTIMER.—She will most surely dare it, doubt it not.
MARY.—And can she thus roll in the very dust,
    Her own, and ev'ry monarch's majesty?
MORTIMER.—She thinks on nothing now but present danger,
    Nor looks to that which is so far removed.
MARY.—And fears she not the dread revenge of France?
MORTIMER.—With France she makes an everlasting peace;
    And gives to Anjou's Duke her throne and hand.
MARY.—Will not the King of Spain rise up in arms?
MORTIMER.—She fears not a collected world in arms,
    If with her people she remain at peace.
MARY.—Were this a spectacle for British eyes?
MORTIMER.—This land, my Queen, has, in these latter days,
    Seen many a royal woman from the throne
    Descend, and mount the scaffold:—her own mother
    And Cath'rine Howard trod this fatal path;
    And was not Lady Grey a crowned head?
MARY [*after a pause*].—No, Mortimer, vain fears have blinded
       you;
    'Tis but the honest care of your true heart,
    Which conjures up these empty apprehensions.
    It is not, Sir, the scaffold that I fear:
    There are so many still and secret means,
    By which her Majesty of England may
    Set all my claims to rest. O, trust me, ere
    An executioner is found for me,
    Assassins will be hir'd to do their work.
    'Tis that which makes me tremble, Mortimer:
    I never lift the goblet to my lips
    Without an inward shudd'ring, lest the draught
    May have been mingled by my sister's love.
MORTIMER.—No:—neither open nor disguised murder
    Shall e'er prevail against you:—fear no more;
    All is prepar'd;—twelve nobles of the land
    Are my confed'rates, and have pledg'd to-day,
    Upon the Sacrament, their faith to free you,
    With dauntless arm, from this captivity.
    Count Aubespine, the French Ambassador,

   Knows of our plot, and offers his assistance:
   'Tis in his palace that we hold our meetings.
MARY.—You make me tremble, Sir, but not for joy;
   An evil boding penetrates my heart.
   Know you, then, what you risk? Are you not scar'd
   By Babington and Tichburn's bloody heads,
   Set up as warnings upon London's bridge?
   Nor by the ruin of those many victims
   Who have, in such attempts, found certain death,
   And only made my chains the heavier?
   Fly hence, deluded, most unhappy youth!
   Fly, if there yet be time for you, before
   That crafty spy, Lord Burleigh, track your schemes,
   And mix his traitors in your secret plots.
   Fly hence:—as yet, success hath never smil'd
   On Mary Stuart's champions.
MORTIMER.—   I'm not scar'd
   By Babington and Tichburn's bloody heads,
   Set up as warnings upon London's bridge;
   Nor by the ruin of those many victims
   Who have, in such attempts, found certain death:
   They also found therein immortal honor,
   And death, in rescuing you, is dearest bliss.
MARY.—It is in vain: nor force nor guile can save me:—
   My enemies are watchful, and the pow'r
   Is in their hands. It is not Paulet only
   And his dependent host; all England guards
   My prison gates; Elizabeth's free will
   Alone can open them.
MORTIMER.—   Expect not that.
MARY.—One man alone on earth can open them.
MORTIMER.—O! let me know his name!
MARY.—   Lord Leicester.
MORTIMER.—   He!
        [*Starts back in wonder.*
   The Earl of Leicester! Your most bloody foe,
   The fav'rite of Elizabeth!—through him——
MARY.—If I am to be sav'd at all, 'twill be
   Through him, and him alone. Go to him, Sir;
   Freely confide in him: and, as a proof

You come from me, present this paper to him.
[*She takes a paper from her bosom; Mortimer draws back,
and hesitates to take it.*
It doth contain my portrait:—take it, Sir;
I've borne it long about me: but your uncle's
Close watchfulness has cut me off from all
Communication with him;—you were sent
By my good angel.   [*He takes it.*
MORTIMER.—   O, my Queen! explain
This mystery.
MARY.—   Lord Leicester will resolve it.
Confide in him, and he'll confide in you.
Who comes?
KENNEDY [*entering hastily*].—'Tis Paulet; and he brings with
him
A nobleman from court.
MORTIMER.—   It is Lord Burleigh.
Collect yourself, my Queen, and strive to hear
The news he brings, with equanimity.
[*He retires through a side door, and Kennedy follows him.*

Scene VII.—The Same

Enter Lord Burleigh and Paulet.

PAULET [*to Mary*].—You wish'd to-day, assurance of your
fate;
My Lord of Burleigh brings it to you now;
Hear it with resignation, as beseems you.
MARY.—I hope with dignity, as it becomes
My innocence, and my exalted station.
BURLEIGH.—I come deputed from the court of justice.
MARY.—Lord Burleigh lends that court his willing tongue,
Which was already guided by his spirit.
PAULET.—You speak as if no stranger to the sentence.
MARY.—Lord Burleigh brings it; therefore do I know it.
PAULET.—It would become you better, Lady Stuart,
To listen less to hatred.
MARY.—   I but name
My enemy: I said not that I hate him.
But to the matter, Sir.

BURLEIGH.—   You have acknowledg'd
    The jurisdiction of the two-and-forty.

MARY.—My Lord, excuse me, if I am oblig'd
    So soon to interrupt you. I acknowledg'd,
    Say you, the competence of the commission?
    I never have acknowledg'd it, my Lord;
    How could I so? I could not give away
    My own prerogative, th' intrusted rights
    Of my own people, the inheritance
    Of my own son, and ev'ry monarch's honor
    The very laws of England say I could not.
    It is enacted by the English laws,
    That ev'ry one who stands arraign'd of crime
    Shall plead before a jury of his equals:
    Who is my equal in this high commission?
    Kings only are my peers.

BURLEIGH.—   But yet you heard
    The points of accusation, answer'd them
    Before the court——

MARY.—   'Tis true, I was deceiv'd
    By Hatton's crafty counsel:—he advis'd me,
    For my own honor, and in confidence
    In my good cause, and my most strong defence,
    To listen to the points of accusation,
    And prove their falsehood. This, my Lord, I did
    From personal respect for the lords' names,
    Not their usurped charge, which I disclaim.

BURLEIGH.—Acknowledge you the court, or not, that is
    Only a point of mere formality,
    Which cannot here arrest the course of justice.
    You breathe the air of England; you enjoy
    The law's protection, and its benefits;
    You therefore are its subject.

MARY.—   Sir, I breathe
    The air within an English prison walls:—
    Is that to live in England; to enjoy
    Protection from its laws? I scarcely know
    And never have I pledg'd my faith to keep them.
    I am no member of this realm; I am
    An independent, and a foreign Queen,

BURLEIGH.—And do you think that the mere name of Queen
  Can serve you as a charter to foment
  In other countries, with impunity,
  This bloody discord? Where would be the state's
  Security, if the stern sword of justice
  Could not as freely smite the guilty brow
  Of the imperial stranger, as the beggar's?

MARY.—I do not wish to be exempt from judgment,
  It is the judges only I disclaim.

BURLEIGH.—The judges? How now, Madam! Are they then
  Base wretches, snatch'd at hazard from the crowd?
  Vile wranglers, that make sale of truth and justice;
  Oppression's willing hirelings, and its tools?
  Are they not all the foremost of this land,
  Too independent to be else than honest,
  And too exalted not to soar above
  The fear of Kings, or base servility?
  Are they not those, who rule a gen'rous people
  In liberty and justice; men, whose names
  I need but mention, to dispel each doubt,
  Each mean suspicion which is rais'd against them?
  Stands not the rev'rend Primate at their head,
  The pious shepherd of his faithful people,
  The learned Talbot, Keeper of the Seals,
  And Howard, who commands our conqu'ring fleets?
  Say, then, could England's sovereign do more
  Than, out of all the monarchy, elect
  The very noblest, and appoint them judges
  In this great suit? And were it probable
  That party hatred could corrupt one heart;
  Can forty chosen men unite to speak
  A sentence just as passion gives command?

MARY [*after a short pause*].—I am struck dumb by that
  tongue's eloquence,
  Which ever was so ominous to me.
  And how shall I, a weak, untutor'd woman,
  Cope with so subtle, learn'd an orator?
  Yes, truly; were these lords as you describe them,
  I must be mute; my cause were lost indeed,
  Beyond all hope, if they pronounc'd me guilty.

But, Sir, these names, which you are pleas'd to praise,
These very men, whose weight you think will crush me,
I see performing in the history
Of these dominions, very different parts:
I see this high nobility of England,
This grave majestic senate of the realm,
Like to an eastern monarch's vilest slaves,
Flatter my uncle Henry's sultan fancies:
I see this noble rev'rend House of Lords,
Venal alike with the corrupted Commons,
Make statutes and annul them, ratify
A marriage and dissolve it, as the voice
Of power commands: to-day it disinherits,
And brands the royal daughters of the realm
With the vile name of bastards, and to-morrow
Crowns them as queens, and leads them to the throne.
I see them in four reigns, with pliant conscience,
Four times abjure their faith; renounce the Pope
With Henry, yet retain the old belief;
Reform themselves with Edward; hear the mass
Again with Mary; with Elizabeth,
Who governs now, reform themselves again.

BURLEIGH.—You say you are not vers'd in England's laws.
You seem well read, methinks, in her disasters.

MARY.—And these men are my judges?

[*As Lord Burleigh seems to wish to speak.*

My Lord Treas'rer,
Tow'rds you I will be just, be you but just
To me.—'Tis said, that you consult with zeal
The good of England, and of England's Queen;
Are honest, watchful, indefatigable:
I will believe it. Not your private ends,
Your Sovereign and your country's weal alone,
Inspire your counsels and direct your deeds.
Therefore, my noble Lord, you should the more
Distrust your heart; should see that you mistake not
The welfare of the government, for justice.
I do not doubt, besides yourself, there are
Among my judges many upright men:
But they are Protestants, are eager all

For England's quiet, and they sit in judgment
On me, the Queen of Scotland, and the Papist.
It is an ancient saying, that the Scots
And English to each other are unjust;
And hence the rightful custom, that a Scot
Against an Englishman, or Englishman
Against a Scot, cannot be heard in judgment.
Necessity prescrib'd this cautious law;
Deep policy oft lies in ancient customs:
My Lord, we must respect them. Nature cast
Into the ocean these two fiery nations
Upon this plank, and she divided it
Unequally, and bade them fight for it.
The narrow bed of Tweed alone divides
These daring spirits; often hath the blood
Of the contending parties dyed its waves.
Threat'ning, and sword in hand, these thousand years,
From both its banks they watch their rival's motions,
Most vigilant and true confederates,
With ev'ry en'my of the neighbor state.
No foe oppresses England, but the Scot
Becomes his firm ally; no civil war
Inflames the towns of Scotland, but the English
Add fuel to the fire: this raging hate
Will never be extinguish'd till, at last,
One parliament in concord shall unite them,
One common sceptre rule throughout the isle.

BURLEIGH.—And from a Stuart, then, should England hope
    This happiness?

MARY.—   Oh! why should I deny it?
Yes, I confess, I cherish'd the fond hope,
I thought myself the happy instrument
To join in freedom, 'neath the olive's shade,
Two gen'rous realms in lasting happiness!
I little thought I should become the victim
Of their old hate, their long-liv'd jealousy,
And the sad flames of that unhappy strife,
I hop'd at last to smother, and forever:
And, as my ancestor, great Richmond, join'd
The rival roses after bloody contest,
To join in peace the Scotch and English crowns.

BURLEIGH.—An evil way you took to this good end,
  To set the realm on fire, and through the flames
  Of civil war to strive to mount the throne.
MARY.—I wish'd not that:—I wish'd it not, by Heaven!
  When did I strive at that?—Where are your proofs?
BURLEIGH.—I came not hither to dispute; your cause
  Is no more subject to a war of words.
  The great majority of forty voices
  Hath found that you have contraven'd the law
  Last year enacted, and have now incurr'd
  Its penalty.   [*Producing the verdict.*
MARY.—   Upon this statute, then,
  My Lord, is built the verdict of my judges?
BURLEIGH [*reading*].—Last year it was enacted, " If a plot
  Henceforth should rise in England, in the name
  Or for the benefit of any claimant
  To England's crown, that justice should be done
  On such pretender, and the guilty party
  Be prosecuted unto death." Now, since
  It has been prov'd——
MARY.—   Lord Burleigh, I can well
  Imagine that a law expressly aim'd
  At me, and fram'd to compass my destruction
  May to my prejudice be used. O! woe
  To the unhappy victim, when the tongue,
  That frames the law, shall execute the sentence.
  Can you deny it, Sir, that this same statute
  Was made for my destruction, and nought else?
BURLEIGH.—It should have acted as a warning to you:
  By your imprudence it became a snare.
  You saw the precipice which yawn'd before you;
  Yet, truly warn'd, you plung'd into the deep.
  With Babington, the traitor, and his bands
  Of murderous companions, were you leagued.
  You knew of all, and from your prison led
  Their treasonous plottings with a deep-laid plan.
MARY.—When did I that, my Lord? Let them produce
  The documents.
BURLEIGH.—   You have already seen them:
  They were, before the court, presented to you.

MARY.—Mere copies written by another hand;
    Show me the proof that they were dictated
    By me, that they proceeded from my lips,
    And in those very terms in which you read them.
BURLEIGH.—Before his execution, Babington
    Confess'd they were the same which he receiv'd.
MARY.—Why was he in his lifetime not produc'd
    Before my face? Why was he then despatch'd
    So quickly, that he could not be confronted
    With her whom he accus'd?
BURLEIGH.—   Besides, my Lady,
    Your secretaries, Curl and Nau, declare
    On oath, they are the very self-same letters
    Which, from your lips, they faithfully transcrib'd.
MARY.—And on my menials' testimony, then,
    I am condemn'd; upon the word of those
    Who have betray'd me, me, their rightful Queen
    Who in that very moment, when they came
    As witnesses against me, broke their faith!
BURLEIGH.—You said yourself, you held your countryman
    To be an upright conscientious man.
MARY.—I thought him such; but 'tis the hour of danger
    Alone, which tries the virtue of a man,
    He ever was an honest man, but weak
    In understanding; and his subtle comrade,
    Whose faith, observe, I never answer'd for,
    Might easily seduce him to write down
    More than he should; the rack may have compell'd him
    To say and to confess more than he knew.
    He hop'd to save himself by this false witness,
    And thought it could not injure *me*—a Queen.
BURLEIGH.—The oath he swore was free and unconstrain'd.
MARY.—But not before my face! How now, my lord,
    The witnesses you name are still alive,
    Let them appear against me, face to face!
    And there repeat what they have testified!
    Why am I then denied that privilege,
    That right, which e'en the murderer enjoys?
    I know from Talbot's mouth, my former keeper,
    That in this reign a statute has been pass'd,

Which orders that the plaintiff be confronted
With the defendant; is it so, good Paulet?
I e'er have known you as an honest man,
Now prove it to me; tell me, on your conscience,
If such a law exist, or not, in England?

PAULET.—Madam, there does: that is the law in England.
I must declare the truth.

MARY.— Well then, my Lord,
If I am treated by the law of England
So hardly, when that law oppresses me,
Say, why avoid this self-same country's law,
When 'tis for my advantage? Answer me;
Why was not Babington confronted with me?
Why not my servants, who are both alive?

BURLEIGH.—Be not so hasty, Lady; 'tis not only
Your plot with Babington——

MARY.— 'Tis that alone
Which arms the law against me; that alone
From which I am call'd upon to clear myself.
Stick to the point, my Lord; evade it not.

BURLEIGH.—It has been prov'd that you have corresponded
With the Ambassador of Spain, Mendoza——

MARY.—Stick to the point, my Lord.

BURLEIGH.— That you have form'd
Conspiracies to overturn the fix'd
Religion of the realm; that you have call'd
Into this kingdom foreign pow'rs, and rous'd
All kings in Europe to a war with England.

MARY.—And were it so, my Lord—though I deny it—
But e'en suppose it were so: I am kept
Imprison'd here against all laws of nations.
I came not into England sword in hand;
I came a suppliant; and at the hands
Of my imperial kinswoman, I claim'd
The sacred rights of hospitality.
When power seized upon me, and prepared
To rivet fetters, where I hop'd protection.
Say, is my conscience bound, then, to this realm?
What are the duties that I owe to England?
I should but exercise a sacred right,

Deriv'd from sad necessity, if I
Warr'd with these bonds, encounter'd might with might,
Roused and incited ev'ry state in Europe,
For my protection, to unite in arms.
Whatever in a rightful war is just
And loyal, 'tis my right to exercise:
Murder alone, the secret bloody deed,
My conscience and my pride alike forbid.
Murder would stain me, would dishonor me:
Dishonor me, my Lord!—but not condemn me,
Nor subject me to England's courts of law:
For 'tis not justice, but mere violence,
Which is the question 'tween myself and England.

BURLEIGH [*significantly*].—Talk not, my Lady, of the dreadful right
    Of pow'r: 'tis seldom on the pris'ner's side.

MARY.—I am weak; she is the mighty one:
    'Tis well, my Lord; let her then use her pow'r;
    Let her destroy me: let me bleed, that she
    May live secure: but let her then confess
    That she hath exercised her pow'r alone,
    And not contaminate the name of justice.
    Let her not borrow, from the laws, the sword
    To rid her of her hated enemy:
    Let her not clothe, in this religious garb,
    The bloody daring of licentious might:
    Let not these juggling tricks deceive the world.—
                        [*Returning the sentence.*
    Though she may murder me, she cannot judge me:—
    Let her no longer strive to join the fruits
    Of vice with virtue's fair and angel show;
    But let her dare to seem the thing she is.   [*Exit.*

Scene VIII.—The Same

Burleigh, Paulet.

BURLEIGH.—She scorns us, she defies us! will defy us,
    Ev'n at the scaffold's foot. This haughty heart
    Is not to be subdued. Say, did the sentence
    Surprise her? Did you see her shed one tear,

Or even change her color? She disdains
To make appeal to our compassion. Well
She knows the wav'ring mind of England's Queen.
Our apprehensions make her bold.
PAULET.   My Lord,
    Take the pretext away which buoys it up,
    And you shall see this proud defiance fail
    That very moment. I must say, my Lord,
    Irregularities have been allowed
    In these proceedings; Babington and Ballard
    Should have been brought, with her two secretaries,
    Before her, face to face.
BURLEIGH.—   No, Paulet, no!
    That was not to be risk'd; her influence
    Upon the human heart is too supreme;
    Too strong the female empire of her tears.
    Her secretary, Curl, if brought before her,
    And call'd upon to speak the weighty word
    On which her life depends, would straight shrink back
    And fearfully revoke his own confession.
PAULET.—Then England's enemies will fill the world
    With evil rumors; and the formal pomp
    Of these proceedings, to the minds of all,
    Will only signalize an act of outrage.
BURLEIGH.—That is the greatest torment of our Queen,
    (That she can never 'scape the blame. O God!)
    Had but this lovely mischief died before
    She set her faithless foot on English ground!
PAULET.—Amen, say I!
BURLEIGH.—   Had sickness but consum'd her!
PAULET.—England had been secur'd from much misfortune.
BURLEIGH.—And yet, if she had died in nature's course,
    The world would still have call'd us murderers.
PAULET.—'Tis true, the world will think, despite of us,
    Whate'er it list.
BURLEIGH.—   Yet could it not be prov'd?
    And it would make less noise.
PAULET.—   Why, let it make
    What noise it may. It is not clam'rous blame,
    'Tis righteous censure only, which can wound.

BURLEIGH.—We know that holy justice cannot 'scape
　　　The voice of censure; and the public cry
　　　Is ever on the side of the unhappy:
　　　Envy pursues the laurell'd conqueror;
　　　The sword of justice, which adorns the man,
　　　Is hateful in a woman's hand; the world
　　　Will give no credit to a woman's justice,
　　　If woman be the victim. Vain that we,
　　　The judges, spoke what conscience dictated;
　　　She has the royal privilege of mercy;
　　　She *must* exert it: 'twere not to be borne,
　　　Should she let justice take its full career.
PAULET.—And therefore——
BURLEIGH.—   Therefore should she live? O! no,
　　　She must not live; it must not be. 'Tis this,
　　　Ev'n this, my friend, which so disturbs the Queen,
　　　And scares all slumber from her couch; I read
　　　Her soul's distracting contest in her eyes;
　　　She fears to speak her wishes, yet her looks,
　　　Her silent looks, significantly ask,
　" Is there not one amongst my many servants,
　　　To save me from this sad alternative?
　　　Either to tremble in eternal fear
　　　Upon my throne, or else to sacrifice
　　　A Queen of my own kindred on the block? "
PAULET.—'Tis even so; nor can it be avoided
BURLEIGH.— Well might it be avoided, thinks the Queen,
　　　If she had only more attentive servants.
PAULET.—How more attentive?
BURLEIGH.—   Such as could interpret
　　　A silent mandate.
PAULET.—   What? A silent mandate!
BURLEIGH.—Who, when a pois'nous adder is deliver'd
　　　Into their hands, would keep the treach'rous charge
　　　As if it were a sacred, precious jewel?
PAULET.—A precious jewel is the Queen's good name,
　　　And spotless reputation: good, my Lord,
　　　One cannot guard it with sufficient care.
BURLEIGH.—When, out of Shrewsb'ry's hand, the Queen of
　　　　　Scots

Was trusted to Sir Amias Paulet's care,
The meaning was——
PAULET.——   I hope to God, my Lord,
The meaning was, to give the weightiest charge
Into the purest hands: my Lord, my Lord!
By Heav'n, I had disdain'd this bailiff's office,
Had I not thought the service claim'd the care
Of the best man that England's realm can boast.
Let me not think I am indebted for it
To anything but my unblemish'd name.
BURLEIGH.—Spread the report, she wastes; grows sicker still,
And sicker; and expires at last in peace;
Thus will she perish in the world's rememb'rance,
And your good name is pure.
PAULET.——   But not my conscience.
BURLEIGH.—Though you refuse us, Sir, your own assistance,
You will not, sure, prevent another's hand.
PAULET.—No murd'rer's foot shall e'er approach her threshold,
Whilst she's protected by my household gods.
Her life's a sacred trust; to me the head
Of Queen Elizabeth is not more sacred.
Ye are the judges; judge, and break the staff;
And when 'tis time, then let the carpenter,
With axe and saw appear to build the scaffold,
My castle's portals shall be open to him,
The sheriff and the executioners:
Till then, she is intrusted to my care;
And, be assur'd, I will fulfil my trust,
She shall not do, nor suffer what's unjust.   [*Exeunt.*

ACT SECOND

Scene I.—London. Hall in Westminster Palace

The Earl of Kent and Sir William Davison, meeting.

DAVISON.—Is that my Lord of Kent? So soon return'd?
    Is then the tourney, the carousal over?
KENT.—How now? Were you not present at the tilt?
DAVISON.—My office kept me here.
KENT.—   Believe me, Sir,
    You've lost the fairest show which ever taste
    Devis'd, or graceful dignity perform'd:
    For beauty's virgin fortress was presented,
    As by Desire invested; the Earl Marshal,
    The Lord High Admiral, and ten other knights,
    Belonging to the Queen, defended it,
    And France's Cavaliers led the attack.
    A herald march'd before the gallant troop,
    And summon'd, in a madrigal, the fortress;
    And from the walls the Chancellor replied;
    And then th' artillery was play'd, and nosegays,
    Breathing delicious fragrance, were discharg'd
    From neat field-pieces; but in vain, the storm
    Was valiantly resisted, and Desire
    Was forc'd, unwillingly, to raise the siege.
DAVISON.—A sign of evil boding, good, my Lord,
    For the French suitors.
KENT.—   Why, you know that this
    Was but in sport; when the attack's in earnest,
    The fortress will, no doubt, capitulate.
DAVISON.—Ha! think you so? I never can believe it.
KENT.—The hardest article of all is now
    Adjusted, and acceded to by France;
    The Duke of Anjou is content to hold
    His holy worship in a private chapel,
    And openly he promises to honor
    And to protect the realm's establish'd faith.
    Had you but heard the people's joyful shouts

Where'er the tidings spread, for it has been
The country's constant fear the Queen might die,
Without immediate issue of her body;
And England bear again the Romish chains,
If Mary Stuart should ascend the throne.

DAVISON.—This fear appears superfluous; she goes
Into the bridal chamber; Mary Stuart
Enters the gates of death.

KENT.—   The Queen approaches.

Scene II.—The Same

Enter Elizabeth, led in by Leicester, Count Aubespine, Bellievre, Lords Shrewsbury and Burleigh, with other French and English gentlemen.

ELIZABETH [*to Aubespine*].—Count, I am sorry for these noblemen,
Whose gallant zeal hath brought them over sea
To visit these our shores, that they, with us,
Must miss the splendor of St. Germain's court.
Such pompous festivals of godlike state
I cannot furnish, as the royal court
Of France. A sober and contented people,
Which crowd around me with a thousand blessings,
Whene'er in public I present myself:
This is the spectacle which I can show,
And not without some pride, to foreign eyes.
The splendor of the noble dames who bloom
In Cath'rine's beauteous garden would, I know,
Eclipse myself, and my more modest merits.

AUBESPINE.—The court of England has one lady only
To show the wond'ring foreigner; but all
That charms our hearts in the accomplish'd sex,
Is seen united in her single person.

BELLIEVRE.—Great Majesty of England, suffer us
To take our leave, and to our royal master,
The Duke of Anjou, bring the happy news.
The hot impatience of his heart would not

Permit him to remain at Paris; he
At Amiens awaits the joyful tidings;
And thence to Calais reach his posts, to bring
With winged swiftness to his tranced ear
The sweet consent which, still we humbly hope,
Your royal lips will graciously pronounce.
ELIZABETH.—Press me no further now, Count Bellievre,
It is not now a time, I must repeat,
To kindle here the joyful marriage torch.
The heav'ns low'r black and heavy o'er this land;
And weeds of mourning would become me better
Than the magnificence of bridal robes.
A fatal blow is aim'd against my heart;
A blow which threatens to oppress my House.
BELLIEVRE.—We only ask your Majesty to promise
Your royal hand when brighter days shall come.
ELIZABETH.—Monarchs are but the slaves of their condition;
They dare not hear the dictates of their hearts.
My wish was ever to remain unmarried,
And I had plac'd my greatest pride in this,
That men hereafter on my tomb might read
"Here rests the virgin Queen." But my good sub-
         jects
Are not content that this should be: they think,
E'en now they often think, upon the time
When I shall be no more. 'Tis not enough
That blessings now are shower'd upon this land;
They ask a sacrifice for future welfare,
And I must offer up my liberty,
My virgin liberty, my greatest good,
To satisfy my people. Thus they'd force
A lord and master on me. 'Tis by this
I see that I am nothing but a woman
In their regard; and yet methought that I
Had govern'd like a man, and like a king.
Well know I that it is not serving God,
To quit the laws of nature; and that those
Who here have rul'd before me merit praise,
That they have op'd the cloister gates, and giv'n
Thousands of victims of ill-taught devotion;

Back to the duties of humanity.
But yet a Queen, who hath not spent her days
In fruitless, idle contemplation; who,
Without a murmur, indefatigably,
Performs the hardest of all duties; she
Should be exempted, from that natural law
Which doth ordain one half of human kind
Shall ever be subservient to the other.

AUBESPINE.—Great Queen, you have upon your throne done
      honor
To ev'ry virtue; nothing now remains,
But to the sex, whose greatest boast you are,
To be the leading star, and give the great
Example of its most consistent duties.
'Tis true, the man exists not who deserves
That you to him should sacrifice your freedom;
Yet if a hero's soul, descent, and rank,
And manly beauty can make mortal man
Deserving of this honor—

ELIZABETH.—   Without doubt,
My Lord Ambassador, a marriage union
With France's royal son would do me honor:
Yes, I acknowledge it without disguise,
If it must be, if I cannot prevent it,
If I must yield unto my people's prayers,
And much I fear they will o'erpower me,
I do not know, in Europe, any prince
To whom with less reluctance I would yield
My greatest treasure, my dear liberty.
Let this confession satisfy your master.

BELLIEVRE.—It gives the fairest hope, and yet it gives,
Nothing but hope; my master wishes more.

ELIZABETH.—What wishes he?
[*She takes a ring from her finger, and thoughtfully examines it.*
                    In this a Queen has not
One privilege above all other women.
This common token marks one common duty,
One common servitude; the ring denotes
Marriage; and 'tis of rings a chain is form'd.
Convey this present to his Highness; 'tis

As yet no chain, it binds me not as yet,
But out of it may grow a link to bind me.

BELLIEVRE [*kneeling*].—This present, in his name, upon my
    knees,
I do receive, great Queen, and press the kiss
Of homage on the hand of her who is
Henceforth my princess.

ELIZABETH [*to the Earl of Leicester, whom she, during the
last speeches, had continually regarded*].—By your
leave, my Lord.

[*She takes the blue riband from his neck,* and invests Bellievre
with it.*

Invest his Highness with this ornament,
As I invest you with it, and receive you
Into the duties of my gallant order.
And, *honi soit qui mal y pense.* Thus perish
All jealousy between our several realms,
And let the bond of confidence unite,
Henceforth, the crowns of Britain and of France.

BELLIEVRE.—Most sov'reign Queen, this is a day of joy;
O that it could be so for all, and no
Afflicted heart within this island mourn.
See! mercy beams upon thy radiant brow;
Let the reflection of its cheering light
Fall on a wretched princess, who concerns
Britain and France alike.

ELIZABETH.—   No further, Count!
Let us not mix two inconsistent things;
If France be truly anxious for my hand,
It must partake my interests, and renounce
Alliance with my foes.

AUBESPINE.—   In thine own eyes
Would she not seem to act unworthily,
If in this joyous treaty, she forgot
This hapless Queen, the widow of her king;
In whose behalf, her honor and her faith
Are bound to plead for grace.

ELIZABETH.—   Thus urged, I know
To rate this intercession at its worth;

---

* Till the time of Charles I, the Knights of the Garter wore the blue riband with
the George, about their necks, as they still do the collars, on great days.

France has discharged her duties as a friend,
I will fulfil my own as England's Queen.
[*She bows to the French Ambassadors, who, with the other
gentlemen, retire respectfully.*

Scene III.—The Same

*Enter Burleigh, Leicester, and Talbot.   The Queen takes her
seat.*

BURLEIGH.—Illustrious sovereign, thou crown'st to-day
        The fervent wishes of thy people: now
        We can rejoice in the propitious days
        Which thou bestow'st upon us; and we look
        No more with fear and trembling tow'rds the time
        Which, charg'd with storms, futurity presented.
        Now, but one only care disturbs this land;
        It is a sacrifice which every voice   .
        Demands; O! grant but this, and England's peace
        Will be establish'd now and evermore.
ELIZABETH.—What wish they still, my Lord? Speak.
BURLEIGH.—   They demand
        The Stuart's head.   If to thy people thou
        Wouldst now secure the precious boon of freedom,
        And the fair light of truth so dearly won,
        Then she must die: if we are not to live
        In endless terror for thy precious life,
        The enemy must fall: for well thou know'st,
        That all thy Britons are not true alike:
        Romish idolatry has still its friends
        In secret, in this island, who foment
        The hatred of our enemies.   Their hearts
        All turn towards this Stuart; they are leagu'd
        With the two plotting brothers of Lorrain,
        The foes invet'rate of thy house and name.
        'Gainst thee this raging faction hath declar'd
        A war of desolation, which they wage
        With the deceitful instruments of hell.
        At Rheims, the Cardinal Archbishop's see,
        There is the arsenal, from which they dart

These lightnings; there the school of regicide;
Thence, in a thousand shapes disguis'd, are sent
Their secret missionaries to this isle;
Their bold and daring zealots; for from thence,
Have we not seen the third assassin come?
And inexhausted is the direful breed
Of secret enemies in this abyss.
While in her castle sits, at Fotheringay,
The Até * of this everlasting war,
Who, with the torch of love, spreads flames around;
For her who sheds delusive hopes on all,
Youth dedicates itself to certain death;
To set her free is the pretence—the aim
Is to establish her upon the throne.
For this accursed House of Guise denies
Thy sacred right; and in their mouths thou art
A robber of the throne, whom chance has crown'd.
By them this thoughtless woman was deluded,
Proudly to style herself the Queen of England:
No peace can be with her, and with her house;
(Their hatred is too bloody, and their crimes
Too great;) thou must resolve to strike, or suffer;—
Her life is death to thee, her death thy life.

ELIZABETH.—My Lord, you bear a melancholy office.
I know the purity which guides your zeal,
The solid wisdom which informs your speech:
And yet I hate this wisdom, when it calls
For blood, I hate it in my inmost soul.
Think of a milder counsel—Good, my Lord
Of Shrewsbury, we crave your judgment here.

TALBOT.—(Desire you but to know, most gracious Queen,
What is for your advantage, I can add

---

* The picture of Até, the Goddess of mischief, we are acquainted with from Homer, Il. v. 91. 130. I. 501. She is a daughter of Jupiter, and eager to prejudice everyone, even the immortal gods. She counteracted Jupiter himself, on which account he seized her by her beautiful hair and hurled her from heaven to the earth, where she now, striding over the heads of men, excites them to evil, in order to involve them in calamity.—HERDER.
Shakespeare has, in Julius Cæsar, made a fine use of this image—

> " And Cæsar's spirit, ranging for revenge,
> With Até by his side, come hot from hell,
> Shall in these confines, with a monarch's voice,
> Cry havoc, and let slip the dogs of war."

There is no need of pointing out to the reader the beautiful propriety of introducing this evil spirit on this occasion.

Nothing to what my Lord High Treasurer
Has urged; then, for your welfare, let the sentence
Be now confirm'd—this much is prov'd already:
There is no surer method to avert
The danger from your head, and from the state.
Should you in this reject our true advice,
You can dismiss your council. We are plac'd
Here as your counsellors, but to consult
The welfare of this land, and with our knowledge,
And our experience, we are bound to serve you!
But in what's good and just, most gracious Queen
You have no need of counsellors, your conscience
Knows it full well, and it is written there.
Nay it were overstepping our commission
If we attempted to instruct you in it.)

ELIZABETH.—(Yet speak, my worthy Lord of Shrewsbury,
'Tis not our understanding fails alone,
Our heart too feels it wants some sage advice.)

TALBOT.—Well did you praise the upright zeal which fires
Lord Burleigh's loyal breast; my bosom too,
Although my tongue be not so eloquent,
Beats with no weaker, no less faithful pulse.
Long may you live, my Queen, to be the joy
Of your delighted people, to prolong
Peace and its envied blessings in this realm.
Ne'er hath this isle beheld such happy days
Since it was govern'd by its native kings.
O let it never buy its happiness
With its good name; at least, may Talbot's eyes
Be clos'd in death, e'er this shall come to pass.

ELIZABETH.—Forbid it, Heaven, that our good name be stain'd.

TALBOT.—Then must you find some other way than this
To save thy kingdom, for the sentence pass'd
Of death against the Stuart is unjust.
You cannot upon her pronounce a sentence,
Who is not subject to you.

ELIZABETH.—   Then, it seems,
My council and my parliament have err'd;
Each bench of justice in the land is wrong,
Which did, with one accord, admit this right.

TALBOT [*after a pause*].—The proof of justice lies not in the
 voice
Of numbers; England's not the world, nor is
Thy parliament the focus, which collects
The vast opinion of the human race.
This present England is no more the future,
Than 'tis the past; as inclination changes,
Thus ever ebbs and flows the unstable tide
Of public judgment. Say not then, that thou
Must act as stern necessity compels,
That thou must yield to the importunate
Petitions of thy people; ev'ry hour
Thou canst experience that thy will is free
Make trial, and declare, thou hatest blood,
And that thou wilt protect thy sister's life;
Show those who wish to give thee other counsels,
That here thy royal anger is not feign'd,
And thou shalt see how stern necessity
Can vanish, and what once was titled justice
Into injustice be converted: thou
Thyself must pass the sentence, thou alone:—
Trust not to this unsteady, trembling reed,
But hear the gracious dictates of thy heart.
God hath not planted rigor in the frame
Of woman; and the founders of this realm,
Who to the female hand have not denied
The reins of government, intend by this
To show that mercy, not severity,
Is the best virtue to adorn a crown.

ELIZABETH.—Lord Shrewsb'ry is a fervent advocate
For mine, and England's enemy; I must
Prefer those counsellors who wish my welfare.

TALBOT.—Her advocates have an invidious task!
None will, by speaking in her favor, dare
To meet thy anger: suffer, then, an old
And faithful counsellor (whom nought on earth
Can tempt, on the grave's brink) to exercise
The pious duty of humanity.
It never shall be said, that, in thy council,
Passion and interest could find a tongue,

While mercy's pleading voice alone was mute,
All circumstances have conspir'd against her;
Thou ne'er hast seen her face, and nothing speaks
Within thy breast for one that's stranger to thee.
I do not take the part of her misdeeds;
They say 'twas she who plann'd her husband's murder:
'Tis true that she espous'd his murderer.
A grievous crime, no doubt; but then it happen'd
In darksome days of trouble and dismay,
In the stern agony of civil war,
When she, a woman, helpless and hemm'd in
By a rude crowd of rebel vassals, sought
Protection in a powerful chieftain's arms.
God knows what arts were used to overcome her!
For woman is a weak and fragile thing.

ELIZABETH.—Woman's not weak; there are heroic souls
Among the sex; and, in my presence, Sir,
I do forbid to speak of woman's weakness.

TALBOT.—Misfortune was for thee a rigid school;
Thou wast not station'd on the sunny side
Of life; thou saw'st no throne, from far, before thee;
The grave was gaping for thee at thy feet.
At Woodstock, and in London's gloomy tower,
'Twas there the gracious father of this land
Taught thee to know thy duty, by misfortune.
No flatt'rer sought thee there: there learn'd thy soul,
Far from the noisy world and its distractions,
To commune with itself, to think apart,
And estimate the real goods of life.
No God protected this poor sufferer:
Transplanted in her early youth to France,
The Court of levity and thoughtless joys,
There, in the round of constant dissipation,
She never heard the earnest voice of truth;
She was deluded by the glare of vice,
And driven onward by the stream of ruin.
Hers was the vain possession of a face,
And she outshone all others of her sex
As far in beauty, as in noble birth.

ELIZABETH.—Collect yourself, my Lord of Shrewsbury;

Bethink you we are met in solemn council.
Those charms must surely be without compare
Which can engender, in an elder's blood,
Such fire. My Lord of Leicester, you alone
Are silent; does the subject which has made
Him eloquent, deprive you of your speech?

LEICESTER.—Amazement ties my tongue, my Queen, to think
That they should fill thy soul with such alarms,
And that the idle tales, which, in the streets
Of London, terrify the people's ears,
Should reach th' enlighten'd circle of thy council,
And gravely occupy our statesmen's minds.
Astonishment possesses me, I own,
To think this lackland Queen of Scotland, she
Who could not save her own poor throne, the jest
Of her own vassals, and her country's refuse,
Who in her fairest days of freedom, was
But thy despised puppet, should become
At once thy terror when a prisoner.
What, in Heaven's name, can make her formidable?
That she lays claim to England? that the Guises
Will not acknowledge thee as Queen? (Did then
Thy people's loyal fealty await
These Guises' approbation?) Can these Guises
With their objections, ever shake the right
Which birth hath given thee; which, with one consent
The votes of parliament have ratified?
And is not she, by Henry's will, pass'd o'er
In silence? Is it probable that England,
And yet so bless'd in the new light's enjoyment,
Should throw itself into this papist's arms?
From thee, the sov'reign it adores, desert
To Darnley's murderess? What will they then,
These restless men, who even in thy lifetime
Torment thee with a successor; who cannot
Dispose of thee in marriage soon enough
To rescue church and state from fancied peril?
Stand'st thou not blooming there in youthful prime
While each step leads her tow'rds th' expecting tomb?
By Heavens, I hope thou wilt full many a year

Walk o'er the Stuart's grave, and ne'er become
Thyself the instrument of her sad end.

BURLEIGH.—Lord Leicester hath not always held this tone.

LEICESTER.—'Tis true, I in the court of justice gave
My verdict for her death; here, in the council,
I may consistently speak otherwise:
Here, right is not the question, but advantage.
Is this a time to feel her power, when France,
Her only succor, has abandon'd her?
When thou preparest with thy hand to bless
The royal son of France, when the fair hope
Of a new, glorious stem of sovereigns
Begins again to blossom in this land?
Why hasten then her death? She's dead already.
Contempt and scorn are death to her; take heed
Lest ill tim'd pity call her into life.
'Tis therefore my advice to leave the sentence,
By which her life is forfeit, in full force.
Let her live on; but let her live beneath
The headsman's axe, and, from the very hour
One arm is lifted for her, let it fall.

ELIZABETH [rises].—My Lords, I now have heard your sev'ral
        thoughts,
And give my ardent thanks for this your zeal.
With God's assistance, who the hearts of kings
Illumines, I will weigh your arguments,
And choose what best my judgment shall approve.

                                    [To Burleigh.

(Lord Burleigh's honest fears, I know it well,
Are but the offspring of his faithful care;
But yet, Lord Leicester has most truly said,
There is no need of haste; our enemy
Hath lost already her most dangerous sting—
The mighty arm of France: the fear that she
Might quickly be the victim of their zeal
Will curb the blind impatience of her friends.)

Scene IV.—The Same

Enter Sir Amias Paulet and Mortimer.

ELIZABETH.—There's Sir Amias Paulet; noble Sir,
    What tidings bring you?
PAULET.—   Gracious Sovereign,
    My nephew, who but lately is return'd
    From foreign travel, kneels before thy feet,
    And offers thee his first and earliest homage.
    Grant him thy royal grace, and let him grow
    And flourish in the sunshine of thy favor.
MORTIMER [*kneeling on one knee*].—Long live my royal mis-
        tress! Happiness
    And glory form a crown to grace her brows!
ELIZABETH.—Arise, Sir Knight; and welcome here in Eng-
        land;
    You've made, I hear, the tour, have been in France
    And Rome, and tarried too some time at Rheims;
    Tell me what plots our enemies are hatching?
MORTIMER.—May God confound them all! And may the darts
    Which they shall aim against my Sovereign,
    Recoiling, strike their own perfidious breasts!
ELIZABETH.—Did you see Morgan, and the wily Bishop
    Of Ross?
MORTIMER.—   I saw, my Queen, all Scottish exiles
    Who forge at Rheims their plots against this realm.
    I stole into their confidence, in hopes
    To learn some hint of their conspiracies.
PAULET.—Private despatches they intrusted to him,
    In ciphers, for the Queen of Scots, which he,
    With loyal hand, hath given up to us.
ELIZABETH.—Say, what are then their latest plans of treason?
MORTIMER.—It struck them all as 'twere a thunderbolt,
    That France should leave them, and with England close
    This firm alliance; now they turn their hopes
    Tow'rds Spain——
ELIZABETH.—   This, Walsingham hath written us.
MORTIMER.—Besides, a bull, which from the Vatican
    Pope Sixtus lately levell'd at thy throne,

Arriv'd at Rheims, as I was leaving it:
With the next ship, we may expect it here.

LEICESTER.—England no more is frighten'd by such arms.

BURLEIGH.—They're always dangerous in bigots' hands.

ELIZABETH [*looking steadfastly at Mortimer*].—Your enemies
        have said, that you frequented
The schools at Rheims, and have abjur'd your faith.

MORTIMER.—So I pretended, that I must confess;
Such was my anxious wish to serve my Queen.

ELIZABETH [*to Paulet, who presents papers to her*].—What
        have you there?

PAULET.—   'Tis from the Queen of Scots.
'Tis a petition, and to thee addressed.

BURLEIGH [*hastily catching at it*].—Give me the paper.

PAULET [*giving it to the Queen*].—By your leave, my Lord
High Treasurer: the Lady order'd me
To bring it to her Majesty's own hands.
She says, I am her enemy; I am
The enemy of her offences only,
And that which is consistent with my duty
I will, and readily, oblige her in.

[*The Queen takes the letter: as she reads it, Mortimer and
Leicester speak some words in private.*

BURLEIGH [*to Paulet*].—What may the purport of the letter be?
Idle complaints, from which one ought to screen
The Queen's too tender heart.

PAULET.—   What it contains,
She did not hide from me; she asks a boon;
She begs to be admitted to the grace
Of speaking with the Queen.

BURLEIGH.—   It cannot be.

TALBOT.—Why not? Her supplication's not unjust.

BURLEIGH.—For her, the base encourager of murder;
Her, who hath thirsted for our sov'reign's blood,
The privilege to see the royal presence
Is forfeited: a faithful counsellor
Can never give this treacherous advice.

TALBOT.—And if the Queen is gracious, Sir, are you
The man to hinder pity's soft emotions?

BURLEIGH.—She is condemn'd to death: her head is laid

Beneath the axe, and it would ill become
The Queen to see a death-devoted head.
The sentence cannot have its execution
If the Queen's Majesty approaches her,
For pardon still attends the royal presence,
As sickness flies the health-dispensing hand.

ELIZABETH [*having read the letter, dries her tears*].—O! what
    is man! What is the bliss of earth!
To what extremities is she reduc'd
Who with such proud and splendid hopes began!
Who, call'd to sit on the most ancient throne
Of Christendom, misled by vain ambition,
Hop'd with a triple crown to deck her brows!
How is her language alter'd, since the time
When she assum'd the arms of England's crown,
And by the flatt'rers of her Court was styled
Sole monarch of the two Britannic isles!
Forgive me, Lords, my heart is cleft in twain,
Anguish possesses me, and my soul bleeds
To think that earthly goods are so unstable,
And that the dreadful fate which rules mankind
Should threaten mine own house, and scowl so near me

TALBOT.—O, Queen! the God of mercy hath inform'd
Your heart; O! hearken to this heav'nly guidance.
Most grievously, indeed, hath she aton'd
Her grievous crime, and it is time that now,
At last, her heavy penance have an end.
Stretch forth your hand, to raise this abject Queen,
And, like the luminous vision of an angel,
Descend into her jail's sepulchral night.

BURLEIGH.—Be steadfast, mighty Queen; let no emotion
Of seeming laudable humanity
Mislead thee; take not from thyself the pow'r
Of acting as necessity commands.
Thou canst not pardon her, thou canst not save her:
Then heap not on thyself the odious blame,
That thou, with cruel and contemptuous triumph,
Didst glut thyself with gazing on thy victim.

LEICESTER.—Let us, my Lords, remain within our bounds;
The Queen is wise, and doth not need our counsels,

To lead her to the most becoming choice.
This meeting of the Queens hath nought in common
With the proceedings of the Court of Justice.
The law of England, not the monarch's will,
Condemns the Queen of Scotland, and 'twere worthy
Of the great soul of Queen Elizabeth,
To follow the soft dictates of her heart,
Though justice swerve not from its rigid path.

ELIZABETH.—Retire, my Lords.—We shall, perhaps, find means
To reconcile the tender claims of pity
With what necessity imposes on us.
And now retire.—

[*The Lords retire: she calls Sir Edward Mortimer back.*
                    Sir Edward Mortimer!

Scene V.—The Same

Elizabeth, Mortimer.

ELIZABETH [*having measured him for some time, with her eyes,
          in silence*].—You've shown a spirit of advent'rous
          courage,
     And self-possession, far beyond your years.
     He who has timely learnt to play so well
     The difficult dissembler's needful task
     Becomes a perfect man before his time,
     And shortens his probationary years.
     Fate calls you to a lofty scene of action;
     I prophesy it, and can, happily
     For you, fulfil, myself, my own prediction.

MORTIMER.—Illustrious mistress, what I am, and all
     I can accomplish, is devoted to you.

ELIZABETH.—You've made acquaintance with the foes of
          England.
     Their hate against me is implacable;
     Their fell designs are inexhaustible.
     As yet, indeed, Almighty Providence
     Hath shielded me; but on my brows the crown
     Forever trembles, while she lives who fans
     Their bigot-zeal, and animates their hopes.

MORTIMER.—She lives no more, as soon as you command it.
ELIZABETH.—O, Sir! I thought I saw my labor's end,
     And I am come no farther than at first.
     I wish'd to let the laws of England act,
     And keep my own hands pure from blood's defilement.
     The sentence is pronounc'd—what gain I by it?
     It must be executed, Mortimer,
     And I must authorize the execution.
     The blame will ever light on me, I must
     Avow it, nor can save appearances.
     That is the worst—
MORTIMER.—   But can appearances
     Disturb your conscience where the cause is just?
ELIZABETH.—You are unpractis'd in the world, Sir Knight;
     What we appear, is subject to the judgment
     Of all mankind, and what we are, of no man.
     No one will be convinc'd that I am right:
     I must take care that my connivance in
     Her death be wrapp'd in everlasting doubt.
     In deeds of such uncertain double visage
     Safety lies only in obscurity.
     Those measures are the worst that stand avow'd,
     What's not abandon'd, is not wholly lost.
MORTIMER [*seeking to learn her meaning*].—Then it perhaps
     were best—
ELIZABETH [*quick*].—Ay, surely 'twere
     The best; O, Sir, my better angel speaks
     Through you;—go on then, worthy Sir, conclude;
     You are in earnest, you examine deep,
     Have quite a different spirit from your uncle.
MORTIMER [*surprised*].—Have you imparted then your wishes
     to him?
ELIZABETH.—I am sorry that I have.
MORTIMER.—   Excuse his age,
     The old man is grown scrupulous; such bold
     Adventures ask the enterprising heart
     Of youth—
ELIZABETH.—   And may I venture then on you—
MORTIMER.—My hand I'll lend thee; save then as thou canst
     Thy reputation—
       VOL. II.—19

ELIZABETH.— Yes, Sir; if you could
But waken me some morning with this news—
" Maria Stuart, your bloodthirsty foe,
Breath'd yesternight her last "—
MORTIMER.— Depend on me.
ELIZABETH.—When shall my head lie calmly down to sleep?
MORTIMER.—The next new moon will terminate thy fears.
ELIZABETH.—And be the self-same happy day the dawn
Of your preferment—so God speed you, Sir:
And be not hurt, if, chance, my thankfulness
Should wear the mask of darkness.—Silence is
The happy suitor's god.—The closest bonds,
The dearest, are the work of secrecy. [*Exit.*

Scene VI.—The Same

Mortimer (alone).

MORTIMER [*alone*].—Go, false deceitful Queen! As thou
deludest
The world, e'en so I cozen thee: 'tis right,
Thus to betray thee; 'tis a worthy deed.
Look I then like a murd'rer? Hast thou read
Upon my brow such base dexterity?
Trust only to my arm, and keep thine own
Conceal'd—assume the pious outward show
Of mercy 'fore the world, while reckoning
In secret on my murd'rous aid; and thus
By gaining time we shall insure her rescue.
Thou wilt exalt me!—show'st me from afar
The costly recompense: but even were
Thyself the prize, and all thy woman's favor,
What art thou, poor one, and what canst thou proffer?
I scorn ambition's avaricious strife,
With her alone is all the charm of life,
O'er her, in rounds of endless glory, hover
Spirits with grace, and youth eternal bless'd,
Celestial joy is thron'd upon her breast.
Thou hast but earthly, mortal goods to offer—
That sov'reign good, for which all else be slighted.

When heart in heart, delighting and delighted;
Together flow in sweet forgetfulness;—
Ne'er didst thou woman's fairest crown possess.
Ne'er hast thou with thy hand a lover's heart requited
—I must attend Lord Leicester, and deliver
Her letter to him—'tis a hateful charge—
I have no confidence in this court puppet—
I can effect her rescue, I alone;
Be danger, honor, and the prize my own.
                    [*As he is going, Paulet meets him.*

Scene VII.—The Same

Mortimer, Paulet.

PAULET.—What said the Queen to you?—
MORTIMER.—   'Twas nothing, Sir;
    Nothing of consequence—
PAULET [*looking at him earnestly*].—Hear, Mortimer!
    It is a false and slipp'ry ground on which
    You tread. The grace of princes is alluring,
    Youth loves ambition—let not yours betray you.
MORTIMER.—Was it not yourself that brought me to the Court?
PAULET.—O, would to God I had not done as much!
    The honor of our house was never reap'd
    In courts—stand fast my nephew—purchase not
    Too dear, nor stain your conscience with a crime.
MORTIMER.—What are these fears? What are you dreaming
        of?
PAULET.—How high soe'er the Queen may pledge herself
    To raise you, trust not her alluring words.
    The spirit of the world's a lying spirit,
    And vice is a deceitful, treach'rous friend.
    She will deny you, if you listen to her;
    And, to preserve her own good name, will punish
    The bloody deed, which she herself enjoin'd.
MORTIMER.—The bloody deed!—
PAULET.—   Away, dissimulation!—
    I know the deed the Queen propos'd to you.
    She hopes that your ambitious youth will prove

More docile than my rigid age. But say,
Have you then pledg'd your promise, have you?—

MORTIMER.—   Uncle!

PAULET.—If you have done so, I abandon you,
And lay my curse upon you—

LEICESTER [*entering*].—   Worthy Sir!
I with your nephew wish a word.—The Queen
Is graciously inclin'd to him; she wills
That to his custody the Scottish Queen
Be with full powers intrusted. She relies
On his fidelity.

PAULET.—   Relies!—'tis well—

LEICESTER.—What say you, Sir?

PAULET.—   Her Majesty relies
On him; and I, my noble Lord, rely
Upon myself, and my two open eyes.   [*Exit.*

Scene VIII.—The Same

Leicester, Mortimer.

LEICESTER [*surprised*].—What ailed the Knight?

MORTIMER.—   My Lord, I cannot tell
What angers him:—the confidence, perhaps,
The Queen so suddenly confers on me.

LEICESTER.—Are you deserving then of confidence?

MORTIMER.—This would I ask of you, my Lord of Leicester.

LEICESTER.—You said you wish'd to speak with me in private.

MORTIMER.—Assure me first that I may safely venture.

LEICESTER.—Who gives me an assurance on your side?
Let not my want of confidence offend you;
I see you, Sir, exhibit at this court
Two diff'rent aspects; one of them must be
A borrow'd one; but which of them is real?

MORTIMER.—The self-same doubts I have concerning you.

LEICESTER.—Which, then, shall pave the way to confidence?

MORTIMER.—He who, by doing it, is least in danger.

LEICESTER.—Well, that are you—

MORTIMER.—   No, you;—the evidence
Of such a weighty, powerful peer as you

Can overwhelm my voice. My accusation
Is weak against your rank and influence.

LEICESTER.—Sir, you mistake. In ev'rything but this
I'm pow'rful here; but in this tender point,
Which I am call'd upon to trust you with,
I am the weakest man of all the Court,
The poorest testimony can undo me.

MORTIMER.—If the all-pow'rful Earl of Leicester deign
To stoop so low to meet me, and to make
Such a confession to me, I may venture
To think a little better of myself,
And lead the way in magnanimity.

LEICESTER.—Lead you the way of confidence, I'll follow.

MORTIMER [*producing suddenly the letter*].—Here is a letter
    from the Queen of Scotland.

LEICESTER [*alarmed, catches hastily at the letter*].—Speak
    softly, Sir!—what see I?—Oh, it is
Her picture!—
    [*Kisses and examines it with speechless joy—a pause.*

MORTIMER [*who has watched him closely the whole time*].—
Now, my Lord, I can believe you.

LEICESTER [*having hastily run through the letter*].—You know
    the purport of this letter, Sir?

MORTIMER.—Not I.—

LEICESTER.—   Indeed! She surely hath informed you.—

MORTIMER.—Nothing hath she informed me of. She said
You would explain this riddle to me—'tis
To me a riddle, that the Earl of Leicester,
The far-famed fav'rite of Elizabeth,
The open, bitter enemy of Mary,
And one of those who spoke her mortal sentence,
Should be the man from whom the Queen expects
Deliv'rance from her woes; and yet it must be;
Your eyes express too plainly, what your heart
Feels for the hapless lady.—

LEICESTER.—   Tell me, Sir,
First, how it comes that you should take so warm
An int'rest in her fate; and what it was
Gain'd you her confidence?—

MORTIMER.—   My Lord, I can,

And in few words, explain this mystery.
I lately have at Rome abjur'd my creed,
And stand in correspondence with the Guises.
A letter from the Cardinal Archbishop
Was my credential with the Queen of Scots.

LEICESTER.—I am acquainted, Sir, with your conversion;
'Twas that which wak'd my confidence towards you.
(Each remnant of distrust be henceforth banish'd;)
Your hand, Sir, pardon me these idle doubts.
I cannot use too much precaution here.
Knowing how Walsingham and Burleigh hate me,
And, watching me, in secret spread their snares;
You might have been their instrument, their creature
To lure me to their toils.

MORTIMER.—   How poor a part
So great a nobleman is forc'd to play
At court! My Lord, I pity you.

LEICESTER.—   With joy
I rest upon the faithful breast of friendship,
Where I can ease me of this long constraint.
You seem surpris'd, Sir, that my heart is turn'd
So suddenly towards the captive Queen.
In truth, I never hated her;—the times
Have forc'd me to appear her enemy.
She was, as you well know, my destined bride,
Long since, ere she bestow'd her hand on Darnley,
While yet the beams of glory round her smil'd.
Coldly I then refused the proffered boon.
Now in confinement, at the gates of death,
I claim her, at the hazard of my life.

MORTIMER.—True magnanimity, my Lord—

LEICESTER.—   The state
Of circumstances, since that time, is chang'd.
Ambition made me all insensible
To youth and beauty.—Mary's hand I held
Too insignificant for me—I hoped
To be the husband of the Queen of England.

MORTIMER.—It is well known she gave you preference
Before all others.

LEICESTER.—   So, indeed, it seem'd.

Now, after ten lost years of tedious courtship,
And hateful self-constraint—O, Sir, my heart
Must ease itself of this long agony.
They call me happy!—Did they only know
What the chains are, for which they envy me!
When I had sacrificed ten bitter years
To the proud idol of her vanity;
Submitted with a slave's humility
To ev'ry change of her despotic fancies;
The plaything of each little wayward whim.
At times by seeming tenderness caressed,
As oft repulsed with proud and cold disdain;
Alike tormented by her grace and rigor:
Watch'd like a pris'ner by the Argus-eyes
Of jealousy; examin'd like a schoolboy,
And rail'd at like a servant.—O, no tongue
Can paint this hell—

MORTIMER.—   My Lord, I feel for you.

LEICESTER.—To lose, and at the very goal, the prize!
Another comes to rob me of the fruits
Of my so anxious wooing. I must lose
To her young blooming husband all those rights
Of which I was so long in full possession;
And I must from the stage descend, where I
So long have play'd the most distinguish'd part.
'Tis not her hand alone this envious stranger
Threatens, he'd rob me of her favor too;
She is a woman, and he form'd to please.

MORTIMER.—He is the son of Cath'rine. He has learnt,
In a good school, the arts of flattery.

LEICESTER.—Thus fall my hopes;—I strove to seize a plank
To bear me in this shipwreck of my fortunes,
And my eye turn'd itself towards the hope
Of former days once more; then Mary's image
Within me was renew'd, and youth and beauty
Once more asserted all their former rights.
No more 'twas cold ambition; 'twas my heart
Which now compar'd, and with regret I felt
The value of the jewel I had lost.
With horror I beheld her in the depths

Of misery, cast down by my transgression;
Then wak'd the hope in me, that I might still
Deliver and possess her; I contriv'd
To send her, through a faithful hand, the news
Of my conversion to her interests;
And in this letter which you brought me, she
Assures me that she pardons me, and offers
Herself as guerdon, if I rescue her.

MORTIMER.—But you attempted nothing for her rescue.
You let her be condemn'd without a word;
You gave, yourself, your verdict for her death;
A miracle must happen, and the light
Of truth must move me, me, her keeper's nephew
And Heav'n must, in the Vatican at Rome,
Prepare for her an unexpected succor,
Else had she never found the way to you.

LEICESTER.—O, Sir! it has tormented me enough!
About this time it was, that they remov'd her
From Talbot's castle, and deliver'd her
Up to your uncle's stricter custody.
Each way to her was shut. I was oblig'd,
Before the world, to persecute her still;
But do not think that I would patiently
Have seen her led to death. No, Sir; I hop'd,
And still I hope, to ward off all extremes,
Till I can find some certain means to save her.

MORTIMER.—These are already found: my Lord of Leicester,
Your gen'rous confidence in me deserves
A like return. I will deliver her.
That is my object here—my dispositions
Are made already, and your pow'rful aid,
Assures us of success in our attempt.

LEICESTER.—What say you?—you alarm me—how?—you
would—

MORTIMER.—I'll open forcibly her prison gates:—
I have confederates, and all is ready.

LEICESTER.—You have confederates, accomplices?
Alas! In what rash enterprise would you
Engage me? And these friends, know they my secret?

MORTIMER.—Fear not; our plan was laid without your help,

Without your help it would have been accomplish'd,
Had she not signified her resolution
To owe her liberty to you alone.

LEICESTER.—And can you then, with certainty, assure me,
That in your plot my name has not been mention'd?

MORTIMER.—You may depend upon it. How, my Lord,
So scrupulous when help is offer'd you?
You wish to rescue Mary, and possess her;
You find confed'rates; sudden, unexpected,
The readiest means fall, as it were from Heav'n,
Yet you show more perplexity than joy.

LEICESTER.—We must avoid all violence; it is
Too dangerous an enterprise.

MORTIMER.—   Delay
Is also dangerous.

LEICESTER.—   I tell you, Sir,
'Tis not to be attempted—

MORTIMER.—   my Lord,
Too hazardous for you who would possess her;
But we, who only wish to rescue her,
We are more bold.

LEICESTER.—   Young man, you are too hasty
In such a thorny, dangerous attempt.

MORTIMER.—And you too scrupulous in honor's cause.

LEICESTER.—I see the trammels that are spread around us.

MORTIMER.—And I feel courage to break through them all.

LEICESTER.—Foolhardiness and madness, is this courage?

MORTIMER.—This prudence is not bravery, my Lord.

LEICESTER.—You surely wish to end like Babington.

MORTIMER. You not to imitate great Norfolk's virtue.

LEICESTER.—Norfolk ne'er won the bride he woo'd so fondly.

MORTIMER.—But yet he prov'd how truly he deserved her.

LEICESTER.—If we are ruin'd, she must fall with us.

MORTIMER.—If we risk nothing, she will ne'er be rescued.

LEICESTER.—You will not weigh the matter, will not hear;
With blind and hasty rashness you destroy
The plans which I so happily had framed.

MORTIMER.—And what were then the plans which you had
fram'd?
What have you done then to deliver her?

And how, if I were miscreant enough
To murder her, as was propos'd to me
This moment by Elizabeth, and which
She looks upon as certain; only name
The measures you have taken to protect her?
LEICESTER.—Did the Queen give you then this bloody order?
MORTIMER.—She was deceiv'd in me, as Mary is
    In you.
LEICESTER.—   And have you promis'd it; say, have you?
MORTIMER.—That she might not engage another's hand,
    I offer'd mine.
LEICESTER.—   Well done, Sir—that was right;—
This gives us leisure, for she rests secure
Upon your bloody service, and the sentence
Is unfulfill'd the while, and we gain time.
MORTIMER [*angrily*].—No, we are losing time.
LEICESTER.—   The Queen depends
On you, and will the readier make a show
Of mercy—and I may prevail on her
To give an audience to her adversary;
And by this stratagem we tie her hands:
Yes! I will make the attempt, strain ev'ry nerve.
MORTIMER.—And what is gain'd by this? When she discovers
That I am cheating her, that Mary lives;
Are we not where we were? She never will
Be free; the mildest doom which can await her
At best, is but perpetual confinement.
A daring deed must one day end the matter;
Why will you not with such a deed begin?
The pow'r is in your hands, would you but rouse
The might of your dependents round about
Your many castles, 'twere an host; and still
Has Mary many secret friends. The Howards'
And Percies' noble houses, though their chiefs
Be fall'n, are rich in heroes; they but wait
For the example of some potent lord.
Away with feigning—act an open part.
And, like a loyal knight, protect your fair;
Fight a good fight for her! You know you are
Lord of the person of the Queen of England,

Whene'er you will: invite her to your castle,
Oft hath she thither follow'd you—then show
That you're a man—then speak as master—keep her
Confin'd till she release the Queen of Scots.
LEICESTER.—I am astonish'd—I am terrified!—
Where would your giddy madness hurry you?
Are you acquainted with this country? Know you
The deeps and shallows of this court? With what
A potent spell this female sceptre binds
And rules men's spirits round her? 'Tis in vain
You seek th' heroic energy which once
Was active in this land!—it is subdued—
A woman holds it under lock and key,
And ev'ry spring of courage is relax'd.
Follow my counsel—venture nothing rashly.
Some one approaches—go—
MORTIMER.—   And Mary hopes—
Shall I return to her with empty comfort?
LEICESTER.—Bear her my vows of everlasting love.
MORTIMER.—Bear them yourself! I offer'd my assistance
As her deliv'rer, not your messenger.   [*Exit.*

Scene IX.—The Same

Elizabeth, Leicester.

ELIZABETH.—Say who was here? I heard the sound of voices.
LEICESTER [*turning round quickly, and perplexed on hearing
      the Queen*].—It was young Mortimer—
ELIZABETH.—   How now, my Lord:
      Why so confus'd?
LEICESTER [*collecting himself*].—Your presence is the cause.
      Ne'er did I see thy beauty so resplendent,
      My sight is dazzled by thy heavenly charms.
      Oh!—
ELIZABETH.—Whence this sigh?
LEICESTER.—   Have I no reason, then,
      To sigh? When I behold you in your glory,
      I feel anew, with pain unspeakable,
      The loss which threatens me.

ELIZABETH.— What loss, my Lord?
LEICESTER.—Your heart—your own inestimable self:
    Soon will you feel yourself within the arms
    Of your young ardent husband, highly bless'd.
    He will possess your heart, without a rival.
    He is of royal blood—that am not I.
    Yet, spite of all the world can say, there lives not
    One on this globe, who with such fervent zeal
    Adores you, as the man who loses you.
    Anjou hath never seen you, can but love
    Your glory, and the splendor of your reign;—
    But I love you—and were you born, of all
    The peasant maids the poorest, I the first
    Of kings, I would descend to your condition,
    And lay my crown and sceptre at your feet!
ELIZABETH.—Oh pity me, my Dudley; do not blame me—
    I cannot ask my heart. Oh, that had chosen
    Far otherwise! Ah, how I envy others
    Who can exalt the object of their love!
    But I am not so blest:—'tis not my fortune
    To place upon the brows of him, the dearest
    Of men to me, the royal crown of England.
    The Queen of Scotland was allow'd to make
    Her hand the token of her inclination;—
    She hath had ev'ry freedom, and hath drunk,
    E'en to the very dregs, the cup of joy.
LEICESTER.—And now she drinks the bitter cup of sorrow.
ELIZABETH.—She never did respect the world's opinion;—
    Life was to her a sport;—she never courted
    The yoke to which I bow'd my willing neck.
    And yet, methinks, I had as just a claim
    As she, to please myself, and taste the joys
    Of life:—but I preferr'd the rigid duties
    Which royalty imposed on me;—yet she
    She was the favorite of all the men,
    Because she only strove to be a woman;
    And youth and age became alike her suitors.
    Thus are the men—voluptuaries all!
    The willing slaves of levity and pleasure;
    Value that least which claims their reverence.

And did not even Talbot, though gray-headed,
Grow young again, when speaking of her charms?
LEICESTER.—Forgive him—for he was her keeper once,
And she has fool'd him with her cunning wiles.
ELIZABETH.—And is it really true, that she's so fair?
So often have I been oblig'd to hear
The praises of this wonder—it were well
If I could learn on what I might depend:
Pictures are flattering, and description lies;—
I will trust nothing, but my own conviction.
Why gaze you at me thus?
LEICESTER.—   I plac'd in thought
You and Maria Stuart, side by side.
Yes! I confess, I oft have felt a wish,
If it could be but secretly contriv'd,
To see you placed beside the Scottish Queen.
Then would you feel, and not till then, the full
Enjoyment of your triumph:—she deserves
To be thus humbled; she deserves to see,
With her own eyes, and envy's glance is keen,
Herself surpass'd, to feel herself o'ermatch'd,
As much by thee in form and princely grace,
As in each virtue that adorns the sex.
ELIZABETH.—In years she has th' advantage—
LEICESTER.—   Has she so?
I never should have thought it. But her griefs,
Her sufferings, indeed! 'tis possible,
Have brought down age upon her ere her time.
Yes, and 'twould mortify her to see thee
As bride—she hath already turn'd her back
On each fair hope of life, and she would see thee
Advancing tow'rds the open arms of joy—
See thee as bride of France's royal son,
She who hath always plumed herself so high
On her connection with the House of France,
And still depends upon its mighty aid.
ELIZABETH [*with a careless air*].—I'm teas'd to grant this in-
    terview.
LEICESTER.—   She asks it
As a favor; grant it as a punishment.

For though you should conduct her to the block,
Yet would it less torment her, than to see
Herself extinguish'd by your beauty's splendor.
Thus can you murder her, as she hath wish'd
To murder you. When she beholds your beauty,
Guarded by modesty, and beaming bright,
In the clear glory of unspotted fame,
(Which she with thoughtless levity discarded,)
Exalted by the splendor of the crown,
And blooming now with tender bridal graces—
Then is the hour of her destruction come.
Yes—when I now behold you—you were never,
No, never were you so prepar'd to seal
The triumph of your beauty. As but now
You enter'd the apartment, I was dazzled
As by a glorious vision from on high.
Could you but now, now as you are, appear
Before her, you could find no better moment.

ELIZABETH.—Now?—no—not now—no Leicester—this must
            be
        Maturely weigh'd—I must with Burleigh—

LEICESTER.—   Burleigh!
        To him you are but Sov'reign, and as such
        Alone he seeks your welfare; but your rights,
        Deriv'd from womanhood, this tender point
        Must be decided by your own tribunal,
        Not by the statesman:—yet e'en policy
        Demands that you should see her, and allure,
        By such a gen'rous deed, the public voice.
        You can hereafter act as it may please you,
        To rid you of the hateful enemy.

ELIZABETH.—But would it then become me to behold
        My kinswoman in infamy and want?
        They say she is not royally attended;
        Would not the sight of her distress reproach me?

LEICESTER.—You need not cross her threshold—hear my
            counsel:—
        A fortunate conjuncture favors it.
        The hunt you mean to honor with your presence
        Is in the neighborhood of Fotheringay;

Permission may be giv'n to Lady Stuart
To take the air; you meet her in the park,
As if by accident; it must not seem
To have been plann'd, and should you not incline,
You need not speak to her.

ELIZABETH.—   If I am foolish,
Be yours the fault, not mine. I would not care
To-day to cross your wishes; for to-day
I've grieved you more than all my other subjects.

[Tenderly.

Let it then be your fancy. Leicester, hence
You see the free obsequiousness of love,
Which suffers that which it cannot approve.

[Leicester prostrates himself before her, and the curtain falls.

ACT THIRD

Scene I.—A Park. In foreground, Trees; distant Prospect

Mary advances, running from behind the trees. Hannah Kennedy follows slowly.

KENNEDY.—You hasten on as if endow'd with wings—
I cannot follow you so swiftly—wait.

MARY.—Freedom returns! O let me enjoy it—
Let me be childish—be thou childish with me!
Freedom invites me! O let me employ it—
Skimming with winged step light o'er the lea;
Have I escaped from this mansion of mourning?
Holds me no more the sad dungeon of care?
Let me, with joy and with eagerness burning,
Drink in the free, the celestial air!

KENNEDY.—O, my dear Lady! but a very little
Is your sad gaol extended; you behold not
The wall that shuts us in: these plaited tufts
Of trees hide from your sight the hated object.

MARY.—Thanks to these friendly trees, that hide from me
My prison walls, and flatter my illusion!
Happy I now may dream myself, and free;

Why wake me from my dream's so sweet confusion?
The extended vault of heaven around me lies.
Free and unfetter'd range my wandering eyes
O'er space's vast immeasurable sea!
From where yon misty mountains rise on high,
I can my empire's boundaries explore;
And those light clouds which, steering southwards, fly,
Seek the mild clime of France's genial shore.

     Fast fleeting clouds! ye meteors that fly;
     Could I but with you sail through the sky.
     Tenderly greet the dear land of my youth!
     Here I am captive! oppress'd by my foes,
     No other than you may carry my woes,
     Free thro' the ether your pathway is seen,
     Ye own not the power of this tyrant Queen.

KENNEDY.—Alas! dear Lady! You're beside yourself,
    This long-lost, long-sought freedom makes you rave.
MARY.—Yonder's a fisher returning to home;—
    Poor though it be, would he lend me his wherry,
    Quick to congenial shores would I ferry.
    Spare is his trade, and labor's his doom—
    Rich would I freight his vessel with treasure,
    Such a draught should be his as he never had seen,
    Wealth should he find in his nets without measure,
    Would he but rescue a poor captive Queen.
KENNEDY.—Fond, fruitless wishes! See you not from far,
    How we are follow'd by observing spies?
    A dismal, barb'rous prohibition scares
    Each sympathetic being from our path.
MARY.—No, gentle Hannah! Trust me, not in vain
    My prison gates are open'd. This small grace
    Is harbinger of greater happiness.
    No! I mistake not—'tis the active hand
    Of love to which I owe this kind indulgence.
    I recognize in this the mighty arm
    Of Leicester. They will by degrees expand
    My prison; will accustom me, through small,
    To greater liberty, until at last
    I shall behold the face of him whose hand
    Will dash my fetters off, and that forever.

KENNEDY.—O, my dear Queen! I cannot reconcile
These contradictions. 'Twas but yesterday
That they announc'd your death, and all at once,
To-day, you have such liberty. Their claims
Are also loos'd, as I have oft been told,
Whom everlasting liberty awaits.

[*Hunting horns at a distance.*

MARY.—Hear'st thou the bugle, so blithely resounding?
Hear'st thou its echoes through wood and through
plain?
Oh, might I now, on my nimble steed bounding,
Join with the jocund, the frolicsome train!

[*Hunting horns again heard.*

Again! O this sad and this pleasing remembrance!
These are the sounds, which, so sprightly and clear,
Oft, when with music the hounds and the horn,
So cheerfully welcom'd the break of the morn,
On the heaths of the Highlands delighted my ear.

Scene II.—The Same

Enter Paulet.

PAULET.—Well! have I acted right at last, my Lady?
Do I for once, at least, deserve your thanks?
MARY.—How! Do I owe this favor, Sir, to you?
PAULET.—Why not to me? I visited the Court,
And gave the Queen your letter.
MARY.— Did you give it?
In very truth did you deliver it?
And is this freedom which I now enjoy,
The happy consequence?
PAULET [*significantly*].— Nor that alone;
Prepare yourself to see a greater still.
MARY.—A greater still! What do you mean by that?
PAULET.—You heard the bugle-horns?
MARY [*starting back with foreboding apprehension*].—You
frighten me—
PAULET.—The Queen is hunting in the neighborhood—
MARY.— What!

VOL. II.—20

PAULET.—In a few moments she'll appear before you.

KENNEDY [*hastening towards Mary, about to fall*].—How
   fare you, dearest Lady?—you grow pale.

PAULET.—How? Is 't not well? Was it not then your pray'r?
   'Tis granted now, before it was expected;
   You who had ever such a ready speech,
   Now summon all your powers of eloquence,
   The important time to use them now is come.

MARY.—O, why was I not told of this before?
   Now I am not prepar'd for it—not now—
   What, as the greatest favor, I besought,
   Seems to me now most fearful:—Hannah, come,
   Lead me into the house, till I collect
   My spirits.

PAULET.—   Stay;—you must await her here.
   Yes!—I believe you may be well alarm'd
   To stand before your judge.

Scene III.—The Same

Enter the Earl of Shrewsbury.

MARY.—   'Tis not for that,
   O God! Far other thoughts possess me now.
   O, worthy Shrewsbury! You come, as though
   You were an angel sent to me from heav'n.
   I cannot, will not see her. Save me, save me
   From the detested sight!

SHREWSBURY.—   Your Majesty,
   Command yourself, and summon all your courage,
   'Tis the decisive moment of your fate.

MARY.—For years I've waited, and prepared myself.
   For this I've studied, weigh'd, and written down
   Each word within the tablet of my mem'ry,
   That was to touch, and move her to compassion.
   Forgotten suddenly, effac'd is all,
   And nothing lives within me at this moment,
   But the fierce, burning feeling of my wrongs.
   My heart is turn'd to direst hate against her;
   All gentle thoughts, all sweet forgiving words

Are gone, and round me stand with grisly mien,
The fiends of hell, and shake their snaky locks!

SHREWSBURY.—Command your wild, rebellious blood;—constrain
The bitterness which fills your heart. No good
Ensues, when hatred is oppos'd to hate.
How much soe'er the inward struggle cost,
You must submit to stern necessity,
The pow'r is in her hand, be therefore humble.

MARY.—To her? I never can.

SHREWSBURY.—   But pray, submit.
Speak with respect, with calmness! Strive to move
Her magnanimity; insist not, now,
Upon your rights, not now—'tis not the season.

MARY.—Ah! woe is me! I've pray'd for my destruction,
And, as a curse to me, my prayer is heard.
We never should have seen each other—never!—
O, this can never, never come to good.
Rather in love could fire and water meet,
The timid lamb embrace the roaring tiger!—
I have been hurt too grievously; she hath
Too grievously oppress'd me; no atonement
Can make us friends!

SHREWSBURY.—   First see her, face to face:
Did I not see how she was mov'd at reading
Your letter? How her eyes were drown'd in tears?
No—she is not unfeeling; only place
More confidence in her. It was for this
That I came on before her, to entreat you,
To be collected—to admonish you—

MARY [seizing his hand].—Oh, Talbot! you have ever been
my friend,
Had I but stay'd beneath your kindly care!
They have, indeed, misused me, Shrewsbury.

SHREWSBURY.—Let all be now forgot, and only think
How to receive her with submissiveness.

MARY.—Is Burleigh with her too, my evil genius?

SHREWSBURY.—No one attends her but the Earl of Leicester.

MARY.—Lord Leicester?

SHREWSBURY.—   Fear not him; it is not he

Who wishes your destruction;—'twas his work,
That here the Queen hath granted you this meeting.
MARY.—Ah! well I knew it.
SHREWSBURY.—   What?
PAULET.—   The Queen approaches.
[*They all draw aside; Mary alone remains, leaning on Kennedy.*

Scene IV.—The Same

Elizabeth, Earl of Leicester, and retinue.

ELIZABETH [*to Leicester*].—What seat is that, my Lord?
LEICESTER.—   'Tis Fotheringay.
ELIZABETH [*to Shrewsbury*].—My Lord, send back our retinue
      to London:
      The people crowd too eager in the roads,
      We'll seek a refuge in this quiet park.
[*Talbot sends the train away. She looks steadfastly at Mary,
      as she speaks further with Paulet.*
      My honest people love me overmuch.
      These signs of joy are quite idolatrous.
      Thus should a God be honor'd, not a mortal.
MARY [*who the whole time had leaned, almost fainting, on
      Kennedy, rises now, and her eyes meet the steady pierc-
      ing look of Elizabeth; she shudders and throws herself
      again upon Kennedy's bosom*].—O God! from out
            these features speaks no heart.
ELIZABETH.—What lady's that?—
                        [*A general, embarrassed silence.*
LEICESTER.—   You are at Fotheringay,
      My Liege.
ELIZABETH [*as if surprised, casting an angry look at Leices-
      ter*].—Who hath done this, my Lord of Leicester?
LEICESTER.—'Tis past, my Queen;—and now that Heav'n hath
      led
      Your footsteps hither, be magnanimous;
      And let sweet pity be triumphant now.
SHREWSBURY.—O royal mistress! yield to our entreaties;
      O cast your eyes on this unhappy one,
      Who stands dissolved in anguish.

[Mary collects herself, and begins to advance towards Eliza-
beth, stops shuddering at half way; her action expresses
the most violent internal struggle.

ELIZABETH.—   How, my Lords!
    Which of you then announc'd to me a prisoner
    Bow'd down by woe? I see a haughty one,
    By no means humbled by calamity.

MARY.—Well be it so:—to this will I submit.
    Farewell high thought, and pride of noble mind!
    I will forget my dignity, and all
    My sufferings; I will fall before her feet
    Who hath reduced me to this wretchedness.

                    [She turns towards the Queen.
    The voice of Heav'n decides for you, my sister.
    Your happy brows are now with triumph crown'd,
    I bless the Power Divine, which thus hath rais'd you.

                          [She kneels.
    But in your turn be merciful, my sister;
    Let me not lie before you thus disgraced;
    Stretch forth your hand, your royal hand, to raise
    Your sister from the depths of her distress.

ELIZABETH [*stepping back*].—You are where it becomes you,
        Lady Stuart;
    And thankfully I prize my God's protection,
    Who hath not suffer'd me to kneel a suppliant
    Thus at your feet, as you now kneel at mine.

MARY [*with increasing energy of feeling*].—Think on all
        earthly things, vicissitudes.
    Oh! there are gods who punish haughty pride;
    Respect them, honor them, the dreadful ones
    Who thus before thy feet have humbled me!
    Before these strangers' eyes, dishonor not
    Yourself in me: profane not, nor disgrace
    The royal blood of Tudor. In my veins
    It flows as pure a stream, as in your own.
    O! for God's pity, stand not so estranged
    And inaccessible, like some tall cliff,
    Which the poor shipwreck'd mariner in vain
    Struggles to seize, and labors to embrace.
    My all, my life, my fortune now depends

Upon the influence of my words and tears;
That I may touch your heart, O! set mine free.
If you regard me with those icy looks,
My shudd'ring heart contracts itself, the stream
Of tears is dried, and frigid horror chains
The words of supplication in my bosom!

ELIZABETH [*cold and severe*].—What would you say to me,
 my Lady Stuart?
You wish'd to speak with me; and I, forgetting
The Queen, and all the wrongs I have sustain'd,
Fulfil the pious duty of the sister,
And grant the boon you wished for of my presence.
Yet I, in yielding to the gen'rous feelings
Of magnanimity, expose myself
To rightful censure, that I stoop so low.
For well you know, you would have had me murder'd.

MARY.—O! how shall I begin? O, how shall I
So artfully arrange my cautious words,
That they may touch, yet not offend your heart?—
Strengthen my words, O Heav'n! and take from them
Whate'er might wound. Alas! I cannot speak
In my own cause, without impeaching you,
And that most heavily, I wish not so;
You have not, as you ought, behav'd to me;
I am a Queen, like you, yet you have held me
Confin'd in prison. As a suppliant
I came to you, yet you in me insulted
The pious use of hospitality;
Slighting in me the holy law of nations,
Immur'd me in a dungeon—tore from me
My friends and servants; to unseemly want
I was exposed, and hurried to the bar
Of a disgraceful, insolent tribunal.
No more of this;—in everlasting silence
Be buried all the cruelties I suffer'd!
See—I will throw the blame of all on fate.
'Twas not your fault, no more than it was mine.
An evil spirit rose from the abyss,
To kindle in our hearts the flames of hate,
By which our tender youth had been divided.

It grew with us, and bad designing men
Fann'd with their ready breath the fatal fire:
Frantics, enthusiasts, with sword and dagger
Arm'd the uncall'd-for hand! This is the curse
Of kings, that they, divided, tear the world
In pieces with their hatred, and let loose
The raging furies of all hellish strife!
No foreign tongue is now between us, sister,
    [*Approaching her confidently, with a flattering tone.*
Now stand we face to face; now, sister, speak;
Name but my crime, I'll fully satisfy you—
Alas! had you vouchsaf'd to hear me then,
When I so earnest sought to meet your eye,
It never would have come to this, nor would,
Here in this mournful place, have happen'd now
This so distressful, this so mournful meeting.
ELIZABETH.—My better stars preserv'd me. I was warn'd,
And laid not to my breast the pois'nous adder!
Accuse not fate! your own deceitful heart
It was, the wild ambition of your house:
As yet no enmities had pass'd between us,
When your imperious uncle, the proud priest,
Whose shameless hand grasps at all crowns, attack'd me
With unprovok'd hostility, and taught
You, but too docile, to assume my arms,
To vest yourself with my imperial title,
And meet me in the lists in mortal strife:
What arms employ'd he not to storm my throne?
The curses of the priests, the people's sword,
The dreadful weapons of religious frenzy;—
Ev'n here in my own kingdom's peaceful haunts,
He fann'd the flames of civil insurrection;—
But God is with me, and the haughty priest
Has not maintain'd the field. The blow was aim'd
Full at my head, but yours it is which falls!
MARY.—I'm in the hand of Heav'n. You never will
Exert so cruelly the pow'r it gives you.
ELIZABETH.—Who shall prevent me? Say, did not your uncle
· Set all the kings of Europe the example,
How to conclude a peace with those they hate.

Be mine the school of Saint Bartholomew;
What's kindred then to me, or nations' laws?
The church can break the bands of ev'ry duty;
It consecrates the regicide, the traitor;
I only practise what your priests have taught!
Say then, what surety can be offer'd me,
Should I magnanimously loose your bonds?
Say, with what lock can I secure your faith,
Which by St. Peter's keys cannot be open'd?
Force is my only surety; no alliance
Can be concluded with a race of vipers.

MARY.—O! this is but your wretched, dark suspicion!
For you have constantly regarded me
But as a stranger, and an enemy,
Had you declar'd me heir to your dominions,
As is my right, then gratitude and love
In me had fix'd, for you, a faithful friend
And kinswoman.

ELIZABETH.—   Your friendship is abroad,
Your house is Papacy, the monk your brother.
Name you my successor! The treach'rous snare!
That in my life you might seduce my people;
And, like a sly Armida, in your net
Entangle all our noble English youth;
That all might turn to the new rising sun,
And I—

MARY.—   O sister, rule your realm in peace:
I give up ev'ry claim to these domains—
Alas! the pinions of my soul are lam'd;
Greatness entices me no more: your point
Is gained; I am but Mary's shadow now—
My noble spirit is at last broke down
By long captivity:—you've done your worst
On me; you have destroy'd me in my bloom!
Now, end your work, my sister;—speak at length
The word, which to pronounce has brought you hither;
For I will ne'er believe, that you are come,
To mock unfeelingly your hapless victim.
Pronounce this word;—say, " Mary, you are free:
You have already felt my pow'r—learn now

To honor too my generosity."
Say this, and I will take my life, will take
My freedom, as a present from your hands.
One word makes all undone;—I wait for it;—
O let it not be needlessly delay'd.
Woe to you, if you end not with this word!
For should you not, like some divinity,
Dispensing noble blessings, quit me now,
Then, sister, not for all this island's wealth,
For all the realms encircled by the deep,
Would I exchange my present lot for yours.

ELIZABETH.—And you confess at last, that you are conquer'd:
    Are all your schemes run out? No more assassins
    Now on the road? Will no adventurer
    Attempt again, for you, the sad achievement?
    Yes, madam, it is over:—You'll seduce
    No mortal more. The world has other cares;
    None is ambitious of the dang'rous honor
    Of being your fourth husband:—You destroy
    Your wooers like your husbands.

MARY [*starling angrily*].—   Sister, sister!—
    Grant me forbearance, all ye pow'rs of heav'n!

ELIZABETH [*regards her with a look of proud contempt*.—
    Those then, my Lord of Leicester, are the charms
    Which no man with impunity can view,
    Near which no woman dare attempt to stand?
    In sooth, this honor has been cheaply gain'd;
    She who to all is common, may with ease
    Become the common object of applause.

MARY.—This is too much!

ELIZABETH [*laughing insultingly*].—You show us now, indeed,
    Your real face; till now 'twas but the mask.

MARY [*burning with rage, yet dignified and noble*].—My sins
            were human, and the faults of youth:
    Superior force misled me. I have never
    Denied or sought to hide it: I despis'd
    All false appearance as became a Queen.
    The worst of me is known, and I can say,
    That I am better than the fame I bear.
    Woe to you! when, in time to come, the world

Shall draw the robe of honor from your deeds,
With which thy arch-hypocrisy has veil'd
The raging flames of lawless secret lust.
Virtue was not your portion from your mother;
Well know we what it was which brought the head
Of Anne Boleyn to the fatal block.

SHREWSBURY [*stepping between both Queens*].—O! Heav'n!
Alas, and must it come to this!
Is this the moderation, the submission,
My Lady?—

MARY.—   Moderation! I've supported
What human nature can support: farewell,
Lamb-hearted resignation, passive patience,
Fly to thy native heaven; burst at length
Thy bonds, come forward from thy dreary cave,
In all thy fury, long-suppressed rancor!
And thou, who to the anger'd basilisk
Impart'st the murd'rous glance, O, arm my tongue
With poison'd darts!

SHREWSBURY.—   She is beside herself!
Exasperated, mad! My Liege, forgive her.

[*Elizabeth, speechless with anger, casts enraged looks at Mary.*

LEICESTER [*in the most violent agitation; he seeks to lead
Elizabeth away*].—Attend not to her rage! Away, away,
From this disastrous place!

MARY [*raising her voice*].—   A bastard soils,
Profanes the English throne! The gen'rous Britons
Are cheated by a juggler, whose whole figure
Is false and painted, heart as well as face!
If right prevail'd, you now would in the dust
Before me lie, for I'm your rightful monarch!

[*Elizabeth hastily quits the stage; the Lords follow her in the
greatest consternation.*

Scene V.—The Same

Mary, Kennedy.

KENNEDY.—What have you done? She has gone hence in
    wrath,
    All hope is over now!
MARY [*still quite beside herself*].—Gone hence in wrath!
    She carries death within her heart! I know it.
                  [*Falling on Kennedy's bosom.*
    Now I am happy, Hannah! and, at last,
    After whole years of sorrow and abasement,
    One moment of victorious revenge!
    A weight falls off my heart, a weight of mountains;
    I plung'd the steel in my oppressor's breast!
KENNEDY.—Unhappy Lady! Frenzy overcomes you.
    Yes, you have wounded your invet'rate foe;
    'Tis she who wields the light'ning, she is Queen,
    You have insulted her before her minion.
MARY.—I have abas'd her before Leicester's eyes;
    He saw it, he was witness of my triumph.
    How did I hurl her from her haughty height,
    He saw it, and his presence strengthen'd me.

Scene VI.—The Same

Enter Mortimer.

KENNEDY.—O Sir! What an occurrence!
MORTIMER.—   I heard all—
[*Gives the nurse a sign to repair to her post, and draws nearer;
his whole appearance expresses the utmost violence of
passion.*
    Thine is the palm;—thou trod'st her to the dust!—
    Thou wast the Queen, she was the malefactor;—
    I am transported with thy noble courage;—
    Yes! I adore thee; like a Deity,
    My sense is dazzled by thy heav'nly beams.
MARY [*with vivacity and expectation*].—You spoke with Lei-
    cester, gave my letter to him.—
    My present too?—O speak, Sir.

MORTIMER [*beholding her with glowing looks*].—How thy
    noble,
  Thy royal indignation shone, and cast
  A glory round thy beauty; yes, by Heavens,
  Thou art the fairest woman upon earth!
MARY.—Sir, satisfy, I beg you, my impatience;
  What says his Lordship? Say, Sir, may I hope?
MORTIMER.—Who?—he?—he is a wretch, a very coward,
  Hope nought from him; despise him, and forget him!
MARY.—What say you?
MORTIMER.—   He deliver, and possess you!
  Why let him dare it:—he!—he must with me
  In mortal contest first deserve the prize!
MARY.—You gave him not my letter? Then, indeed,
  My hopes are lost!
MORTIMER.—   The coward loves his life.
  Whoe'er would rescue you, and call you his,
  Must boldly dare affront e'en death itself!
MARY.—Will he do nothing for me?
MORTIMER.—   Speak not of him.
  What can he do? What need have we of him?
  I will release you; I alone.
MARY.—   Alas!
  What pow'r have you?
MORTIMER.—   Deceive yourself no more;
  Think not your case is now as formerly;
  The moment that the Queen thus quitted you,
  And that your interview had ta'en this turn,
  All hope was lost, each way of mercy shut.
  Now deeds must speak, now boldness must decide;
  To compass all must all be hazarded;
  You must be free before the morning break.
MARY.—What say you, Sir—to-night?—impossible!
MORTIMER.—Hear what has been resolv'd:—I led my friends
  Into a private chapel, where a priest
  Heard our confession, and, for ev'ry sin
  We had committed, gave us absolution;
  He gave us absolution too, beforehand,
  For ev'ry crime we might commit in future,
  He gave us too the final sacrament,
  And we are ready for the final journey.

MARY.—O! what an awful, dreadful preparation.

MORTIMER.—We scale, this very night, the castle's walls;
    The keys are in my pow'r; the guards we murder!
    Then from thy chamber bear thee forcibly.
    Each living soul must die beneath our hands,
    That none remain who might disclose the deed.

MARY.—And Drury, Paulet, my two keepers, they
    Would sooner spill their dearest drop of blood.

MORTIMER.—They fall the very first beneath my steel.

MARY.—What, Sir! Your uncle? How! Your second father!

MORTIMER.—Must perish by my hand—I murder him!

MARY.—O, bloody outrage!

MORTIMER.—   We have been absolv'd
    Beforehand; I may perpetrate the worst;—
    I can, I will do so!

MARY.—   O dreadful, dreadful!

MORTIMER.—And should I be oblig'd to kill the Queen,
    I've sworn upon the host, it must be done!

MARY.—No, Mortimer; ere so much blood for me—

MORTIMER.—What is the life of all, compar'd to thee,
    And to my love? The bond which holds the world
    Together may be loos'd, a second deluge
    Come rolling on, and swallow all creation!
    Henceforth I value nothing; ere I quit
    My hold on thee, may earth and time be ended!

MARY [retiring].—Heav'ns! Sir, what language, and what
        looks! They scare,
    They frighten me!

MORTIMER [with unsteady looks, expressive of madness].—
    Life's but a moment—death
    Is but a moment too. Why! let them drag me
    To Tyburn, let them tear me limb from limb,
    With red-hot pincers—
            [Violently approaching her with extended arms.
                    If I clasp but thee
    Within my arms, thou fervently belov'd!

MARY.—Madman, avaunt!

MORTIMER.—   To rest upon this bosom,
    To press upon this passion-breathing mouth—

MARY.—Leave me, for God's sake, Sir; let me go in—

MORTIMER.—He is a madman who neglects to clasp
    His bliss in folds that never may be loosed,
    When Heav'n has kindly giv'n it to his arms.
    I will deliver you, and though it cost
    A thousand lives, I do it: but I swear,
    As God's in Heav'n, I will possess you too!

MARY.—O! Will no God, no angel shelter me?
    Dread destiny! thou throw'st me, in thy wrath,
    From one tremendous terror to the other!
    Was I then born to waken nought but frenzy?
    Do hate and love conspire alike to fright me?

MORTIMER.—Yes, glowing as their hatred is my love;
    They would behead thee, they would wound this neck
    So dazzling white, with the disgraceful axe!
    O! offer to the living god of joy
    What thou must sacrifice to bloody hate!
    Inspire thy happy lover with those charms
    Which are no more thine own. Those golden locks
    Are forfeit to the dismal pow'rs of death,
    O! use them to entwine thy slave forever!

MARY.—Alas! alas! what language must I hear!
    My woe, my suff'rings should be sacred to you,
    Although my royal brows are so no more.

MORTIMER.—The crown is fallen from thy brows, thou hast
    No more of earthly majesty. Make trial,
    Raise thy imperial voice, see if a friend,
    If a deliverer will rise to save you.
    Thy moving form alone remains, the high,
    The godlike influence of thy heav'nly beauty;
    This bids me venture all, this arms my hand
    With might, and drives me tow'rds the headsman's axe.

MARY.—O! Who will save me from his raging madness?

MORTIMER.—Service that's bold, demands a bold reward.
    Why shed their blood the daring? Is not life
    Life's highest good? And he a madman, who
    Casts life away? First will I take my rest,
    Upon that breast that glows with love's own fire!
                      [He presses her violently to his bosom.

MARY.—Oh, must I call for help against the man
    Who would deliver me!

MORTIMER.—   Thou'rt not unfeeling,
The world ne'er censur'd thee for frigid rigor;
The fervent pray'r of love can touch thy heart.
Thou mad'st the minstrel Rizzio blest, and gavest
Thyself a willing prey to Bothwell's arms.
MARY.—Presumptuous man!
MORTIMER.—   He was indeed thy tyrant,
Thou trembled at his rudeness, whilst thou lov'd him;
Well then—if only terror can obtain thee—
By the infernal gods!
MARY.—   Away—you're mad!
MORTIMER.—I'll teach thee then before me too to tremble—
KENNEDY [*entering suddenly*].—They're coming—they ap-
    proach—the Park is fill'd
With men in arms.
MORTIMER [*starting, and catching at his sword*].—I will de-
    fend you—I—
MARY.—O Hannah! save me, save me from his hands.
Where shall I find, poor suff'rer, an asylum?
O! to what saint shall I address my pray'rs?
Here force assails me, and within is murder!
    [*She flies towards the house, Kennedy follows her.*

Scene VII.—The Same

Mortimer, Paulet, and Drury rush in in the greatest consterna-
    tion.—Attendants hasten over the stage.

PAULET.—Shut all the portals—draw the bridges up—
MORTIMER.—What is the matter, uncle?
PAULET.—   Where is the murd'ress?
Down with her, down into the darkest dungeon!
MORTIMER.—What is the matter? What has pass'd?
PAULET.—   The Queen!
Accursed hand! Infernal machination!
MORTIMER.—The Queen! What Queen?
PAULET.—   What Queen!
                    The Queen of England;—
She has been murder'd on the road to London.
    [*Hastens into the house.*

Scene VIII.—The Same

Mortimer, soon after, O'Kelly.

MORTIMER [*after a pause*].—Am I then mad? Came not one
    running by
    But now, and cried aloud, The Queen is murder'd!
    No, no! I did but dream. A fev'rish fancy
    Paints that upon my mind as true and real,
    Which but existed in my frantic thoughts.
    Who's there? It is O'Kelly. So dismay'd!
O'KELLY [*rushing in*].—Flee, Mortimer, O! flee—for all is
    lost!
MORTIMER.—What then is lost?
O'KELLY.—   Stand not on question. Think
    On speedy flight.
MORTIMER.—   What has occurred?
O'KELLY.—   Sauvage,
    That madman, struck the blow.
MORTIMER.—   It is then true!
O'KELLY.—True, true—O! save yourself.
MORTIMER [*exultingly*].—   The Queen is murder'd—
    And Mary shall ascend the English throne!
O'KELLY.—Is murder'd! Who said that?
MORTIMER.—   Yourself.
O'KELLY.—   She lives,
    And I, and you, and all of us, are lost.
MORTIMER.—She lives!
O'KELLY.—   The blow was badly aim'd, her cloak
    Receiv'd it. Shrewsbury disarm'd the murd'rer.
MORTIMER.—She lives!
O'KELLY.—   She lives to whelm us all in ruin;
    Come, they surround the park already; come—
MORTIMER.—Who did this frantic deed?
O'KELLY.—   It was the monk
    From Toulon, whom you saw immers'd in thought,
    As in the chapel the Pope's bull was read,
    Which pour'd anathemas upon the Queen.
    He wish'd to take the nearest, shortest way,
    To free, with one bold stroke, the church of God,

And gain the crown of martyrdom:—he trusted
His purpose only to the priest, and struck
The fatal blow upon the road to London.
MORTIMER [*after a long silence*].—Alas! a fierce destructive
    fate pursues thee,
Unhappy one! Yes—now thy death is fix'd;
Thy very angel has prepar'd thy fall!
O'KELLY.—Say, whither will you take your flight? I go
To hide me in the forests of the north.
MORTIMER.—Fly thither, and may God attend your flight;
I will remain, and still attempt to save
My love; if not, my bed shall be upon her grave.

                  [*Exeunt at different sides.*

ACT FOURTH

Scene I.—Ante-chamber

Count Aubespine, the Earls of Kent and Leicester.

AUBESPINE.—How fares her Majesty? My Lords, you see me
Still stunn'd, and quite beside myself for terror?
How happen'd it? How was it possible
That, in the midst of this most loyal people—
LEICESTER.—The deed was not attempted by the people.
The assassin was a subject of your king,
A Frenchman.
AUBESPINE.—   Sure a lunatic.
LEICESTER.—   A Papist,
Count Aubespine!

Scene II.—The Same

Enter Burleigh in conversation with Davison.

BURLEIGH.—   Sir; let the death-warrant
Be instantly made out, and pass the seal;
Then let it be presented to the Queen;

Her Majesty must sign it. Hasten, Sir,
We have no time to lose.

DAVISON.—   It shall be done.   [*Exit.*

AUBESPINE.—My Lord High Treasurer, my faithful heart
Shares in the just rejoicings of the realm.
Prais'd be almighty Heaven, who hath averted
Assassination from our much-lov'd Queen!

BURLEIGH.—Prais'd be his name, who thus hath turn'd to scorn
The malice of our foes!

AUBESPINE.—   May Heav'n confound
The perpetrator of this cursed deed!

BURLEIGH.—Its perpetrator and its base contriver!

AUBESPINE.—Please you, my Lord, to bring me to the Queen,
That I may lay the warm congratulations
Of my imperial master at her feet.

BURLEIGH.—There is no need of this.

AUBESPINE [*officiously*].—   My Lord of Burleigh,
I know my duty.

BURLEIGH.—   Sir, your duty is
To quit, and that without delay, this kingdom.

AUBESPINE [*stepping back with surprise*].—What! How is
    this?

BURLEIGH.—   The sacred character
Of an Ambassador to-day protects you,
But not to-morrow.

AUBESPINE.—   What's my crime?

BURLEIGH.—   Should I
Once name it, there were then no pardon for it.

AUBESPINE.—I hope, my Lord, my charge's privilege—

BURLEIGH.—Screens not a traitor.

LEICESTER and KENT.—   Traitor! How?

AUBESPINE.—   My Lord,
Consider well—

BURLEIGH.—   Your passport was discover'd
In the assassin's pocket.

KENT.—   Righteous Heaven!

AUBESPINE.—Sir, many passports are subscrib'd by me,
I cannot know the secret thoughts of men.

BURLEIGH.—He in your house confess'd, and was absolv'd—

AUBESPINE.—My house is open—

BURLEIGH.—   To our enemies.

AUBESPINE.—I claim a strict inquiry—

BURLEIGH.—   Tremble at it—

AUBESPINE.—My monarch in my person is insulted,
    He will annul the marriage contract.

BURLEIGH.—   That
    My royal mistress has annull'd already;
    England will not unite herself with France.
    My Lord of Kent, I give to you the charge
    To see Count Aubespine embark'd in safety.
    The furious populace has storm'd his palace,
    Where a whole arsenal of arms was found;
    Should he be found, they'll tear him limb from limb,
    Conceal him till their fury is abated—
    You answer for his life.

AUBESPINE.—   I go—I leave
    This kingdom, where they sport with public treaties,
    And trample on the laws of nations. Yet
    My monarch, be assur'd, will vent his rage
    In direst vengeance!

BURLEIGH.—   Let him seek it here.
                  [*Exeunt Kent and Aubespine.*

Scene III.—The Same

Leicester, Burleigh.

LEICESTER.—And thus you loose, yourself, the knot of union
    Which you, officiously, uncall'd for, bound!
    You have deserv'd but little of your country,
    My Lord; this trouble was superfluous.

BURLEIGH.—My aim was good, though fate declared against it;
    Happy is he who has so fair a conscience!

LEICESTER.—Well know we the mysterious mien of Burleigh,
    When he is on the hunt for deeds of treason.
    Now you are in your element, my Lord;
    A monstrous outrage has been just committed,
    And darkness veils, as yet, its perpetrators:—
    Now will a court of inquisition rise;
    Each word, each look be weigh'd; men's very thoughts

Be summon'd to the bar. You are, my Lord,
The mighty man, the Atlas of the state,
All England's weight lies upon your shoulders.

BURLEIGH.—In you my Lord, I recognize my master;
For such a victory as your eloquence
Has gain'd I cannot boast.

LEICESTER.—　　　　　　　What means your lordship?

BURLEIGH.—You were the man who knew, behind my back,
To lure the Queen to Fotheringay castle.

LEICESTER.—Behind your back! When did I fear to act
Before your face?

BURLEIGH.—　　　　　You led her Majesty?
O, no—you led her not—it was the Queen
Who was so gracious as to lead you thither.

LEICESTER.—What mean you, my Lord, by that?

BURLEIGH.—　　　　　　　　　The noble part
You forc'd the Queen to play! The glorious triumph
Which you prepar'd for her! Too gracious princess!
So shamelessly, so wantonly to mock
Thy unsuspecting goodness, to betray thee
So pitiless to thy exulting foe!
This, then, is the magnanimity, the grace
Which suddenly possess'd you in the council!
The Stuart is for this so despicable,
So weak an enemy, that it would scarce
Be worth the pains to stain us with her blood.
A specious plan! and sharply pointed too;
'Tis only pity this sharp point is broken.

LEICESTER.—Unworthy wretch!—this instant follow me,
And answer at the throne this insolence.

BURLEIGH.—You'll find me there, my Lord; and look you well,
That there your eloquence desert you not.　　　[Exit.

Scene IV.—The Same

Leicester, alone; then Mortimer.

LEICESTER.—I am detected! All my plot's disclos'd!
How has my evil genius track'd my steps!
Alas! if he has proofs, if she should learn

That I have held a secret correspondence
With her worst enemy; how criminal
Shall I appear to her! How false will then
My counsel seem, and all the fatal pains
I took to lure the Queen to Fotheringay!
I've shamefully betray'd, I have exposed her
To her detested enemy's revilings!
O! never, never can she pardon that.
All will appear as if premeditated.
The bitter turn of this sad interview,
The triumph and the tauntings of her rival;
Yes, e'en the murd'rous hand, which had prepar'd
A bloody, monstrous, unexpected fate;
All, all will be ascrib'd to my suggestions!
I see no rescue!—nowhere—Ha! Who comes?

[*Mortimer enters, in the most violent uneasiness, and looks
with apprehension round him.*

MORTIMER.—Lord Leicester! Is it you? Are we alone?
LEICESTER.—Ill-fated wretch, away! What seek you here?
MORTIMER.—They are upon our track—upon yours too,
    Be vigilant!
LEICESTER.—   Away, away!
MORTIMER.—   ·   They know,
    That private conferences have been held
    At Aubespine's—
LEICESTER.—   What's that to me?
MORTIMER.—   They know, too,
    That the assassin—
LEICESTER.—   That is your affair—
    Audacious wretch! to dare to mix my name
    In your detested outrage: go; defend
    Your bloody deeds yourself!
MORTIMER.—   But only hear me.
LEICESTER [*violently enraged*].—Down, down to hell! Why
    cling you at my heels
    Like an infernal spirit! I disclaim you—
    I know you not—I make no common cause
    With murderers!
MORTIMER.—   You will not hear me, then!
    I came to warn you—you too are detected.

LEICESTER.—How! What?

MORTIMER.—   Lord Burleigh went to Fotheringay,
Just as the luckless deed had been attempted:
Search'd with strict scrutiny the Queen's apartments,
And found there—

LEICESTER.—   What?

MORTIMER.—   A letter, which the Queen
Had just addressed to you—

LEICESTER.—   Unhappy woman!—

MORTIMER.—In which she calls on you to keep your word,
Renews the promise of her hand, and mentions
The picture which she sent you.

LEICESTER.—   Death and hell!

MORTIMER.—Lord Burleigh has the letter—

LEICESTER.—   I am lost!

[*During the following speech of Mortimer, Leicester goes up
and down, as in despair.*

MORTIMER.—Improve the moment; be beforehand with him,
And save yourself—save her! An oath can clear
Your fame; contrive excuses to avert
The worst. I am disarm'd, can do no more;
My comrades are dispers'd—to pieces fall'n
Our whole confed'racy. For Scotland I,
To rally such new friends as there I may.
'Tis now your turn, my Lord—try what your weight,
What bold assurance can effect.

LEICESTER [*stops suddenly, as if resolved*].—I will—
                    [*Goes to the door, opens it, and calls.*
Who waits without? Guards! seize this wretched
    traitor!
            [*To the Officer, who comes in with soldiers.*
And guard him closely! A most dreadful plot
Is brought to light—I'll to her Majesty.

MORTIMER [*stands for a time petrified with wonder; collects
himself soon, and follows Leicester with his looks ex-
pressive of the most sovereign contempt for him*].—
Infamous wretch!—But I deserve it all.
Who told me then to trust this practis'd villain?
Now o'er my head he strides, and on my fall
He builds the bridge of safety!—be it so,

Go, save thyself—my lips are seal'd forever;—
I will not join e'en thee in my destruction—
I would not own thee, no, not e'en in death;
Life is the faithless villain's only good!
[*To the Officer of the Guard, who steps forward to seize him.*
What wilt thou, slave of tyranny, with me?
I laugh to scorn thy threat'nings—I am free.
[*Drawing a dagger.*
OFFICER.—He's arm'd;—rush in, and wrest his weapon from
    him.   [*They rush upon him, he defends himself.*
MORTIMER [*raising his voice*].—And in this latest moment,
    shall my heart
Expand itself in freedom, and my tongue
Shall break this long constraint. Curse and destruction
Light on you all, who have betray'd your faith,
Your God, and your true Sov'reign! Who, alike
To earthly Mary false as to the heav'nly,
Have said your duties to this bastard Queen!
OFFICER.—Hear you these blasphemies? Rush forward—
    seize him!
MORTIMER.—Beloved Queen! I could not set thee free;
Yet take a lesson from me how to die.
Mary, thou holy one, O! pray for me!
And take me to thy heav'nly home on high!
    [*Stabs himself, and falls into the arms of the Guard.*

Scene V.—Apartment of the Queen

Elizabeth, with a letter in her hand, Burleigh.

ELIZABETH.—To lure me thither! trifle with me thus!
The traitor! Thus to lead me, as in triumph,
Into the presence of his paramour!
O, Burleigh! ne'er was woman so deceiv'd.
BURLEIGH.—I cannot yet conceive what potent means,
What magic he exerted, to surprise
My Queen's accustom'd prudence.
ELIZABETH.—   O, I die
For shame! How must he laugh to scorn my weakness!
I thought to humble her, and was myself
The object of her bitter scorn.

BURLEIGH.—   By this
    You see how faithfully I counsell'd you.

ELIZABETH.—O, I am sorely punish'd, that I turn'd
    My ear from your wise counsels; yet I thought
    I might confide in him. Who could suspect,
    Beneath the vows of faithfulest devotion,
    A deadly snare? In whom can I confide,
    When he deceives me? He, whom I have made
    The greatest of the great, and ever set
    The nearest to my heart, and in this court
    Allow'd to play the master and the king.

BURLEIGH.—Yet in that very moment he betray'd you,
    Betray'd you to this wily Queen of Scots.

ELIZABETH.—O, she shall pay me for it with her life!
    Is the death-warrant ready?

BURLEIGH.—   'Tis prepar'd
    As you commanded.

ELIZABETH.—   She shall surely die—
    He shall behold her fall, and fall himself!
    I've driven him from my heart. No longer love,
    Revenge alone is there: and high as once
    He stood, so low and shameful be his fall!
    A monument of my severity,
    As once the proud example of my weakness.
    Conduct him to the Tower; let a commission
    Of peers be nam'd to try him. He shall feel
    In its full weight the rigor of the law.

BURLEIGH.—But he will seek thy presence; he will clear—

ELIZABETH.—How can he clear himself? Does not the letter
    Convict him? O, his crimes are manifest!

BURLEIGH.—But thou art mild and gracious! His appearance,
    His pow'rful presence—

ELIZABETH.—   I will never see him;
    No never, never more. Are orders giv'n,
    Not to admit him, should he come?

BURLEIGH.—   'Tis done.

PAGE [entering].—The Earl of Leicester!

ELIZABETH.—   The presumptuous man!
    I will not see him. Tell him that I will not.

PAGE.—I am afraid to bring my Lord this message,
    Nor would he credit it.

ELIZABETH.—   And I have raised him
   So high, that my own servants tremble more
   At him than at me!
BURLEIGH [*to the Page*].—The Queen forbids his presence.
               [*The Page retires slowly.*
ELIZABETH [*after a pause*].—Yet, if it still were possible?
   If he
   Could clear himself? Might it not be a snare
   Laid by the cunning one, to sever me
   From my best friend—the ever treach'rous harlot!
   She might have writ the letter but to raise
   Pois'nous suspicion in my heart, to ruin
   The man she hates.
BURLEIGH.—   Yet, gracious Queen, consider—

Scene VI.—The Same

Leicester bursts open the door with violence, and enters with
an imperious air.

LEICESTER.—Fain would I see the shameless man, who dares
   Forbid me the apartments of my Queen!—
ELIZABETH [*avoiding his sight*].—Audacious slave!
LEICESTER.—   To turn me from the door!
   If for a Burleigh she be visible,
   She must be so to me!
BURLEIGH.—   My Lord, you are
   Too bold, without permission to intrude—
LEICESTER.—My Lord, you are too arrogant, to take
   The lead in these apartments. What! Permission!
   I know of none, who stands so high at court
   As to permit my doings, or refuse them.
            [*Humbly approaching Elizabeth.*
   'Tis from my Sov'reign's lips alone that I—
ELIZABETH [*without looking at him*].—Out of my sight, de-
   ceitful, worthless traitor!
LEICESTER.—'Tis not my gracious Queen I hear, but Burleigh,
   My enemy, in these ungentle words.
   To my imperial mistress I appeal;
   Thou hast lent him thine ear; I ask the like,

ELIZABETH.—Speak, shameless wretch! Increase your crime
        —deny it—
LEICESTER.—   Dismiss this troublesome intruder first.
        Withdraw, my Lord; it is not of your office
        To play the third man here: between the Queen
        And me there is no need of witnesses.
        Retire—
ELIZABETH [*to Burleigh*].—Remain, my Lord; 'tis my com-
        mand.
LEICESTER.—What has a third to do 'twixt thee and me?
        I have to clear myself before my Queen,
        My worshipp'd Queen; I will maintain the rights
        Which thou hast given me: these rights are sacred,
        And I insist upon it, that my Lord
        Retire.
ELIZABETH.— This haughty tone befits you well.
LEICESTER.—It well befits me; and not I the man,
        The happy man, to whom thy gracious favor
        Has giv'n the highest station? this exalts me
        Above this Burleigh, and above them all.
        Thy heart imparted me this rank, and what
        Thy favor gave, by Heav'ns I will maintain
        At my life's hazard! Let him go, it needs
        Two moments only to exculpate me.
ELIZABETH.—Think not, with cunning words, to hide the truth.
LEICESTER.—That fear from him, so voluble of speech:
        But what I say, is to the heart address'd;
        And I will justify what I have dar'd
        To do, confiding in thy gen'rous favor,
        Before thy heart alone. I recognize
        No other jurisdiction.
ELIZABETH.—   Base deceiver!
        'Tis this, e'en this, which above all condemns you.
        My Lord, produce the letter.   [*To Burleigh.*
BURLEIGH.—   Here it is.
LEICESTER [*running over the letter without losing his presence
        of mind*].—'Tis Mary Stuart's hand—
ELIZABETH.—   Read, and be dumb!
LEICESTER [*having read it quietly*].—Appearance is against
        me; yet I hope
        I shall not by appearances be judg'd,

ELIZABETH.—Can you deny your secret correspondence
    With Mary?—that she sent, and you receiv'd
    Her picture, that you gave her hopes of rescue?
LEICESTER.—It were an easy matter, if I felt
    That I were guilty of a crime, to challenge
    The testimony of my enemy:
    Yet bold is my good conscience. I confess
    That she hath said the truth.
ELIZABETH.—   Well then, thou wretch!
BURLEIGH.—His own words sentence him—
ELIZABETH.—   Out of my sight!
    Away! Conduct the traitor to the tow'r!
LEICESTER.—I am no traitor; it was wrong, I own,
    To make a secret of this step to thee;—
    Yet pure was my intention, it was done
    To search into her plots and to confound them.
ELIZABETH.—Vain subterfuge!
BURLEIGH.—   And do you think, my Lord—
LEICESTER.—I've play'd a dang'rous game, I know it well,
    And none but Leicester dare be bold enough
    To risk it at this court. The world must know
    How I detest this Stuart, and the rank
    Which here I hold, my monarch's confidence,
    With which she honors me, must sure suffice
    To overturn all doubt of my intentions.
    Well may the man thy favor above all
    Distinguishes, pursue a daring course
    To do his duty!
BURLEIGH.—   If the course was good,
    Wherefore conceal it?
LEICESTER.—   You are us'd, my Lord,
    To prate before you act—the very chime
    Of your own deeds. This is your manner, Lord.
    But mine, is first to act, and then to speak.
BURLEIGH.—Yes; now you speak, because you must.
LEICESTER [*measuring him proudly and disdainfully with his
    eyes*].—   And you
    Boast of a wonderful, a mighty action,
    That you have sav'd the Queen, have snatch'd away
    The mask from treach'ry:—all is known to you;

You think, forsooth, that nothing can escape
Your penetrating eyes. Poor, idle boaster!
In spite of all your cunning, Mary Stuart
Was free to-day, had I not hinder'd it.

BURLEIGH.—How? you?

LEICESTER.—   Yes I, my Lord: the Queen confided
In Mortimer; she open'd to the youth
Her inmost soul! Yes, she went farther still;
She gave him too a secret bloody charge,
Which Paulet had before refus'd with horror.
Say, is it so, or not?

[*The Queen and Burleigh look at one another with astonishment.*

BURLEIGH.—   Whence know you this?

LEICESTER.—Nay, is it not a fact? Now answer me!
And where, my Lord, where were your thousand eyes,
Not to discover Mortimer was false?
That he, the Guise's tool, and Mary's creature,
A raging Papist, daring fanatic,
Was come to free the Stuart and to murder
The Queen of England!

ELIZABETH [*with the utmost astonishment*].—How! This
Mortimer?

LEICESTER.—'Twas he through whom our correspondence
pass'd:
This plot it was which introduc'd me to him.
This very day she was to have been torn
From her confinement; he, this very moment,
Disclos'd his plan to me: I took him pris'ner,
And gave him to the guard, when in despair
To see his work o'erturn'd, himself unmask'd,
He slew himself!

ELIZABETH.—   O, I indeed have been
Deceiv'd beyond example, Mortimer!

BURLEIGH.—This happen'd then but now? Since last we
parted?

LEICESTER.—For my own sake, I must lament the deed—
That he was thus cut off. His testimony,
Were he alive, had fully clear'd my fame,
And freed me from suspicion:—'twas for this

That I surrender'd him to open justice.
I thought to choose the most impartial course
To verify and fix my innocence
Before the world.
BURLEIGH.—   He kill'd himself, you say!
Is 't so? Or did you kill him?
LEICESTER.—   Vile suspicion!
Hear but the guard who seiz'd him.
> [*He goes to the door, and calls.*
> Ho! Who waits?
> [*Enter the Officer of the guard.*
Sir, tell the Queen how Mortimer expir'd.
OFFICER.—I was on duty in the palace porch,
When suddenly my Lord threw wide the door,
And order'd me to take the knight in charge,
Denouncing him a traitor: upon this
He grew enrag'd, and with most bitter curses
Against our sov'reign, and our holy faith,
He drew a dagger, and before the guards
Could hinder his intention, plung'd the steel
Into his heart, and fell a lifeless corpse.
LEICESTER —'Tis well, you may withdraw. Her Majesty
Has heard enough.   [*The Officer withdraws.*
ELIZABETH.—   O! what a deep abyss
Of monstrous deeds!
LEICESTER.—   Who was it then, my Queen,
Who sav'd you? Was it Burleigh? Did he know
The dangers which surrounded you? Did he
Avert them from your head? Your faithful Leicester
Was your good angel.
BURLEIGH.—   This same Mortimer
Died most conveniently for you, my Lord.
What I should say I know not. I believe you,
And I believe you not:—I think you guilty,
And yet I think you not. A curse on her
Who caus'd me all this anguish!
LEICESTER.—   She must die—
I now myself consent unto her death.
I formerly advis'd you to suspend
The sentence, till some arm should rise anew

On her behalf; the case has happen'd now,
And I demand her instant execution.

BURLEIGH.—You give this counsel? You?

LEICESTER.— How'er it wound
My feelings to be forc'd to this extreme,
Yet now I see most clearly, now I feel
That the Queen's welfare asks this bloody victim.
'Tis my proposal, therefore, that the writ
Be drawn at once, to fix the execution.

BURLEIGH [*to the Queen*].—Since then his Lordship shows
such earnest zeal,
Such loyalty, 'twere well, were he appointed
To see the execution of the sentence.

LEICESTER.—Who? I?

BURLEIGH.— Yes, you; you surely ne'er could find
A better means to shake off the suspicion
Which rests upon you still, than to command
Her, whom 'tis said you love, to be beheaded.

ELIZABETH [*looking steadfastly at Leicester*].—My Lord ad-
vises well. So be it then!

LEICESTER.—It were but fit that my exalted rank
Should free me from so mournful a commission,
Which would indeed, in ev'ry sense, become
A Burleigh better than the Earl of Leicester.
The man who stands so near the royal person
Should have no knowledge of such fatal scenes:
But yet, to prove my zeal, to satisfy
My Queen, I waive my charge's privilege,
And take upon myself this hateful duty.

ELIZABETH.—Lord Burleigh shall partake this duty with you.
[*To Burleigh.*
So be the warrant instantly prepar'd.
[*Burleigh withdraws; a tumult heard without.*

Scene VII.—The Same

The Queen, the Earl of Kent.

ELIZABETH.—How now, my Lord of Kent? What uproar's
    this,
    I hear without?
KENT.—   My Queen, it is thy people,
    Who, round the palace rang'd, impatiently
    Demand to see their sov'reign.
ELIZABETH.—   What's their wish?
KENT.—A panic terror has already spread
    Through London, that thy life has been attempted;
    That murderers commission'd from the Pope
    Beset thee; that the Catholics have sworn
    To rescue from her prison Mary Stuart,
    And to proclaim her Queen. Thy loyal people
    Believe it, and are mad—her head alone
    Can quiet them—this day must be her last.
ELIZABETH.—How! Will they force me then?
KENT.—   They are resolv'd—

Scene VIII.—The Same

Enter Burleigh and Davison, with a paper.

ELIZABETH.—Well, Davison?
DAVISON [*approaches earnestly*].—Your orders are obey'd,
    My Queen—
ELIZABETH.—   What orders, Sir?
[*As she is about to take the paper, she shudders, and starts
    back.*
                       O God!—
BURLEIGH.—   Obey
    Thy people's voice; it is the voice of God.
ELIZABETH [*irresolute, as if in contest with herself*].—O my
    good Lord, who will assure me now
    That what I hear is my whole people's voice,
    The voice of all the world! Ah! much I fear,
    That, if I now should listen to the wish
    Of the wild multitude, a diff'rent voice

Might soon be heard;—and that the very men,
Who now by force oblige me to this step,
May, when 'tis taken, heavily condemn me!

Scene IX.—The Same

Enter the Earl of Shrewsbury, with great emotion.

SHREWSBURY.—Hold fast, my Queen, they wish to hurry thee;
                    [*Seeing Davison with the paper.*
Be firm—Or is it then decided?—is it
Indeed decided? I behold a paper
Of ominous appearance in his hand;
Let it not at this moment meet thy eyes,
My Queen!—
ELIZABETH.—   Good Shrewsbury! I am constrain'd—
SHREWSBURY.—Who can constrain thee? Thou art Queen of
        England,
Here must thy Majesty assert its rights:
Command those savage voices to be silent,
Who take upon themselves to put constraint
Upon thy royal will, to rule thy judgment.
Fear only, blind conjecture, moves thy people;
Thou art thyself beside thyself; thy wrath
Is grievously provok'd: thou art but mortal,
And canst not thus ascend the judgment seat.
BURLEIGH.—Judgment has long been past. It is not now
The time to speak, but execute the sentence.
KENT [*who, on Shrewsbury's entry, had retired, comes back*]
        —The tumult gains apace; there are no means
To moderate the people.
ELIZABETH [*to Shrewsbury*].—See, my Lord,
How they press on.
SHREWSBURY.—   I only ask a respite;
A single word trac'd by thy hand decides
The peace, the happiness of all thy life!
Thou hast for years consider'd, let not then
A moment rul'd by passion hurry thee—
But a short respite—recollect thyself!
Wait for a moment of tranquillity.

BURLEIGH [*violently*].—Wait for it—pause—delay—till flames
     of fire
    Consume the realm; until the fifth attempt
    Of murder be successful! God, indeed,
    Hath thrice deliver'd thee; thy late escape
    Was marvellous, and to expect again
    A miracle, would be to tempt thy God!
SHREWSBURY.—That God, whose potent hand hath thrice pre-
     serv'd thee,
    Who lent my aged feeble arm the strength
    To overcome the madman:—he deserves
    Thy confidence. I will not raise the voice
    Of justice now, for now is not the time;
    Thou canst not hear it in this storm of passion.
    Yet listen but to this! Thou tremblest now
    Before this living Mary—tremble rather
    Before the murder'd, the beheaded Mary.
    She will arise, and quit her grave, will range
    A fiend of discord, an avenging ghost
    Around thy realm, and turn thy people's hearts
    From their allegiance. For as yet the Britons
    Hate her, because they fear her; but most surely
    Will they avenge her, when she is no more.
    They will no more behold the enemy
    Of their belief, they will but see in her
    The much-lamented issue of their kings
    A sacrifice to jealousy and hate.
    Then quickly shalt thou see the sudden change
    When thou hast done the bloody deed; then go
    Through London, seek thy people, which till now
    Around thee swarm'd delighted; thou shalt see
    Another England, and another people;
    For then no more the godlike dignity
    Of justice, which subdued thy subjects' hearts,
    Will beam around thee. Fear, the dread ally
    Of tyranny, will shudd'ring march before thee,
    And make a wilderness in ev'ry street—
    The last, extremest crime thou hast committed.
    What head is safe, if the anointed fall?
ELIZABETH.—Ah! Shrewsbury, you sav'd my life, you turn'd

The murd'rous steel aside; why let you not
The dagger take its course? then all these broils
Would have been ended; then, releas'd from doubt,
And free from blame, I should be now at rest
In my still peaceful grave. In very sooth,
I'm weary of my life, and of my crown.
If Heav'n decree that one of us two Queens
Must perish, to secure the other's life—
And sure it must be so—Why should not I
Be she who yields? My people must decide;
I give them back the Sovereignty they gave.
God is my witness, that I have not liv'd
For my own sake, but for my people's welfare.
If they expect from this false, fawning Stuart,
The younger sovereign, more happy days,
I will descend with pleasure from the throne,
Again repair to Woodstock's quiet bowers,
Where once I spent my unambitious youth;
Where far remov'd from all the vanities
Of earthly power, I found within myself
True Majesty. I am not made to rule—
A ruler should be made of sterner stuff:
My heart is soft and tender. I have govern'd
These many years, this kingdom happily,
But then I only needed to make happy:
Now, comes my first important regal duty,
And now I feel how weak a thing I am.

BURLEIGH.—Now by mine honor, when I hear my Queen,
My royal liege, speak such unroyal words,
I should betray my office, should betray
My country, were I longer to be silent.
You say you love your people 'bove yourself,
Now prove it. Choose not peace for your own heart,
And leave your kingdom to the storms of discord.
Think on the church. Shall, with this Papist Queen,
The ancient superstition be renew'd?
The monk resume his sway, the Roman legate
In pomp march hither; lock our churches up,
Dethrone our monarchs? I demand of you
The souls of all your subjects—as you now

Shall act, they all are sav'd, or all are lost!
Here is no time for mercy;—to promote
Your people's welfare is your highest duty.
If Shrewsbury has sav'd your life, then I
Will save both you, and England—that is more!
ELIZABETH.—I would be left alone. No consolation,
No counsel, can be drawn from human aid
In this conjecture:—I will lay my doubts
Before the Judge of all:—I am resolv'd
To act as He shall teach. Withdraw, my Lords.
       [*To Davison, who lays the paper on the table.*
You, Sir, remain in waiting—close at hand.
[*The Lords withdraw; Shrewsbury alone stands for a few
moments before the Queen, regards her significantly,
then withdraws slowly, and with an expression of the
deepest anguish.*

Scene X.—The Same

Elizabeth alone.

ELIZABETH.—O! servitude of popularity!
    Disgraceful slavery! How weary am I
Of flattering this idol, which my soul
Despises in its inmost depth! O! when
Shall I once more be free upon this throne?
I must respect the people's voice, and strive
To win the favor of the multitude,
And please the fancies of a mob, whom nought
But jugglers' tricks delight. O call not him
A king, who needs must please the world: 'tis he
Alone, who in his actions does not heed
The fickle approbation of mankind.
Have I then practis'd justice, all my life
Shunn'd each despotic deed; have I done this.
Only to bind my hands against this first,
This necessary act of violence?
My own example now condemns myself!
Had I but been a tyrant, like my sister,
My predecessor, I could fearless then

Have shed this royal blood:—but am I now
Just by my own free choice? No—I was forc'd
By stern necessity to use this virtue;
Necessity, which binds e'en monarch's wills.
Surrounded by my foes, my people's love
Alone supports me on my envied throne.
All Europe's pow'rs confederate to destroy me;
The Pope's inveterate decree declares me
Accurst and excommunicated. France
Betrays me with a kiss, and Spain prepares
At sea a fierce exterminating war;
Thus stand I, in contention with the world,
A poor defenceless woman: I must seek
To veil the spot in my imperial birth,
By which my father cast disgrace upon me:
In vain with princely virtues would I hide it;
The envious hatred of my enemies
Uncovers it, and places Mary Stuart
A threat'ning fiend before me evermore!
    [*Walking up and down, with quick and agitated steps.*
O no! this fear must end. Her head must fall!
I will have peace. She is the very fury
Of my existence; a tormenting demon,
Which destiny has fasten'd on my soul.
Wherever I had planted me a comfort,
A flatt'ring hope, my way was ever cross'd
By this infernal viper! She has torn
My fav'rite, and my destined bridegroom from me.
The hated name of ev'ry ill I feel
Is Mary Stuart—were but she no more
On earth, I should be free as mountain air.
                            [*Standing still.*
With what disdain did she look down on me,
As if her eye should blast me like the lightning!
Poor feeble wretch! I bear far other arms,
Their touch is mortal, and thou art no more.
        [*Advancing to the table hastily, and taking the pen.*
I am a bastard am I? Hapless wretch,
I am but so the while thou liv'st and breath'st.
Thy death will make my birth legitimate.

The moment I destroy thee, is the doubt
Destroy'd, which hangs o'er my imperial right.
As soon as England has no other choice,
My mother's honor and my birthright triumphs!

[*She signs with resolution; lets her pen then fall, and steps
back with an expression of terror.—After a pause she
rings.*

Scene XI.—The Same

Elizabeth, Davison.

ELIZABETH.—Where are their Lordships?
DAVISON.— They are gone to quell
The tumult of the people. The alarm
Was instantly appeas'd, when they beheld
The Earl of Shrewsbury. That's he! exclaim'd
A hundred voices—that's the man—he sav'd
The Queen; hear him—the bravest man in England!
And now began the gallant Talbot, blam'd
In gentle words the people's violence,
And used such strong, persuasive eloquence,
That all were pacified, and silently
They slunk away.
ELIZABETH.— The fickle multitude!
Which turns with ev'ry wind. Unhappy he
Who leans upon this reed! 'Tis well, Sir William;
You may retire again—
[*As he is going towards the door.*
And, Sir, this paper,
Receive it back; I place it in your hands.
DAVISON [*casts a look upon the paper, and starts back*].—My
gracious Queen—thy name!—'tis then decided.
ELIZABETH.—I had but to subscribe it—I have done so—
A paper sure cannot decide—a name
Kills not—
DAVISON.— Thy name, my Queen, beneath this paper,
Is most decisive—kills—'tis like the lightning,
Which blasteth as it flies! This fatal scroll
Commands the Sheriff and Commissioners
To take departure straight for Fotheringay,

And to the Queen of Scots announce her death,
Which must at dawn be put in execution.
There is no respite, no discretion, here—
As soon as I have parted with this writ,
Her race is run—

ELIZABETH.—   Yes, Sir, the Lord has plac'd
This weighty bus'ness in your feeble hands;
Seek him in pray'r, to light you with his wisdom;
I go—and leave you, Sir, to do your duty.   [*Going.*

DAVISON.—No; leave me not, my Queen, till I have heard
Your will. The only wisdom that I need
Is, word for word, to follow your commands.
Say, have you plac'd this warrant in my hands,
To see that it be speedily enforced?

ELIZABETH.—That you must do, as your own prudence dictates.

DAVISON [*interrupting her quickly, and alarmed*].—Not mine
        —O God forbid! Obedience is
My only prudence here. No point must now
Be left to be decided by your servant.
A small mistake would here be regicide,
A monstrous crime, from which my soul recoils!
Permit me, in this weighty act, to be
Your passive instrument, without a will;—
Tell me in plain undoubted terms your pleasure,
What with the bloody mandate I should do.

ELIZABETH.—Its name declares its meaning.

DAVISON.—   Do you, then,
My Liege, command its instant execution?

ELIZABETH.—I said not that; I tremble but to think it.

DAVISON.—Shall I retain it, then, 'till further orders?

ELIZABETH.—At your own risk; you answer the event.

DAVISON.—I!—gracious Heavens!—O speak, my Queen, your
        pleasure!

ELIZABETH.—My pleasure is, that this unhappy bus'ness
Be no more mention'd to me; that at last
I may be freed from it, and that forever.

DAVISON.—It costs you but a word—determine then;
What shall I do with this mysterious scroll?

ELIZABETH.—I have declar'd it, plague me, Sir, no longer.

DAVISON.—You have declar'd it? say you? O, my Queen,

You have said nothing. Please my gracious mistress
But to remember—

ELIZABETH [*stamps on the ground*].—Insupportable!

DAVISON.—O, be indulgent to me! I have enter'd
Unwittingly, not many months ago,
Upon this office; I know not the language
Of courts and kings. I ever have been rear'd
In simple, open wise, a plain blunt man.
Be patient with me; nor deny your servant
A light to lead him clearly to his duty.

[*He approaches her in a supplicating posture; she turns her
back on him; he stands in despair; then speaks with a
tone of resolution.*
Take, take again this paper—take it back!
Within my hands, it is a glowing fire.
Select not me, my Queen; select not me
To serve you, in this terrible conjuncture.

ELIZABETH.—Go, Sir;—fulfil the duty of your office!   [*Exit.*

Scene XII.—The Same

Davison, then Burleigh.

DAVISON.—She goes! She leaves me doubting, and perplex'd
With this dread paper! How to act I know not;
Should I retain it, should I forward it?
                              [*To Burleigh, who enters.*
Oh! I am glad that you are come, my Lord,
'Tis you who have preferr'd me to this charge;
Now free me from it, for I undertook it,
Unknowing how responsible it made me.
Let me then seek again th' obscurity
In which you found me; this is not my place.

BURLEIGH.—How now? Take courage, Sir! Where is the
        warrant?
The Queen was with you.

DAVISON.—   She has quitted me
In bitter anger. O advise me, help me,
Save me from this fell agony of doubt!
My Lord, here is the warrant: it is sign'd!

BURLEIGH.—Indeed? O give it, give it me!

DAVISON.— I may not.

BURLEIGH.—How!

DAVISON.— She has not yet explain'd her final will.

BURLEIGH.—Explain'd! She has subscrib'd it;—give it me.

DAVISON.—I am to execute it, and I am not.

Great Heavens! I know not what I am to do!

BURLEIGH [*urging more violently*].—It must be now, this moment, executed—

The warrant, Sir. You're lost if you delay.

DAVISON.—So am I also, if I act too rashly.

BURLEIGH.—What strange infatuation. Give it me.

[*Snatches the paper from him, and exit with it.*

DAVISON.—What would you? Hold! You will be my destruction!

ACT FIFTH

Scene I.—Apartment in Castle of Fotheringay

Hannah Kennedy in deep mourning, her eyes still red from weeping in great but quiet anguish, is employed in sealing letters and parcels. Her sorrow often interrupts her occupation, and she is seen at such intervals to pray in silence. Paulet and Drury, also in mourning, enter, followed by many servants, who bear golden and silver vessels, mirrors, paintings, and other valuables, and fill the back part of the stage with them: Paulet delivers to the Nurse a box of jewels and a paper, and seems to inform her by signs, that it contains the inventory of the effects the Queen had brought with her. At the sight of these riches, the anguish of the Nurse is renewed; she sinks into a deep, gloomy melancholy, during which Drury, Paulet, and the Servants, silently retire.

Enter Melvil.

KENNEDY [*screams aloud, as soon as she observes him*].—Melvil! Is 't you? Behold I you again?

MELVIL.—Yes, faithful Kennedy, we meet once more.

KENNEDY.—After this long, long, painful separation!
MELVIL.—A most unhappy, bitter meeting, this!
KENNEDY.—You come—
MELVIL.—   To take an everlasting leave
Of my dear Queen—to bid a last farewell!
KENNEDY.—And now at length, now on the fatal morn
Which brings her death, they grant our royal Lady
The presence of her friends. O, worthy Sir,
I will not question you, how you have far'd,
Nor tell you all the suff'rings we've endured,
Since you were torn away from us:—alas!
There will be time enough for that hereafter.
O, Melvil, Melvil, why was it our fate
To see the dawn of this unhappy day!
MELVIL.—Let us not melt each other with our grief.
Throughout my whole remaining life, as long
As ever it may be, I'll sit and weep;
A smile shall never more light up these cheeks,
Ne'er will I lay this sable garb aside,
But lead henceforth a life of endless mourning.
Yet on this last sad day, I will be firm;
Pledge me your word to moderate your grief;
And when the rest, of comfort all bereft,
Abandon'd to despair, wail round her, we
Will lead her with heroic resolution,
And be her staff upon the road to death!
KENNEDY.—Melvil! You are deceiv'd, if you suppose
The Queen has need of our support to meet
Her death with firmness. She it is, my friend,
Who will exhibit the undaunted heart.
O! trust me, Mary Stuart will expire
As best becomes a Heroine and Queen!
MELVIL.—Receiv'd she firmly, then, the sad decree
Of death?—'tis said, that she was not prepar'd.
KENNEDY.—She was not; yet they were far other terrors
Which made our Lady shudder: 'twas not death,
But her deliverer, which made her tremble.
Freedom was promis'd us; this very night
Had Mortimer engag'd to bear us hence:
And thus the Queen, perplex'd 'twixt hope and fear,

And doubting still if she should trust her honor
And royal person to th' advent'rous youth,
Sat waiting for the morning. On a sudden
We hear a boist'rous tumult in the castle;
Our ears are startled by repeated blows
Of many hammers, and we think we hear
The approach of our deliv'rers:—hope salutes us,
And suddenly and unresisted, wakes
The sweet desire of life. And now at once
The portals are thrown open—it is Paulet,
Who comes to tell us—that—the carpenters
Erect beneath our feet the murd'rous scaffold!
  [*She turns aside, overpowered by excessive anguish.*
MELVIL.—O God in Heav'n! O tell me then, how bore
The Queen this terrible vicissitude?
KENNEDY [*after a pause, in which she has somewhat collected
        herself*].—Not by degrees can we relinquish life;
Quick, sudden, in the twinkling of an eye
The separation must be made, the change
From temporal, to eternal life;—and God
Imparted to our mistress at this moment
His grace, to cast away each earthly hope,
And firm and full of faith to mount the skies.
No sign of pallid fear dishonor'd her;
No word of mourning, 'till she heard the tidings
Of Leicester's shameful treach'ry, the sad fate
Of the deserving youth, who sacrificed
Himself for her: the deep, the bitter anguish
Of that old knight, who lost, through her, his last,
His only hope; till then she shed no tear—
'Twas then her tears began to flow, 'twas not
Her own, but others' woe which wrung them from her.
MELVIL.—Where is she now? Can you not lead me to her?
KENNEDY.—She spent the last remainder of the night
In pray'r, and from her dearest friends she took
Her last farewell in writing:—then she wrote
Her will * with her own hand. She now enjoys
A moment of repose, the latest slumber
Refreshes her weak spirits.

    *The document is now in the British Museum.

MELVIL.— Who attends her?
KENNEDY.—None but her women and physician Burgoyne:
    You seem to look around you with surprise;
    Your eyes appear to ask me what should mean
    This show of splendor in the house of death.
    O, Sir, while yet we lived we suffer'd want;
    But at our death plenty returns to us.

Scene II.—The Same

Enter Margaret Curl.

KENNEDY.—How, Madam, fares the Queen? Is she awake?
CURL [*drying her tears*].—She is already dressed—she asks
    for you.
KENNEDY.—I go;—
    [*To Melvil, who seems to wish to accompany her.*
               But follow not, until the Queen
Has been prepar'd to see you. [*Exit.*
CURL.— Melvil, sure,
    The ancient steward?
MELVIL.— Yes, the same.
CURL.— O, Sir,
    This is a house which needs no steward now!
    Melvil, you come from London; can you give
    No tidings of my husband?
MELVIL.— It is said
    He will be set at liberty, as soon—
CURL.—As soon as our dear Queen shall be no more.
    O, the unworthy, the disgraceful traitor!
    He is our Lady's murderer—'tis said
    It was his testimony which condemn'd her.
MELVIL.—'Tis true.
CURL.— O, curse upon him!—be his soul
    Condemn'd forever!—he has borne false witness—
MELVIL.—Think, Madam, what you say.
CURL.— I will maintain it,
    With ev'ry sacred oath, before the court,
    I will repeat it in his very face;

The world shall hear of nothing else.   I say
That she dies innocent!
MELVIL.—   God grant it true!

Scene III.—The Same

Enter Hannah Kennedy.

KENNEDY [*to Curl*].—Go, Madam, and require a cup of wine—
'Tis for our Lady.
MELVIL.—   Is the Queen then sick?
KENNEDY.—She thinks that she is strong; she is deceiv'd
By her heroic courage; she believes
She has no need of nourishment; yet still
A hard and painful task 's allotted her.
Her enemies shall not enjoy the triumph;
They shall not say that fear hath blanch'd her cheeks,
When her fatigues have conquer'd human weakness.
MELVIL.—May I approach her?
KENNEDY.—   She will come herself.

Scene IV.—The Same

Enter Burgoyne; two women of the chamber follow him, weeping, and in deep mourning.

BURGOYNE.—O, Melvil!
MELVIL.—   O, Burgoyne!   [*They embrace silently.*
FIRST WOMAN [*to the Nurse*].—She chose to be
Alone:—she wishes, at this awful moment,
For the last time, to commune with her God.

Scene V.—The Same

Enter Margaret Curl, bearing a golden cup of wine; she places it hastily upon the table, and leans, pale and trembling, against a chair.

MELVIL.—How, Madam! What has frighten'd you?
KENNEDY.—   O God!

BURGOYNE.—Speak, Madam.

CURL.— What, alas! have I beheld!

MELVIL.—Come to yourself, and say what you have seen!

CURL.—As I went down the staircase which conducts
To the great hall below, a door stood open;
I look'd into the chamber, and I saw—
O Heav'n!

MELVIL.— What saw you?

CURL.— All the walls were hung
With black; a spacious scaffold too o'erspread
With sable cloth, was rais'd above the floor,
And in the middle of the scaffold stood
A dreadful sable block! upon it lay
A naked, polish'd axe:—the hall was full
Of cruel people, crowding round the scaffold;
Who, with a horrid thirst for human blood,
Seem'd waiting for the victim!

THE WOMEN.— Gracious Heav'n
Protect our Queen!

MELVIL.— Be calm; the Queen approaches.

Scene VI.—The Same

Enter Mary in white and sumptuously arrayed, as for a festival: she wears hanging from her neck, on a row of small beads an Agnus Dei; a rosary hangs from her girdle; she bears a crucifix in her hand, and a diadem of precious stones binds her hair; her large black veil is thrown back. On her entrance, all present fall back on both sides with the most violent expressions of anguish. Melvil falls involuntarily upon his knees.

MARY [*with quiet majesty, looking round the whole circle*].—
Why these complaints? Why weep ye? Ye should rather
Rejoice with me, that now at length the end
Of my long woe approaches; that my shackles
Fall off, my prison opens, and my soul
Delighted mounts on seraph's wings, and seeks
The land of everlasting liberty.

When I was offer'd up to the oppression
Of my proud enemy, was forc'd to suffer
Ignoble taunts, and insults most unfitting
A free and sov'reign Queen, then was the time
To weep for me; but, as an earnest friend,
Beneficent and healing Death approaches.
All the indignities which I have suffer'd
On earth, are cover'd by his sable wings.
The most degraded criminal 's ennobled
By his last suff'rings, by his final exit;
I feel again the crown upon my brows,
And dignity possess my swelling soul!

       [Advancing a few steps.

How! Melvil here! My worthy Sir, not so;
Arise; you rather come in time to see
The triumph of your mistress, than her death.
One comfort, which I never had expected,
Is granted me; that, after death, my name
Will not be quite abandon'd to my foes;
One friend at least, one partner of my faith,
Will be my witness in the hour of death.
Say, honest Melvil, how you far'd the while
In this inhospitable, hostile land?
For since the time they tore you from my side,
My fears for you have oft depress'd my soul.

MELVIL.—No other evil gall'd me, but my grief
 For thee, and that I wanted pow'r to serve thee.

MARY.—How fares my chamberlain, old Didier?
 But sure the faithful servant long has slept
 The sleep of death, for he was full of years.

MELVIL.—God hath not granted him as yet this grace;
 He lives to see the grave o'erwhelm thy youth.

MARY.—O! Could I but have felt before my death,
 The happiness of pressing one descendant
 Of the dear blood of Stuart to my bosom.
 But I must suffer in a foreign land,
 None but my servants to bewail my fate!
 Sir; to your loyal bosom I commit
 My latest wishes. Bear then, Sir, my blessing
 To the most Christian king, my royal brother,

And the whole royal family of France.
I bless the cardinal, my honor'd uncle,
And also Henry Guise, my noble cousin.
I bless the holy Father, the vicegerent
Of Christ on earth, who will, I trust, bless me.
I bless the King of Spain, who nobly offer'd
Himself as my deliv'rer, my avenger.
They are remember'd in my will: I hope
That they will not despise, how poor soe'er
They be, the presents of a heart which loves them.

[*Turning to her servants.*

I have bequeath'd you to my royal brother
Of France; he will protect you, he will give you
Another country, and a better home;
And if my last desire have any weight,
Stay not in England; let no haughty Briton
Glut his proud heart with your calamities,
Nor see those in the dust, who once were mine.
Swear by this image of our suff'ring Lord,
To leave this fatal land, when I'm no more.

MELVIL [*touching the crucifix*].—I swear obedience, in the
name of all.

MARY.—What I, though poor and plunder'd, still possess,
Of which I am allow'd to make disposal,
Shall be amongst you shar'd; for I have hope
In this at least, my will may be fulfill'd.
And what I wear upon the way to death,
Is yours—nor envy me on this occasion,
The pomp of earth upon the road to heav'n.

[*To the ladies of her chamber.*

To you, my Alice, Gertrude, Rosamund,
I leave my pearls, my garments: you are young,
And ornament may still delight your hearts.
You, Margaret, possess the nearest claims,
To you I should be gen'rous: for I leave you
The most unhappy woman of them all.
That I have not aveng'd your husband's fault
On you, I hope my legacy will prove.
The worth of gold, my Hannah, charms not thee;
Nor the magnificence of precious stones:

My memory, I know will be to thee
The dearest jewel; take this handkerchief,
I work'd it for thee, in the hours of sorrow,
With my own hands, and my hot scalding tears
Are woven in the texture:—you will bind
My eyes with this, when it is time: this last
Sad service I would wish but from my Hannah.
KENNEDY.—O Melvil! I cannot support it.
MARY.—   Come,
Come all, and now receive my last farewell.

[*She stretches forth her hands; the women violently weeping, fall successively at her feet, and kiss her outstretched hand.*

Marg'ret, farewell—my Alice, fare thee well;
Thanks, Burgoyne, for thy honest faithful service—
Thy lips are hot, my Gertrude:—I have been
Much hated, yet have been as much belov'd.
May a deserving husband bless my Gertrude,
For this warm glowing heart is form'd for love.
Bertha, thy choice is better, thou hadst rather
Become the chaste and pious bride of heav'n;—
O! haste thee to fulfil thy vows;—the goods
Of earth are all deceitful;—thou may'st learn
This lesson from thy Queen. No more; farewell,
Farewell, farewell, my friends, farewell forever.

[*She turns suddenly from them; all but Melvil retire at different sides.*

Scene VII.—The Same

Mary, Melvil.

MARY [*after the others are all gone*].—I have arrang'd all
        temporal concerns,
And hope to leave the world in debt to none;
Melvil, one thought alone there is, which binds
My troubled soul, nor suffers it to fly
Delighted, and at liberty, to heav'n.
MELVIL.—Disclose it to me; ease your bosom, trust
Your doubts, your sorrows to your faithful friend.

MARY.—I see eternity's abyss before me;—
    Soon must I stand before the highest judge
    And have not yet appeas'd the Holy One.
    A priest of my religion is denied me.
    And I disdain to take the sacrament,
    The holy, heav'nly nourishment, from priests
    Of a false faith; I die in the belief
    Of my own church, for that alone can save.

MELVIL.—Compose your heart; the fervent pious wish
    Is priz'd in heaven as high as the performance.
    The might of tyrants can but bind the hands,
    The heart's devotion rises free to God,
    The word is dead—'tis faith which brings to life.

MARY.—The heart is not sufficient of itself;
    Our faith must have some earthly pledge to ground
    Its claims to the high bliss of heav'n. For this
    Our God became incarnate, and enclos'd
    Mysteriously his unseen heav'nly grace
    Within the outward figure of a body.
    The church it is, the holy one, the high one,
    Which rears for us the ladder up to heav'n:—
    'Tis call'd the Catholic—apostolic church
    For 'tis but gen'ral faith can strengthen faith;
    Where thousands worship and adore, the heat
    Breaks out in flame, and borne on eagle wings,
    The soul mounts upwards to the heav'n of heav'ns.
    Ah! happy they, who for the glad communion
    Of pious pray'r, meet in the house of God!
    The altar is adorn'd, the tapers blaze,
    The bell invites, the incense soars on high,
    The bishop stands enrob'd, he takes the cup,
    And blessing it declares the solemn mystery,
    The transformation of the elements;
    And the believing people fall delighted
    To worship and adore the present Godhead.
    Alas! I only am debarr'd from this;
    The heav'nly benediction pierces not
    My prison walls: its comfort is denied me.

MELVIL.—Yes! it can pierce them—put thy trust in Him
    Who is almighty—in the hand of faith,

The wither'd staff can send forth verdant branches;
And he who from the rock call'd living water,
He can prepare an altar in this prison,
Can change—
                    [*Seizing the cup, which stands upon the table.*
                    The earthly contents of this cup
Into a substance of celestial grace.

MARY.—Melvil! O yes, I understand you, Melvil!
Here is no priest, no church, no sacrament;
But the Redeemer says, " When two or three
Are in my name assembled, I am with them."
What consecrates the priest? Say, what ordains him
To be the Lord's interpreter?—a heart
Devoid of guile, and a reproachless conduct.
Well, then, though unordain'd, be you my priest;
To you will I confide my last confession,
And take my absolution from your lips.

MELVIL.—If then thy heart be with such zeal inflam'd,
I tell thee, that for thine especial comfort,
The Lord may work a miracle. Thou say'st
Here is no priest, no church, no sacrament—
Thou err'st—here is a priest—here is a God;
A god descends to thee in real presence.

[*At these words he uncovers his head, and shows a host in a golden vessel.*
I am a priest—to hear thy last confession,
And to announce to thee the peace of God
Upon thy way to death. I have receiv'd
Upon my head the seven consecrations.
I bring thee, from his Holiness, this host,
Which, for thy use, himself has deign'd to bless.

MARY.—Is then a heav'nly happiness prepar'd
To cheer me on the very verge of death?
As an immortal one on golden clouds
Descends, as once the angel from on high,
Deliver'd the Apostle from his fetters:—
He scorns all bars, he scorns the soldier's sword,
He steps undaunted through the bolted portals,
And fills the dungeon with his native glory;
Thus here the messenger of Heav'n appears,

When ev'ry earthly champion had deceiv'd me.
And you, my servant once, are now the servant
Of the Most High, and his immortal Word!
As before me your knees were wont to bend,
Before you humbled, now I kiss the dust.

                  [She sinks before him on her knees.

MELVIL [*making over her the sign of the cross*].—Hear, Mary
      Queen of Scotland:—in the name
Of God the Father, Son, and Holy Ghost,
Hast thou examin'd carefully thy heart,
Swear'st thou, art thou prepar'd in thy confession
To speak the truth before the God of truth?

MARY.—Before my God and thee, my heart lies open.

MELVIL.—What calls thee to the presence of the Highest?

MARY.—I humbly do acknowledge to have err'd
Most grievously, I tremble to approach,
Sullied with sin, the God of purity.

MELVIL.—Declare the sin which weighs so heavily
Upon thy conscience, since thy last confession.

MARY.—My heart was fill'd with thoughts of envious hate,
And vengeance took possession of my bosom.
I hope forgiveness of my sins from God,
Yet could I not forgive my enemy.

MELVIL.—Repent'st thou of the sin? Art thou, in sooth,
Resolv'd to leave this world at peace with all?

MARY.—As surely as I wish the joys of heav'n.

MELVIL.—What other sin hath arm'd thy heart against thee?

MARY.—Ah! not alone through hate; through lawless love
Have I still more abus'd the sov'reign good.
My heart was vainly turn'd towards the man,
Who left me in misfortune, who deceiv'd me.

MELVIL.—Repent'st thou of the sin? And hast thou turn'd
Thy heart, from this idolatry, to God?

MARY.—It was the hardest trial I have pass'd;
This last of earthly bonds is torn asunder.

MELVIL.—What other sin disturbs thy guilty conscience?

MARY.—A bloody crime, indeed of ancient date,
And long ago confess'd; yet with new terrors
It now attacks me, black and grisly steps
Across my path, and shuts the gates of heav'n:

By my connivance fell the king, my husband—
I gave my hand and heart to a seducer—
By rigid penance I have made atonement;
Yet in my soul the worm is gnawing still.

MELVIL.—Has then thy heart no other accusation,
Which hath not been confess'd and wash'd away?

MARY.—All you have heard, with which my heart is charg'd.

MELVIL.—Think on the presence of Omniscience;
Think on the punishments, with which the church
Threatens imperfect, and reserv'd confession!
This is the sin to everlasting death,
For this is sinning 'gainst his Holy Spirit.

MARY.—So may eternal grace with victory
Crown my last contest, as I wittingly
Have nothing hid—

MELVIL.—   How? Wilt thou then conceal
The crime from God, for which thou art condemn'd?
Thou tell'st me nothing of the share thou hadst
In Babington and Parry's bloody treason:
Thou diest for this a temporal death; for this
Wilt thou too die the everlasting death?

MARY.—I am prepar'd to meet eternity;
Within the narrow limits of an hour,
I shall appear before my judge's throne;
But, I repeat it, my confession's ended.

MELVIL.—Consider well—the heart is a deceiver.
Thou hast perhaps, with sly equivocation,
The word avoided, which would make thee guilty,
Although thy will was party to the crime.
Remember, that no juggler's tricks can blind
The eye of fire which darts through ev'ry breast.

MARY.—'Tis true, that I have call'd upon all princes
To free me from unworthy chains; yet 'tis
As true, that neither by intent or deed,
Have I attempted my oppressor's life.

MELVIL.—Your secretaries then have witness'd falsely.

MARY.—It is, as I have said;—what they have witness'd
The Lord will judge.

MELVIL.—   Thou mount'st then, satisfied
Of thy own innocence, the fatal scaffold?

MARY.—God suffers me in mercy to atone,
> By undeserved death, my youth's transgressions.

MELVIL [*making over her the sign of the cross*].—Go, then,
> and expiate them all by death;
> Sink a devoted victim on the altar,
> Thus shall thy blood atone the blood thou'st spilt.
> From female frailty were deriv'd thy faults,
> Free from the weakness of mortality,
> The spotless spirit seeks the blest abodes.
> Now then, by the authority which God
> Hath unto me committed, I absolve thee
> From all thy sins—be as thy faith thy welfare!

> > [*He gives her the host.*
> Receive the body which for thee was offer'd—

[*He takes the cup which stands upon the table, consecrates it
with silent prayer, then presents it to her; she hesitates
to take it, and makes signs to him to withdraw it.*
> Receive the blood, which for thy sins was shed—
> Receive it—'tis allow'd thee by the Pope,
> To exercise in death the highest office
> Of kings, the holy office of the priesthood.

> > [*She takes the cup.*
> And as thou now in this his earthly body
> Hast held with God mysterious communion,
> So may'st thou henceforth, in his realm of joy,
> Where sin no more exists, nor tears of woe,
> A fair transfigur'd spirit, join thyself
> Forever with the Godhead, and forever.

[*He sets down the cup; hearing a noise, he covers his head,
and goes to the door; Mary remains in silent devotion,
on her knees.*

MELVIL [*returning*].—A painful conflict is in store for thee;
> Feel'st thou within thee strength enough to smother
> Each impulse of malignity and hate?

MARY.—I fear not a relapse. I have to God
> Devoted both my hatred, and my love.

MELVIL.—Well, then, prepare thee to receive my Lords
> Of Leicester and of Burleigh. They are here.

Scene VIII.—The Same

Enter Burleigh, Leicester, and Paulet.

[*Leicester remains in the background, without raising his eyes;
Burleigh, who remarks his confusion, steps between him
and the Queen.*

BURLEIGH.—I come, my Lady Stuart, to receive
    Your last commands and wishes.
MARY.—   Thanks, my Lord.
BURLEIGH.—It is the pleasure of my royal mistress,
    That nothing reasonable be denied you.
MARY.—My will, my Lord, declares my last desires;
    I've plac'd it in the hand of Sir Amias,
    And humbly beg, that it may be fulfill'd.
PAULET.—You may rely on this.
MARY.—   I beg that all
    My servants unmolested may return
    To France, or Scotland, as their wishes lead.
BURLEIGH.—It shall be as you wish.
MARY.—   And since my body
    Is not to rest in consecrated ground,
    I pray you suffer this my faithful servant
    To bear my heart to France, to my relations—
    Alas! 'twas ever there.
BURLEIGH.—   It shall be done.
    What wishes else?
MARY.—   Unto her Majesty
    Of England bear a sister's salutation;
    Tell her, that from the bottom of my heart
    I pardon her my death: most humbly too
    I crave her to forgive me for the passion
    With which I spoke to her. May God preserve her
    And bless her with a long and prosp'rous reign!
BURLEIGH.—Say, do you still adhere to your resolve,
    And still refuse assistance from the Dean?
MARY.—My Lord, I've made my peace with God.
                         [*To Paulet.*] Good Sir,
    I have unwittingly caused you much sorrow—

Bereft you of your age's only stay.
Oh, let me hope you do not hate my name.
PAULET [*giving her his hand*].—The Lord be with you! go
    your way in peace.

Scene IX.—The Same

*Hannah Kennedy, and the other women of the Queen crowd
    into the room, with marks of horror. The Sheriff fol-
    lows them, a white staff in his hand; behind are seen,
    through the open doors, men under arms.*

MARY.—What ails thee, Hannah?—Yes—my hour is come—
    The Sheriff comes to lead me to my fate.
    And part we must—farewell!—
KENNEDY and CURL.—   We will not leave thee—
    We will not part from thee.
MARY [*to Melvil*].—   You, worthy Sir,
    And my dear faithful Hannah, shall attend me,
    In my last moments. I am sure my Lord
    Will not refuse my heart this consolation.
BURLEIGH.—For this I have no warrant.
MARY.—   How, my Lord;
    Can you deny me then this small petition?
    Respect my sex; who shall attend me else,
    And yield me the last service?—sure it never
    Can be my sister's pleasure, that in me
    My sex should be insulted; that these men
    With their rude hands, should touch my royal person.
BURLEIGH.—'Tis order'd that no woman shall ascend
    The scaffold steps with you—their tears and moans—
·MARY.—She shall not weep, my Lord, she shall not moan;
    I answer for my Hannah's resolution,
    Be merciful; divide me not so soon
    From my true foster-mother, from my friend.
    She bore me on her arms into this life,
    Let her then gently lead me to my death.
PAULET [*to Burleigh*].—Yield to her wishes.
BURLEIGH.—   Be it so.
MARY.—   I now

Have nothing in this world to wish for more.

                [*She takes the crucifix, and kisses it.*

My God! My Comforter! My blest Redeemer!
As once thy arms were stretch'd upon the cross,
Let them be now extended to receive me!

[*She turns round to go, at the same moment her eyes fall upon
    Leicester, who, on her going, starts involuntarily and
    turns his eyes towards her: at this sight Mary trembles,
    her knees fail her, she is about to fall, when Leicester
    catches at her, and receives her in his arms; she regards
    him for some time earnestly, and in silence; he cannot
    support her looks; at length she speaks.*

You keep your word, my Lord of Leicester: for
You promised me your arm to lead me forth
From prison, and you lend it to me now.
At length the wish'd for day is come, and what
Was oft the object of my fondest dreams
Is now accomplish'd: and the Earl of Leicester,
The long expected, the long wish'd for friend,
Appears at length in Fotheringay Castle.
I see him standing in my prison; all
Is ready for the journey; all the gates
Stand open, and at length I cross the threshold
Conducted by his hand; and now I leave
These dismal walls behind me, and forever.
All is fulfill'd, and you have sav'd your honor.

[*He stands as if annihilated; she continues, with a gentle voice.*

Yes, Leicester; not for liberty alone
I wish'd to be indebted to your hands.
You should have made me bless that liberty.
Led by your hand, and happy in your love,
I hop'd once more to taste the joys of life.
Yes; now that I'm prepar'd from all the world
To part, and to become a happy spirit,
Whom earthly inclinations tempt no more,
Now, Leicester, I may venture to confess
Without a blush, the frailty I have conquer'd—
Farewell, my lord; and, if you can, be happy!
To woo two Queens has been your daring aim;
You have disdain'd a tender, loving heart;

Betray'd it, in the hope to win a proud one:
Kneel at the feet of Queen Elizabeth!
,   May your reward not prove your punishment.
Farewell; I now have nothing more on earth.

[*She goes, preceded by the Sheriff, at her side Melvil and her
Nurse, Burleigh and Paulet follow, the others wailing,
follow her with their eyes till she disappears; they then
retire through the other two doors.*

Scene X.—The Same

LEICESTER [*remaining alone*].—Do I live still? Can I still
bear to live?
Will not this roof fall down and bury me?
Yawns no abyss, to swallow in its gulf
The veriest wretch on earth? What have I lost?
Oh, what a pearl have I not cast away!
What bliss celestial madly dash'd aside!
She's gone, a spirit purged from earthly stain,
And the despair of hell remains for me!
Where is the purpose now with which I came,
To stifle my heart's voice in callous scorn?
To see her head descend upon the block
With unaverted and indifferent eyes?
How doth her presence wake my slumb'ring shame?
Must she in death surround me with Love's toils?
Lost, wretched man! No more it suits thee now
To melt away, in womanly compassion:
Love's golden bliss lies not upon thy path,
Then arm thy breast in panoply of steel,
And henceforth be thy brows of adamant!
Wouldst thou not lose the guerdon of thy guilt,
Thou must uphold, complete it daringly!
Pity be dumb; mine eyes be petrified!
I'll see—I will be witness of her fall.

[*He advances with resolute steps towards the door, through
which Mary passed; but stops suddenly half way.*
No! No! The terrors of all Hell possess me.
I cannot look upon the dreadful deed;
I cannot see her die!—Hark! What was that?

They are already there.   Beneath my feet
The bloody business is preparing.   Hark!
I hear their voices—Hence!—Away—Away—
From this abode of misery and death!

[*He attempts to escape by another door; finds it locked, and
returns.*

How! Does some demon chain me to this spot?
To hear, what I would shudder to behold?
That voice—it is the Dean's, exhorting her;
She interrupts him.   Hark—she prays aloud—
Her voice is firm—now all is still, quite still!
And sobs and women's moans are all I hear.
Now, they undress her—they remove the stool—
She kneels upon the cushion—lays her head—

[*Having spoken these last words, and paused awhile, he is
seen with a convulsive motion suddenly to shrink, and
faint away; a confused hum of voices is heard at the
same moment from below, and continues for some time.*

Scene XI.—Apartment of the Queen

ELIZABETH [*entering from a side door; her gait and action
expressive of the most violent uneasiness*].—No mes-
sage yet arrived! What! no one here!
Will evening never come! Stands the sun still
In its ethereal course? I can no more
Remain upon the rack of expectation!
Is it accomplish'd?—Is it not?—I shudder
At both events, and do not dare to ask.
My Lord of Leicester comes not—Burleigh too,
Whom I appointed to fulfil the sentence.
If they have quitted London, then 'tis done,
The bolt has left its rest—it cuts the air—
It strikes;—has struck already:—were my realm
At stake, I could not now arrest its course.
Who's there?

Scene XII.—The Same

Enter a Page.

ELIZABETH.—   Return'd alone? Where are the Lords?
PAGE.—My Lord High Treasurer, and the Earl of Leicester—
ELIZABETH.—Where are they?
PAGE.—   They are not in London.
ELIZABETH.—   No!
    Where are they then?
PAGE.—   That no one could inform me;
    Before the dawn, mysteriously, in haste,
    They quitted London.
ELIZABETH [*exultingly*].—   I am Queen of England!
    [*Walking up and down in the greatest agitation.*
    Go—call me—no, remain, boy! She is dead—
    Now have I room upon the earth at last,
    Why do I shake? Whence comes this agueish dread?
    My fears are cover'd by the grave; who dares
    To say I did it?—I have tears enough
    In store to weep her fall.—Are you still here?
                                        [*To the Page.*
    Command my secretary Davison
    To come to me this instant. Let the Earl
    Of Shrewsbury be summon'd. Here he comes.
                                        [*Exit Page.*

Scene XIII.—The Same

Enter Shrewsbury.

ELIZABETH.—Welcome, my noble Lord. What tidings—say—
    It cannot be a trifle which hath led
    Your footsteps hither at so late an hour.
SHREWSBURY.—My Liege, the doubts that hung upon my heart,
    And dutiful concern for your fair fame,
    Directed me this morning to the Tower,
    Where Mary's secretaries, Nau and Curl,
    Are now confined as pris'ners, for I wish'd
    Once more to put their evidence to proof.
    On my arrival the lieutenant seem'd
    Embarras'd and perplex'd; refus'd to show me

His pris'ners; but my threats obtain'd admittance.   .
God! what a sight was there! With frantic looks
With hair dishevell'd, on his pallet lay
The Scot, like one tormented by a fury.
The miserable man no sooner saw me,
Than at my feet he fell, and there, with screams,
Clasping my knees, and writhing like a worm,
Implored, conjured me to acquaint him with
His sov'reign's destiny, for vague reports
Had somehow reach'd the dungeons of the tow'r,
That she had been condemn'd to suffer death.
When I confirm'd these tidings, adding too,
That on his evidence she had been doom'd—
He started wildly up—caught by the throat
His fellow pris'ner; with the giant strength
Of madness tore him to the ground, and tried
To strangle him. No sooner had we sav'd
The wretch from his fierce grapple, than at once
He turn'd his rage against himself, and beat
His breasts with savage fists; then curs'd himself
And his companions to the depths of hell!
His evidence was false; the fatal letters
To Babington, which he had sworn were true,
He now denounc'd as forgeries—for he
Had set down words the Queen had never spoken.
The traitor Nau had led him to this treason.
Then ran he to the casement, threw it wide
With frantic force, and cried into the street
So loud, that all the people gather'd round.
I am the man, Queen Mary's secretary,
The traitor, who accus'd his mistress falsely;
I bore false witness, and am cursed forever!
ELIZABETH.—You said yourself, that he had lost his wits;
    A madman's words prove nothing.
SHREWSBURY.—   Yet this madness
    Serves in itself to swell the proof. My Liege,
    Let me conjure thee; be not over hasty;
    Pri'thee, give order for a new inquiry!
ELIZABETH.—I will, my Lord, because it is your wish,
    Not that I can believe my noble peers

Have in this case pronounced a hasty judgment.
To set your mind at rest, the inquiry shall
Be straight renew'd. Well, that 'tis not too late!—
Upon the honor of our royal name
No, not the shadow of a doubt shall rest.

Scene XIV.—The Same

Enter Davison.

ELIZABETH.—The sentence, Sir, which I but late intrusted
    Unto your keeping;—where is it?
DAVISON [*in utmost astonishment*].—   The sentence!
ELIZABETH [*more urgent*].—Which yesterday I gave into your
    charge.
DAVISON.—Into my charge, my Liege!
ELIZABETH.—   The people urged
    And baited me to sign it. I perforce
    Was driven to yield obedience to their will.
    I did so; did so, on extreme constraint,
    And in your hands deposited the paper.
    To gain time was my purpose; you remember,
    What then I told you. Now, the paper, Sir!
SHREWSBURY.—Restore it, Sir, affairs have changed since then,
    The inquiry must be set on foot anew.
DAVISON.—Anew! Eternal mercy!
ELIZABETH.—   Why this pause,
    This hesitation? Where, Sir, is the paper?
DAVISON.—I am undone! Undone! My fate is sealed.
ELIZABETH [*interrupting him violently*].—Let me not fancy,
    Sir—
DAVISON.—   O, I am lost!
    I have it not.
ELIZABETH.—   How? What?
SHREWSBURY.—   O, God in heav'n!
DAVISON.—It is in Burleigh's hands—since yesterday.
ELIZABETH.—Wretch! Is it thus you have obeyed my orders?
    Did I not lay my strict injunction on you
    To keep it carefully?
DAVISON.—   No such injunction
    Was laid on me, my Liege.

ELIZABETH.—   Give me the lie?
        Opprobrious wretch! When did I order you
        To give the paper into Burleigh's hands?
DAVISON.—Never expressly in so many words.—
ELIZABETH.—And, paltering villain! dare you then presume
        To construe, as you list, my words—and lay
        Your bloody meaning on them? Woe betide you,
        If evil come of this officious deed!
        Your life shall answer the event to me.
        Earl Shrewsbury, you see how my good name
        Has been abused!
SHREWSBURY.—   I see! O, God in heav'n!
ELIZABETH.—What say you?
SHREWSBURY.—   If the Knight has dar'd to act
        In this, upon his own authority,
        Without the knowledge of your majesty,
        He must be cited to the Court of Peers
        To answer there for subjecting thy name
        To the abhorrence of all after time.

Scene XV.—The Same

Enter Burleigh.

BURLEIGH [*bowing his knee before the Queen*].—Long life
        and glory to my royal mistress,
        And may all enemies of her dominions
        End like this Stuart.
[*Shrewsbury hides his face.—Davison wrings his hands in
        despair.*
ELIZABETH.—   Speak, my Lord; did you
        From me receive the warrant?
BURLEIGH.—   No, my Queen,
        From Davison.
ELIZABETH.—   And did he in my name
        Deliver it?
BURLEIGH.—   No, that I cannot say.
ELIZABETH.—And dar'd you then to execute the writ
        Thus hastily, nor wait to know my pleasure?
Just was the sentence—we are free from blame

Before the world; yet it behooved thee not
To intercept our natural clemency.
For this, my Lord, I banish you my presence;
And as this forward will was yours alone,
Bear you alone the curse of the misdeed!

        [*To Davison.*

For you, Sir; who have trait'rously o'erstepp'd
The bounds of your commission, and betray'd
A sacred pledge entrusted to your care,
A more severe tribunal is prepar'd:
Let him be straight conducted to the Tow'r,
And capital arraignments fil'd against him.
My honest Talbot, you alone have prov'd,
'Mongst all my counsellors, an upright man:
You shall henceforward be my guide—my friend.

SHREWSBURY.—O! banish not the truest of your friends;
Nor cast those into prison, who for you
Have acted; who for you are silent now.
But suffer me, great Queen, to give the seal,
Which, these twelve years, I've borne unworthily,
Back to your royal hands, and take my leave.

ELIZABETH [*surprised*].—No, Shrewsbury; you surely would
   not now
Desert me? No; not now.

SHREWSBURY.—   Pardon, I am
Too old, and this right hand is grown too stiff
To set the seal upon your later deeds.

ELIZABETH.—Will he forsake me, who has sav'd my life?

SHREWSBURY.—'Tis little I have done;—I could not save
Your nobler part. Live—govern happily!
Your rival's dead. Henceforth you've nothing more
To fear—henceforth, to nothing pay regard. [*Exit.*

ELIZABETH [*to the Earl of Kent, who enters*].—Send for the
   Earl of Leicester.

KENT.—   He desires
To be excused—he is embark'd for France.

        [*The curtain drops.*

CHOICE EXAMPLES OF EARLY PRINTING AND ENGRAVING.

Fac-similes from Rare and Curious Books.

THE DANCE OF DEATH.

The " Dance of Death," in mediæval legend, means the visit of Death and his summons to people in every rank and profession of life. This was a favorite subject with mediæval painters and poets. Such a series of pictures was set up on the walls of St. Paul's Cathedral, London, in the sixteenth century. The present Dance of Death is a page from a volume printed at Lyons in 1499. It represents the visit of the Destroyer to a printing-house, where the compositors and pressmen are each being summoned to their account. In the other compartment of the picture Death lays his icy hand on a book-seller. Nothing can be more clever than these drawings, the animation and expression of which will appeal at once to the connoisseur.

Mors resecat/mors omne necat quod carne creatur
Magnificos premit et modicos/cunctis dominatur.

Nobilium tenet imperiu nulli reueretur
Tam ducibus q̈ principib⁹ comuuis habetur.

Nunc ibi ius/ibi lex/ibi vox/ibi flos iuuenilis.hic nisi pus/nisi fex/nisi terre precio vilis.

Le mort

Venez danser vng tourdion
Imprimeurs sus legierement
Venez tost/pour conclusion
Mourir vous fault certainement
Faictes vng sault habillement
Presses/z capses vous fault laisser
Reculer ny fault nullement
A louurage on congnoist louurier.

Les imprimeurs

Helas ou aurons nous recours
Puis que la mort nous espie
Imprime auons tous les cours
De la saincte theologie
Loix/decret/z poeterie/
Par nre art plusieurs sont grans clers
Releuee en est clergie
Les vouloirs des gens sont diuers

Le mort

Sus auant vous ires apres
Maistre libraire marchez auant
Vous me regardez de bien pres
Laissez voz liures maintenant
Danser vous fault/a quel galant
Mettez icy vostre pensee
Comment vous reculez marchant
Comencement nest pas fusee

Le libraire

Me fault il maulgre moy danser
Ie croy que ouy/mort me presse
Et me contrainct de me auancer
Nesse pas dure destresse
Mes liures il fault que ie laisse
Et ma boutique desormais
Dont ie pers toute lpesse
Tel est blece qui nen peult mais.

ꝑ

A DOLL'S HOUSE

—

BY

HENRIK IBSEN

[Translation by William Archer]

DRAMATIS PERSONÆ

Torvald Helmer.

Nora, his wife.

Doctor Rank.

Mrs. Linden.

Nils Krogstad.

The Helmers' Three Children.

Anna, their nurse.

Maid-servant and Porter.

The scene is in Helmer's house (a flat), at Christiania, Norway.

A DOLL'S HOUSE

ACT FIRST

SCENE.—*A room, comfortably and tastefully, but not expensively furnished. In the back, to the right, a door leads to the hall; to the left another door leads to Helmer's study. Between the two doors a pianoforte. In the middle of the left wall a door, and nearer the front a window. Near the window a round table with armchairs and a small sofa. In the right wall, somewhat to the back, a door, and against the same wall, further forward, a porcelain stove; in front of it a couple of armchairs and a rocking-chair. Between the stove and the side door a small table. Engravings on the walls. A what-not with china and bric à brac. A small bookcase of handsomely-bound books. Carpet. A fire in the stove. It is a winter day.*

A bell rings in the hall outside. Presently the outer door is heard to open. Then Nora enters, humming gayly. She is in outdoor dress, and carries several parcels which she lays on the right-hand table. She leaves the door into the hall open behind her, and a porter is seen outside, carrying a Christmas tree and a basket, which he gives to the maid-servant who has opened the door.

NORA. Hide the Christmas tree carefully, Ellen; the children mustn't see it before this evening, when it's lighted up. [*To the porter, taking out her purse*] How much?

PORTER. Fifty öre.*

NORA. There is a crown. No, keep the change.

---

* About sixpence. There are 100 öre in a krone or crown, which is worth thirteenpence halfpenny.

[*The Porter thanks her and goes. Nora shuts the door. She continues smiling in quiet glee as she takes off her walking things. Then she takes from her pocket a bag of macaroons, and eats one or two. As she does so, she goes on tip-toe to her husband's door and listens.*

NORA. Yes, he is at home. [*She begins humming again, going to the table on the right.*

HELMER [*in his room*]. Is that my lark twittering there?

NORA [*busy opening some of her parcels*]. Yes, it is.

HELMER. Is it the squirrel skipping about?

NORA. Yes!

HELMER. When did the squirrel get home?

NORA. Just this minute. [*Hides the bag of macaroons in her pocket and wipes her mouth.*] Come here, Torvald, and see what I've bought.

HELMER. Don't disturb me. [*A little later he opens the door and looks in, pen in hand.*] " Bought," did you say? What! All that? Has my little spendthrift been making the money fly again?

NORA. Why, Torvald, surely we can afford to launch out a little now! It's the first Christmas we haven't had to pinch.

HELMER. Come, come; we can't afford to squander money.

NORA. O yes, Torvald, do let's squander a little—just the least little bit, won't you? You know you'll soon be earning heaps of money.

HELMER. Yes, from New Year's Day. But there's a whole quarter before my first salary is due.

NORA. Never mind; we can borrow in the meantime.

HELMER. Nora! [*He goes up to her and takes her playfully by the ear.*] Thoughtless as ever! Supposing I borrowed a thousand crowns to-day, and you spent it during Christmas week, and then on New Year's Eve a tile blew off the roof and knocked my brains out——

NORA [*laying her hand on his mouth*]. Hush! How can you talk so horribly?

HELMER. But supposing it were to happen—what then?

NORA. If anything so dreadful happened, I shouldn't care whether I was in debt or not.

HELMER. But what about the creditors?

NORA. They! Who cares for them? They're only strangers.

HELMER. Nora, Nora! What a woman you are! But seriously, Nora, you know my principles on these points. No debts! No credit! Home-life ceases to be free and beautiful as soon as it is founded on borrowing and debt. We two have held out bravely till now, and we won't give in at the last.

NORA [*going to the fire-place*]. Very well—as you please, Torvald.

HELMER [*following her*]. Come, come; my little lark mustn't let her wings droop like that. What? Is the squirrel pouting there? [*Takes out his purse.*] Nora, what do you think I've got here?

NORA [*turning round quickly*]. Money!

HELMER. There! [*Gives her some notes.*] Of course I know all sorts of things are wanted at Christmas.

NORA [*counting*]. Ten, twenty, thirty, forty. Oh! Thank you, thank you, Torvald. This will go a long way.

HELMER. I should hope so.

NORA. Yes, indeed; a long way! But come here, and see all I've been buying. And so cheap! Look, here's a new suit for Ivar, and a little sword. Here are a horse and a trumpet for Bob. And here are a doll and a cradle for Emmy. They're only common; but she'll soon pull them all to pieces. And dresses and neckties for the servants; only I should have got something better for dear old Anna.

HELMER. And what's in that other parcel?

NORA [*crying out*]. No, Torvald, you're not to see that until this evening!

HELMER. Oh! Ah! But now tell me, you little rogue, what have you got for yourself?

NORA. For myself? Oh, I don't want anything.

HELMER. Nonsense! Just tell me something sensible you would like to have.

NORA. No, really I want nothing—— Well, listen, Torvald——

HELMER. Well?

NORA [*playing with his coat buttons, without looking him in the face*]. If you really want to give me something, you might, you know, you might——

HELMER. Well well? Out with it!

NORA [*quickly*]. You might give me money, Torvald. Only just what you think you can spare; then I can buy myself something with it later.

HELMER. But, Nora——

NORA. Oh, please do, dear Torvald, please do! Then I would hang the money in lovely gilt paper on the Christmas tree. Wouldn't that be fun?

HELMER. What do they call the birds that are always making the money fly?

NORA. Yes, I know—spendthrifts,* of course. But please do as I say, Torvald. Then I shall have time to think what I want most. Isn't that very sensible now?

HELMER [*smiling*]. Certainly; that is to say, if you really kept the money I gave you, and really bought yourself something with it. But it all goes in housekeeping, and for all sorts of useless things, and then I have to find more.

NORA. But, Torvald——

HELMER. Can you deny it, Nora dear? [*He puts his arm round her.*] It's a sweet little lark; but it gets through a lot of money. No one would believe how much it costs a man to keep such a little bird as you.

NORA. For shame! How can you say so? Why, I save as much as ever I can.

HELMER [*laughing*]. Very true—as much as you can—but you can't.

NORA [*hums and smiles in quiet satisfaction*]. Hm! You should just know, Torvald, what expenses we larks and squirrels have.

HELMER. You're a strange little being! Just like your father —always eager to get hold of money, but the moment you have it, it seems to slip through your fingers; you never know what becomes of it. Well, one must take you as you are. It's in the blood. Yes, Nora, that sort of thing is inherited.

NORA. I wish I had inherited many of my father's qualities.

HELMER. And I don't wish you anything but just what you are—my own, sweet little song-bird. But, I say—it strikes me—you look so, so—what shall I call it?—so suspicious to-day——

* " Spillefugl," literally, " playbird," means a gambler.

NORA. Do I?

HELMER. You do, indeed. Look me full in the face.

NORA [*looking at him*]. Well?

HELMER [*threatening with his finger*]. Hasn't the little sweet-tooth been breaking the rules to-day?

NORA. No; how can you think of such a thing!

HELMER. Didn't she just look in at the confectioner's?

NORA. No, Torvald; really——

HELMER. Not to sip a little jelly?

NORA. *No;* certainly not.

HELMER. Hasn't she even nibbled a macaroon or two?

NORA. No, Torvald, indeed, indeed!

HELMER. Well well well; of course I'm only joking.

NORA [*goes to the table on the right*]. I shouldn't think of doing what you disapprove of.

HELMER. No, I'm sure of that; and, besides, you've given me your word. [*Going towards her.*] Well, keep your little Christmas secrets to yourself, Nora darling. The Christmas tree will bring them all to light, I dare say.

NORA. Have you remembered to ask Dr. Rank?

HELMER. No. But it's not necessary; he'll come as a matter of course. Besides, I shall invite him when he looks in to-day. I've ordered some capital wine. Nora, you can't think how I look forward to this evening!

NORA. And I too. How the children will enjoy themselves, Torvald!

HELMER. Ah! It's glorious to feel that one has an assured position and ample means. Isn't it delightful to think of?

NORA. Oh, it's wonderful!

HELMER. Do you remember last Christmas? For three whole weeks beforehand you shut yourself up till long past midnight to make flowers for the Christmas tree, and all sorts of other marvels that were to have astonished us. I was never so bored in my life.

NORA. I didn't bore myself at all.

HELMER [*smiling*]. And it came to so little after all, Nora.

NORA. Oh! Are you going to tease me about that again? How could I help the cat getting in and spoiling it all?

HELMER. To be sure you couldn't, my poor little Nora. You did your best to amuse us all, and that's the main thing. But, all the same, it's a good thing the hard times are over.

NORA. Oh, isn't it wonderful?

HELMER. Now I needn't sit here boring myself all alone; and you needn't tire your dear eyes and your delicate little fingers——

NORA [*clapping her hands*]. No, I needn't need I, Torvald? Oh! it's wonderful to think of! [*Takes his arm.*] And now I'll tell you how I think we ought to manage, Torvald. As soon as Christmas is over—— [*The hall-door bell rings.*] Oh, there's a ring! [*Arranging the room.*] That's somebody come to call. How vexing!

HELMER. I'm " not at home " to callers; remember that.

ELLEN [*in the doorway*]. A lady to see you, ma'am.

NORA. Show her in.

ELLEN [*to Helmer*]. And the doctor has just come, sir.

HELMER. Has he gone into my study?

ELLEN. Yes, sir.

[*Helmer goes into his study. Ellen ushers in Mrs. Linden, in travelling costume, and shuts the door behind her.*

MRS. LINDEN [*timidly and hesitatingly*]. How do you do, Nora?

NORA [*doubtfully*]. How do you do?

MRS. LINDEN. I dare say you don't recognize me?

NORA. No, I don't think—oh, yes!—I believe—— [*Effusively.*] What! Christina! Is it really you?

MRS. LINDEN. Yes; really I!

NORA. Christina! and to think I didn't know you! But how could I—— [*More softly.*] How changed you are, Christina!

MRS. LINDEN. Yes, no doubt. In nine or ten years——

NORA. Is it really so long since we met? Yes, so it is. Oh! the last eight years have been a happy time, I can tell you. And now you've come to town? All that long journey in mid-winter! How brave of you!

MRS. LINDEN. I arrived by this morning's steamer.

NORA. To keep Christmas, of course. Oh, how delightful! What fun we shall have! Take your things off. Aren't you frozen? [*Helping her.*] There; now we'll sit cosily by the fire. No, you take the arm-chair; I'll sit in this rocking-chair. [*Seizes her hands.*] Yes, now I can see the dear old face again. It was only at the first glance.—

But you're a little paler, Christina, and perhaps a little thinner.

MRS. LINDEN. And much, much older, Nora.

NORA. Yes, perhaps a little older—not much—ever so little. [*She suddenly stops; seriously.*] Oh! what a thoughtless wretch I am! Here I sit chattering on, and—— Dear, dear Christina, can you forgive me?

MRS. LINDEN. What do you mean, Nora?

NORA [*softly*]. Poor Christina! I forgot: you are a widow?

MRS. LINDEN. Yes; my husband died three years ago.

NORA. I know, I know; I saw it in the papers. Oh! believe me, Christina, I did mean to write to you, but I kept putting it off, and something always came in the way.

MRS. LINDEN. I can quite understand that, Nora dear.

NORA. No, Christina; it was horrid of me. Oh, you poor darling! how much you must have gone through! And he left you nothing?

MRS. LINDEN. Nothing.

NORA. And no children?

MRS. LINDEN. None.

NORA. Nothing, nothing at all?

MRS. LINDEN. Not even a sorrow or a longing to dwell upon.

NORA [*looking at her incredulously*]. My dear Christina, how is that possible?

MRS. LINDEN [*smiling sadly and stroking her hair*]. Oh, it happens sometimes, Nora.

NORA. So utterly alone! How dreadful that must be! I have three of the loveliest children. I can't show them to you just now; they're out with their nurse. But now you must tell me everything.

MRS. LINDEN. No, no; I want you to tell me——

NORA. No, you must begin; I won't be egotistical to-day. To-day I'll think only of you. Oh! I must tell you one thing —but perhaps you've heard of our great stroke of fortune?

MRS. LINDEN. No. What is it?

NORA. Only think! my husband has been made Manager of the Joint Stock Bank.

MRS. LINDEN. Your husband! Oh, how fortunate!

NORA. Yes; isn't it? A lawyer's position is so uncertain, you see, especially when he won't touch any business that's the

least bit—shady, as of course Torvald won't; and in that
I quite agree with him. Oh! you can't imagine how glad
we are. He's to enter on his new position at the New
Year, and then he'll have a large salary, and percentages.
In future we shall be able to live quite differently—just as
we please, in fact. Oh, Christina, I feel so light and happy!
It's splendid to have lots of money, and no need to worry
about things, isn't it?

MRS. LINDEN. Yes; it must be delightful to have what you
need.

NORA. No, not only what you need, but heaps of money—
heaps!

MRS. LINDEN [*smiling*]. Nora, Nora, haven't you learnt reason yet? In our school-days you were a shocking little
spendthrift!

NORA [*quietly smiling*]. Yes; Torvald says I am still.
[*Threatens with her finger.*] But " Nora, Nora " is not so
silly as you all think. Oh! I haven't had the chance to be
much of a spendthrift. We have both had to work.

MRS. LINDEN. You too?

NORA. Yes, light fancy work: crochet, and embroidery, and
things of that sort [*significantly*], and other work too.
You know, of course, that Torvald left the Government
service when we were married. He had little chance of
promotion, and of course he required to make more money.
But in the first year of our marriage he overworked himself terribly. He had to undertake all sorts of odd jobs,
you know, and to work early and late. He couldn't stand
it, and fell dangerously ill. Then the doctors declared he
must go to the South.

MRS. LINDEN. Yes; you spent a whole year in Italy, didn't
you?

NORA. We did. It wasn't easy to manage, I can tell you. It
was just after Ivar's birth. But of course we had to go.
Oh, it was a delicious journey! And it saved Torvald's
life. But it cost a frightful lot of money, Christina.

MRS. LINDEN. So I should think.

NORA. Twelve hundred dollars! Four thousand eight hundred
crowns! * Isn't that a lot of money?

* The dollar (4s. 6d.) was the old unit of currency in Norway. The crown was
substituted for it shortly before the date of this play.

MRS. LINDEN. How lucky you had the money to spend!

NORA. We got it from father, you must know.

MRS. LINDEN. Ah, I see. He died just about that time, didn't he?

NORA. Yes, Christina, just then. And only think! I couldn't go and nurse him! I was expecting little Ivar's birth daily; and then I had my poor sick Torvald to attend to. Dear, kind old father! I never saw him again, Christina. Oh! that's the hardest thing I've had to bear since my marriage.

MRS. LINDEN. I know how fond you were of him. And then you went to Italy?

NORA. Yes; we had the money, and the doctors insisted. We started a month later.

MRS. LINDEN. And your husband returned completely cured?

NORA. Sound as a bell.

MRS. LINDEN. But—the doctor?

NORA. What about him?

MRS. LINDEN. I thought as I came in your servant announced the doctor——

NORA. Oh, yes; Doctor Rank. But he doesn't come as a doctor. He's our best friend, and never lets a day pass without looking in. No, Torvald hasn't had an hour's illness since that time. And the children are so healthy and well, and so am I. [*Jumps up and claps her hands.*] Oh, Christina, Christina, it's lovely to live and to be happy? Oh! but it's really too horrid of me! Here am I talking about nothing but my own concerns. [*Sits down upon a footstool close to her and lays her arms on Christina's lap.*] Oh! don't be angry with me! Now just tell me, is it really true that you didn't love your husband? What made you take him then?

MRS. LINDEN. My mother was then alive, bedridden and helpless; and then I had my two younger brothers to think of. I thought it my duty to accept him.

NORA. Perhaps it was. I suppose he was rich then?

MRS. LINDEN. Very well off, I believe. But his business was uncertain. It fell to pieces at his death, and there was nothing left.

NORA. And then——?

MRS. LINDEN. Then I had to fight my way by keeping a shop, a little school, anything I could turn my hand to. The last three years have been one long struggle for me. But now it's over, Nora. My poor mother no longer needs me; she is at rest. And the boys are in business, and can look after themselves.

NORA. How free your life must feel!

MRS. LINDEN. No, Nora; only inexpressibly empty. No one to live for! [*Stands up restlessly.*] That's why I couldn't bear to stay any longer in that out-of-the-way corner. Here it must be easier to find something really worth doing—something to occupy one's thoughts. If I could only get some settled employment—some office work.

NORA. But, Christina, that's such drudgery, and you look worn out already. You should rather go to some watering-place and rest.

MRS. LINDEN [*going to the window*]. I have no father to give me the money, Nora.

NORA [*rising*]. Oh! don't be vexed with me.

MRS. LINDEN [*going towards her*]. My dear Nora, don't you be vexed with me. The worst of a position like mine is that it makes one bitter. You have no one to work for, yet you have to be always on the strain. You must live; and so you become selfish. When I heard of the happy change in your circumstances—can you believe it?—I rejoiced more on my own account than on yours.

NORA. How do you mean? Ah! I see. You mean Torvald could perhaps do something for you.

MRS. LINDEN. Yes, I thought so.

NORA. And so he shall, Christina. Just you leave it all to me. I shall lead up to it beautifully, and think of something pleasant to put him in a good humor! Oh! I should so love to do something for you.

MRS. LINDEN. How good of you, Nora! And doubly good in you, who know so little of the troubles of life.

NORA. I? I know so little of——?

MRS. LINDEN [*smiling*]. Oh, well! a little fancy-work, and so forth. You're a mere child, Nora.

NORA [*tosses her head and paces the room*]. Oh, come, you mustn't be so patronizing!

MRS. LINDEN. No?

NORA. You're like the rest. You all think I'm fit for nothing really serious——

MRS. LINDEN. Well——

NORA. You think I've had no troubles in this weary world.

MRS. LINDEN. My dear Nora, you've just told me all your troubles.

NORA. Pooh—those trifles! [*Softly.*] I haven't told you the great thing.

MRS. LINDEN. The great thing? What do you mean?

NORA. I know you look down upon me, Christina; but you've no right to. You're proud of having worked so hard and so long for your mother.

MRS. LINDEN. I'm sure I don't look down upon any one; but it's true I'm both proud and glad when I remember that I was able to make my mother's last days free from care.

NORA. And you're proud to think of what you have done for your brothers.

MRS. LINDEN. Have I not the right to be?

NORA. Yes, surely. But now let me tell you, Christina—I, too, have something to be proud and glad of.

MRS. LINDEN. I don't doubt it. But what do you mean?

NORA. Hush! Not so loud. Only think, if Torvald were to hear! He mustn't—not for worlds! No one must know about it, Christina—no one but you.

MRS. LINDEN. What can it be?

NORA. Come over here. [*Draws her down beside her on the sofa.*] Yes—I, too, have something to be proud and glad of. *I* saved Torvald's life!

MRS. LINDEN. Saved his life? How?

NORA. I told you about our going to Italy. Torvald would have died but for that.

MRS. LINDEN. Yes—and your father gave you the money.

NORA [*smiling*]. Yes, so Torvald and every one believes; but——

MRS. LINDEN. But——?

NORA. Father didn't give us one penny. I found the money.

MRS. LINDEN. You? All that money?

NORA. Twelve hundred dollars. Four thousand eight hundred crowns. What do you say to that?

MRS. LINDEN. My dear Nora, how did you manage it? Did
you win it in the lottery?

NORA [*contemptuously*]. In the lottery? Pooh! Any fool
could have done that!

MRS. LINDEN. Then where ever did you get it from?

NORA [*hums and smiles mysteriously*]. Hm; tra-la-la-la!

MRS. LINDEN. Of course you couldn't borrow it.

NORA. No? Why not?

MRS. LINDEN. Why, a wife can't borrow without her husband's
consent.

NORA [*tossing her head*]. Oh! when the wife knows a little
of business, and how to set about things, then——

MRS. LINDEN. But, Nora, I don't understand——

NORA. Well, you needn't. I never said I borrowed the money.
Perhaps I got it another way. [*Throws herself back on
the sofa.*] I may have got it from some admirer. When
one is so—attractive as I am——

MRS. LINDEN. You're too silly, Nora.

NORA. Now I'm sure you're dying of curiosity, Christina——

MRS. LINDEN. Listen to me, Nora dear: haven't you been a
little rash?

NORA [*sitting upright again*]. Is it rash to save one's husband's life?

MRS. LINDEN. I think it was rash of you, without his knowledge——

NORA. But it would have been fatal for him to know! Can't
you understand that? He was never to suspect how ill
he was. The doctors came to me privately and told me
his life was in danger—that nothing could save him but
a trip to the South. Do you think I didn't try diplomacy
first? I told him how I longed to have a trip abroad, like
other young wives; I wept and prayed; I said he ought to
think of my condition, and not to thwart me; and then I
hinted that he could borrow the money. But then, Christina, he got almost angry. He said I was frivolous, and
that it was his duty as a husband not to yield to my whims
and fancies—so he called them. Very well, thought I, but
saved you must be; and then I found the way to do it.

MRS. LINDEN. And did your husband never learn from your
father that the money was not from him?

NORA. No; never. Father died at that very time. I meant to have told him all about it, and begged him to say nothing. But he was so ill—unhappily, it wasn't necessary.

MRS. LINDEN. And you've never confessed to your husband?

NORA. Good heavens! What can you be thinking of? Tell him, when he has such a loathing of debt! And besides— how painful and humiliating it would be for Torvald, with his manly self-reliance, to know that he owed anything to me! It would utterly upset the relation between us; our beautiful, happy home would never again be what it is.

MRS. LINDEN. Will you never tell him?

NORA [*thoughtfully, half-smiling*]. Yes, some time perhaps— after many years, when I'm—not so pretty. You mustn't laugh at me. Of course I mean when Torvald is not so much in love with me as he is now; when it doesn't amuse him any longer to see me skipping about, and dressing up and acting. Then it might do well to have something in reserve. [*Breaking off.*] Nonsense! nonsense! That time will never come. Now, what do you say to my grand secret, Christina? Am I fit for nothing now? You may believe it has cost me a lot of anxiety. It has been no joke to meet my engagements punctually. You must know, Christina, that in business there are things called instalments, and quarterly interest, that are terribly hard to provide for. So I had to pinch a little here and there, wherever I could. I couldn't save anything out of the housekeeping, for of course Torvald had to live well. And I couldn't let the children go about badly dressed; all I got for them, I spent on them, the darlings.

MRS. LINDEN. Poor Nora! So it had to come out of your own pocket-money.

NORA. Yes, of course. After all, the whole thing was my doing. When Torvald gave me money for clothes and so on, I never spent more than half of it; I always bought the simplest things. It's a mercy that everything suits me so well, Torvald never noticed anything. But it was often very hard, Christina dear. For it's nice to be beautifully dressed—now, isn't it?

MRS. LINDEN. Indeed it is.

NORA. Well, and besides that, I made money in other ways. Last winter I was so lucky—I got a heap of copying to do. I shut myself up every evening and wrote far into the night. Oh, sometimes I was so tired, so tired. And yet it was splendid to work in that way and earn money. I almost felt as if I was a man.

MRS. LINDEN. Then how much have you been able to pay off?

NORA. Well, I can't precisely say. It's difficult to keep that sort of business clear. I only know that I've paid everything I could scrape together. Sometimes I really didn't know where to turn. [*Smiles.*] Then I used to sit here and imagine that a rich old gentleman was in love with me——

MRS. LINDEN. What! What gentleman?

NORA. Oh, nobody!—that he was now dead, and that when his will was opened, there stood in large letters: Pay over at once everything of which I die possessed to that charming person, Mrs. Nora Helmer.

MRS. LINDEN. But, my dear Nora, what gentleman do you mean?

NORA. Dear dear, can't you understand? There wasn't any old gentleman: it was only what I used to dream and dream when I was at my wits' end for money. But it's all over now—the tiresome old creature may stay where he is for me: I care nothing for him, or his will; for now my troubles are over. [*Springing up.*] Oh, Christina, how glorious it is to think of! Free from cares! Free, quite free. To be able to play and romp about with the children; to have things tasteful and pretty in the house, exactly as Torvald likes it! And then the spring is coming, with the great blue sky. Perhaps then we shall have a short holiday. Perhaps I shall see the sea again. Oh, what a wonderful thing it is to live and to be happy!

[*The hall-door bell rings.*

MRS. LINDEN [*rising*]. There's a ring. Perhaps I had better go.

NORA. No; do stay. It's sure to be some one for Torvald.

ELLEN [*in the doorway*]. If you please, ma'am, there's a gentleman to speak to Mr. Helmer.

NORA. Who is the gentleman?

KROGSTAD [*in the doorway to the hall*]. It is I, Mrs. Helmer.
[*Ellen goes.*
[*Mrs. Linden starts and turns away to the window.*
NORA [*goes a step towards him, anxiously, half aloud*]. You?
What is it? What do you want with my husband?
KROGSTAD. Bank business—in a way. I hold a small post in
the Joint Stock Bank, and your husband is to be our new
chief, I hear.
NORA. Then it is——?
KROGSTAD. Only tiresome business, Mrs. Helmer; nothing
more.
NORA. Then will you please go to his study.
[*Krogstad goes. She bows indifferently while she closes the
door into the hall. Then she goes to the fireplace and
looks to the fire.*
MRS. LINDEN. Nora—who was that man?
NORA. A Mr. Krogstad. Do you know him?
MRS. LINDEN. I used to know him—many years ago. He was
in a lawyer's office in our town.
NORA. Yes, so he was.
MRS. LINDEN. How he has changed!
NORA. I believe his marriage was unhappy.
MRS. LINDEN. And he's a widower now?
NORA. With a lot of children. There! Now it'll burn up.
[*She closes the stove, and pushes the rocking-chair a little
aside.*
MRS. LINDEN. His business is not of the most creditable, they
say.
NORA. Isn't it? I dare say not. I don't know. But don't let
us think of business—it's so tiresome.
[*Doctor Rank comes out of Helmer's room.*
RANK [*still in the doorway*]. No, no; I won't keep you. I'll
just go and have a chat with your wife. [*Shuts the door
and sees Mrs. Linden.*] Oh, I beg your pardon. I'm *de
trop* here too.
NORA. No, not in least. [*Introduces them.*] Doctor Rank—
Mrs. Linden.
RANK. Oh, indeed; I've often heard Mrs. Linden's name; I
think I passed you on the stairs as I came up.

VOL. II.—25

Mrs. Linden. Yes; I go so very slowly. Stairs try me so
much.

Rank. You're not very strong?

Mrs. Linden. Only overworked.

Rank. Ah! Then you've come to town to find rest in a round
of dissipation?

Mrs. Linden. I have come to look for employment.

Rank. Is that an approved remedy for overwork?

Mrs. Linden. One must live, Doctor Rank.

Rank. Yes, that seems to be the general opinion.

Nora. Come, Doctor Rank, you yourself want to live.

Rank. To be sure I do. However wretched I may be, I want
to drag on as long as possible. And my patients have all
the same mania. It's just the same with people whose
complaint is moral. At this very moment Helmer is talking to such a wreck as I mean.

Mrs. Linden [softly]. Ah!

Nora. Whom do you mean!

Rank. Oh, a fellow named Krogstad, a man you know nothing about—corrupt to the very core of his character. But
even he began by announcing solemnly that he must live.

Nora. Indeed? Then what did he want with Torvald?

Rank. I really don't know; I only gathered that it was some
bank business.

Nora. I didn't know that Krog—that this Mr. Krogstad had
anything to do with the Bank?

Rank. He has some sort of place there. [To Mrs. Linden.]
I don't know whether, in your part of the country, you
have people who go rooting and sniffing around in search
of moral rottenness—whose policy it is to fill good places
with men of tainted character whom they can keep under
their eye and in their power? The honest men they leave
out in the cold.

Mrs. Linden. Well, I suppose the—delicate characters require
most care.

Rank [shrugs his shoulders]. There we have it! It's that
notion that makes society a hospital.

[Nora, deep in her own thoughts, breaks into half-stifled
laughter and claps her hands.

Rank. What are you laughing at? Have you any idea what
society is?

Nora. What do I care for your tiresome society? I was laughing at something else—something awfully amusing. Tell me, Dr. Rank, are all the employees at the Bank dependent on Torvald now?

Rank. Is that what strikes you as awfully amusing?

Nora [*smiles and hums*]. Never mind, never mind! [*Walks about the room.*] Yes, it *is* amusing to think that we—that Torvald has such power over so many people. [*Takes the bag from her pocket.*] Doctor Rank, will you have a macaroon?

Rank. Oh, dear dear—macaroons! I thought they were contraband here.

Nora. Yes; but Christina brought me these.

Mrs. Linden. What! I?

Nora. Oh, well! Don't be frightened. You couldn't possibly know that Torvald had forbidden them. The fact is, he's afraid of me spoiling my teeth. But, oh bother, just for once!—That's for you, Doctor Rank! [*Puts a macaroon into his mouth.*] And you too, Christina. And I'll have one at the same time—only a tiny one, or at most two. [*Walks about again.*] Oh dear, I *am* happy! There's only one thing in the world I really want.

Rank. Well; what's that?

Nora. There's something I should so like to say—in Torvald's hearing.

Rank. Then why don't you say it?

Nora. Because I daren't, it's so ugly.

Mrs. Linden. Ugly?

Rank. In that case you'd better not. But to us you might. What is it you would so like to say in Helmer's hearing?

Nora. I should so love to say " Damn! " *

Rank. Are you out of your mind?

Mrs. Linden. Good gracious, Nora!

Rank. Say it—there he is!

Nora [*hides the macaroons*]. Hush—sh—sh!

[*Helmer comes out of his room, hat in hand, with his overcoat on his arm.*

Nora [*going towards him*]. Well, Torvald dear, have you got rid of him?

* " Död og pine," literally " death and torture "; but by usage a comparatively mild oath.

HELMER. Yes; he's just gone.

NORA. May I introduce you? This is Christina, who has come to town——

HELMER. Christina? Pardon me, but I don't know——

NORA. Mrs. Linden, Torvald dear—Christina Linden.

HELMER [to Mrs. Linden]. A school-friend of my wife's, no doubt?

MRS. LINDEN. Yes; we knew each other as girls.

NORA. And, only think! she has taken this long journey on purpose to speak to you.

HELMER. To speak to me!

MRS. LINDEN. Well, not quite——

NORA. You see, Christina is tremendously clever at accounts, and she's so anxious to work under a first-rate man of business in order to learn still more——

HELMER [to Mrs. Linden]. Very sensible indeed.

NORA. And when she heard you were appointed manager—it was telegraphed, you know—she started off at once, and —Torvald dear, for my sake, you must do something for Christina. Now can't you?

HELMER. It's not impossible. I presume you are a widow?

MRS. LINDEN. Yes.

HELMER. And have already had some experience in office-work?

MRS. LINDEN. A good deal.

HELMER. Well, then, it's very likely I may find a place for you.

NORA [clapping her hands]. There now! There now!

HELMER. You have come at a lucky moment, Mrs. Linden.

MRS. LINDEN. Oh, how can I thank you——?

HELMER [smiling]. There is no occasion. [Puts on his over-coat.] But for the present you must excuse me——

RANK. Wait; I'll go with you. [Fetches his fur coat from the hall and warms it at the fire.

NORA. Don't be long, Torvald dear.

HELMER. Only an hour; not more.

NORA. Are you going too, Christina?

MRS. LINDEN [putting on her walking things]. Yes; I must set about looking for lodgings.

HELMER. Then perhaps we can go together?

NORA [helping her]. What a pity we haven't a spare room for you; but it's impossible——

MRS. LINDEN. I shouldn't think of troubling you. Good-by, dear Nora, and thank you for all your kindness.

NORA. Good-by for a little while. Of course you'll come back this evening. And you too, Doctor Rank. What! If you're well enough? Of course you'll be well enough. Only wrap up warmly. [*They go out, talking, into the hall. Outside on the stairs are heard children's voices.*] There they are! There they are! [*She runs to the door and opens it.*] Come in! Come in! [*Bends down and kisses the children.*] Oh, my sweet darlings! Do you see them, Christina? Aren't they lovely?

RANK. Don't let's stand here chattering in the draught.

HELMER. Come, Mrs. Linden; only mothers can stand such a temperature.

[*Doctor Rank, Helmer, and Mrs. Linden go down the stairs; Anna enters the room with the children; Nora also, shutting the door.*

NORA. How fresh and bright you look! And what red cheeks you have! Like apples and roses. [*The children chatter to her during the following.*] Have you had great fun? That's splendid. Oh, really! You've been giving Emmy and Bob a ride on your sledge!—both at once, only think! Why, you're quite a man, Ivar. Oh, give her to me a little, Anna. My sweet little dolly! [*Takes the smallest from the nurse and dances with her.*] Yes, yes; mother will dance with Bob too. What! Did you have a game of snow-balls? Oh, I wish I'd been there. No; leave them, Anna; I'll take their things off. Oh, yes, let me do it; it's such fun. Go to the nursery; you look frozen. You'll find some hot coffee on the stove.

[*The Nurse goes into the room on the left. Nora takes off the children's things and throws them down anywhere, while the children talk to each other and to her.*

Really! A big dog ran after you all the way home? But he didn't bite you? No; dogs don't bite dear little dolly children. Don't peep into those parcels, Ivar. What is it? Wouldn't you like to know? Oh, take care—it'll bite! What! Shall we have a game? What shall we play at? Hide-and-seek? Yes, let's play hide-and-seek. Bob shall hide first. Am I to? Yes, let me hide first.

[*She and the children play, with laughter and shouting, in the
room and the adjacent one to the right. At last Nora
hides under the table; the children come rushing in,
look for her, but cannot find her, hear her half-choked
laughter, rush to the table, lift up the cover and see her.
Loud shouts. She creeps out, as though to frighten
them. Fresh shouts. Meanwhile there has been a knock
at the door leading into the hall. No one has heard
it. Now the door is half opened and Krogstad appears.
He waits a little; the game is renewed.*

KROGSTAD. I beg your pardon, Mrs. Helmer——

NORA [*with a suppressed cry turns round and half jumps up*].
Ah! What do you want?

KROGSTAD. Excuse me, the outer door was ajar—somebody
must have forgotten to shut it——

NORA [*standing up*]. My husband is not at home.

KROGSTAD. I know it.

NORA. Then what do you want here?

KROGSTAD. To say a few words to you.

NORA. To me? [*To the children, softly.*] Go in to Anna.
What? No, the strange man won't hurt mamma. When
he's gone we'll go on playing. [*She leads the children
into the left-hand room, and shuts the door behind them.
Uneasy, in suspense.*] It's with me you wish to speak?

KROGSTAD. Yes.

NORA. To-day? But it's not the first yet——

KROGSTAD. No, to-day is Christmas Eve. It will depend upon
yourself whether you have a merry Christmas.

NORA. What do you want? I'm not ready to-day——

KROGSTAD. Never mind that just now. It's about another matter. You have a minute to spare?

NORA. Oh, yes, I suppose so; although——

KROGSTAD. Good. I was sitting in the restaurant opposite, and
I saw your husband go down the street.

NORA. Well?

KROGSTAD. With a lady.

NORA. What then?

KROGSTAD. May I ask if the lady was a Mrs. Linden?

NORA. Yes.

KROGSTAD. Who has just come to town?

NORA. Yes. To-day.

KROGSTAD. I believe she's an intimate friend of yours?

NORA. Certainly. But I don't understand——

KROGSTAD. I used to know her too.

NORA. I know you did.

KROGSTAD. Ah, you know all about it! I thought as much. Now, frankly, is Mrs. Linden to have a place in the Bank?

NORA. How dare you catechise me in this way, Mr. Krogstad —you, a subordinate of my husband's? But since you ask, you shall know. Yes, Mrs. Linden is to be employed. And it's I who recommended her, Mr. Krogstad. Now you know.

KROGSTAD. Then my guess was right.

NORA [*walking up and down*]. You see one has a little wee bit of influence. It doesn't follow because one's only a woman that—when one is in a subordinate position, Mr. Krogstad, one ought really to take care not to offend anybody who—hm——

KROGSTAD. Who has influence?

NORA. Exactly!

KROGSTAD [*taking another tone*]. Mrs. Helmer, will you have the kindness to employ your influence on my behalf?

NORA. What? How do you mean?

KROGSTAD. Will you be so good as to see that I retain my subordinate position in the Bank?

NORA. What do you mean? Who wants to take it from you?

KROGSTAD. Oh, you needn't pretend ignorance. I can very well understand that it cannot be pleasant for your friend to meet me; and I can also understand now for whose sake I am to be hounded out.

NORA. But I assure you——

KROGSTAD. Come now, once for all: there's time yet, and I advise you to use your influence to prevent it.

NORA. But, Mr. Krogstad, I have absolutely no influence.

KROGSTAD. None? I thought you just said——

NORA. Of course not in that sense. I! How should I have such influence over my husband?

KROGSTAD. Oh, I know your husband from our college days. I don't think he's firmer than other husbands.

NORA. If you talk disrespectfully of my husband, I must request you to go.

KROGSTAD. You are bold, madam.

NORA. I'm afraid of you no longer. When New Year's Day is over, I shall soon be out of the whole business.

KROGSTAD [*controlling himself*]. Listen to me, Mrs. Helmer. If need be, I shall fight as though for my life to keep my little place in the Bank.

NORA. Yes, so it seems.

KROGSTAD. It's not only for the money: that matters least to me. It's something else. Well, I'd better make a clean breast of it. Of course you know, like everyone else, that some years ago I—got into trouble.

NORA. I think I've heard something of the sort.

KROGSTAD. The matter never came into court; but from that moment all paths were barred to me. Then I took up the business you know about. I was obliged to grasp at something; and I don't think I've been one of the worst. But now I must clear out of it all. My sons are growing up; for their sake I must try to win back as much respectability as I can. This place in the Bank was the first step; and now your husband wants to kick me off the ladder back into the mire.

NORA. But I assure you, Mr. Krogstad, I haven't the power to help you.

KROGSTAD. You haven't the will; but I can compel you.

NORA. You won't tell my husband that I owe you money?

KROGSTAD. Hm; suppose I were to?

NORA. It would be shameful of you. [*With tears in her voice.*] This secret, which is my joy and my pride—that he should learn it in such an ugly, coarse way—and from you! It would involve me in all sorts of unpleasantness.

KROGSTAD. Only unpleasantness?

NORA [*hotly*]. But just do it. It will be worst for you, for then my husband will see what a bad man you are, and then you certainly won't keep your place.

KROGSTAD. I asked if it was only domestic unpleasantness you feared?

NORA. If my husband gets to know about it, he will of course pay you off at once, and then we'll have nothing more to do with you.

KROGSTAD [*stepping a pace nearer*]. Listen, Mrs. Helmer:

either you have a weak memory, or you don't know much
about business. I must make the position clear to you.

NORA. How so?

KROGSTAD. When your husband was ill, you came to me to
borrow twelve hundred dollars.

NORA. I knew of nobody else.

KROGSTAD. I promised to find you the money——

NORA. And you did find it.

KROGSTAD. I promised to find you the money, under certain
conditions. You were then so much taken up about your
husband's illness, and so eager to have the wherewithal
for your journey, that you probably didn't give much
thought to the details. Let me remind you of them. I
promised to find you the amount in exchange for a note of
hand which I drew up.

NORA. Yes, and I signed it.

KROGSTAD. Quite right. But then I added a few lines, making your father security for the debt. Your father was to
sign this.

NORA. Was to? He did sign it!

KROGSTAD. I had left the date blank. That is to say, your
father was himself to date his signature. Do you recollect that?

NORA. Yes, I believe——

KROGSTAD. Then I gave you the paper to send to your father.
Is not that so?

NORA. Yes.

KROGSTAD. And of course you did so at once? For within
five or six days you brought me back the paper, signed by
your father; and I gave you the money.

NORA. Well? Haven't I made my payments punctually?

KROGSTAD. Fairly—yes. But to return to the point: You
were in great trouble at the time, Mrs. Helmer.

NORA. I was indeed!

KROGSTAD. Your father was very ill, I believe?

NORA. He was on his death-bed.

KROGSTAD. And died soon after?

NORA. Yes.

KROGSTAD. Tell me, Mrs. Helmer: do you happen to recollect
the day of his death? The day of the month, I mean?

NORA. Father died on the 29th of September.

KROGSTAD. Quite correct. I have made inquiries. And here comes in the remarkable point—[*produces a paper*] which I cannot explain.

NORA. What remarkable point? I don't know——

KROGSTAD. The remarkable point, madam, that your father signed this paper three days after his death!

NORA. What! I don't understand——

KROGSTAD. Your father died on the 29th of September. But look here: he has dated his signature October 2d! Is not that remarkable, Mrs. Helmer? [*Nora is silent.*] Can you explain it? [*Nora continues silent.*] It is noteworthy, too, that the words "October 2d" and the year are not in your father's handwriting, but in one which I believe I know. Well, this may be explained; your father may have forgotten to date his signature; and somebody may have added the date at random, before the fact of your father's death was known. There's nothing wrong in that. Everything depends on the signature. Of course it is genuine, Mrs. Helmer? It was really your father who, with his own hand, wrote his name here?

NORA [*after a short silence, throws her head back and looks defiantly at him*]. No; I wrote father's name there.

KROGSTAD. Ah! Are you aware, madam, that that is a dangerous admission?

NORA. Why? you'll soon get your money.

KROGSTAD. May I ask you one more question? Why did you not send the paper to your father?

NORA. It was impossible. Father was ill. If I had asked him for his signature I should have had to tell him why I wanted the money; but he was so ill I really could not tell him that my husband's life was in danger. It was impossible.

KROGSTAD. Then it would have been better to have given up your tour.

NORA. No, I couldn't do that; my husband's life depended on that journey. I couldn't give it up.

KROGSTAD. And did you not consider that you were playing me false?

NORA. That was nothing to me. I didn't care in the least about you. I couldn't endure you for all the cruel difficulties you made, although you knew how ill my husband was.

KROGSTAD. Mrs. Helmer, you have evidently no clear idea of what you have really done. But I can assure you it is nothing more and nothing worse that made me an outcast from society.

NORA. You! You want me to believe that you did a brave thing to save your wife's life?

KROGSTAD. The law takes no account of motives.

NORA. Then it must be a very bad law.

KROGSTAD. Bad or not, if I lay this document before a court of law you will be condemned according to law.

NORA. I don't believe that. Do you mean to tell me that a daughter has no right to spare her dying father anxiety? —that a wife has no right to save her husband's life? I don't know much about the law, but I'm sure you'll find, somewhere or another, that *that* is allowed. And you don't know that—you, a lawyer! You must be a bad one, Mr. Krogstad.

KROGSTAD. Possibly. But business—such business as ours—I do understand. You believe that? Very well; now do as you please. But this I may tell you, that if I'm flung into the gutter a second time, you shall keep me company.

[*Bows and goes out through hall.*

NORA [*stands awhile thinking, then tosses her head*]. Never! He wants to frighten me. I'm not so foolish as that. [*Begins folding the children's clothes. Pauses.*] But ——? No, it's impossible. I did it for love!

CHILDREN [*at the door, left*]. Mamma, the strange man has gone now.

NORA. Yes, yes, I know. But don't tell any one about the strange man. Do you hear? Not even papa!

CHILDREN. No, mamma; and now will you play with us again?

NORA. No, no, not now.

CHILDREN. Oh do, mamma; you know you promised.

NORA. Yes, but I can't just now. Run to the nursery; I've so much to do. Run along, run along, and be good, my darlings! [*She pushes them gently into the inner room, and closes the door behind them. Sits on the sofa, embroiders a few stitches, but soon pauses.*] No! [*Throws*

down work, rises, goes to the hall door and calls out.]
Ellen, bring in the Christmas tree! [*Goes to table, left,
and opens the drawer; again pauses.*] No, it's quite impossible!

ELLEN [*with Christmas tree*]. Where shall I stand it, ma'am?

NORA. There, in the middle of the room.

ELLEN. Shall I bring in anything else?

NORA. No, thank you, I have all I want.

　　　　　　　　　[*Ellen having put down the tree, goes out.*

NORA [*busy dressing the tree*]. There must be a candle here,
and flowers there. The horrid man! Nonsense, nonsense! there's nothing in it. The Christmas tree shall be
beautiful. I'll do everything to please you, Torvald; I'll
sing and dance, and——

[*Enter Helmer by the hall door, with bundle of documents.*

NORA. Oh! You're back already?

HELMER. Yes. Has anybody been here?

NORA. Here? No.

HELMER. Curious! I saw Krogstad come out of the house.

NORA. Did you? Oh, yes, by the bye, he was here for a minute.

HELMER. Nora, I can see by your manner that he has been
asking you to put in a good word for him?

NORA. Yes.

HELMER. And you were to do it of your own accord? You
were to say nothing to me of his having been here! Didn't
he suggest that too?

NORA. Yes, Torvald; but——

HELMER. Nora, Nora! And you could condescend to that!
To speak to such a man, to make him a promise! And
then to tell me an untruth about it!

NORA. An untruth!

HELMER. Didn't you say nobody had been here? [*Threatens
with his finger.*] My little bird must never do that again!
A song-bird must never sing false notes. [*Puts his arm
round her.*] That's so, isn't it? Yes, I was sure of it.
[*Lets her go.*] And now we'll say no more about it.
[*Sits down before the fire.*] Oh, how cosey and quiet it is
here! [*Glances into his documents.*

NORA [*busy with the tree, after a short silence*]. Torvald.

HELMER. Yes.

NORA. I'm looking forward so much to the Stenborg's fancy ball the day after to-morrow.

HELMER. And I'm on tenterhooks to see what surprise you have in store for me.

NORA. Oh, it's too tiresome!

HELMER. What is?

NORA. I can't think of anything good. Everything seems so foolish and meaningless.

HELMER. Has little Nora made that discovery?

NORA [behind his chair, with her arms on the back]. Are you very busy, Torvald?

HELMER. Well——

NORA. What sort of papers are those?

HELMER. Bank business.

NORA. Already?

HELMER. I got the retiring manager to let me make some changes in the staff, and so forth. This will occupy Christmas week. Everything will be straight by the New Year.

NORA. Then that's why that poor Krogstad——

HELMER. Hm.

NORA [still leaning over the chair back and slowly stroking his hair]. If you hadn't been so very busy I should have asked you a great, great favor, Torvald.

HELMER. What can it be? Let's hear it.

NORA. Nobody has such exquisite taste as you; and I should so love to look well at the fancy ball. Torvald, dear, couldn't you take me in hand, and settle what I'm to be, and arrange my costume for me?

HELMER. Aha! So my wilful little woman is at a loss, and making signals of distress.

NORA. Yes, please, Torvald. I can't get on without you.

HELMER. Well, well, I'll think it over, and we'll soon hit upon something.

NORA. Oh, how good that is of you! [Goes to the tree again; pause.] How well the red flowers show. Tell me, was it anything so very dreadful this Krogstad got into trouble about?

HELMER. Forgery, that's all. Don't you know what that means?

NORA. Mayn't he have been driven to it by need?

HELMER. Yes, or like so many others, he may have done it in pure heedlessness. I'm not so hard-hearted as to condemn a man absolutely for a single fault.

NORA. No, surely not, Torvald.

HELMER. Many a man can retrieve his character, if he owns his crime and takes the punishment.

NORA. Crime?

HELMER. But Krogstad didn't do that. He resorted to tricks and dodges, and it's that that has corrupted him.

NORA. Do you think that——?

HELMER. Just think how a man with a thing of that sort on his conscience must be always lying and canting and shamming. Think of the mask he must wear even towards his own wife and children. It's worst for the children, Nora!

NORA. Why?

HELMER. Because such a dust-cloud of lies poisons and contaminates the whole air of home. Every breath the children draw contains some germ of evil.

NORA [close behind him]. Are you sure of that?

HELMER. As a lawyer, my dear, I've seen it often enough. Nearly all cases of early corruption may be traced to lying mothers.

NORA. Why—mothers?

HELMER. It generally comes from the mother's side; but of course the father's influence may act in the same way. And this Krogstad has been poisoning his own children for years past by a life of lies and hypocrisy—that's why I call him morally ruined. [Stretches out his hands towards her.] So my sweet little Nora must promise not to plead his cause. Shake hands upon it. Come, come, what's this? Give me your hand. That's right. Then it's a bargain. I assure you it would have been impossible for me to work with him. It gives me a positive sense of physical discomfort to come in contact with such people.

[Nora snatches her hand away, and moves to the other side of the Christmas tree.

NORA. How warm it is here; and I have so much to do.

HELMER. Yes, and I must try to get some of these papers looked through before dinner; and I'll think over your

costume too. Perhaps I may even find something to hang
in gilt paper on the Christmas tree! [*Lays his hand on
her head.*] My precious little song-bird!

    [*He goes into his room and shuts the door behind him.*

NORA [*softly, after a pause*]. It can't be. It's impossible. It
must be impossible!

ANNA [*at the door, left*]. The little ones are begging so prettily to come to mamma. .

NORA. No, no, don't let them come to me! Keep them with
you, Anna.

ANNA. Very well, ma'am.   [*Shuts the door.*

NORA [*pale with terror*]. Corrupt my children!—Poison my
home! [*Short pause. She raises her head.*] It's not true!
It can never, never be true!

ACT SECOND

SCENE.—*The same room. In the corner, beside the piano,
    stands the Christmas tree, stripped, and with the candles
    burnt out. Nora's out-door things lie on the sofa.*

[*Nora discovered, walking about restlessly. She stops by the
    sofa, takes up her cloak, then lays it down again.*

NORA. There's somebody coming. [*Goes to hall door, listens.*]
Nobody; nobody's likely to come to-day, Christmas-day;
nor to-morrow either. But perhaps—— [*Opens the door
and looks out.*] No, nothing in the letter-box; quite
empty. [*Comes forward.*] Stuff and nonsense! Of
course he only meant to frighten me. There's no fear of
any such thing. It's impossible! Why, I have three little
children.

    [*Enter Anna from the left with a large cardboard box.*

ANNA. At last I've found the box with the fancy dress.

NORA. Thanks, put it down on the table.

ANNA [*does so*]. But it's very much out of order.

NORA. Oh, I wish I could tear it into a hundred thousand
pieces.

ANNA. Oh, no. It can easily be put to rights—just a little
patience.

NORA. I'll go and get Mrs. Linden to help me.

ANNA. Going out again? In such weather as this! You'll catch cold, ma'am, and be ill.

NORA. Worse things might happen. What are the children doing?

ANNA. They're playing with their Christmas presents, poor little dears; but——

NORA. Do they often ask for me?

ANNA. You see they've been so used to having their mamma with them.

NORA. Yes; but Anna, in future I can't have them so much with me.

ANNA. Well, little children get used to anything.

NORA. Do you think they do? Do you believe they would forget their mother if she went quite away?

ANNA. Gracious me! Quite away?

NORA. Tell me, Anna—— I've so often wondered about it— how could you bring yourself to give your child up to strangers?

ANNA. I had to when I came to nurse my little Miss Nora.

NORA. But how could you make up your mind to it?

ANNA. When I had the chance of such a good place? A poor girl who's been in trouble must take what comes. That wicked man did nothing for me.

NORA. But your daughter must have forgotten you.

ANNA. Oh, no, ma'am, that she hasn't. She wrote to me both when she was confirmed and when she was married.

NORA [embracing her]. Dear old Anna—you were a good mother to me when I was little.

ANNA. My poor little Nora had no mother but me.

NORA. And if my little ones had nobody else, I'm sure you would—— Nonsense, nonsense! [Opens the box.] Go in to the children. Now I must—— To-morrow you shall see how beautiful I'll be.

ANNA. I'm sure there will be no one at the ball so beautiful as my Miss Nora. [She goes into the room on the left.

NORA [takes the costume out of the box, but soon throws it down again]. Oh, if I dared go out. If only nobody would come. If only nothing would happen here in the meantime. Rubbish; nobody will come. Only not to think. What a delicious muff! Beautiful gloves, beautiful gloves! Away with it all—away with it all! One, two, three, four, five, six—[*with a scream*]. Ah, there they come— [*Goes towards the door, then stands undecided.*

[*Mrs. Linden enters from the hall, where she has taken off her things.*

NORA. Oh, it's you, Christina. Is nobody else there? How delightful of you to come.

MRS. LINDEN. I hear you called at my lodgings.

NORA. Yes, I was just passing. I did so want you to help me. Let's sit here on the sofa—so. To-morrow evening there's to be a fancy ball at Consul Stenborg's overhead, and Torvald wants me to appear as a Neapolitan fisher-girl, and dance the tarantella; I learned it at Capri.

MRS. LINDEN. I see—quite a performance.

NORA. Yes, Torvald wishes it. Look, this is the costume. Torvald had it made for me in Italy; but now it's all so torn, I don't know——

MRS. LINDEN. Oh! We'll soon set that to rights. It's only the trimming that's got loose here and there. Have you a needle and thread? Ah, here's the very thing.

NORA. Oh, how kind of you.

MRS. LINDEN. So you're to be in costume to-morrow, Nora? I'll tell you what—I shall come in for a moment to see you in all your glory. But I've quite forgotten to thank you for the pleasant evening yesterday.

NORA [*rises and walks across room*]. Oh, yesterday, it didn't seem so pleasant as usual. You should have come a little sooner, Christina. Torvald has certainly the art of making home bright and beautiful.

MRS. LINDEN. You too, I should think, or you wouldn't be your father's daughter. But tell me—is Doctor Rank always so depressed as he was last evening?

NORA. No, yesterday it was particularly striking. You see he has a terrible illness. He has spinal consumption, poor fellow. They say his father led a terrible life—kept mistresses and all sorts of things—so the son has been sickly from his childhood, you understand.

MRS. LINDEN [*lets her sewing fall into her lap*]. Why, my darling Nora, how do you learn such things?

NORA [*walking*]. Oh! When one has three children, one has visits from women who know something of medicine—and they talk of this and that.

MRS. LINDEN [*goes on sewing; a short pause*]. Does Doctor Rank come here every day?

NORA. Every day. He's been Torvald's friend from boyhood, and he's a good friend of mine too. Doctor Rank is quite one of the family.

MRS. LINDEN. But tell me—is he quite sincere? I mean, doesn't he like to say flattering things to people?

NORA. On the contrary. Why should you think so?

MRS. LINDEN. When you introduced us yesterday he declared he had often heard my name; but I noticed your husband had no notion who I was. How could Dr. Rank——?

NORA. Yes, he was quite right, Christina. You see, Torvald loves me so indescribably, he wants to have me all to himself, as he says. When we were first married he was almost jealous if I even mentioned one of the people at home; so I naturally let it alone. But I often talk to Doctor Rank about the old times, for he likes to hear about them.

MRS. LINDEN. Listen to me, Nora! You're still a child in many ways. I'm older than you, and have had more experience. I'll tell you something: You ought to get clear of the whole affair with Doctor Rank.

NORA. What affair?

MRS. LINDEN. You were talking yesterday of a rich admirer who was to find you money——

NORA. Yes, one who never existed, worse luck. What then?

MRS. LINDEN. Has Doctor Rank money?

NORA. Yes, he has.

MRS. LINDEN. And nobody to provide for?

NORA. Nobody. But——

MRS. LINDEN. And he comes here every day?

NORA. Yes, every day.

MRS. LINDEN. I should have thought he'd have had better taste.

NORA. I don't understand you.

MRS. LINDEN. Don't pretend, Nora. Do you suppose I don't guess who lent you the twelve hundred dollars?

NORA. Are you out of your senses? You think that! A friend who comes here every day! How painful that would be!

MRS. LINDEN. Then it really is not he?

NORA. No, I assure you. It never for a moment occurred to me—— Besides, at that time he had nothing to lend; he came into his property afterwards.

MRS. LINDEN. Well, I believe that was lucky for you, Nora dear.

NORA. No, really, it would never have struck me to ask Doctor Rank. But I'm certain that if I did——

MRS. LINDEN. But of course you never would?

NORA. Of course not. It's inconceivable that it should ever be necessary. But I'm quite sure that if I spoke to Doctor Rank——

MRS. LINDEN. Behind your husband's back?

NORA. I must get out of the other thing; that's behind his back too. I must get out of that.

MRS. LINDEN. Yes, yes, I told you so yesterday; but——

NORA [*walking up and down*]. A man can manage these things much better than a woman.

MRS. LINDEN. One's own husband, yes.

NORA. Nonsense. [*Stands still.*] When everything is paid, one gets back the paper?

MRS. LINDEN. Of course.

NORA. And can tear it into a hundred thousand pieces, and burn it, the nasty, filthy thing!

MRS. LINDEN [*looks at her fixedly, lays down her work, and rises slowly*]. Nora, you're hiding something from me.

NORA. Can you see it in my face?

MRS. LINDEN. Something has happened since yesterday morning. Nora, what is it?

NORA [*going towards her*]. Christina—— [*Listens.*] Hush! There's Torvald coming home. Here, go into the nursery. Torvald can't bear to see dressmaking. Get Anna to help you.

MRS. LINDEN [*gathers some of the things together*]. Very well; but I shan't go away until you've told me all about it.

[*She goes out to the left, as Helmer enters from the hall.*

NORA [*runs to meet him*]. Oh, how I've been longing for you to come, Torvald dear!

HELMER. Was the dressmaker here?

NORA. No, Christina. She's helping me with my costume. You'll see how nice I shall look.

HELMER. Yes, wasn't that a lucky thought of mine?

NORA. Splendid. But isn't it good of me, too, to have given in to you?

HELMER [*takes her under the chin*]. Good of you! To give in to your own husband? Well well, you little madcap, I know you don't mean it. But I won't disturb you. I dare say you want to be "trying on."

NORA. And you're going to work, I suppose?

HELMER. Yes. [*Shows her a bundle of papers.*] Look here [*Goes towards his room.*] I've just come from the Bank.

NORA. Torvald.

HELMER [*stopping*]. Yes?

NORA. If your little squirrel were to beg you for something so prettily——

HELMER. Well?

NORA. Would you do it?

HELMER. I must know first what it is.

NORA. The squirrel would skip about and play all sorts of tricks if you would only be nice and kind.

HELMER. Come, then, out with it.

NORA. Your lark would twitter from morning till night——

HELMER. Oh, that she does in any case.

NORA. I'll be an elf and dance in the moonlight for you, Torvald.

HELMER. Nora—you can't mean what you were hinting at this morning?

NORA [*coming nearer*]. Yes, Torvald, I beg and implore you.

HELMER. Have you really the courage to begin that again?

NORA. Yes, yes; for my sake, you must let Krogstad keep his place in the Bank.

HELMER. My dear Nora, it's his place I intend for Mrs. Linden.

NORA. Yes, that's so good of you. But instead of Krogstad, you could dismiss some other clerk.

HELMER. Why, this is incredible obstinacy! Because you thoughtlessly promised to put in a word for him, I am to——

NORA. It's not that, Torvald. It's for your own sake. This man writes for the most scurrilous newspapers; you said so yourself. He can do you such a lot of harm. I'm terribly afraid of him.

HELMER. Oh, I understand; it's old recollections that are frightening you.

NORA. What do you mean?

HELMER. Of course you're thinking of your father.

NORA. Yes, of course. Only think of the shameful things wicked people used to write about father. I believe they'd have got him dismissed if you hadn't been sent to look into the thing, and been kind to him and helped him.

HELMER. My dear Nora, between your father and me there is all the difference in the world. Your father was not altogether unimpeachable. I am; and I hope to remain so.

NORA. Oh, no one knows what wicked men can hit upon. We could live so happily now, in our cosey, quiet home, you and I and the children, Torvald! That's why I beg and implore you——

HELMER. And it's just by pleading his cause that you make it impossible for me to keep him. It's already known at the Bank that I intend to dismiss Krogstad. If it were now reported that the new manager let himself be turned round his wife's little finger——

NORA. What then?

HELMER. Oh, nothing, so long as a wilful woman can have her way—I am to make myself the laughing-stock of every one, and set people saying I'm under petticoat government? Take my word for it, I should soon feel the consequences. And besides, there's one thing that makes Krogstad impossible for me to work with.

NORA. What thing?

HELMER. I could perhaps have overlooked his shady character at a pinch——

NORA. Yes, couldn't you, Torvald?

HELMER. And I hear he's good at his work. But the fact is, he was a college chum of mine—there was one of those rash friendships between us that one so often repents of later. I don't mind confessing it—he calls me by my Christian name; * and he insists on doing it even when

* In the original " We say ' thou ' to each other."

others are present. He delights in putting on airs of familiarity—Torvald here, Torvald there! I assure you it's most painful to me. He would make my position at the Bank perfectly unendurable.

NORA. Torvald, you're not serious?

HELMER. No? Why not?

NORA. That's such a petty reason.

HELMER. What! Petty! Do you consider me petty?

NORA. No, on the contrary, Torvald dear; and that's just why——

HELMER. Never mind, you call my motives petty; then I must be petty too. Petty! Very well. Now we'll put an end to this, once for all. [*Goes to the door into the hall and calls.*] Ellen!

NORA. What do you want?

HELMER [*searching among his papers*]. To settle the thing. [*Ellen enters.*] There, take this letter, give it to a messenger. See that he takes it at once. The address is on it. Here's the money.

ELLEN. Very well, sir.   [*Goes with the letter.*

HELMER [*putting his papers together*]. There, Madam Obstinacy.

NORA [*breathless*]. Torvald, what was in that letter?

HELMER. Krogstad's dismissal.

NORA. Call it back again, Torvald! There's still time. Oh, Torvald, get it back again! For my sake, for your own, for the children's sake! Do you hear, Torvald? Do it. You don't know what that letter may bring upon us all.

HELMER. Too late.

NORA. Yes, too late.

HELMER. My dear Nora, I forgive your anxiety, though it's anything but flattering to me. Why should I be afraid of a blackguard scribbler's spite? But I forgive you all the same, for it's a proof of your great love for me. [*Takes her in his arms.*] That's as it should be, my own dear Nora. Let what will happen—when the time comes, I shall have strength and courage enough. You shall see; my shoulders are broad enough to bear the whole burden.

NORA [*terror-struck*]. What do you mean by that?

HELMER. The whole burden, I say.

Nora [*with decision*]. That you shall never, never do!

Helmer. Very well; then we'll share it, Nora, as man and wife. [*Petting her.*] Are you satisfied now? Come, come, come, don't look like a scared dove. It is all nothing—fancy. Now you must play the tarantella through and practise with the tambourine. I shall sit in my inner room and shut both doors, so that I shall hear nothing. You can make as much noise as you please. [*Turns round in doorway.*] And when Rank comes, just tell him where I'm to be found.

[*He nods to her, and goes with his papers into his room, closing the door.*

Nora [*bewildered with terror, stands as though rooted to the ground, and whispers*]. He would do it. Yes, he would do it. He would do it, in spite of all the world. No, never that, never, never! Anything rather than that! Oh, for some way of escape! What to do! [*Hall bell rings.*] Doctor Rank——! Anything rather than that—anything, anything!

[*Nora draws her hands over her face, pulls herself together, goes to the door and opens it. Rank stands outside hanging up his great-coat. During the following it grows dark.*

Nora. Good afternoon, Doctor Rank. I knew you by your ring. But you mustn't go to Torvald now. I believe he's busy.

Rank. And you?

Nora. Oh, you know very well, I've always time for you.

Rank. Thank you. I shall avail myself of your kindness as long as I can!

Nora. What do you mean? As long as you can?

Rank. Yes. Does that frighten you?

Nora. I think it's an odd expression. Do you expect anything to happen?

Rank. Something I have long been prepared for; but I didn't think it would come so soon.

Nora [*seizing his arm*]. What is it, Doctor Rank? You must tell me.

Rank [*sitting down by the stove*]. I am running down hill. There's no help for it.

Nora [*draws a long breath of relief*]. It's you——?

Rank. Who else should it be?—Why lie to one's self? I'm the most wretched of all my patients, Mrs. Helmer. I've been auditing my life account—bankrupt! Before a month is over I shall lie rotting in the churchyard.

Nora. Oh! What an ugly way to talk!

Rank. The thing itself is so confoundedly ugly, you see. But the worst of it is, so many other ugly things have to be gone through first. There's one last investigation to be made, and when that's over I shall know exactly when the break-up will begin. There's one thing I want to say to you: Helmer's delicate nature shrinks so from all that is horrible; I will not have him in my sick-room.

Nora. But, Doctor Rank——

Rank. I won't have him, I say—not on any account! I shall lock my door against him. As soon as I've ascertained the worst, I shall send you my visiting-card with a black cross on it; and then you'll know that the horror has begun.

Nora. Why, you're perfectly unreasonable to-day; and I did so want you to be in a really good humor.

Rank. With death staring me in the face? And to suffer thus for another's sin! Where's the justice of it? And in every family you can see some such inexorable retribution.

Nora [*stopping her ears*]. Nonsense, nonsense; now cheer up.

Rank. Well, after all, the whole thing's only worth laughing at. My poor innocent spine must do penance for my father's wild oats.

Nora [*at table, left*]. I suppose he was too fond of asparagus and Strasbourg pâté, wasn't he?

Rank. Yes; and truffles.

Nora. Yes, truffles, to be sure. And oysters, I believe?

Rank. Yes, oysters; oysters, of course.

Nora. And then all the port and champagne! It's sad all these good things should attack the spine.

Rank. Especially when the spine attacked never had any good of them.

Nora. Yes, that's the worst of it.

Rank [*looks at her searchingly*]. Hm——

Nora [*a moment later*]. Why did you smile?

RANK. No; it was you that laughed.

NORA. No; it was you that smiled, Doctor Rank.

RANK [*standing up*]. You're deeper than I thought.

NORA. I'm in such a crazy mood to-day.

RANK. So it seems.

NORA [*with her hands on his shoulders*]. Dear, dear Doctor Rank, death shall not take you away from Torvald and me.

RANK. Oh, you'll easily get over the loss. The absent are soon forgotten.

NORA [*looks at him anxiously*]. Do you think so?

RANK. People make fresh ties, and then——

NORA. Who make fresh ties?

RANK. You and Helmer will, when I'm gone. You yourself are taking time by the forelock, it seems to me. What was that Mrs. Linden doing here yesterday?

NORA. Oh, you're surely not jealous of Christina?

RANK. Yes, I am. She will be my successor in this house. When I'm gone, this woman will perhaps——

NORA. Hush! Not so loud; she's in there.

RANK. To-day as well? You see!

NORA. Only to put my costume in order—how unreasonable you are! [*Sits on sofa.*] Now do be good, Doctor Rank! To-morrow you shall see how beautifully I'll dance; and then you may fancy that I'm doing it all to please you— and of course Torvald as well. [*Takes various things out of box.*] Doctor Rank, sit here, and I'll show you something.

RANK [*sitting*]. What is it?

NORA. Look here. Look!

RANK. Silk stockings.

NORA. Flesh-colored. Aren't they lovely? Oh, it's so dark here now; but to-morrow—No, no, no, you must only look at the feet. Oh, well, I suppose you may look at the rest too.

RANK. Hm——

NORA. What are you looking so critical about? Do you think they won't fit me?

RANK. I can't possibly have any valid opinion on that point.

NORA [*looking at him a moment*]. For shame! [*Hits him lightly on the ear with the stockings.*] Take that.

[*Rolls them up again.*

RANK. And what other wonders am I to see?

NORA. You shan't see any more, for you don't behave nicely.
  [*She hums a little and searches among the things.*

RANK [*after a short silence*]. When I sit here gossiping with
  you, I simply can't imagine what would have become of
  me if I had never entered this house.

NORA [*smiling*]. Yes, I think you do feel at home with us.

RANK [*more softly—looking straight before him*]. And now
  to have to leave it all——

NORA. Nonsense. You shan't leave us.

RANK [*in the same tone*]. And not to be able to leave behind
  the slightest token of gratitude; scarcely even a passing
  regret—nothing but an empty place, that can be filled by
  the first comer.

NORA. And if I were to ask you for——? No——

RANK. For what?

NORA. For a great proof of your friendship.

RANK. Yes—yes?

NORA. No, I mean—for a very, very great service.

RANK. Would you really for once make me so happy?

NORA. Oh, you don't know what it is.

RANK. Then tell me.

NORA. No, I really can't; it's far, far too much—not only a
  service, but help and advice besides——

RANK. So much the better. I can't think what you can mean.
  But go on. Don't you trust me?

NORA. As I trust no one else. I know you are my best and
  truest friend. So I will tell you. Well then, Doctor Rank,
  you must help me to hinder something. You know how
  deeply, how wonderfully Torvald loves me; he wouldn't
  hesitate a moment to give his very life for my sake.

RANK [*bending towards her*]. Nora, do you think he is the
  only one who——

NORA [*with a slight start*]. Who——?

RANK. Who would gladly give his life for you?

NORA [*sadly*]. Oh!

RANK. I have sworn that you shall know it before I—go. I
  shall never find a better opportunity.—Yes, Nora, now
  you know it; and now you know too that you can trust
  me as you can no one else.

NORA [*standing up simply and calmly*]. Let me pass, please.

RANK [*makes way for her, but remains sitting*]. Nora——

NORA [*in the doorway*]. Ellen, bring the lamp. [*Crosses to the stove.*] Oh dear, Doctor Rank, that was too bad of you.

RANK [*rising*]. That I have loved you as deeply as—any one else? Was that too bad of me?

NORA. No, but that you should have told me so. It was so unnecessary——

RANK. What do you mean? Did you know——?

[*Ellen enters with the lamp; sets it on the table and goes out again.*

RANK. Nora—Mrs. Helmer—I ask you, did you know?

NORA. Oh, how can I tell what I knew or didn't know? I really can't say. How could you be so clumsy, Doctor Rank? It was all so nice!

RANK. Well, at any rate, you know now that I am yours, soul and body. And now, go on.

NORA [*looking at him*]. Go on—now?

RANK. I beg you to tell me what you want.

NORA. I can tell you nothing now.

RANK. Yes, yes! You mustn't punish me in that way. Let me do for you whatever a man can.

NORA. You can do nothing for me now. Besides, I really want no help. You'll see it was only my fancy. Yes, it must be so. Of course! [*Sits in the rocking-chair, smiling at him.*] You're a nice one, Doctor Rank! Aren't you ashamed of yourself, now the lamp's on the table?

RANK. No, not exactly. But perhaps I ought to go—forever.

NORA. No, indeed you mustn't. Of course you must come and go as you've always done. You know very well that Torvald can't do without you.

RANK. Yes, but you?

NORA. Oh, you know I always like to have you here.

RANK. That's just what led me astray. You're a riddle to me. It has often seemed to me as if you liked being with me almost as much as being with Helmer.

NORA. Yes; don't you see? There are people one loves, and others one likes to talk to.

RANK. Yes—there's something in that.

NORA. When I was a girl I naturally loved papa best. But it always delighted me to steal into the servants' room. In the first place they never lectured me, and in the second it was such fun to hear them talk.

RANK. Oh, I see; then it's their place I have taken?

NORA [*jumps up and hurries towards him*]. Oh, my dear Doctor Rank, I don't mean that. But you understand, with Torvald it's the same as with papa——

[*Ellen enters from the hall.*

ELLEN. Please, ma'am——

[*Whispers to Nora, and gives her a card.*

NORA [*glancing at card*]. Ah! [*Puts it in her pocket.*

RANK. Anything wrong?

NORA. No, not in the least. It's only—it's my new costume——

RANK. Why, it's there.

NORA. Oh, that one, yes. But it's another that—I ordered it —Torvald mustn't know——

RANK. Aha! So that's the great secret.

NORA. Yes, of course. Do just go to him; he's in the inner room. Do keep him as long as you can.

RANK. Make yourself easy; he shan't escape.

[*Goes into Helmer's room.*

NORA [*to Ellen*]. Is he waiting in the kitchen?

ELLEN. Yes, he came up the back stair——

NORA. Didn't you tell him I was engaged?

ELLEN. Yes, but it was no use.

NORA. He won't go away?

ELLEN. No, ma'am, not until he has spoken with you.

NORA. Then let him come in; but quietly. And, Ellen—say nothing about it; it's a surprise for my husband.

ELLEN. Oh yes, ma'am, I understand. [*She goes out.*

NORA. It's coming. It's coming, after all. No, no, no, it can never be; it shall not!

[*She goes to Helmer's door and slips the bolt. Ellen opens the hall-door for Krogstad, and shuts it after him. He wears a travelling coat, high boots, and a fur cap.*

NORA. Speak quietly; my husband is at home.

KROGSTAD. All right. I don't care.

NORA. What do you want?

KROGSTAD. A little information.

NORA. Be quick, then. What is it?

KROGSTAD. You know I've got my dismissal.

NORA. I couldn't prevent it, Mr. Krogstad. I fought for you to the last, but it was no good.

KROGSTAD. Does your husband care for you so little? He knows what I can bring upon you, and yet he dares——

NORA. How can you think I should tell him?

KROGSTAD. I knew very well you hadn't. It wasn't like my friend Torvald Helmer to show so much courage——

NORA. Mr. Krogstad, be good enough to speak respectfully of my husband.

KROGSTAD. Certainly, with all due respect. But since you're so anxious to keep the matter secret, I suppose you're a little clearer than yesterday as to what you have done.

NORA. Clearer than you could ever make me.

KROGSTAD. Yes, such a bad lawyer as I——

NORA. What is it you want?

KROGSTAD. Only to see how you're getting on, Mrs. Helmer. I've been thinking about you all day. A mere money-lender, a penny-a-liner, a—in short, a creature like me—has a little bit of what people call " heart."

NORA. Then show it; think of my little children.

KROGSTAD. Did you and your husband think of mine? But enough of that. I only wanted to tell you that you needn't take this matter too seriously. I shan't lodge any information, for the present.

NORA. No, surely not. I knew you wouldn't.

KROGSTAD. The whole thing can be settled quite quietly. Nobody need know. It can remain among us three.

NORA. My husband must never know.

KROGSTAD. How can you prevent it? Can you pay off the debt?

NORA. No, not at once.

KROGSTAD. Or have you any means of raising the money in the next few days?

NORA. None, that I will make use of.

KROGSTAD. And if you had, it would be no good to you now. If you offered me ever so much ready money you should not get back your I.O.U.

NORA. Tell me what you want to do with it.

KROGSTAD. I only want to keep it, to have it in my possession. No outsider shall hear anything of it. So, if you've got any desperate scheme in your head——

NORA. What if I have?

KROGSTAD. If you should think of leaving your husband and children——

NORA. What if I do?

KROGSTAD. Or if you should think of—something worse——

NORA. How do you know that?

KROGSTAD. Put all that out of your head.

NORA. How did you know what I had in my mind?

KROGSTAD. Most of us think of that at first. I thought of it, too; but I hadn't the courage——

NORA [*voicelessly*]. Nor I.

KROGSTAD [*relieved*]. No, one hasn't. You haven't the courage either, have you?

NORA. I haven't, I haven't.

KROGSTAD. Besides, it would be very silly—when the first storm's over——! I have a letter in my pocket for your husband——

NORA. Telling him everything?

KROGSTAD. Sparing you as much as possible.

NORA [*quickly*]. He must never have that letter. Tear it up. I will get the money somehow.

KROGSTAD. Pardon me, Mrs. Helmer, but I believe I told you——

NORA. Oh, I'm not talking about the money I owe you. Tell me how much you demand from my husband—I'll get it.

KROGSTAD. I demand no money from your husband.

NORA. What do you demand then?

KROGSTAD. I'll tell you. I want to regain my footing in the world. I want to rise; and your husband shall help me to do it. For the last eighteen months my record has been spotless; I've been in bitter need all the time; but I was content to fight my way up, step by step. Now, I've been thrust down, and I won't be satisfied with merely being allowed to sneak back again. I want to rise, I tell you. I must get into the Bank again, in a higher position than before. Your husband shall create a place on purpose for me——

NORA. He will never do that!

KROGSTAD. He will do it; I know him—he won't dare to refuse! And when I'm in, you'll soon see! I shall be the manager's right hand. It won't be Torvald Helmer, but Nils Krogstad, that manages the Joint Stock Bank.

NORA. That will never be.

KROGSTAD. Perhaps you'll——?

NORA. Now I have the courage for it.

KROGSTAD. Oh, you don't frighten me! A sensitive, petted creature like you——

NORA. You shall see, you shall see!

KROGSTAD. Under the ice, perhaps? Down into the cold, black water? And next spring to come up again, ugly, hairless, unrecognizable——

NORA. You can't terrify me.

KROGSTAD. Nor you me. People don't do that sort of thing, Mrs. Helmer. And, after all, what good would it be? I have your husband in my pocket, all the same.

NORA. Afterwards? When I am no longer——?

KROGSTAD. You forget, your reputation remains in my hands! [*Nora stands speechless, and looks at him.*] Well, now you're prepared. Do nothing foolish. So soon as Helmer has received my letter, I shall expect to hear from him. And remember that it's your husband himself who has forced me back again into such paths. That I will never forgive him. Good-by, Mrs. Helmer.

[*Goes through hall. Nora hurries to the door, opens it a little, and listens.*

NORA. He's going. He's not putting the letter into the box. No, no, it would be impossible. [*Opens the door further and further.*] What's that? He's standing still; not going down stairs. Is he changing his mind? Is he——? [*A letter falls into the box. Krogstad's footsteps are heard gradually receding down the stair. Nora utters a suppressed shriek; pause.*] In the letter-box! [*Slips shrinkingly up to the door.*] There it lies—Torvald, Torvald— now we are lost!

[*Mrs. Linden enters from the left with the costume.*

MRS. LINDEN. There, I think it's all right now. Shall we just try it on?

Nora [*hoarsely and softly*]. Christina, come here.

Mrs. Linden [*throws dress on sofa*]. What's the matter? You look quite aghast.

Nora. Come here. Do you see that letter? There, see— through the glass of the letter-box.

Mrs. Linden. Yes, yes, I see it.

Nora. That letter is from Krogstad——

Mrs. Linden. Nora— it was Krogstad who lent you the money!

Nora. Yes; and now Torvald will know everything.

Mrs. Linden. Believe me, Nora, it's the best thing for you both.

Nora. You don't know all yet. I have forged a name——

Mrs. Linden. Good heavens!

Nora. Now, listen to me, Christina; you shall bear me witness——

Mrs. Linden. How " witness "? What am I to——?

Nora. If I should go out of my mind—it might easily happen——

Mrs. Linden. Nora!

Nora. Or if anything else should happen to me—so that I couldn't be here myself——!

Mrs. Linden. Nora, Nora, you're quite beside yourself!

Nora. In case any one wanted to take it all upon himself— the whole blame—you understand——

Mrs. Linden. Yes, but how can you think——?

Nora. You shall bear witness that it's not true, Christina. I'm not out of my mind at all; I know quite well what I'm saying; and I tell you nobody else knew anything about it; I did the whole thing, I myself. Don't forget that.

Mrs. Linden. I won't forget. But I don't understand what you mean——

Nora. Oh, how should you? It's the miracle coming to pass.

Mrs. Linden. The miracle?

Nora. Yes, the miracle. But it's so terrible, Christina; it mustn't happen for anything in the world.

Mrs. Linden. I'll go straight to Krogstad and talk to him.

Nora. Don't; he'll do you some harm.

Mrs. Linden. Once he would have done anything for me.

Nora. He?

MRS. LINDEN. Where does he live?

NORA. Oh, how can I tell——? Yes [*feels in her pocket*]. Here's his card; but the letter, the letter——!

HELMER [*knocking outside*]. Nora!

NORA [*shrieks in terror*]. What is it? What do you want?

HELMER. Don't be frightened, we're not coming in; you've bolted the door. Are you trying on your dress?

NORA. Yes, yes, I'm trying it on. It suits me so well, Torvald.

MRS. LINDEN [*who has read the card*]. Then he lives close by here?

NORA. Yes, but it's no use now. The letter is there in the box.

MRS. LINDEN. And your husband has the key?

NORA. Always.

MRS. LINDEN. Krogstad must demand his letter back, unread. He must make some excuse——

NORA. But this is the very time when Torvald generally——

MRS. LINDEN. Prevent him. Keep him occupied. I'll come back as quickly as I can.

[*She goes out quickly through the hall door.*

NORA [*opens Helmer's door and peeps in*]. Torvald!

HELMER. Well, now may one come back into one's own room? Come, Rank, we'll have a look—— [*In the doorway.*] But how's this?

NORA. What, Torvald dear?

HELMER. Rank led me to expect a grand dressing-up.

RANK [*in the doorway*]. So I understood. I suppose I was mistaken.

NORA. No, no one shall see me in my glory till to-morrow evening.

HELMER. Why, Nora dear, you look so tired. Have you been practising too hard?

NORA. No, I haven't practised at all yet.

HELMER. But you'll have to——

NORA. Oh yes, I must, I must! But, Torvald, I can't get on without your help. I've forgotten everything.

HELMER. Oh, we'll soon freshen it up again.

NORA. Yes, do help me, Torvald. You must promise me—— Oh, I'm so nervous about it. Before so many people—— This evening you must give yourself up entirely to me.

You mustn't do a stroke of work! Now promise, Torvald dear!

HELMER. I promise. All this evening I'll be your slave. Little helpless thing——! But, by the bye, I must first——
                                        [*Going to hall door.*

NORA. What do you want there?

HELMER. Only to see if there are any letters.

NORA. No, no, don't do that, Torvald.

HELMER. Why not?

NORA. Torvald, I beg you not to. There are none there.

HELMER. Let me just see.   [*Is going.*
        ·[*Nora, at the piano, plays the first bars of the tarantella.*

HELMER [*at the door, stops*]. Aha!

NORA. I can't dance to-morrow if I don't rehearse with you first.

HELMER [*going to her*]. Are you really so nervous, dear Nora?

NORA. Yes, dreadfully! Let me rehearse at once. We have time before dinner. Oh! do sit down and accompany me, Torvald dear; direct me as you used to do.

HELMER. With all the pleasure in life, if you wish it.
                                        [*Sits at piano.*

[*Nora snatches the tambourine out of the box, and hurriedly drapes herself in a long parti-colored shawl; then, with a bound, stands in the middle of the floor.*

NORA. Now play for me! Now I'll dance!

·[*Helmer plays and Nora dances. Rank stands at the piano behind Helmer and looks on.*

HELMER [*playing*]. Slower! Slower!

NORA. I can't do it slower!

HELMER. Not so violently, Nora.

NORA. I must! I must!

HELMER [*stops*]. Nora—that'll never do.

NORA [*laughs and swings her tambourine*]. Didn't I tell you so!

RANK. Let me accompany her.

HELMER [*rising*]. Yes, do—then I can direct her better.

[*Rank sits down to the piano and plays; Nora dances more and more wildly. Helmer stands by the stove and addresses frequent corrections to her; she seems not to hear. Her hair breaks loose, and falls over her shoul-*

ders. She does not notice it, but goes on dancing. Mrs. Linden enters and stands spell-bound in the doorway.

MRS. LINDEN. Ah——!

NORA [*dancing*]. We're having such fun here, Christina!

HELMER. Why, Nora dear, you're dancing as if it were a matter of life and death.

NORA. So it is.

HELMER. Rank, stop! This is the merest madness. Stop, I say!

[*Rank stops playing, and Nora comes to a sudden standstill.*

HELMER [*going towards her*]. I couldn't have believed it. You've positively forgotten all I taught you.

NORA [*throws tambourine away*]. You see for yourself.

HELMER. You really do want teaching.

NORA. Yes, you see how much I need it. You must practise with me up to the last moment. Will you promise me, Torvald?

HELMER. Certainly, certainly.

NORA. Neither to-day nor to-morrow must you think of anything but me. You mustn't open a single letter—mustn't look at the letter-box!

HELMER. Ah, you're still afraid of that man——

NORA. Oh yes, yes, I am.

HELMER. Nora, I can see it in your face—there's a letter from him in the box.

NORA. I don't know, I believe so. But you're not to read anything now; nothing must come between us until all is over.

RANK [*softly, to Helmer*]. You mustn't contradict her.

HELMER [*putting his arm around her*]. The child shall have her own way. But to-morrow night, when the dance is over——

NORA. Then you will be free.

[*Ellen appears in the doorway, right.*

ELLEN. Dinner is ready, ma'am.

NORA. We'll have some champagne, Ellen!

ELLEN. Yes, ma'am. [*Goes out.*

HELMER. Dear me! Quite a feast.

NORA. Yes, and we'll keep it up till morning. [*Calling out.*] And macaroons, Ellen—plenty—just this once.

HELMER [*seizing her hand*]. Come, come, don't let's have this wild excitement! Be my own little lark again.

Nora. Oh yes, I will. But now go into the dining-room; and
you too, Doctor Rank. Christina, you must help me to
do up my hair.

Rank [*softly, as they go*]. There's nothing in the wind?
Nothing—I mean——?

Helmer. Oh no, nothing of the kind. It's merely this baby-
ish anxiety I was telling you about.

[*They go out to the right.*

Nora. Well?

Mrs. Linden. He's gone out of town.

Nora. I saw it in your face.

Mrs. Linden. He comes back to-morrow evening. I left a
note for him.

Nora. You shouldn't have done that. Things must take their
course. After all, there's something glorious in waiting
for the miracle.

Mrs. Linden. What is it you're waiting for?

Nora. Oh, you can't understand. Go to them in the dining-
room; I'll come in a moment.

[*Mrs. Linden goes into the dining-room. Nora stands for a
moment as though collecting her thoughts; then looks
at her watch.*

Nora. Five. Seven hours till midnight. Then twenty-four
hours till the next midnight. Then the tarantella will be
over. Twenty-four and seven? Still thirty-one hours to
live.

[*Helmer appears at the door, right.*

Helmer. What's become of my little lark?

Nora [*runs to him with open arms*]. Here she is!

ACT THIRD

SCENE.—*The same room. The table, with the chairs around it, in the middle. A lamp lit on the table. The door to the hall stands open. Dance music is heard from the floor above.*

[*Mrs. Linden sits by the table and absently turns the pages of a book. She tries to read, but seems unable to fix her attention; she frequently listens and looks anxiously towards the hall door.*

MRS. LINDEN [*looks at her watch*]. Not here yet; and the time's nearly up. If only he hasn't—— [*Listens again.*] Ah, there he is—— [*She goes into the hall and cautiously opens the outer door; soft footsteps are heard on the stairs; she whispers.*] Come in; there's no one here.

KROGSTAD [*in the doorway*]. I found a note from you at my house. What does it mean?

MRS. LINDEN. I must speak to you.

KROGSTAD. Indeed? and in this house?

MRS. LINDEN. I could not see you at my rooms. They have no separate entrance. Come in; we are quite alone. The servants are asleep, and the Helmers are at the ball up stairs.

KROGSTAD [*coming into the room*]. Ah! So the Helmers are dancing this evening. Really?

MRS. LINDEN. Yes. Why not?

KROGSTAD. Quite right. Why not?

MRS. LINDEN. And now let us talk a little.

KROGSTAD. Have we anything to say to each other?

MRS. LINDEN. A great deal.

KROGSTAD. I shouldn't have thought so.

MRS. LINDEN. Because you have never really understood me.

KROGSTAD. What was there to understand? The most natural thing in the world—a heartless woman throws a man over when a better match offers.

MRS. LINDEN. Do you really think me so heartless? Do you think I broke with you lightly?

KROGSTAD. Did you not?

MRS. LINDEN. Do you really think so?

KROGSTAD. If not, why did you write me that letter?

MRS. LINDEN. Was it not best? Since I had to break with you, was it not right that I should try to put an end to your love for me?

KROGSTAD [*pressing his hands together*]. So that was it? And all this—for the sake of money!

MRS. LINDEN. You ought not to forget that I had a helpless mother and two little brothers. We could not wait for you, as your prospects then stood.

KROGSTAD. Did that give you the right to discard me for another?

MRS. LINDEN. I don't know. I have often asked myself whether I did right.

KROGSTAD [*more softly*]. When I had lost you, the very ground seemed to sink from under my feet. Look at me now. I am a shipwrecked man clinging to a spar.

MRS. LINDEN. Rescue may be at hand.

KROGSTAD. It was at hand; but then you stood in the way.

MRS. LINDEN. Without my knowledge, Nils. I did not know till to-day that it was you I was to replace in the Bank.

KROGSTAD. Well, I take your word for it. But now you do know, do you mean to give way?

MRS. LINDEN. No, for that wouldn't help you.

KROGSTAD. Oh, help, help——! I should do it whether or no.

MRS. LINDEN. I have learnt prudence. Life and bitter necessity have schooled me.

KROGSTAD. And life has taught me not to trust fine speeches.

MRS. LINDEN. Then life has taught you a very sensible thing. But deeds you will trust?

KROGSTAD. What do you mean?

MRS. LINDEN. You said you were a shipwrecked man, clinging to a spar.

KROGSTAD. I have good reason to say so.

MRS. LINDEN. I am a shipwrecked woman, clinging to a spar. I have no one to care for.

KROGSTAD. You made your own choice.

MRS. LINDEN. I had no choice.

KROGSTAD. Well, what then?

MRS. LINDEN. How if we two shipwrecked people could join hands?

KROGSTAD. What!

MRS. LINDEN. Two on a raft have a better chance than if each clings to a separate spar.

KROGSTAD. Christina!

MRS. LINDEN. What do you think brought me to town?

KROGSTAD. Had you any thought of me?

MRS. LINDEN. I must have work or I can't live. All my life, as long as I can remember, I have worked; work has been my one great joy. Now I stand quite alone in the world, so terribly aimless and forsaken. There's no happiness in working for one's self. Nils, give me somebody and something to work for.

KROGSTAD. No, no; that can never be. It's simply a woman's romantic notion of self-sacrifice.

MRS. LINDEN. Have you ever found me romantic?

KROGSTAD. Would you really——? Tell me, do you know my past?

MRS. LINDEN. Yes.

KROGSTAD. And do you know what people say of me?

MRS. LINDEN. Didn't you say just now that with me you could have been another man?

KROGSTAD. I am sure of it.

MRS. LINDEN. Is it too late?

KROGSTAD. Christina, do you know what you are doing? Yes, you do; I see it in your face. Have you the courage——?

MRS. LINDEN. I need some one to tend, and your children need a mother. You need me, and I—I need you. Nils, I believe in your better self. With you I fear nothing.

KROGSTAD [seizing her hand]. Thank you—thank you, Christina. Now I shall make others see me as you do. Ah, I forgot——

MRS. LINDEN [listening]. Hush! The tarantella! Go! go!

KROGSTAD. Why? What is it?

MRS. LINDEN. Don't you hear the dancing overhead? As soon as that's over they'll be here.

KROGSTAD. Oh yes, I'll go. But it's too late now. Of course you don't know the step I've taken against the Helmers.

MRS. LINDEN. Yes, Nils, I do know.

KROGSTAD. And yet you have the courage to——

MRS. LINDEN. I know what lengths despair can drive a man to.

KROGSTAD. Oh, if I could only undo it!

MRS. LINDEN. You can—— Your letter is still in the box.

KROGSTAD. Are you sure?

MRS. LINDEN. Yes, but——

KROGSTAD [*looking at her searchingly*]. Ah, now I understand. You want to save your friend at any price. Say it out— is that your idea?

MRS. LINDEN. Nils, a woman who has once sold herself for the sake of others, doesn't do so again.

KROGSTAD. I'll demand my letter back again.

MRS. LINDEN. No, no.

KROGSTAD. Yes, of course. I'll wait till Helmer comes; I'll tell him to give it back to me—that it's only about my dismissal—that I don't want it read——

MRS. LINDEN. No, Nils, you must not recall the letter.

KROGSTAD. But tell me, wasn't that just why you got me to come here?

MRS. LINDEN. Yes, in my first terror. But a day has passed since then, and in that day I have seen incredible things in this house. Helmer must know everything; there must be an end to this unhappy secret. These two must come to a full understanding. They can't possibly go on with all these shifts and concealments.

KROGSTAD. Very well, if you like to risk it. But one thing I can do, and at once——

MRS. LINDEN [*listening*]. Make haste, go, go! The dance is over; we're not safe another moment.

KROGSTAD. I'll wait for you in the street.

MRS. LINDEN. Yes, do; you must take me home.

KROGSTAD. I never was so happy in all my life!

[*Krogstad goes out by the outer door. The door between the room and hall remains open.*

MRS. LINDEN [*setting furniture straight and getting her outdoor things together*]. What a change! What a change! To have some one to work for; a home to make happy! I shall have to set to work in earnest. I wish they would come. [*Listens.*] Ah, here they are! I must get my things on.

[*Takes bonnet and cloak. Helmer's and Nora's voices are heard outside, a key is turned in the lock, and Helmer*

*drags Nora almost by force into the hall. She wears
the Italian costume with a large black shawl over it.
He is in evening dress and wears a black domino.*

NORA [*struggling with him in the doorway*]. No, no, no! I
won't go in! I want to go upstairs again; I don't want
to leave so early!

HELMER. But, my dearest girl——!

NORA. Oh, please, please, Torvald, only one hour more!

HELMER. Not one minute more, Nora dear; you know what
we agreed! Come, come in; you're catching cold here!
[*He leads her gently into the room in spite of her resistance.*

MRS. LINDEN. Good evening.

NORA. Christina!

HELMER. What, Mrs. Linden! You here so late?

MRS. LINDEN. Yes, pardon me. I did so want to see Nora in
her costume.

NORA. Have you been sitting here waiting for me?

MRS. LINDEN. Yes; unfortunately I came too late. You had
already gone upstairs, and I couldn't go away without seeing you.

HELMER [*taking Nora's shawl off*]. Well then, just look at
her! I think she's worth looking at. Isn't she lovely, Mrs.
Linden?

MRS. LINDEN. Yes, I must say——

HELMER. Isn't she exquisite? Every one said so. But she's
dreadfully obstinate, dear little creature. What's to be
done with her? Just think, I had almost to force her
away.

NORA. Oh, Torvald, you'll be sorry some day you didn't let
me stop, if only for one half hour.

HELMER. There! You hear her, Mrs. Linden? She dances
her tarantella with wild applause, and well she deserved
it, I must say—though there was, perhaps, a little too
much nature in her rendering of the idea—more than was,
strictly speaking, artistic. But never mind—she made a
great success, and that's the main thing. Ought I to let
her stop after that—to weaken the impression? Not if I
know it. I took my sweet little Capri girl—my capricious
little Capri girl, I might say—under my arm; a rapid
turn round the room, a courtesy to all sides, and—as they

say in novels—the lovely apparition vanished! An exit should always be effective, Mrs. Linden; but I can't get Nora to see it. By Jove, it's warm here. [*Throws his domino on a chair, and opens the door to his room.*] What! No light here? Oh, of course! Excuse me——
[*Goes in and lights candles.*

NORA [*whispers breathlessly*]. Well?

MRS. LINDEN [*softly*]. I've spoken to him.

NORA. And——?

MRS. LINDEN. Nora—you must tell your husband everything——

NORA [*almost voiceless*]. I knew it!

MRS. LINDEN. You have nothing to fear from Krogstad; but you must speak out.

NORA. I shall not speak!

MRS. LINDEN. Then the letter will.

NORA. Thank you, Christina. Now I know what I have to do. Hush!

HELMER [*coming back*]. Well, Mrs. Linden, have you admired her?

MRS. LINDEN. Yes; and now I'll say good-night.

HELMER. What, already? Does this knitting belong to you?

MRS. LINDEN [*takes it*]. Yes, thanks; I was nearly forgetting it.

HELMER. Then you do knit?

MRS. LINDEN. Yes.

HELMER. Do you know, you ought to embroider instead?

MRS. LINDEN. Indeed! Why?

HELMER. Because it's so much prettier. Look now! You hold the embroidery in the left hand, so, and then work the needle with the right hand, in a long, easy curve, don't you?

MRS. LINDEN. Yes, I suppose so.

HELMER. But knitting is always ugly. Just look—your arms close to your sides, and the needles going up and down—there's something Chinese about it.—They really gave us splendid champagne to-night.

MRS. LINDEN. Well, good-night, Nora, and don't be obstinate any more.

HELMER. Well said, Mrs. Linden!

Mrs. Linden. Good-night, Mr. Helmer.

Helmer [*going with her to the door*]. Good-night, good-night; I hope you'll get safely home. I should be glad to—but really you haven't far to go. Good-night, good-night! [*She goes; Helmer shuts the door after her and comes forward again.*] At last we've got rid of her; she's an awful bore.

Nora. Aren't you very tired, Torvald?

Helmer. No, not in the least.

Nora. Nor sleepy?

Helmer. Not a bit. I feel particularly lively. But you? You do look tired and sleepy.

Nora. Yes, very tired. I shall soon sleep now.

Helmer. There, you see. I was right after all not to let you stop longer.

Nora. Oh, everything you do is right.

Helmer [*kissing her forehead*]. Now my lark is speaking like a reasonable being. Did you notice how jolly Rank was this evening?

Nora. Was he? I had no chance of speaking to him.

Helmer. Nor I, much; but I haven't seen him in such good spirits for a long time. [*Looks at Nora a little, then comes nearer her.*] It's splendid to be back in our own house, to be quite alone together! Oh, you enchanting creature!

Nora. Don't look at me in that way, Torvald.

Helmer. I am not to look at my dearest treasure?—at the loveliness that is mine, mine only, wholly and entirely mine?

Nora [*goes to the other side of the table*]. You mustn't say these things to me this evening.

Helmer [*following*]. I see you have the tarantella still in your blood—and that makes you all the more enticing. Listen! the other people are going now. [*More softly.*] Nora—soon the whole house will be still.

Nora. I hope so.

Helmer. Yes, don't you, Nora darling? When we're among strangers do you know why I speak so little to you, and keep so far away, and only steal a glance at you now and then—do you know why I do it? Because I am fancying that we love each other in secret, that I am secretly be-

trothed to you, and that no one guesses there is anything
between us.

NORA. Yes, yes, yes. I know all your thoughts are with me.

HELMER. And then, when we have to go, and I put the shawl
about your smooth, soft shoulders, and this glorious neck
of yours, I imagine you are my bride, that our marriage
is just over, that I am bringing you for the first time to my
home, and that I am alone with you for the first time, quite
alone with you, in your trembling loveliness. All this
evening I was longing for you, and you only. When I
watched you swaying and whirling in the tarantella—my
blood boiled—I could endure it no longer; and that's why
I made you come home with me so early.

NORA. Go now, Torvald! Go away from me! I won't have
all this.

HELMER. What do you mean? Ah, I see you're teasing me!
Won't—won't! Am I not your husband?

                                        [A knock at the outer door.

NORA [starts]. Did you hear?

HELMER [going towards the hall]. Who's there?

RANK [outside]. It's I; may I come in a moment?

HELMER [in a low tone, annoyed]. Oh! what can he want?
[Aloud.] Wait a moment. [Opens door.] Come, it's
nice of you to give us a look in.

RANK. I thought I heard your voice, and that put it into my
head. [Looks round.] Ah, this dear old place! How
cosey you two are here!

HELMER. You seemed to find it pleasant enough upstairs, too.

RANK. Exceedingly. Why not? Why shouldn't one get all
one can out of the world? All one can for as long as one
can. The wine was splendid——

HELMER. Especially the champagne.

RANK. Did you notice it? It's incredible the quantity I con-
trived to get down.

NORA. Torvald drank plenty of champagne too.

RANK. Did he?

NORA. Yes, and it always puts him in such spirits.

RANK. Well, why shouldn't one have a jolly evening after a
well-spent day?

HELMER. Well-spent! Well, I haven't much to boast of.

RANK [*slapping him on the shoulder*]. But I have, don't you see?

NORA. I suppose you've been engaged in a scientific investigation, Doctor Rank?

RANK. Quite right.

HELMER. Bless me! Little Nora talking about scientific investigations!

NORA. Am I to congratulate you on the result?

RANK. By all means.

NORA. It was good, then?

RANK. The best possible, both for doctor and patient—certainty.

NORA [*quickly and searchingly*]. Certainty?

RANK. Absolute certainty. Wasn't I right to enjoy myself after that?

NORA. Yes, quite right, Doctor Rank.

HELMER. And so say I, provided you don't have to pay for it to-morrow.

RANK. Well, in this life nothing's to be had for nothing.

NORA. Doctor Rank, aren't you very fond of masquerades?

RANK. Yes, when there are plenty of comical disguises.

NORA. Tell me, what shall we two be at our next masquerade?

HELMER. Little insatiable! Thinking of your next already!

RANK. We two? I'll tell you. You must go as a good fairy.

HELMER. Ah, but what costume would indicate that?

RANK. She has simply to wear her every-day dress.

HELMER. Capital! But don't you know what you will be yourself?

RANK. Yes, my dear friend, I'm perfectly clear upon that point.

HELMER. Well?

RANK. At the next masquerade I shall be invisible.

HELMER. What a comical idea!

RANK. There's a big black hat—haven't you heard of the invisible hat? It comes down all over you, and then no one can see you.

HELMER [*with a suppressed smile*]. No, you're right there.

RANK. But I'm quite forgetting what I came for. Helmer, give me a cigar, one of the dark Havanas.

HELMER. With the greatest pleasure. [*Hands case.*

RANK [*takes one and cuts the end off*]. Thanks.

NORA [*striking a wax match*]. Let me give you a light.

RANK. A thousand thanks.

> [*She holds match. He lights his cigar at it.*

RANK. And now, good-by!

HELMER. Good-by, good-by, my dear fellow.

NORA. Sleep well, Doctor Rank.

RANK. Thanks for the wish.

NORA. Wish me the same.

RANK. You? Very well, since you ask me—Sleep well; and thanks for the light. [*He nods to them both and goes out.*

HELMER [*in an undertone*]. He's been drinking a good deal.

NORA [*absently*]. I dare say. [*Helmer takes his bunch of keys from his pocket and goes into the hall.*] Torvald, what are you doing there?

HELMER. I must empty the letter-box, it's quite full; there will be no room for the newspapers to-morrow morning.

NORA. Are you going to work to-night?

HELMER. Not very likely! Why, what's this? Some one's been at the lock.

NORA. The lock——?

HELMER. I'm sure of it. What does it mean? I can't think that the servants——? Here's a broken hair-pin. Nora, it's one of yours.

NORA [*quickly*]. It must have been the children.

HELMER. Then you must break them of such tricks. Hm, hm! There! At last I've got it open. [*Takes contents out and calls into the kitchen.*] Ellen, Ellen, just put the hall door lamp out.

[*He returns with letters in his hand, and shuts the inner door.*

HELMER. Just see how they've accumulated. [*Turning them over.*] Why, what's this?

NORA [*at the window*]. The letter! Oh no, no, Torvald!

HELMER. Two visiting-cards—from Rank.

NORA. From Doctor Rank?

HELMER [*looking at them*]. Doctor Rank. They were on the top. He must just have put them in.

NORA. Is there anything on them?

HELMER. There's a black cross over the name. Look at it. What a horrid idea! It looks just as if he were announcing his own death.

NORA. So he is.

HELMER. What! Do you know anything? Has he told you anything?

NORA. Yes. These cards mean that he has taken his last leave of us. He intends to shut himself up and die.

HELMER. Poor fellow! Of course I knew we couldn't hope to keep him long. But so soon—and then to go and creep into his lair like a wounded animal——

NORA. What must be, must be, and the fewer words the better. Don't you think so, Torvald?

HELMER [*walking up and down*]. He had so grown into our lives, I can't realize that he's gone. He and his sufferings and his loneliness formed a sort of cloudy background to the sunshine of our happiness. Well, perhaps it's best so—at any rate for him. [*Stands still.*] And perhaps for us too, Nora. Now we two are thrown entirely upon each other. [*Takes her in his arms.*] My darling wife! I feel as if I could never hold you close enough. Do you know, Nora, I often wish some danger might threaten you, that I might risk body and soul, and everything, everything, for your dear sake.

NORA [*tears herself from him and says firmly*]. Now you shall read your letters, Torvald.

HELMER. No, no; not to-night. I want to be with you, sweet wife.

NORA. With the thought of your dying friend?

HELMER. You are right. This has shaken us both. Unloveliness has come between us thoughts of death and decay. We must seek to cast them off. Till then we will remain apart.

NORA [*her arms round his neck*]. Torvald! Good-night, good-night.

HELMER [*kissing her forehead*]. Good-night, my little bird. Sleep well, Nora. Now I'll go and read my letters.

[*He goes into his room and shuts the door.*

NORA [*with wild eyes, gropes about her, seizes Helmer's domino, throws it round her, and whispers quickly, hoarsely, and brokenly*]. Never to see him again. Never, never, never. [*Throws her shawl over head.*] Never to see the children again. Never, never. Oh that black, icy water!

Oh that bottomless——! If it were only over! Now he has it; he's reading it. Oh no, no, no, not yet. Torvald, good-by——! Good-by, my little ones——!

[*She is rushing out by the hall; at the same moment Helmer tears his door open, and stands with open letter in his hand.*

HELMER. Nora!

NORA [*shrieking*]. Ah——!

HELMER. What is this? Do you know what is in this letter?

NORA. Yes, I know. Let me go! Let me pass!

HELMER [*holds her back*]. Where do you want to go?

NORA [*tries to get free*]. You shan't save me, Torvald.

HELMER [*falling back*]. True! Is it true what he writes? No, no, it cannot be true.

NORA. It is true. I have loved you beyond all else in the world.

HELMER. Pshaw—no silly evasions!

NORA [*a step nearer him*]. Torvald——!

HELMER. Wretched woman! What have you done?

NORA. Let me go—you shall not save me! You shall not take my guilt upon yourself!

HELMER. I don't want any melodramatic airs. [*Locks the door.*] Here you shall stay and give an account of yourself. Do you understand what you have done? Answer. Do you understand it?

NORA [*looks at him fixedly, and says with a stiffening expression*]. Yes; now I begin fully to understand it.

HELMER [*walking up and down*]. Oh, what an awful awakening! During all these eight years—she who was my pride and my joy—a hypocrite, a liar—worse, worse—a criminal. Oh, the hideousness of it! Ugh! Ugh!

[*Nora is silent, and continues to look fixedly at him.*

HELMER. I ought to have foreseen something of the kind. All your father's dishonesty—be silent! I say your father's dishonesty! you have inherited—no religion, no morality, no sense of duty. How I am punished for shielding him! I did it for your sake, and you reward me like this.

NORA. Yes—like this!

HELMER. You have destroyed my whole happiness. You have ruined my future. Oh, it's frightful to think of! I am in the power of a scoundrel; he can do whatever he pleases with me, demand whatever he chooses, and I must submit. And all this disaster is brought upon me by an un-principled woman.

NORA. When I am gone, you will be free.

HELMER. Oh, no fine phrases. Your father, too, was always ready with them. What good would it do me, if you were "gone," as you say? No good in the world! He can publish the story all the same; I might even be suspected of collusion. People will think I was at the bottom of it all and egged you on. And for all this I have you to thank —you whom I have done nothing but pet and spoil during our whole married life. Do you understand now what you have done to me?

NORA [with cold calmness]. Yes.

HELMER. It's impossible. I can't grasp it. But we must come to an understanding. Take that shawl off. Take it off, I say! I must try to pacify him in one way or other— the secret must be kept, cost what it may. As for ourselves, we must live as we have always done; but of course only in the eyes of the world. Of course you will continue to live here. But the children cannot be left in your care. I dare not trust them to you.—Oh, to have to say this to one I have loved so tenderly—whom I still —but that must be a thing of the past. Henceforward there can be no question of happiness, but merely of saving the ruins, the shreds, the show of it! [A ring; Helmer starts.] What's that? So late! Can it be the worst? Can he——? Hide yourself, Nora; say you are ill.

[Nora stands motionless. Helmer goes to the door and opens it.

ELLEN [half-dressed, in the hall]. Here is a letter for you, ma'am.

HELMER. Give it to me. [Seizes letter and shuts the door.] Yes, from him. You shall not have it. I shall read it.

NORA. Read it!

HELMER [by the lamp]. I have hardly courage to. We may both be lost, both you and I. Ah! I must know. [Hastily tears the letter open; reads a few lines, looks at an enclosure; a cry of joy.] Nora!

[Nora looks inquiringly at him.

HELMER. Nora! Oh! I must read it again. Yes, yes, it is so. I am saved! Nora, I am saved!

NORA. And I?

HELMER. You too, of course; we are both saved, both of us. Look here, he sends you back your promissory note. He writes that he regrets and apologizes; that a happy turn in his life—— Oh, what matter what he writes. We are saved, Nora! No one can harm you. Oh, Nora, Nora——; but first to get rid of this hateful thing. I'll just see—— [*Glances at the I.O.U.*] No, I won't look at it; the whole thing shall be nothing but a dream to me. [*Tears the I.O.U. and both letters in pieces. Throws them into the fire and watches them burn.*] There! it's gone! He wrote that ever since Christmas Eve—— Oh, Nora, they must have been three awful days for you!

NORA. I have fought a hard fight for the last three days.

HELMER. And in your agony you saw no other outlet but—— no; we won't think of that horror. We will only rejoice and repeat—it's over, all over! Don't you hear, Nora? You don't seem able to grasp it. Yes, it's over. What is this set look on your face? Oh, my poor Nora, I understand; you can't believe that I have forgiven you. But I have, Nora; I swear it. I have forgiven everything. I know that what you did was all for love of me.

NORA. That's true.

HELMER. You loved me as a wife should love her husband. It was only the means you misjudged. But do you think I love you the less for your helplessness? No, no. Only lean on me; I will counsel and guide you. I should be no true man if this very womanly helplessness didn't make you doubly dear in my eyes. You mustn't think of the hard things I said in my first moment of terror, when the world seemed to be tumbling about my ears. I have forgiven you, Nora—I swear I have forgiven you.

NORA. I thank you for your forgiveness.

[*Goes out right.*

HELMER. No, stay! [*Looks in.*] What are you going to do?

NORA [*inside*]. To take off my doll's dress.

HELMER [*in the doorway*]. Yes, do, dear. Try to calm down, and recover your balance, my scared little song-bird. You may rest secure. I have broad wings to shield you. [*Walking up and down near the door.*] Oh, how lovely —how cosey our home is, Nora! Here you are safe; here I can shelter you like a hunted dove, whom I have saved from the claws of the hawk. I shall soon bring your poor beating heart to rest; believe me, Nora, very soon. To-morrow all this will seem quite different—everything will be as before. I shall not need to tell you again that I for-give you; you will feel for yourself that it is true. How could I find it in my heart to drive you away, or even so much as to reproach you? Oh, you don't know a true man's heart, Nora. There is something indescribably sweet and soothing to a man in having forgiven his wife —honestly forgiven her, from the bottom of his heart. She becomes his property in a double sense. She is as though born again; she has become, so to speak, at once his wife and his child. That is what you shall henceforth be to me, my bewildered, helpless darling. Don't worry about anything, Nora; only open your heart to me, and I will be both will and conscience to you. [*Nora enters, crossing to table, in every-day dress.*] Why, what's this? Not gone to bed? You have changed your dress?

NORA. Yes, Torvald; now I have changed my dress.

HELMER. But why now, so late?

NORA. I shall not sleep to-night.

HELMER. But, Nora dear——

NORA [*looking at her watch*]. It's not so late yet. Sit down, Torvald; you and I have much to say to each other.

[*She sits on one side of the table.*]

HELMER. Nora, what does this mean? Your cold, set face——

NORA. Sit down. It will take some time; I have much to talk over with you.

[*Helmer sits at the other side of the table.*]

HELMER. You alarm me; I don't understand you.

NORA. No, that's just it. You don't understand me; and I have never understood you—till to-night. No, don't in-terrupt. Only listen to what I say. We must come to a final settlement, Torvald!

HELMER. How do you mean?

NORA [*after a short silence*]. Does not one thing strike you as we sit here?

HELMER. What should strike me?

NORA. We have been married eight years. Does it not strike you that this is the first time we two, you and I, man and wife, have talked together seriously?

HELMER. Seriously! Well, what do you call seriously?

NORA. During eight whole years, and more—ever since the day we first met—we have never exchanged one serious word about serious things.

HELMER. Was I always to trouble you with the cares you could not help me to bear?

NORA. I'm not talking of cares. I say that we have never yet set ourselves seriously to get to the bottom of anything.

HELMER. Why, my dear Nora, what have you to do with serious things?

NORA. There we have it! You have never understood me. I have had great injustice done me, Torvald; first by father, and then by you.

HELMER. What! By your father and me?—By us who have loved you more than all the world?

NORA [shaking her head]. You have never loved me. You only thought it amusing to be in love with me.

HELMER. Why, Nora, what a thing to say!

NORA. Yes, it is so, Torvald. While I was at home with father, he used to tell me all his opinions, and I held the same opinions. If I had others I concealed them, because he wouldn't have liked it. He used to call me his doll-child, and played with me as I played with my dolls. Then I came to live in your house——

HELMER. What an expression to use about our marriage!

NORA [undisturbed]. I mean I passed from father's hands into yours. You settled everything according to your taste; and I got the same tastes as you; or I pretended to—I don't know which—both ways, perhaps. When I look back on it now, I seem to have been living here like a beggar, from hand to mouth. I lived by performing tricks for you, Torvald. But you would have it so. You and father have done me a great wrong. It's your fault that my life has been wasted.

HELMER. Why, Nora, how unreasonable and ungrateful you are. Haven't you been happy here?

NORA. No, never; I thought I was, but I never was.

HELMER. Not—not happy?

NORA. No, only merry. And you've always been so kind to me. But our house has been nothing but a play-room. Here I have been your doll-wife, just as at home I used to be papa's doll-child. And the children, in their turn, have been my dolls. I thought it fun when you played with me, just as the children did when I played with them. That has been our marriage, Torvald.

HELMER. There is some truth in what you say, exaggerated and overstrained though it be. But henceforth it shall be different. Play-time is over; now comes the time for education.

NORA. Whose education? Mine, or the children's?

HELMER. Both, my dear Nora.

NORA. Oh, Torvald, you can't teach me to be a fit wife for you.

HELMER. And you say that?

NORA. And I—am I fit to educate the children?

HELMER. Nora!

NORA. Didn't you say yourself, a few minutes ago, you dared not trust them to me?

HELMER. In the excitement of the moment! Why should you dwell upon that?

NORA. No—you were perfectly right. That problem is beyond me. There's another to be solved first—I must try to educate myself. You are not the man to help me in that. I must set about it alone. And that's why I am now leaving you!

HELMER [jumping up]. What—do you mean to say——

NORA. I must stand quite alone to know myself and my surroundings; so I cannot stay with you.

HELMER. Nora! Nora!

NORA. I am going at once. Christina will take me in for to-night——

HELMER. You are mad. I shall not allow it. I forbid it.

NORA. It's no use your forbidding me anything now. I shall take with me what belongs to me. From you I will accept nothing, either now or afterwards.

HELMER. What madness!

NORA. To-morrow I shall go home.

HELMER. Home!

NORA. I mean to what was my home. It will be easier for me to find some opening there.

HELMER. Oh, in your blind inexperience——

NORA. I must try to gain experience, Torvald.

HELMER. To forsake your home, your husband, and your children! You don't consider what the world will say.

NORA. I can pay no heed to that! I only know that I must do it.

HELMER. It's exasperating! Can you forsake your holiest duties in this way?

NORA. What do you call my holiest duties?

HELMER. Do you ask me that? Your duties to your husband and your children.

NORA. I have other duties equally sacred.

HELMER. Impossible! What duties do you mean?

NORA. My duties towards myself.

HELMER. Before all else you are a wife and a mother.

NORA. That I no longer believe. I think that before all else I am a human being, just as much as you are—or at least I will try to become one. I know that most people agree with you, Torvald, and that they say so in books. But henceforth I can't be satisfied with what most people say, and what is in books. I must think things out for myself, and try to get clear about them.

HELMER. Are you not clear about your place in your own home? Have you not an infallible guide in questions like these? Have you not religion?

NORA. Oh, Torvald, I don't know properly what religion is.

HELMER. What do you mean?

NORA. I know nothing but what our clergyman told me when I was confirmed. He explained that religion was this and that. When I get away from here and stand alone, I will look into that matter too. I will see whether what he has taught me is true, or, at any rate, whether it is true for me.

HELMER. Oh, this is unheard of! But if religion cannot keep you right, let me appeal to your conscience—for I suppose you have some moral feeling? Or, answer me: perhaps you have none?

NORA. Well, Torvald, it's not easy to say. I really don't know

—I'm all at sea about these things. I only know that I think quite differently from you about them. I hear, too, that the laws are different from what I thought; but I can't believe that they are right. It appears that a woman has no right to spare her dying father, or to save her husband's life. I don't believe that.

HELMER. You talk like a child. You don't understand the society in which you live.

NORA. No, I don't. But I shall try to. I must make up my mind which is right—society or I.

HELMER. Nora, you are ill, you are feverish. I almost think you're out of your senses.

NORA. I have never felt so much clearness and certainty as to-night.

HELMER. You are clear and certain enough to forsake husband and children?

NORA. Yes, I am.

HELMER. Then there's only one explanation possible.

NORA. What is that?

HELMER. You no longer love me.

NORA. No; that is just it.

HELMER. Nora! Can you say so?

NORA. Oh, I'm so sorry, Torvald; for you've always been so kind to me. But I can't help it. I do not love you any longer.

HELMER [*keeping his composure with difficulty*]. Are you clear and certain on this point too?

NORA. Yes, quite. That is why I won't stay here any longer.

HELMER. And can you also make clear to me how I have forfeited your love?

NORA. Yes, I can. It was this evening, when the miracle did not happen; for then I saw you were not the man I had taken you for.

HELMER. Explain yourself more clearly; I don't understand.

NORA. I have waited so patiently all these eight years; for of course I saw clearly enough that miracles don't happen every day. When this crushing blow threatened me, I said to myself confidently, "Now comes the miracle!" When Krogstad's letter lay in the box, it never occurred to me that you would think of submitting to that man's conditions. I was convinced that you would say to him, " Make it known to all the world; " and that then——

HELMER. Well? When I had given my own wife's name up to disgrace and shame——?

NORA. Then I firmly believed that you would come forward, take everything upon yourself, and say, " I am the guilty one."

HELMER. Nora!

NORA. You mean I would never have accepted such a sacrifice? No, certainly not. But what would my assertions have been worth in opposition to yours? That was the miracle that I hoped for and dreaded. And it was to hinder that that I wanted to die.

HELMER. I would gladly work for you day and night, Nora— bear sorrow and want for your sake—but no man sacrifices his honor, even for one he loves.

NORA. Millions of women have done so.

HELMER. Oh, you think and talk like a silly child.

NORA. Very likely. But you neither think nor talk like the man I can share my life with. When your terror was over— not for me, but for yourself—when there was nothing more to fear—then it was to you as though nothing had happened. I was your lark again, your doll—whom you would take twice as much care of in future, because she was so weak and fragile. [*Stands up.*] Torvald, in that moment it burst upon me that I had been living here these eight years with a strange man, and had borne him three children. Oh! I can't bear to think of it—I could tear myself to pieces!

HELMER [*sadly*]. I see it, I see it; an abyss has opened between us. But, Nora, can it never be filled up?

NORA. As I now am, I am no wife for you.

HELMER. I have strength to become another man.

NORA. Perhaps—when your doll is taken away from you.

HELMER. To part—to part from you! No, Nora, no; I can't grasp the thought.

NORA [*going into room, right*]. The more reason for the thing to happen.

[*She comes back with out-door things and a small travelling-bag, which she puts on a chair.*

HELMER. Nora, Nora, not now! Wait till to-morrow.

NORA [*putting on cloak*]. I can't spend the night in a strange man's house.

HELMER. But can't we live here, as brother and sister?

NORA [*fastening her hat*]. You know very well that wouldn't last long. Good-by, Torvald. No, I won't go to the children. I know they're in better hands than mine. As I now am, I can be nothing to them.

HELMER. But some time, Nora; some time——

NORA. How can I tell? I have no idea what will become of me.

HELMER. But you are my wife, now and always!

NORA. Listen, Torvald—when a wife leaves her husband's house, as I am doing, I have heard that in the eyes of the law he is free from all duties towards her. At any rate, I release you from all duties. You must not feel yourself bound any more than I shall. There must be perfect freedom on both sides. There, there is your ring back. Give me mine.

HELMER. That too?

NORA. That too.

HELMER. Here it is.

NORA. Very well. Now it's all over. Here are the keys. The servants know about everything in the house, better than I do. To-morrow, when I have started, Christina will come to pack up my things. I will have them sent after me.

HELMER. All over! all over! Nora, will you never think of me again?

NORA. Oh, I shall often think of you, and the children, and this house.

HELMER. May I write to you, Nora?

NORA. No, never. You must not.

HELMER. But I must send you——

NORA. Nothing, nothing.

HELMER. I must help you if you need it.

NORA. No, I say. I take nothing from strangers.

HELMER. Nora, can I never be more than a stranger to you?

NORA [*taking her travelling-bag*]. Oh, Torvald, then the miracle of miracles would have to happen.

HELMER. What is the miracle of miracles?

NORA. Both of us would have to change so that—— Oh, Torvald, I no longer believe in miracles.

HELMER. But I will believe. We must so change that——

NORA. That communion between us shall be a marriage. Good-by. [*She goes out.*

HELMER [*sinks in a chair by the door with his face in his hands*]. Nora! Nora! [*He looks round and stands up.*] Empty. She's gone. [*A hope inspires him.*] Ah! The miracle of miracles——?!

[*From below is heard the reverberation of a heavy door closing.*

LES PATTES DE MOUCHE

(Called " A Scrap of Paper " on the British and American Stage)

—

BY

VICTORIEN SARDOU

[Translation by Léonie Gilmour]

DRAMATIS PERSONÆ

PROSPER BLOCK.

VANHOVE.

BUSONIER.

THIRION.

PAUL.

BAPTISTE.

HENRI.

SUZANNE.

COLOMBA.

CLARISSE.

MARTHE.

SOLANGE.

CLAUDINE.

The scene is in the environs of Chinon, France

LES PATTES DE MOUCHE

ACT FIRST

Scene I.—A Salon of the Time of Louis XVI

Enter Baptiste, Henri, and Claudine.

CLAUDINE [*contemptuously whirling around an arm-chair that she is dusting*].—Just look at that, will you! Is that old-fashioned enough for you—that ridiculous piece of furniture!

HENRI [*nailing the carpet down*].—You must come to the suburbs of Chinon* to see such rubbish.

BAPTISTE.—Yes, that's another of monsieur's fine ideas—to come out here to the country to hunt. . . . [*Stretching himself on a settee.*] And I had thought to take him to some watering-place—for my sciatica.

HENRI [*stopping and sitting cross-legged on the carpet*].— I'm beginning to have enough of this! Here we've been swallowing dust ever since five o'clock this morning!

BAPTISTE.—Yes, and for people who've been trundled over a railroad for a whole day.

CLAUDINE.—Second-class, too—and that's anything but comfortable.

Enter Madame Solange.

SOLANGE.—Well! I declare! You won't wear your shoes out in a hurry at that pace, you three.

CLAUDINE.—Hello! To whom have we the honor of speaking?

---

* [Chinon is an historic spot. It is situated in the department of Indre-et-Loire (France), on the River Vienne, twenty-six miles southwest of Tours. It contains a ruined castle, a royal residence from the twelfth century to the reign of Henry IV. The remains of the castle occupy a large rock-platform. The exterior walls are ruinous, except the high towers. The royal apartments are chiefly of the twelfth century, and include armory, kitchen and other commons, the King's room, and the great hall—where Charles VII first saw Joan of Arc. The great keep is of the thirteenth century.—EDITOR'S NOTE.]

445

SOLANGE.—You have the honor of speaking to Madame Solange, housekeeper of the château, my dear, and nurse
to madame.

BAPTISTE.—My compliments to your nursing, Madame Solange; but as to your housekeeping—

SOLANGE.—Well! What about it?

BAPTISTE.—It won't kill you. It must be two years since
you've handled a broom in this room, hey?

SOLANGE.—No! Three!

BAPTISTE, HENRI, CLAUDINE [*laughing*].—Three!

SOLANGE.—Yes, three years! . . . Since the departure of
my old mistress, Madame de Crussolles (the mother of
madame; ah, you didn't know her). . . . Since her
departure for Paris, with Mademoiselle Clarisse, who
was going there to marry M. Vanhove! . . . Stay!
It all comes back to me! It was at daybreak; they had
gone for the post-horses to harness them to the old
barouche; and madame said to me, in a low voice, from
the coach-door: "Solange, shut up everything tight,
my girl, for fear of burglars!" (That was her mania,
poor woman, to be afraid of burglars!) "And you are
not to open the salon again until my return, do you
hear?" "Yes, madame." "Whip up, driver." Then I
did as I was told—I shut everything under bolt and bar,
awaiting the return of madame. Alas! She didn't return, poor lady. A year after the wedding she was no
longer of this world; and so the apartment has never
been touched until yesterday evening, when Mademoiselle Clarisse, now Madame Vanhove, arrives at midnight with her husband, without a word of warning, and
says, as she jumps from the carriage: "Hurry, nurse,
open the salon and have it cleaned early in the morning: I have company to-morrow, to lunch, to dinner!"
So I opened the room, and that good and early; for,
say what you please, I always obey orders.

HENRI.—And so that's why the salon was all upside down,
as if the folks had just left yesterday!

SOLANGE.—Yes, that's the reason; only, instead of standing
there chattering, you'd better finish your work.

HENRI.—Bah! two touches of the feather duster and it's done!
[*He starts to dust a statuette of Flora.*

SOLANGE.—Wretch! Don't touch Flora!

HENRI.—But she's covered with dust, your Flora!

SOLANGE [*stopping him*].—Never mind! Don't touch it! It's forbidden! Since the accident to Zephyr——

ALL.—Zephyr!

SOLANGE.—Yes, it was the companion piece to the Flora. See!
> [*She points to the other pedestal.*]

CLAUDINE.—Well, where is it?

SOLANGE.—Ah, poor thing! broken to a thousand bits. And madame cherished it as the apple of her eye! A real old Sèvres! And so nobody was to touch it! And when madame became paralyzed in both arms, it was always Mademoiselle Clarisse who dusted it. No one else! [*To Henri, taking the duster.*] Here, give me that, I'll finish this job.

CLAUDINE.—So! There's nothing more to do here; I'm going to take my cup of chocolate.

HENRI.—And I my bath.

BAPTISTE.—And I to get my letters ready!

HENRI [*with a mock courtesy to Solange*].—Adieu, Lady Solange.

BAPTISTE [*bowing*].—Housekeeper of the château.

CLAUDINE [*bowing*].—And nurse!
> [*Exeunt Claudine, Baptiste, and Henri, laughing.*]

SOLANGE [*alone*].—A fine lot! So devoted to their masters! A pity about his " chocolate "!

Enter Paul, tiptoeing.

PAUL [*in a low voice*].—Solange!

SOLANGE.—Monsieur Paul! Here, in the house of M. Vanhove!

PAUL.—She sleeps?

SOLANGE.—Who? Madame Vanhove?

PAUL [*timidly*].—No, Mademoiselle Marthe.

SOLANGE.—What! You know Mademoiselle Marthe, then?

PAUL.—Oh, yes.

SOLANGE.—There's no need of blushing about it.

PAUL.—But I'm not blushing. [*Aside.*] What a tiresome woman! [*Aloud.*] It was the suddenness of your question——

SOLANGE.—Yes. . . . And pray where did you make the acquaintance of Mademoiselle Marthe, who hasn't been at the château since she was eight years old?

PAUL.—Why, at Paris, two months ago, when I went there with my tutor, M. Thirion.

SOLANGE.—Ah! It was our neighbor, M. Thirion, who introduced you to Madame Vanhove?

PAUL.—And to Mademoiselle Marthe.

SOLANGE [*laughing*].—Ah! That's it!

PAUL [*embarrassed*].—Yes, that's it!

SOLANGE.—What a boy! There's no need of asking him what's up. It's plain enough.

PAUL [*quickly*].—Plain! what is plain? I didn't say anything.

SOLANGE.—No, but you've told everything.

Enter Marthe, in riding-habit.

MARTHE.—Good-morning, Monsieur Paul.

PAUL.—Mademoiselle Marthe!

SOLANGE.—He thought you still asleep.

MARTHE.—Asleep! I've already made the tour of the village twice on horseback, all alone, English fashion. Here, nurse! [*She gives her her hat and whip.*

SOLANGE [*aside*].—With a young man like that—I can leave them alone, with an easy conscience. [*Exit.*

PAUL [*eagerly*].—Ah! Mademoiselle!

MARTHE [*mimicking*].—Ah, Monsieur Paul!

PAUL.—How have you been since last I had the happiness of seeing you?

MARTHE [*still mimicking*].—Oh, pretty well, I thank you. And you?

PAUL.—There you are making fun of me again, just as you did at Paris.

MARTHE.—Oh, no! Not at all! What good have you been doing these two months?

PAUL.—Good? Oh, nothing.

MARTHE.—What else?

PAUL.—Writing poetry.

MARTHE.—Verses! You must let me see them.

PAUL.—Oh, no!

MARTHE.—Why not?

PAUL.—Because there are things in them that I shouldn't like to say.

MARTHE.—Well, you needn't say them. I'll read them.

PAUL.—Never! No, mademoiselle, let me take my hat and go. I feel as though I were sliding down a precipice. You can say anything without fearing to vex me, while I —no! Decidedly, mademoiselle, another time, later—

[*He takes his hat.*

MARTHE.—Then you've finished? I may go?

[*Pretends to go.*

PAUL.—So soon?

MARTHE.—But, gracious, if you've nothing more to say to me——

PAUL.—Ah! If I dared——a thousand things.

MARTHE.—That's too many. You are embarrassed. Do you know what you ought to do, Monsieur Paul?

PAUL.—What, mademoiselle?

MARTHE.—You should go walk in the park for an hour or two, to calm yourself. And above all, don't make verses. No! you must reason with yourself in simple prose, and then you'll say something like this: " It must be admitted that I am a great bungler."

PAUL.—Very true.

MARTHE.—" Here I've been waiting for some one, a friend, with a certain degree of impatience."

PAUL.—Yes, indeed, counting every second.

MARTHE.—" Counting every second. And when she arrives, I dare not tell her what is in my heart."

PAUL.—Most true.

MARTHE.—" As if all that were not perfectly proper and polite "—

PAUL.—Oh, perfectly.

MARTHE.—" As if Mademoiselle Marthe could be vexed by that."

PAUL.—Ah, mademoiselle, that is——

MARTHE.—That is what you are going to say to yourself under the trees—then you'll come back—you'll speak—I'll listen!——

PAUL.—Ah, permit me!

MARTHE.—And we shall see whether I am vexed. Good-morning, Monsieur Paul. [*Exit.*

PAUL.—Well, truly—it's over.—I've said it—that is—no; it was she who made me say it. But it comes to the same thing. Ah, I should never have believed that I could have gotten through it so well. But that's what it is to be plucky.

COLOMBA [*from without*].—Paul!

PAUL.—My guardian, and his wife! Let me escape with my happiness! They'd spoil it for me.

[*Exit precipitately towards the park.*

Enter Thirion, Colomba.

COLOMBA.—Paul! Paul! Where can he be?

THIRION [*holding up a net with a butterfly in it*].—The butter-fly? Here he is.

COLOMBA.—Who's thinking of your butterfly? I'm speaking of Paul. I saw him in this salon.

THIRION.—Paul, always Paul! You've nothing but Paul in your head.

COLOMBA.—And you—you'd better be looking after him than be forever chasing flies and butterflies.

THIRION [*sitting down by the table*].—Entomology is a pas-sion which hurts no one.

[*Sticks the butterfly on to his hat with a pin.*

COLOMBA.—I tell you you're not living up to your duty as guardian to that child.

THIRION.—" That child " is twenty years old.

COLOMBA.—His wits have gone wool-gathering since you took him to Paris on that ridiculous journey—against my wishes, mind you.

THIRION.—It was to make the acquaintance of his lawyer, my dear. He's got to know his lawyer some time. My guar-dianship will come to an end; and when the time comes for him to marry——

COLOMBA.—To marry! What, he's going to be married, then?

THIRION [*astonished*].—What's the matter? If——

COLOMBA.—I forbid you to put such ideas into his head.

THIRION.—Pshaw!

COLOMBA.—The mere fact of having seen those frivolous décolleté Parisian women at the ball, at the theatre—

THIRION.—Oh, as to the décolleté—the fact is—but indeed he's only seen very respectable women—Madame Vanhove, for instance.

COLOMBA.—Ah, truly! a coquette—who got herself talked about nicely at Chinon—before her marriage. And I suspect that odd friend of yours, M. Prosper, knows something about that, too. Just arrived from India the other day to pay you a visit and hasn't even come to say good-morning to me to-day.

THIRION.—What does Prosper know? A mere bit of girlish folly. Really, to hear you talk——

COLOMBA.—I don't care who hears me! It's just trouble wasted trying to bring up this young man to a sense of decorum and modesty, if he's to be spoiled by those Parisian women.

THIRION.—Oh, as to that! You don't imagine that boy will remain forever—Confound it—— You make me forget myself. But in fact, even I, who speak to you, I, Madame Thirion—— Hang it. But at his age—I, too——

COLOMBA [aside].—You too!

THIRION.—And what if this young man should have an intrigue——

COLOMBA.—An intrigue with a woman! Speak!

THIRION [aside, biting his lips].—Ah, blockhead! and Colomba such a prude! What an idiot I am!

COLOMBA.—But continue—go on—speak!

THIRION.—No, no, my dear, I was jesting.

COLOMBA.—Monsieur Thirion! You are hiding something from me.

THIRION.—No, no, I tell you.

COLOMBA.—But I shall force you to tell me. I will know it, whatever comes of it.

Enter Prosper, at the back.

THIRION.—Come, come, Colomba.

COLOMBA.—I will know everything. Speak!

THIRION.—But——

COLOMBA.—But speak, I tell you.

PROSPER [*clad in white, with a Chinese parasol*].—No, don't
speak, Thirion.

THIRION.—Prosper!

PROSPER.—Don't speak! After trying violence, Madame Thirion will be forced to have recourse to persuasiveness.
Turn and turn about. Let yourself be persuaded, my
friend, and don't speak.

THIRION [*to Prosper*].—Would you believe it?

COLOMBA.—Enough! [*To Prosper.*] Have you been going
around the village in that garb?

PROSPER.—Just as I went around the world, madame, and always with the greatest success. Just now, for instance,
I met a lady on horseback who didn't attempt to hide
her extreme delight at the sight of me. A most charming creature.

COLOMBA.—To be frank—for a man—that fan, that parasol
—it's very bad form.

PROSPER.—What do you mean by *form*, my dear lady?

COLOMBA.—Why, the fashion.

PROSPER.—Talk of fashion to a man who has just traversed
two hemispheres, running across men and women of
every color. It's not good form at Chinon; but it's good
form at Peking—and that's all there is to it.

THIRION.—Ugh! the Chinese!

PROSPER [*imitating him*].—Ugh! the Chinese. That's my
good European, who thinks all is said when he disdainfully exclaims *the Chinese!* But to them, you are the
Chinese, you Chinonese! With your side-whiskers and
your stove-pipe hat in broad daylight!

THIRION.—I!

PROSPER.—Yes, you, and madame, and all like you. Just so
many Chinese, in another China, and with as many ridiculous Chinese customs. Thirion's Chinese. He doesn't
eat larks' nests but he devours pickled oysters, and snails
à la provençal. And madame's Chinese; she doesn't
imprison her little feet in thimbles, but she mutilates her
figure with a tight corset. And Prosper Block, here,
is Chinese. He doesn't smoke opium, but he smokes
twenty cigars a day, ruins himself, makes an offensive
brute of himself. Chinese! Bah!

Enter Busonier.

BUSONIER.—And Busonier, too! Here's one you haven't mentioned.

THIRION.—Busonier! you here!

BUSONIER [*shaking hands*].—Here I am! I heard of Madame Vanhove's arrival and started for the country the first thing in the morning, so as to be the first to announce to her the great news.

THIRION.—The great news? What news?

BUSONIER.—What! You don't know? [*Bursts out laughing.*] Bah! you really don't know?

THIRION.—What is it?

BUSONIER [*laughing*].—You're certainly the only ones—— Such a thing to happen to me—customhouse inspector— why, my friend, it's the only topic in the cafés, in the theatres, in the papers, everywhere. Why, man, I'm famous, thanks to Madame Busonier.

THIRION.—Your wife! I understand.

BUSONIER.—You catch on? And you, Prosper?

PROSPER [*grasping his hand*].—I'm with you.

THIRION [*enthusiastically*] —I'm delighted!

BUSONIER.—Eh?

THIRION.—You deserved it long ago. I always said to Madame Thirion: "That's all he lacks. But it will come to that finally."

BUSONIER [*to Madame Thirion*].—He told you that——

THIRION.—A woman like Madame Busonier, so intelligent, so clever! Ah, I was sure——

BUSONIER.—Hold on! Allow me! What is it you think has happened?

THIRION.—Why, an increase in the family!

BUSONIER.—An increase in the family? Well, yes. But not as you understand it!

COLOMBA.—Ah! I understand. Madame Busonier——

BUSONIER.—Heavens! She's had herself abducted.

COLOMBA.—Horrors!

THIRION.—My dear fellow, before Colomba!

BUSONIER.—Faith! Madame Thirion can't take it tragically no more than I; and seeing that I turn the thing into a jest——

THIRION.—A jest!

BUSONIER.—What! Do you think I'm going to be such a fool as to tear my hair, to draw more ridicule upon myself! Hardly! Busonier is not such a fool as to give his friends the satisfaction of pitying him! At the first news, another man would have hidden himself! But I —took my cane, put on my hat, and went straight to my club. As I enter, some one holds out his hand to me with an air of condolence. I burst out laughing. The crowd retorts. But I was the first to laugh, and my laugh killed theirs. Let a hunch-back forget his hump, and nobody thinks of it!

COLOMBA.—You take it philosophically!

BUSONIER.—Do you want me to take it like a hoodwinked husband? Am I so joined to the frivolities of Madame Busonier that my thirty years of well-known probity should become bankrupt owing to the loss of her virtue? Thank God, my honor is my own—as her dishonor is hers. I was an honest husband! I remain an honest man! She loses both.—So much the worse for her!

PROSPER.—There's a man without prejudices for you!

BUSONIER.—To be sure; and that is also the opinion of a sensible and intelligent woman to whom I related the affair this morning.

THIRION.—Who's that?

BUSONIER.—Mademoiselle Suzanne.

THIRION.—She here!

BUSONIER.—At Chinon, where I left her in the midst of her trunks. She has come to spend the autumn at the château.

COLOMBA.—Who is this Mademoiselle Suzanne?

BUSONIER.—Ah, true! Madame doesn't know her. Mademoiselle Suzanne is a Parisian, a little cousin of Madame Vanhove's and godmother to her younger sister, who, coming into a snug little fortune on the death of her parents, has steadily refused the best matches, out of sheer love of independence.

COLOMBA.—An old maid!

BUSONIER.—A charming woman, just verging on thirty, and who, consequently, has the right to know in theory

many things which young girls are supposed not to
know. Spirituelle, with a frankness of manner that
would perhaps be offensive in another—but which she
renders amiable; moving among the best people in
Paris; and more virtuous in her liberty than many another in chains—as Madame Busonier can testify.

PROSPER.—Bah! don't talk of Madame Busonier; it's laugh-
able.

THIRION.—Oh, she! Gad! She'd shrug her shoulders at such
trifles.

PROSPER.—That she would.

THIRION.—Yes, in China it's tolerated indulgently.

PROSPER.—And in the Marquesas Islands it's quite an honor.

THIRION [*trying to hush him*].—Softly, my friend. Colomba!

PROSPER.—An honor! Intrigued for! Solicited! Implored!

THIRION.—My friend, Colomba! Colomb——

PROSPER [*continuing and rising*].—Bah! Madame will soon
understand all that. It's a matter of latitude. What is
honor, in such a case? A mere shadow! Now all
travellers will tell you that the nearer you come to the
equator, the shorter the shadows, on account of the
perpendicularity of the rays of the sun. At Java, for
instance, a deer, an elk, or Busonier, might walk with
impunity in broad daylight without blushing at their
shadows. But let them go northward, and presto!—
there is the shadow——which lengthens, lengthens——
and the fear of ridicule grows with the length of the
shadow.

THIRION.—Then that is why Vanhove is so jealous.

PROSPER.—He is from the North?

THIRION.—A Hollander.

PROSPER.—He is afraid of his shadow.

Enter Vanhove crossing through the park at the back.

COLOMBA.—Good-morning, Monsieur Vanhove. Did you have
a good night?

VANHOVE.—Thanks. Yes.

BUSONIER.—Is Madame Vanhove down yet?

VANHOVE.—I believe so.

THIRION.—Then we'll go say good-morning to her with Monsieur. M. Prosper Block—the friend of whom I spoke last night. He would like to have an interview with you.

VANHOVE.—Very well.

PROSPER [aside].—What ice!

THIRION.—We'll see you later.   [Exeunt Colomba, Thirion.

VANHOVE.—You've come to join us in the chase, sir?

PROSPER.—The chase? No. That is, yes, but another sort of chase.

VANHOVE [coldly].—Indeed.

PROSPER.—Let me come to the point at once. I am a bachelor, and, you'll be surprised to hear, have just come from India for the purpose of getting married. But I will say at the outset that my hand is forced.

VANHOVE.—Indeed.

PROSPER.—I'll tell you how: I am only heir to a very rich uncle, who's even more pig-headed than he is rich. And as for my patrimony—swallowed up, shipwrecked, in the course of long voyages.

VANHOVE.—Indeed.

PROSPER.—You'll perhaps want to know why I undertook such long and expensive journeys?

VANHOVE.—No.

PROSPER.—No! Then perhaps you wouldn't like to hear about woman's treachery and the cruel mishap that forced me to seek oblivion on the foamy brine?

VANHOVE.—No.

PROSPER.—No! But still you must be impatient to learn the causes that make marriage a necessity to me?

VANHOVE.—No.

PROSPER.—Excuse me—But it's absolutely indispensable that you should be impatient to learn about them. Otherwise I should have no reason for telling you about them.

VANHOVE [coolly].—As you will. I'm all impatience.

PROSPER.—Then I will yield to your desire, and begin; but don't be alarmed, I'll make a short story of it. A month ago, after three years of wandering over land and sea, I turn up, with my whole cargo of stuffed crocodiles and parrots, at the house of the uncle of whom I spoke to you, who lives alone in a kind of a dove-cote, about a mile from here. He opens his door, and, instead of embracing me: "Ah vagabond," he cries, "is it you"? "It's myself, uncle!" "At least you're married"? I rack my brains to recall whether in Oceania or elsewhere—"No, uncle, no, I'm not married." "What, you heartless knave——here I've condemned myself to celibacy, all on your account, in the hope that your house would be mine, that your wife would cook my gruel—and instead of that, you leave me alone in my pigeon-house, with Athénaïs." Athénaïs is his housekeeper. "Do me the favor to go and get yourself a wife, at once." "But where shall I find her?" "Why, anywhere, vagabond! There are adorable girls everywhere." "But, uncle!"—— "I give you six weeks, and if by that time you don't bring me your betrothed, I'll publish the bans for my marriage with Athénaïs—— Be off!" With that he slams the door in my face, leaving me in the street, with all my traps. Now what do you say to that?

VANHOVE.—Nothing.

PROSPER.—Nothing! Then don't let's talk of it any more. So then I made up my mind to take up my quarters with your neighbor, my friend Thirion, who has kept my room ready for me these ten years. "I have it!" says he—— "Just the thing for you! M. Vanhove has just arrived with his wife and his little sister-in-law. She's a pearl. Go find him, make your request, and it's done." I come to you, make my request for the hand of your sister-in-law—is it done?

VANHOVE.—Well, I don't say no.

PROSPER.—Then it is yes?

VANHOVE.—Oh, no.

PROSPER.—Then what is it, my good sir?

VANHOVE.—Go see my wife—her sister. It concerns her more than me. [Rings.

PROSPER.—You are right. And I am the more pleased, because three years ago, when I was on a visit to my friend, Thirion, I had the honor of making the acquaintance of Madame de Crussolles; and if I've never seen Mademoiselle Marthe, who was then at the convent, I am well-known to Madame Vanhove.

VANHOVE.—Ah, indeed! [Rings.

Enter Claudine.

VANHOVE [*to Claudine*].—Tell madame some one wishes to see her.

PROSPER.—Wait! Give her this card!   [*Exit Claudine.*

VANHOVE.—You'll stay to lunch and to dinner?

PROSPER.—You are too kind.

VANHOVE [*looking at his watch*].—Nine o'clock! I am going to see whether my dogs are here. I'll be back directly.

PROSPER [*alone*].—Don't hurry! Well, now I'm sure of the husband, and I have no doubt about his wife. His wife! What memories! And how many changes in three years! But the salon at least hasn't changed; there is the little table, the lamp, the Flora. Even the bit of embroidery—God bless me—is the same. And this book —the very book. Oh, we were just going to look up " Genevieve." [*Reading.*] " Genev—" What a strange sensation. [*Coldly.*] Very surprising—— Surely it's the castle of the Sleeping Beauty. Everything has been asleep.

Enter Clarisse.

CLARISSE.—And you come to awaken us!

PROSPER.—Clarisse! Madame!

CLARISSE.—I couldn't believe the card. Is it indeed yourself?

PROSPER.—Come, like the prince in the fairy tale, through a thousand brambles and briars, to see what has survived the grand trumpet-blast.

CLARISSE.—Oh, nothing.

PROSPER.—Nothing! In your heart, perhaps; but mine will never forget three months of the most budding, tenderest, purest love—born among flowers and sunshine!

CLARISSE.—It is dead!

PROSPER.—Dead?

CLARISSE.—Sit down and tell me where in the world you come from, so early in the morning—to talk of all that again.

PROSPER.—I come from the other world, madame, and to speak of other things!

CLARISSE.—Indeed. Of what?

PROSPER.—Of my marriage, madame.

CLARISSE.—With whom?

PROSPER.—With your sister Marthe, if you will permit it.

CLARISSE.—Marthe. What folly! A mere child!

PROSPER.—Oh, there are no more children. Only little women.

CLARISSE.—She hasn't even met you.

PROSPER.—A tremendous advantage. The unforeseen!

CLARISSE.—But how do you know she doesn't love another?

PROSPER.—O, I am counting on that.

CLARISSE.—What, you count upon her loving—

PROSPER.—To be sure. Will you permit an Oriental simile to a man just come from Calcutta? How did you use to make tea every evening, in this same salon? First you poured a few drops of boiling water on the leaves to soften them and take out the bitterness; and after throwing away this first water, the next infusion was the more savory! So it is with the first love of a young girl. It's thrown off and all the fragrance remains for the first cup.

CLARISSE.—You always were a crack-brained fellow!

PROSPER.—Besides, are you happy?

CLARISSE.—Perfectly.

PROSPER.—You perhaps repent of having married M. Vanhove?

CLARISSE.—Not in the least! I love him, and I have only one regret—to have believed for an instant that I ever loved another.

PROSPER.—You've found the true recipe for happiness—to throw overboard the man you love in order to marry the one you don't love! Then why not give me Mademoiselle Marthe? She'll follow in your footsteps and become the happiest woman in the world.

CLARISSE.—You want to know the truth?

PROSPER.—The real truth?

CLARISSE.—The real truth! Here it is. I should be most unhappy if this marriage should take place;—I won't deceive you—it will not take place.

PROSPER.—Why not?

CLARISSE.—Why not? How can you ask? You've known me as a light, frivolous woman—a flirt, if you will. And, however little cause I have to blush for that school girl

love of which you spoke just now, still it cannot give me
pleasure to recall it. Can you not understand that I
should be most reluctant to see in my husband's house,
the man whom I permitted to say to me, before he did—

PROSPER.—Ah—what you replied to me: "I love you."

CLARISSE [*hastily rising*].—You see you give me reason for
my prejudice. Come, be chivalrous, I ask no sacrifice
of you. You don't love my sister; you haven't met her.
Withdraw your request. Let us say good-by and you
will carry away with you not only the consciousness of
having done a good deed but also the assurance that
you have in me a true friend.

PROSPER.—Ah, but that is what I can't believe.

CLARISSE.—You can't believe——?

PROSPER.—In your friendship. No more than I advise you to
believe in mine—for under the ashes of love I have kept
a smouldering brand—what a glowing brand!—an in-
extinguishable hatred—which I've carefully kept alive
these three years, all by myself. I'm not sorry to draw
some sparks of it from your eyes; for really a woman
can't trifle with a man as you trifled with me—in the
space of five hours!

CLARISSE.—I!

PROSPER.—Listen. We are here in this room again; all the
surroundings are the same. It's only you who prevent
these three years from seeming like one night and that
last night we saw each other——yesterday. Ah, yesterday. You were there and I here. And I was reading
aloud from this book—see, it's still here. And you were
embroidering this bit of tapestry—(there's witchcraft
in it; everything is the same)—and in this arm-chair sat
your mother, apparently asleep, but her watchful eye
followed us everywhere, and reduced our love-making
to the mute interchange of glances and little scraps of
notes. Ah, those little notes! You remember them—
faintly scented, charming—I burned them as I received
them—as I had sworn to do—in my divine candor. And
the letter-box, so well chosen—for none touched it but
you and I—our Flora is there still, as it was yesterday. Yesterday, Mademoiselle Clarisse, I left you say-

VICTORIEN SARDOU.

Photogravure from a photograph by Reutlinger, Paris.

This is the portrait of a man of wit and humor, and the most superficial glance would recognize the whole-souled geniality and kindly benevolence that beam from Sardou's face. The mobile, expressive features and clean-shaven chin suggest the actor rather than the man of letters. Sardou is the most eminent of living French dramatists.

ing: "Until to-morrow" — "To-morrow," you answered. And this morning you are Madame Vanhove.
That's what I call rather abrupt.

CLARISSE.—Who willed it so? You!

PROSPER.—I?

CLARISSE.—Were you beside me to prevent it? Where were
you?

PROSPER.—Where was I? That's just what I am going to explain to you. When I left you, madame, last night, or
three years ago, as you will, instead of going straight to
Thirion's, I take a turn under the trees. I light a cigar,
and after the fashion of platonic lovers, lean against a
tree and gaze at the light in your window, giving vent
to a thousand sighs. Suddenly——

CLARISSE.—Suddenly?

PROSPER.—Two steps away, I see shining under the trees a
little glowing light—not a glow-worm—a cigar!

CLARISSE.—A cigar!

PROSPER.—With, of course, a man at the end of it: one of
my good friends and your admirers—M. de Rivière.
Mutual astonishment and stupefaction at the discovery
of a new light in the mass of rhododendrons. Third
cigar, M. Tonnerieux, secretary to the prefect.

CLARISSE.—Ah!

PROSPER.—Three hearts on fire, burning their incense under
your windows. I drag these gentlemen off to my room.
Stormy explanations ensue. Each claims that he has
the right to give you this little serenade. Sarcasm and
retort discourteous. Two duels on my hands!

CLARISSE.—Good Heavens!

PROSPER.—We take down our swords, make for the duelling
ground, and there in the moonlight I wound Tonnerieux
—a mere scratch; de Rivière stabs me through the
arm; I fall, am carried away,—and that's where I was:
in bed, with fever and delirium.

CLARISSE.—But I never knew——

PROSPER.—Naturally. Except for Thirion everyone thought
it was a hemorrhage of the lungs; and, moreover, to
add to the dramatic situation, at the very moment when
I fell a post-chaise was carrying Madame de Crussolles

and her daughter to Paris, where M. Vanhove awaited them. Your marriage was the first news to greet my convalescence: result—a relapse, followed by my first voyage to the Marquesas Isles.

CLARISSE.—But—my letter?

PROSPER.—Your letter!

CLARISSE.—The letter I wrote—at the very moment when you were waiting under my window. The letter in which I told you everything—M. Vanhove's proposal—the implacable will of my mother—our departure at night for Paris! That letter which told you to join us in Paris at any price—that I was ready!—oh, a thousand foolish things that I should blush to repeat and which you know very well.

PROSPER.—It's the first time I ever heard of it.

CLARISSE.—Ah, do not say that! I slipped down here in the night to put the letter in the usual place, sure of your finding it in the morning, as you had the others.

PROSPER.—But in the morning—I was in bed with a fever, madame.

CLARISSE [*rising, frightened*].—But then, the letter! If you haven't it, where is it?

PROSPER.—Why, where you put it—under the Flora—unless some one—

CLARISSE.—My writing. Oh, if my husband! Fortunately this salon has not been opened.

PROSPER.—Then it must be there.

CLARISSE.—Oh, you've frightened me so! I dare not look!

PROSPER.—I will look.

CLARISSE.—No, no—let me.

PROSPER [*stopping short*].—Someone——

CLARISSE.—My husband!

Enter Vanhove, Busonier, Thirion, Madame Thirion, Colomba, finally Paul and Marthe.

PROSPER.—Well, sir, are your hounds ready?

VANHOVE.—Yes. [*To Clarisse.*] What's the matter?

CLARISSE.—Nothing—the excitement—what monsieur was telling me——

VANHOVE.—This marriage?

PROSPER.—Precisely. My marriage.

VANHOVE [*to Clarisse*].—Well?

PROSPER [*to Clarisse*].—Well, as I understand it, the matter is settled, is it not?

CLARISSE.—Entirely! Monsieur understands my reasons. He withdraws his request.

[*Movement of surprise on the part of Prosper.*

VANHOVE.—Indeed!

PROSPER.—But pardon me, madame. I cannot so easily renounce the honor of an alliance with your family. I should like first—I should be glad——

MARTHE [*embracing Clarisse*].—Good-morning, sister.

PROSPER [*aside*].—Ha! my enchantress—the lady on horseback—[*Aloud.*] But no, no, no. I don't withdraw. Not at all!

CLARISSE [*uneasy*].—Ah!

PROSPER.—And I implore madame to permit me to offer my suit before judging it unacceptable.

VANHOVE.—Naturally.   [*Moves to one side.*

CLARISSE [*aside to Prosper*].—Your conduct is neither charitable nor courteous—and it is utterly useless.

COLOMBA [*aside to Paul*].—I forbid you to speak to Mademoiselle Marthe.

PROSPER [*looking after Clarisse*].—What great thinker was it who said: "When a woman ceases to love us she hates us." I'd like to have lived before that gentleman so as to have said it first; for it is an incontrovertible truth.

THIRION.—What is that you are saying?

PROSPER.—I say that it's confoundedly rough on a fellow to make the tour of the world all for the sake of a coquette who treats you like a lackey when you return—under the pretext that in the interval she has become as virtuous as Cornelia, mother of the Gracchi!

THIRION.—A refusal?

PROSPER.—Worse—a dismissal! And as a result I am now madly enamoured of the charming creature, who was an object of utter indifference to me this morning. Plague take it! Shall I go back like this, with my parasol?

THIRION.—Gad! A husband who is both jealous and brutal; a woman who hates you. Better give it up!

PROSPER [*looking at Clarisse who softly moves up toward the mantel-piece*].—No, by Heavens! I hold her under my thumb. I shall stay, and I shall do my courting in spite of her.

THIRION.—What's that?

PROSPER.—What's that? Did you ever see two hunters after one partridge?

THIRION.—Well?

PROSPER.—Well! Just watch Madame Vanhove prowling around the Flora. The partridge is there.—She is watching it—I too. And I'm thinking it will be a strange kind of a game.

THIRION.—A partridge?

PROSPER [*turning and seeing Clarisse on the point of lifting the Flora and taking the letter*].—Confound it! Too late! She's taking aim!

Enter Suzanne.

SUZANNE [*gayly*].—It is I! [*All turn abruptly and Clarisse withdraws her hand without having taken the letter.*

BUSONIER.—Mademoiselle Suzanne!

MARTHE [*running up to Suzanne*].—My godmother!

PROSPER [*seeing Clarisse go to embrace Suzanne*].—Saved! My turn now!

[*He starts towards the Flora, but Colomba stops him midway.*

SUZANNE.—Good-morning, dear friend! Good-morning, pet!

MARTHE.—I'm going to get your room ready. [*Exit.*

SUZANNE [*embracing every one*].—Good-morning, cousin Vanhove. You're a bear. But I'll permit you to embrace me. I don't make my arrival every day. And M. Thirion, too. And M. Busonier—Oh, not you—I've seen you before, this morning. Who else?

THIRION [*presenting Paul*].—My pupil whom you saw in Paris!

COLOMBA [*stopping Paul*].—I forbid you to kiss——

SUZANNE [*drawing Paul to her*].—Ah, M. Paul! He will blush! [*Kisses him.*] He did blush! [*Bowing to Colomba.*] Madame!

COLOMBA [*drily*].—Mademoiselle! [*Talks apart with Paul.*

SUZANNE [*turning and seeing Prosper, who is about to lift*

the Flora and take out the letter unperceived].—Who is this gentleman in white?

PROSPER.—Missed! Try again.

CLARISSE [*hastening to introduce him so as to force him to come forward*].—M. Prosper Block! A friend!

[*Moving past him.*

SUZANNE [*looking at them*].—Ah, indeed! [*Aside.*] There's something in the wind.

PROSPER.—I have long coveted the honor of being introduced to madame!

SUZANNE.—You are interested in curiosities?

THIRION.—Oh, tremendously! He has just returned from Asia, Oceania, the ends of the earth.

SUZANNE.—How fortunate to be a man! But to run about the world in skirts!

BUSONIER.—They didn't embarrass Madame Busonier.

SUZANNE.—Tell me, sir traveller, what is the most curious thing you have seen in the world?

PROSPER.—The most curious? Woman.

SUZANNE.—Ah, you are a student of the species?

PROSPER.—Exclusively! As Thirion studies insects, and others mushrooms.

SUZANNE.—You wish to imply that there are some venomous kinds?

PROSPER [*watching Clarisse as she hovers about the Flora*].— Some, and they are generally the most beautiful. [*Aside.*] Ah! We begin to beat about the bush again.

SUZANNE.—And like a true naturalist, you stick little labels on us as they do with the stuffed birds in the *Jardin des Plantes*.

PROSPER.—Just what I was saying to Madame Vanhove. Excuse me. [*Every one turns towards Clarisse who comes forward without the letter; Prosper offers her a seat which she is obliged to accept.*] Woman is a bird with a very slender beak, long claws, plumage of a greater or less degree of brilliancy, which she is constantly occupied in keeping bright.

SUZANNE.—And wings?

PROSPER.—The wings are wanting. She has nothing in common with the angels. [*Everybody protests.*

VOL. II.—30

SUZANNE.—Oh, sir, think of your mother, who perhaps hadn't so much wit as you, but who had heart enough to rock your cradle all night long—and your sister, a bit of a coquette perhaps, but who pawns her jewels to pay your gambling debts—and your wife?—

PROSPER [*interrupting*].—Now there's where you spoil the simile.

SUZANNE.—No, there's where you spoil us! For it's you who make our faults; but you don't make our virtues. And some day, when poverty and disease cast you upon a hospital cot—then it is you find your natural history at fault. For there beside you is neither wife, nor beak, nor claws; only a sister of charity—with wings.

PROSPER.—The exception proves the rule. And in the case of woman, it is a general rule—

SUZANNE.—General rule! There are only exceptions.

PROSPER.—Well, madame, twice I thought I had met with exceptions—in Java and in Borneo; and do you know what happened? I was poisoned twice! And even in our own country, where poisons change their nature and are transformed into every sort of treachery and backbiting, I've sworn never to take a step without an antidote.

THIRION.—An antidote? Of what sort?

PROSPER.—Oh, any little object that might scare the enemy and hold him off—— Such as, for instance, a letter.

CLARISSE [*aside*].—He wants the letter.

SUZANNE [*aside*].—There's a letter in the case!

BUSONIER.—Fie! Such a weapon—and against a woman.

PROSPER.—Pardon me. I spoke of defense, not of attack. The shield is legitimate where it would be infamous to use a sword. Among all peoples——

THIRION.—He's going to cite the Chinese. Just see if he doesn't!

PROSPER [*quickly*].—Our masters in many things—even the manufacture of porcelain. Show me any object in this salon comparable to their masterpieces. Take this little Sèvres, for instance. [*To Clarisse.*] A Flora, is it not?
[*Taking the Flora.*

CLARISSE [*trying to stop him*].—Sir!

PROSPER.—Oh, don't be alarmed—I know its value.

CLARISSE [*frightened*].—Give it to me. It's covered with dust.

PROSPER.—Don't give yourself the trouble. [*Aside.*] I feel the letter.

CLARISSE [*taking a handkerchief, as if to dust it herself*].— Let me——

PROSPER.—A thousand thanks! By just blowing—
> [*Turns aside, under the pretext of blowing off the dust.*

SUZANNE [*staying Clarisse's hand*].—Vanhove is watching.

CLARISSE.—Oh, if you knew! [*The letter falls.*] Ah!
> [*Prosper quickly puts his foot on the letter.*

SUZANNE [*aside*].—A letter! I was sure of it.

PROSPER [*handing the Flora to Clarisse*].—It is evident you are alarmed for this little work of art.

CLARISSE [*in a low voice*].—Oh, this is infamous!

PROSPER [*softly*].—A shield, madame! All is fair in love and war. [*The bell rings for luncheon.*

Enter Marthe.

MARTHE.—Luncheon is ready!

THIRION [*rising*].—Well, I'm not sorry for that!

BUSONIER.—Nor I!

PAUL.—Nor I!

COLOMBA [*aside to Paul*].—You are not to sit beside Mademoiselle Marthe!

PAUL.—But—

COLOMBA.—I forbid you.

MARTHE.—Give me your arm, Monsieur Paul!

COLOMBA.—I forbid you.
> [*Turns and finds herself facing Busonier.*

BUSONIER.—Madame!
> [*Colomba takes his arm, Clarisse Thirion's.*

SUZANNE [*to Prosper, who stands with his foot on the letter*]. Aren't you going to offer me your arm?

PROSPER.—Beg pardon! I just dropped——

SUZANNE.—What?

PROSPER [*letting his handkerchief fall*].—My handkerchief.

SUZANNE [*in a low tone*].—Come, give it up with a good grace—

PROSPER.—Give what up?

SUZANNE.—The letter.

PROSPER.—My antidote! Never.

SUZANNE.—I shall force you to give it up.

PROSPER.—I'll wager you don't.

SUZANNE.—I'll wager I do.

PROSPER.—A declaration of war?

SUZANNE.—To the death!

PROSPER.—And we are to begin hostilities?—

SUZANNE.—After luncheon. But give me your arm—her husband is watching us.

PROSPER [*offering his arm*].—Madame, may I?

SUZANNE [*aloud*].—And so you like the Chinese; and do you eat with little sticks too? [*Exeunt.*

ACT SECOND

Scene I.—Prosper's Room at Thirion's

PROSPER [*seated before an open fire, wrapped in a fur dressing-gown*].—A nice climate, upon my word! In the morning it's hot as Senegal—at two o'clock cold as Lapland. [*Throws a log into the fire.*] Disgusting! [*Another stick. Shooting heard in the distance.*] Ah, shooting! The gentlemen are hunting. Much joy to them!

Enter a servant.

What do you want? I didn't ring.

SERVANT.—A letter for you, sir. They're waiting for an answer.

PROSPER.—Ah, from my uncle. Good! I know his letter by heart. Every morning he writes the same thing: "Vagabond, have you found a wife?" [*Reading.*] "Vagabond, have you found"—— Just so. Fifteenth edition. [*Throws it in the fire.*] Say I'll take the answer myself, within an hour, and have my horse ready at three.

SERVANT.—Very well, sir. [*Exit.*

PROSPER.—A quarter of an hour to go, another to return. I'd
rather make the run and see that savage uncle myself.
I'll tell him I've found my wife—[*Looks for a cigar.*]
—that she is a charming blonde, and adores me! [*Rolling a cigarette.*] As for Mademoiselle Suzanne, I don't
know whether she is as virtuous as her friend; but one
thing there's no doubt about, and that's her challenge—
" I will have the letter by force! " Did you ever hear
the like! So you're going to outwit me—bless your
little heart!—and filch my letter—American fashion.
Clever Suzanne! But far more clever Prosper! We'll
see who wins—— Once in possession of the letter,
there were several ways of defending it—First, to keep
it on my person, day and night. At night I hardly think
the young lady—No! But day and night there are a
thousand ambushes to be feared. To hide it in the lin-
ing of my hat! I tried that at Surinam with the love-
letter of a pretty little Dutch woman—but of course I
managed to leave the hat at the house of her husband,
who serenely took possession of it and has worn it ever
since. I didn't dare claim it. So the hat won't do.
Now from the moment I gave up the plan of carrying the
letter about with me, I had no other resource but my
room with its furniture or a friend—or the hollow
trunk of a tree. But as to the tree-trunk—out of the
question; for first you must find your tree, and then,
having found it, you mustn't use it, for fear of rats.
Then for the friend.—There is only Thirion, married,
consequently allied to the fair sex, and not to be trusted.
Third, there's my bedroom.—Nothing in it mine, nothing to be trusted—neither servants nor locks. Supposing I should put it in this casket with the secret lock.
The casket can't be opened. But the windows are only
six feet from the ground, and a casket of this shape has
wings. Just see how an apparently simple problem may
become complicated! All for a wicked little scrap of
paper, no bigger than that. In short, another man than
Prosper Block would have been at his wits' end. And so
it is with almost delirious enthusiasm that I proclaim
myself a genius in hiding it in the only place that will

never be suspected, in—— [*A knock at the door.*]
Some one knocks—Come in!

Enter Paul.

PROSPER.—Ah, it's you, my young friend. Then you didn't
go shooting with the rest?

PAUL [*embarrassed, and trying to be dignified*].—No, sir.

PROSPER.—I understand. Madame Thirion is afraid. Good.
Sit down and have a cigar. [*Offering cigars.*

PAUL.—Thank you. I don't smoke.

PROSPER.—Ah, indeed. Madame Thirion objects to the odor?

PAUL.—Sir, I didn't come here to smoke, but to talk seriously
with you.

PROSPER.—Indeed!

PAUL.—This morning I learned, from a chance word dropped
by M. Thirion, that you had asked M. Vanhove for the
hand of Mademoiselle Marthe in marriage.

PROSPER.—Well?

PAUL.—Well, sir, I will not conceal from you that I love
Mademoiselle Marthe, and that my greatest desire is to
obtain her hand in marriage.

PROSPER.—Provided Madame Thirion consents.

PAUL [*gently*].—Sir, there is no question of Madame Thirion
here. It's between you and me. Kindly tell me whether
you persist in your suit, yes or no?

PROSPER [*aside*].—The boy is amusing. [*Aloud.*] Well, yes,
I persist.

PAUL.—Then, sir, since one of us must necessarily yield his
place to the other, and since I am not disposed to do
that, it is indispensable that we fight.

PROSPER.—Indispensable?

PAUL.—I leave you to judge of that.

PROSPER.—Well, granted. Only you know, my dear young
man, there are many modes of fighting: which do you
prefer?

PAUL.—It is for you to choose, sir.

PROSPER.—I confess to a weakness for the custom of Japan.

PAUL.—I agree to the custom of Japan. I shall have the honor
to send you my seconds, and——

PROSPER.—Oh, that's quite unnecessary. The matter can be

decided between ourselves, with closed doors, and immediately, if you wish it.   [*He goes to his wardrobe.*

PAUL [*laying aside his hat and gloves*].—It's contrary to all rules, but I'm your man.

PROSPER [*presenting two Malayan daggers*].—Here are two daggers.   Be so kind as to choose.

PAUL.—What are those?

PROSPER.—The weapons.   [*Paul takes one.*]   And now [*sitting down*] be good enough to begin.

PAUL [*turns quickly, weapon in hand, but stops short on seeing Prosper seated*].—To begin!

PROSPER.—Certainly.   You provoke the quarrel; it's for you to begin.

PAUL.—All alone?   How shall I begin?

PROSPER.—Why, by ripping open your stomach.

PAUL.—My stomach?

PROSPER.—The custom of Japan—Invariable rule: the aggressor is to rip open his stomach before his adversary, and the latter is bound to do likewise at the very same instant.   You are the aggressor.   Begin!   I'll follow suit.

PAUL.—You are making sport of me, sir!   We are not in Japan, but in France, and your custom is utterly absurd.

PROSPER.—A question of appreciation.   I find your custom detestable.

PAUL.—Detestable for one who has neither courage nor honor.

PROSPER [*gayly*].—Oh, as for courage, young man, I've fought with tigers—quite as dangerous as you; and as for honor, you see every one hasn't the same opinion about that, since in Japan it's different from what it is here. And mark, the Japanese reason far better than you; for supposing we were to fight in the French fashion: I should inevitably kill you.

PAUL.—Oh!

PROSPER.—Oh, I'll answer for that!   And afterwards I should be only the more sure to marry: there you are away off from your object!   On the other hand, suppose we fight like the Japanese.   You rip yourself open—I rip myself open.—You won't get married, that's sure; but neither will I!   And you can rest in peace.

PAUL.—You treat me like a child, sir.

PROSPER [*rising and holding out his hand*].—Rather, like a friend, young man. For, to make an end of the matter, the two methods are equally unreasonable; and the man who has washed his honor in blood can say with Diogenes on coming from a bath of questionable purity, "Where can I wash myself clean after this?" But what is welcome in all places and at all times, what suits every age and stature, is the fair and courteous competition—with the head and heart for weapons—that I offer you. You love Mademoiselle Marthe. She, perhaps, loves you. So much the better for you—for I swear I will not marry her against her will. But since you have found means to please her, permit me to believe that I shall not be less skilful, and allow me to go through my term of probation.

PAUL.—In what manner?

PROSPER.—Ah! I haven't asked you your methods. The young lady will choose, the vanquished will retire from the field—and intact.—Consolation ready at hand!

PAUL.—And how long do you require for this trial, sir?

PROSPER.—My dear friend, don't haggle over the time. You are not of age, you haven't the consent of your guardian, and I am certain you never will get it.

PAUL.—Never? Why not?

PROSPER.—Why not?

COLOMBA [*from without, knocking*].—M. Prosper!

PROSPER.—Listen—That's why! I am not presentable; let me get out of the way.

COLOMBA AND MARTHE [*from without*].—May we come in?

PROSPER.—Yes, you're quite welcome, ladies.

[*He enters his dressing-room.*

Enter Colomba and Marthe.

COLOMBA [*looking around for Prosper*].—Well?

MARTHE.—Where's M. Prosper?

PROSPER [*from within*].—Excuse me. I am a bear. I should have frightened you.

COLOMBA.—We beg your pardon. We thought we should find Mademoiselle Suzanne and the gentlemen here. They wish to visit your museum.

PROSPER.—Visit it, ladies, by all means.

MARTHE.—Oh, what pretty things! [*Frightened.*] Oh! a mummy!

COLOMBA [*aside to Paul*].—You know I don't wish you to associate with M. Prosper. He is a very undesirable acquaintance for you.

PAUL.—But really, if I listened to you, I shouldn't speak to anybody. Now it's M. Prosper, now Mademoiselle Suzanne, then Mademoiselle Marthe——

COLOMBA.—Especially the latter. And I must say you pay great attention to my wishes. You never fail to sit beside her at table and to chatter with her in an undertone in a most improper manner—in spite of my disapproving looks——

PAUL.—But madame——

COLOMBA.—But I give you warning, that if you don't mend your ways, I'll have you sent back to Chinon this very evening, to study for your degree.

PAUL.—But, madame!

MARTHE.—Monsieur Paul!

COLOMBA.—And as a beginning, I here formally command you to give your whole attention to me.

MARTHE.—Monsieur Paul!

COLOMBA [*to Paul*].—You hear? [*Sitting down by a table.*

MARTHE.—Must I come for you, then? [*She sits down on a divan.*] Ah! I understand. Madame Thirion has been making eyes at you ever since this morning, and now she has forbidden you to speak to me.

PAUL.—Oh! madame——

COLOMBA.—Paul, bring me a footstool, please.

PAUL.—Yes, madame.

MARTHE [*aside to Paul*].—I forbid you to give it to her.

PAUL [*footstool in hand*].—But——

MARTHE [*pointing to her feet*].—And put it there at once.

COLOMBA.—Paul, don't you hear me? A footstool.

PAUL.—Pardon! but I——don't know——

COLOMBA.—Why, you've got it in your hand!

PAUL [*looking at Marthe, who points to her feet*].—Yes, but Mademoiselle Marthe asked me——

MARTHE.—What's that? If madame wishes it, give it to her, by all means.

COLOMBA.—You are too kind!

MARTHE.—Don't mention it, madame. It is a deference that my age owes to yours.

COLOMBA [*pushing away the footstool which Paul presents*].— The difference is too slight for me to accept it.

MARTHE.—Then take it as a delicate attention of Monsieur Paul—which I yield to you.

COLOMBA [*aside, rising*].—Which she yields! What insolence!

MARTHE [*aside, rising*].—Checkmated!

COLOMBA [*to Paul*].—You shall go this very evening.

PAUL.—But——

MARTHE [*aside to Paul*].—If you answer her, I'll never speak to you again.

PAUL.—Then—I— [*Sits down on the footstool.*] Ah!

Enter Thirion, Busonier, Suzanne, and several hunters, with their rifles.

THIRION [*at the door*].—May we come in?

PROSPER [*coming from his room, dressed*].—Come in! Come in!

SUZANNE.—Beat the drums! Blow the trumpets! [*To Prosper.*] I hope to make a good fight. Was it rash to come upon you in your stronghold with an armed force?

PROSPER [*bowing*].—I can only answer in Oriental phrase:— " A ray of sunshine has the right to enter everywhere!"

MARTHE.—And when one isn't a ray of sunshine?

PROSPER.—Perfume of roses has the same privilege.

MARTHE [*to Paul*].—He is more gallant than you.

PROSPER [*to Thirion and Busonier*].—I thought you had both gone hunting?

BUSONIER.—Yes, yes. But this is between the acts.

PROSPER.—And what have you killed since noon?

THIRION.—Between the two of us, we've killed one dog.

PROSPER.—And Vanhove?

BUSONIER.—Oh, Vanhove! He's a mighty hunter before the Lord, as a rule. But to-day I don't know what's the matter with him. He is moody and absent-minded. Misses every shot.

COLOMBA.—Madame Vanhove didn't come with you?

BUSONIER.—No, she is not feeling well.

THIRION [*coming upon Paul*].—Hello! What's he doing here?

COLOMBA.—It is imperative that this young man should go to Chinon.

THIRION.—How's that? Why?

COLOMBA.—To prepare for his examinations.

THIRION.—Pshaw! I don't see the necessity of it.

PAUL.—Nor do I.

COLOMBA.—But I do.

THIRION.—Why?

COLOMBA.—I have good reason to.

THIRION.—That's another matter. He shall go. [*Colomba moves away.*] [*Aside.*] Some pranks, I'll wager. What a simpleton it is! Can't manage his affairs without Colomba's knowledge. [*To Paul.*] Oh, you are a simpleton!

PAUL.—Sir?

THIRION.—Go pack your trunk.

PAUL [*sighing*].—Ah! When a woman takes a grudge against you! But I'm not at Chinon yet.

THIRION.—What's that? [*Exit Paul.*

SUZANNE.—A truly remarkable collection this—and collector.

PROSPER.—All *bric-à-brac*. It's the fashion, you know. Our furniture, our books, our ideas and customs—*bric-à-brac*—mere *bric-à-brac*. We only care for what is foreign.

SUZANNE.—Show me a man seated in an American rocking chair, like this one, before a Flemish table covered with an Algerian cloth, drinking Chinese drinks out of Saxon porcelain, smoking Turkish tobacco, after a Russian dinner, where he talked sport to his wife in English, while she answered with Italian music—I'll tell you at once—This is a Frenchman!

MARTHE.—Just look at these little shells!

PROSPER.—Souvenir of a Honolulu lady.

COLOMBA.—A bracelet!

PROSPER [*in an undertone to Suzanne and Colomba*].—A dress, rather.

COLOMBA [*rising*].—Oh, monsieur!

SUZANNE [*aside*].—Too much virtue to be virtuous.

MARTHE.—Monsieur Paul! What, is he gone?

SUZANNE [*aside*].—Oh! Monsieur Paul again!

MARTHE [*to Prosper*].—A thousand thanks for your kindness. Are you coming, godmother!

SUZANNE.—Run along. I'm coming.

THIRION [*seeing Marthe go towards the little door at the right*].—You're not going out that way?

MARTHE.—Yes, it's the shortest road to the château. [*Aside.*] And he went out by this door. [*Aloud.*] Good-day, gentlemen. [*Exit.*

THIRION [*to Busonier*].—Supposing we resume our shooting.

BUSONIER.—And kill another dog?

COLOMBA [*about to go out by the door at the rear*].—Aren't you coming, mademoiselle?

SUZANNE.—No, madame. I shall go with Marthe.

THIRION AND BUSONIER.—Good-by.

[*Exeunt Thirion, Busonier, Colomba.*

SUZANNE.—Good sport, gentlemen! [*To Prosper.*] Monsieur, I have the honor—

[*Prosper bows and shuts the door after Busonier and Thirion. Suzanne quickly closes the little door at the right and returns.*

SUZANNE [*taking a seat*].—to salute you.

PROSPER.—Indeed! I thought you were beating a retreat.

SUZANNE.—Before the battle? It's clear you don't know me. But are you still holding on to the letter?

PROSPER.—Yes, I'm holding on to it!

SUZANNE.—Well then, before coming to open hostilities, suppose we exchange a few diplomatic notes.

PROSPER [*sitting down by the table*].—By all means.

SUZANNE.—First note: We appeal to the honor of our adversary and ask him whether simple probity authorizes him to keep a letter which he has—how shall I express myself——

PROSPER.—Stolen!

SUZANNE.—Let us be parliamentary and say—intercepted! What have you to answer?

PROSPER.—I answer that the letter, being addressed to me, taken by me, is in possession of its rightful owner.

SUZANNE.—You didn't receive it, therefore it belongs to us.

PROSPER.—You sent it to me, therefore it belongs to me.

SUZANNE.—There was no emissary.

PROSPER.—Pardon me. A point of good faith. The Flora represents in this case the letter-box, and the point in dispute is this: Does a letter dropped into a letter-box belong to the sender or to the person to whom it is addressed?

SUZANNE.—To the sender.

PROSPER.—To the person addressed.

SUZANNE.—Let us say to both.

PROSPER.—Then it's mine.

SUZANNE.—But it's also ours.

PROSPER.—Where rights are equal, possession gives the title Let us go on to the next point.

SUZANNE.—We ask what you purpose to do with our handwriting?

PROSPER.—I have already replied categorically on that point. Observe strict neutrality, and on the day when I give up all hopes of Mademoiselle Marthe, I will bid an eternal farewell to Madame Vanhove, and burn the letter before her eyes.

SUZANNE.—You will do that?

PROSPER.—On my word of honor—and I swear I should have done it this morning, without telling you, of course, if your challenge hadn't provoked me to combat.

SUZANNE.—Well, then, I withdraw my challenge. Burn it before me. See, here's a pretty fire. Clarisse will know nothing about it, and the effect will be the same for you. Come, a good deed!

PROSPER [smiling].—I'd lose too much.

SUZANNE.—But what?

PROSPER.—The immense satisfaction that I promise to my artistic instincts in seeing you find the letter where I have hidden it.

SUZANNE.—Surely wit spoils the heart.

PROSPER.—Not always, mademoiselle. You are a proof to the contrary.

SUZANNE.—And that is your last word?

PROSPER.—The last.—Negotiations broken off!

SUZANNE.—At least I hope I have observed all the forms, and given you three summonses.

PROSPER.—Yes.

SUZANNE.—Then let the trumpets sound for battle. Since it is I who prevented your destroying this scrap of paper, I shall be forced to repair the injury I've done you, and to make you destroy it before my eyes.

PROSPER.—As you please. The letter is here.

SUZANNE.—Here?

PROSPER.—Here! Find it, and I'll authorize you to burn it yourself.

SUZANNE.—Oh, I'm something of an artist, too. And I shall not be satisfied unless you burn it with your own hands —in that fire.

PROSPER.—Madame, I swear that if you succeed I will renounce Mademoiselle Marthe—and I will start this evening, madame, this very evening, to find a wife in the Marquesas Islands.

SUZANNE.—You swear?

PROSPER.—I swear it.

SUZANNE.—A coward he who retracts! I warn you I am obstinate.

PROSPER.—I too!

SUZANNE.—That the fear of gossip will never deter me.

PROSPER.—Nor me!

SUZANNE.—Especially when there's a good deed to be done.

PROSPER.—Oh, for my part, in the matter of good deeds— don't mention it!

SUZANNE.—And I'm going to begin by a regular siege. I shall attach myself to you, bore you to death with my presence. I shall be tiresome, unendurable, altogether odious. I will never leave you until you say—" What a nuisance of a woman! I'd rather burn the letter than have her around."

PROSPER.—Was ever any one threatened with so delightful a punishment! My soul is intoxicated with joy to think of the many pleasant hours we shall spend together. Do me the honor to sit in this arm-chair and make yourself at home. Here is a fire, books, and some sketches to which I venture to call your attention. The cases are open—here are my shells; there, Thirion's insects. All the keys are in their locks. Let me see, are they?

[*Looks.*] Yes—excepting this little casket, which contains papers on matters of no interest to you. Open and rummage through everything—turn everything topsy-turvy—I shall be only too delighted if they charm your leisure during a little visit that I am obliged to make to my uncle; and if you're still here when I return I hope to continue our most entertaining conversation. Would it were never to end!

SUZANNE.—But——

PROSPER.—Good-day, madame. [*Exit.*

SUZANNE [*alone*].—What? Gone? He's decidedly interesting. Did you ever hear such insolence! "Search, madame, search!—Everything is open—excepting this casket." How particular he was to emphasize the casket—with his important papers. Poor man! I can be sure at least his letter isn't in the casket. But it is in this room—Where can he have hidden it? [*Some one knocks at the little door to the right.*] Already! No. It is the little door leading to the park. [*Louder knocking.*] Who's there?—I'm compromised!—Come to my aid! [*She opens the door.*

Enter Clarisse.

CLARISSE.—You are alone?

SUZANNE.—Clarisse!

CLARISSE [*shutting the door*].—I saw him pass my windows on horseback, and as you didn't return—why, I couldn't keep still. I threw this shawl over my shoulders and came over.

SUZANNE.—Rash woman! What if your husband had seen you!—Or Madame Colomba, that embodiment of charity!

CLARISSE [*throwing her shawl on the sofa*].—Pshaw! Since we are alone, tell me. Have you got it?

SUZANNE.—The letter? No, he refuses to surrender it.

CLARISSE.—Oh, Suzanne, he's left it somewhere around here. Find it, I implore you. I no longer dare look M. Vanhove in the face. He acts as if he had guessed everything—as if he knew all.

SUZANNE.—My poor friend! What a lesson to young girls, if they could only hear you.

CLARISSE.—Oh, they'd never do any more writing, I assure you.

SUZANNE.—Avoid all double-dealing, there's a simple rule of conduct for you.

CLARISSE.—Oh, don't lose any time!—Let us search.

SUZANNE.—But I am searching!

CLARISSE.—Like that?

SUZANNE.—With my head. It does better work than my hands could.

CLARISSE.—But we must rummage over everything—examine everything.

SUZANNE.—Do so—I have permission. But that's not my way of doing it.

CLARISSE.—What!—you're just going to sit still?

SUZANNE.—My dear child—Nature, in making us women did us such an ill turn that she tried to recompense us by giving us a sixth sense—like the butterflies. Have you ever examined a butterfly?

CLARISSE.—Oh, I don't know. What a question!

SUZANNE.—Well, just look in that case there. Let's see! [*Clarisse quickly picks up the case and takes it to her.*] That is Thirion's collection. Just examine their heads. How pretty they are! They have two long slender horns to feel and to touch things at a distance.

CLARISSE.—Well?

SUZANNE.—Well, my dear, it's the same way with us women. We, too, have little horns all around our heads—so fine that no one perceives them, so delicate that they find out everything. Some are like tendrils, to twine around the men, others are sharp-pointed, to blind them.

CLARISSE [*pettishly, putting back the case*].—And that's how you're going to find my letter?

SUZANNE.—Search!—I'll show you how to make use of your horns.

CLARISSE.—I'd rather trust my two hands.

[*Begins to open all the drawers.*

SUZANNE.—That's right—Go ahead! Upset everything. Don't forget to search the mouth of the lizard, and the hollow of the guitar. What a child!

CLARISSE.—Could he have hidden it in the book-case, perhaps?

SUZANNE.—Three hundred volumes to examine—Look at the edges of the shelves!

CLARISSE.—Why?

SUZANNE.—Are they dusty?

CLARISSE [*climbing on a chair to see*].—Yes.

SUZANNE.—All along?

CLARISSE.—All along.

SUZANNE.—Then it isn't there. In pulling out a book he would have disturbed the dust.

CLARISSE.—That's so.

SUZANNE.—Now look there—at that little bit of paper folded under one foot of the table.

CLARISSE.—This?

SUZANNE.—Yes—no, it's not worth the trouble.

CLARISSE—Why not?

SUZANNE.—Because the edge of the paper is worn and discolored.

CLARISSE.—And besides, that wouldn't have been clever— right in plain sight. [*She continues to hunt about.*]

SUZANNE.—For that very reason it would have been extremely clever. It's clear you don't know how to use your little horns, my dear. You confound the hiding places of simpletons with those of clever people. A clever man will take so little pains to conceal an object that you'd never think of hunting for it where it is. And I'll wager that if we don't find this wretched letter it's because it's staring us in the face.

CLARISSE [*after hunting awhile*].—Nothing! But there's still another room.

SUZANNE [*smiling*].—Go ahead! I am privileged to look everywhere.

CLARISSE.—But if he should come back—Well, I don't care—I can defend myself. [*Enters the bedroom.*]

SUZANNE.—Now where can it be? He's clever enough to have simply put it—under his paper-weight—[*She lifts the paper-weight.*] Nothing there! Or here, in the tobacco jar—[*Looks into the jar.*] Cards, a stick of sealing wax—paper for cigarettes—tobacco—some torn and crumpled letters. [*Reading.*] " To Monsieur Prosper Block—To monsieur, monsieur "—[*Going over the letters.*] And here'ş an odd-looking one, all covered with stamps. It must have done considerable travelling. [*Starts to put it into the other hand, with the rest, but changes her mind.*] "To Monsieur Prosper Block, care of the Reverend Sir Edward, Honolulu, Island of Oahou "—[*Reflecting.*] Honolulu! But that can't be of recent date. Why is it here? Very odd! [*Weighs the letter.*] Who could have sent a little *billet-doux,* weighing no more than that, to Monsieur Prosper Block, at Honolulu? Make a man pay five francs postage just to bid him good-morning! It's certainly very odd. [*Holds the letter up to the light.*] It's a little square piece of paper. [*Calling.*] Clarisse!

CLARISSE [*from the other room*].—I can find nothing.

SUZANNE.—Tell me, my dear—Was your letter very big?

CLARISSE.—No—a half sheet, folded once.

SUZANNE [*feeling the letter. Aside*].—A half sheet, folded once!—yes. [*Aloud.*] White paper?

CLARISSE.—No, blue. I saw it this morning.

SUZANNE [*peeping into the envelope*].—It is blue!

CLARISSE [*from the other room*].—Oh, Suzanne!—A box full of papers!

SUZANNE.—All right. So much the better. [*Smelling the envelope.*] Perfume—but very faint. [*Looking more closely through the envelope.*] Let's see the handwriting. [*Makes a movement to take out the letter. Stops short.*] Softly! This is a matter of honor. Have I the right to read it? Why not? He gave me permission to look at everything that was open—everything. This envelope is open—It's not quite the thing—and it's not my custom, although a woman. [*Fingering the envelope.*] But if it should be the letter! My fingers twitch!

CLARISSE [*coming out from the bedroom, in despair*].—Ah, my dear friend—It's no use—I give it up. We shall never find it—never!

SUZANNE.—I can't see her cry like that! [*Snatches the paper from the envelope and presents it to Clarisse.*] Clarisse! Was your letter anything like that?

CLARISSE [*unfolding the letter*].—It's my letter!

SUZANNE [*laughing*].—Ah, my dear—My little horns! What did I tell you?

CLARISSE.—Oh, yes, it's the very letter. [*Reading.*] " I leave to-night; but far or near, my love—" my love! If Monsieur Vanhove——

[*Violent knocking at the little door.*

SUZANNE.—Some one knocks!

CLARISSE.—Some one knocks?

VANHOVE [*from without, knocking louder*].—Open the door!

SUZANNE.—Vanhove! Give it here! [*Takes the letter.*

CLARISSE.—Oh, where shall I hide?

SUZANNE [*sotto-voce, going to open the door*].—Always the same! Don't hide—Stay.

CLARISSE [*losing her wits*].—No, no. He would see my agitation—He would guess. [*Looks around.*] Ah, in this room! [*Vanhove knocks again.*

SUZANNE [*her hand on the door-knob*].—Stay here!

CLARISSE.—No! [*Enters the bedroom and closes the door.*

SUZANNE.—Oh, foolish woman! [*Opens the door.*

Enter Vanhove in shooting-dress, with his gun.

VANHOVE.—You?

SUZANNE [*calm and smiling*].—Yes, I. What an uproar you've been making, cousin.

VANHOVE.—You here?

SUZANNE.—As you see—Looking at the collection.

VANHOVE [*looking around him*].—Alone?

SUZANNE.—As you see. [*She sits down before the cases of shells.*] There's a wonderful collection of shells!— Just look!

VANHOVE [*putting down his gun*].—I thought I heard talking in here.

SUZANNE.—Yes—I was trying to decipher these labels aloud. These scientific men give such outlandish names to things. Here, just look at that. Isn't it pretty?

VANHOVE.—Suzanne, you weren't alone—Clarisse was here!

SUZANNE.—Clarisse! What should she be doing here?

VANHOVE.—No good, evidently, since she has fled.

SUZANNE [*laughing and still looking at the shells*].—Indeed! Are you often taken that way, cousin?

VANHOVE.—I tell you she was here.

SUZANNE.—Then, why shouldn't she be here still? Come, my friend, do you think she has hidden herself under the table?

VANHOVE.—Then why didn't you open at once?

SUZANNE.—Because I thought the knocking was at the other door, and opened that door first.

VANHOVE.—You opened it to let Clarisse make her escape. That's the way she went!

SUZANNE.—How tiresome you are! If she went out that way, go and satisfy yourself, and leave me in peace with my shells.

VANHOVE.—Suzanne, I noticed that my wife was very much agitated this morning, after talking with this man—who knew her in the past. They spoke to each other in an undertone before lunch. What did they have to say to each other during that affair of the statuette?

SUZANNE.—They probably were saying that M. Vanhove was a funny kind of a man with his jealousies.

VANHOVE.—He asked for the hand of Marthe without even having seen her. How transparent! A mere pretext for introducing himself into this house in order to see her again. This marriage is merely a blind to divert my suspicions. [Seizing Suzanne's hand.] Look me in the face, and tell me that it isn't.

SUZANNE.—Of course it isn't.—But let go my hand, Vanhove, —you hurt me. And see what a mess you've made of my shells. [Opens her hand and shows a shell in powder.] This isn't nice of you.

VANHOVE.—Do you want to know what I have done? I left off shooting abruptly, to return to the château. I asked for madame. She had gone out. I had with me my dog Myrrha, who is as much attached to her mistress as to me. I said: "Search, Myrrha, search for her."

SUZANNE.—Oh—if it is possible.

VANHOVE.—Oh! [Mocking her.] And Myrrha darted into the park and came straight to Thirion's house, stopping at the door at the foot of this stairway. I tell you my wife is here, Suzanne. Where is she?—Where is she?

SUZANNE.—How do I know? Call Myrrha, my dear friend. If you're going to hunt your wife with dogs——

VANHOVE [*falling into a chair*].—Ah, Suzanne! You are
right. What a miserable wretch I am! This jealousy
is a frightful passion—It blinds and maddens me. My
head is on fire—I am no longer a man, but a wild beast,
without understanding or reason. [*Weeping.*] Oh, let
me weep. It will relieve me. Oh, my God, what torture!

SUZANNE.—Why, Vanhove!—My friend! Now I'm going to
scold you—you great baby! Spoiling your happiness
in that fashion, when you have the most charming, the
most lovable wife—who thinks of no one but you, who
lives only for you.

VANHOVE.—I know it!—I know it! I am reasonable again,
Suzanne. I am calm. But the first occasion—if I
should ever believe—[*Sees Clarisse's shawl and leaps
upon it.*] Ah, you see she's been here—That's her
shawl!

SUZANNE.—Her shawl!

VANHOVE.—Don't deny it. Who put it there?

SUZANNE.—I did—I took the first that came to hand.

VANHOVE.—I don't believe you. The shawl is here—She hasn't
gone. She is hidden somewhere. But I swear that I'll
find her.

SUZANNE.—Vanhove!—Stop!

VANHOVE [*searching, in spite of her*].—Leave me!

SUZANNE [*trying to stop him*].—Think of what you are doing!

VANHOVE [*finding the door to the other room*].—A door!—
She's there! [*Suzanne throws herself between him and
the door.*] She's hidden in that man's room! Let me
pass, I say! And on my life—[*picks up his gun*] I'll
kill lover and mistress together.

SUZANNE.—Ah, wretch! Then kill me! For I am his mistress.

VANHOVE.—You!

SUZANNE.—You drive me to say it, madman! since by your
uproar you are turning it into a public scandal. What!
You didn't understand at once, from my confusion, my
agitation—Do you think a woman comes to visit a man
alone, to look at his butterflies and shells? I didn't
open the door at once, it's true—because I was afraid of

being found here. Your dog stopped at the door—because it had tracked Clarisse's shawl. Clarisse refused to give Marthe to Prosper—because she knows of our liaison. Prosper wants to marry—because he thinks I've deceived him and wants to be revenged on me. Clarisse spoke low to him—to try to move him and prevent this marriage—which will never take place. For I, too, am jealous, Vanhove—jealous as you. And I can tell you that when once I am aroused! Well!

VANHOVE.—Is it possible! You, Suzanne! So virtuous!

SUZANNE [*sighing*].—Ah, my poor friend. There are days and moments——

VANHOVE.—Yes, yes. He spoke this morning of having fallen in love with a woman three years ago.

SUZANNE [*sighing*].—It was I.

VANHOVE.—He spoke of treachery!

SUZANNE [*sighing*].—My treachery!

VANHOVE.—But why did you not tell me that at once?

SUZANNE.—You are so good! And do you think a woman makes such a confession voluntarily? But you were in such a rage—and your outcry! You can't imagine it! Then the terrible fright, and then—but it's all told now, isn't it? And my reputation, my position—you understand, Vanhove? [*Aside.*] And ta ra ta ta ta! I'm in such a muddle I don't know what I'm saying.

VANHOVE.—Calm yourself, Suzanne—No one shall know what you have confided to me. And from this wrong great good may result.

SUZANNE.—How?

VANHOVE.—For now it is no longer Marthe whom Monsieur Prosper shall marry—it is you.

SUZANNE.—Me? [*Aside.*] I never thought of that!

VANHOVE.—Trust me. I'll take it upon myself.

SUZANNE.—But, my friend——

VANHOVE.—No, no. I will see him myself. I will speak to him—and that at once. Where is the gentleman to be found?

SUZANNE.—Oh, my dear friend. Not before I—at least you'll grant me the joy of luring him back. Come now! [*Insisting.*] Ah, Vanhove!

VANHOVE.—Well, as you will. But I swear that if he hasn't made up his mind before dinner, I'll take him by the collar—

SUZANNE.—Oh, Heavens.

VANHOVE.—And make him marry you—I'll answer for it! Dead or alive! A woman like you to be suspected, accused! It's like Clarisse! My good, pure Clarisse! Whom I—[*Laughing.*] What a fool I am! But he shall marry you! I am so happy I want everybody else to be happy. He shall marry you!—And we'll dance at your wedding! By Saint Hubert!—Suzanne, you shall be happy! I am entirely satisfied. Now, to my shooting! [*Taking his gun.*] Come, Myrrha, we're going a-hunting, my girl.

SUZANNE [*aside*].—And they say this man can't talk.

VANHOVE.—But not a word to Clarisse, Suzanne.

SUZANNE.—Be at ease, my friend. She shall know no more about it than she knows at this minute.

VANHOVE.—To the hunt, Myrrha! Ah! What a joyful day!

SUZANNE.—Ah, what a joyful day! [*Exit Vanhove.*] Oh!

CLARISSE [*coming from the bedroom*].—Gone?

SUZANNE.—Hush!   [*Clarisse draws back.*

VANHOVE [*from without*].—To the hunt, Myrrha! Come, my girl!

SUZANNE.—He's gone.

CLARISSE.—Oh, Suzanne!—My friend, my sister! Blessings on you! You've saved me twice.

SUZANNE.—Nonsense! We must stand by each other against the common enemy. Only, I am lost.

CLARISSE.—Lost?

SUZANNE.—If I've got to marry this man I'll kill him first. I'll kill him on the wedding-night.

CLARISSE.—Good heavens! If my husband persists in seeing him, in speaking to him, everything will be found out. We must get him out of the way.

SUZANNE.—He shall go. But be off, quickly! Vanhove may go to the house again.

CLARISSE.—Burn the letter. I'd like to stop to see it burn, at least.

SUZANNE.—Hurry, I tell you. You must be there before him.

CLARISSE.—Some one may see me.

SUZANNE [*opens the little door*].—Go this way. The road is clear.

CLARISSE.—I will escape this way.

SUZANNE [*snatching her shawl from her*].—Leave the shawl!

CLARISSE.—That's so! Oh, I'll go quickly—I'm lighter than when I came.   [*Exit.*

SUZANNE [*draws the letter from her pocket*].—Easy enough to burn the letter—But how to make him go? . That's another matter. He'll want his revenge. [*Looks at the clock.*] Half-past four. He would still have time to pack up and take the nine o'clock train this evening. [*Crumples the letter to throw it in the fire.*] Wouldn't that be fine! [*Stops and looks at the letter.*] But there's the envelope—Give unto Cæsar what is Cæsar's. [*Takes the paper from the envelope.*] I'll just slip in the first scrap of paper that comes to hand. [*Picks up a scrap of paper from the table and puts it in the envelope.*] There!—right in the midst of the tobacco—"To M. Prosper Block, Honolulu." [*Places it among the other letters in the tobacco jar.*] That's done! Now for the billet-doux. [*Approaches the fire-place.*] It's not just what I had counted on ; it would have been such a joy— [*Holds it over the fire*] to make him burn it himself. [*The paper catches fire. She pulls it back and blows it out.*] Himself! Stay! What was it he swore?—" If you make me burn it with my own hands, in this fire, I give you my word of honor that I'll leave this evening to go look for a wife in the Marquesas Islands." That would just suit us! Has he a word of honor, a man like that? He must have. Poor head and weak brain—but I'll trust to his word of honor. Let's see—Would it be very difficult to make him burn that?—[*Looks around the fire-place.*] If I put it there, near the fire! [*Twists the paper and puts it near the fire-place.*] Looks as if it had already been used to light a cigar. [*Goes off, and looks at it from every side.*] This whets my appetite— I do love these little contests of skill. Here's a paper to be burned! Now, for a change, he shall amuse me ; for he has bored me enough ever since morning. [*Lis-*

tens.] Some one coming up stairs. It is he. Oh, I forgot the matches! [*Throws them all into the fire.*] There! [*Sits down in an arm-chair.*] Let me appear worn out, utterly worn out. [*Pretends to be dozing. Prosper knocks softly.*] Ah! All right!—go on knocking.

Enter Prosper, softly opening the little door at the right.

PROSPER.—Asleep! Fatigue! Exhaustion! Despair! [*Looks around him.*] Well, she's managed to turn everything topsy-turvy. [*Looks into bedroom and laughs.*] And the letter?—Have we found it? [*Suzanne watches him from the corners of her eyes, while he looks into the tobacco jar and perceives the envelope.*] It's there. Ha! ha! The cunning sex is beaten! [*Looking closely at Suzanne.*] Beat—[*Breaking off.*] But asleep, like that—she's pretty—remarkably—[*looks closer*] pretty. Exquisite! [*Turns around her.*] As for her eyes!——

SUZANNE [*opens her eyes wide, and looks at him*].—What did you say?

PROSPER [*drawing back*].—Oh! dazzling!

SUZANNE [*pretending to awake*].—I beg your pardon. I must have fallen asleep.

PROSPER.—Pray consider yourself at home, madame.

SUZANNE.—What time is it?

PROSPER.—Five o'clock.

SUZANNE.—So late!

PROSPER.—Tell me, joking aside, have you found it?

SUZANNE.—No, but I haven't given up. You see I am at my post—and I shall stay here.

PROSPER.—All the evening?

SUZANNE.—All the evening.

PROSPER.—And the night?

SUZANNE.—And—bah! I'll have it before then.

PROSPER [*laughing*].—On my soul, madame, that's very fine and chivalrous of you. The most heroic obstinacy I've ever seen in my life.

SUZANNE.—Obstinacy? You call it obstinacy.

PROSPER.—Call it pride!

SUZANNE.—Neither the one nor the other.

PROSPER.—Don't defend yourself. You have a reputation for cleverness to save. This contest, that you've so rashly entered upon, may tarnish its lustre by a defeat. You make a desperate appeal to all your forces, you swear to die in the breach. That is fine! It's great! Sublime! If the chances of war hadn't made me your enemy, I'd like to fight under your standard and help you recover this wretched letter. [*Suzanne shivers.*] You are cold—pardon me!

[*Throws a stick into the fire.*]

SUZANNE.—Seriously, do you imagine my only motive is the silly vanity of outwitting you?

PROSPER.—Don't call it vanity—call it pride, madame! And legitimate pride! You're pitted against a man who has fought with red Indians. Here's a tomahawk that I captured from a great chief—" The sachem who weeps over his posterity." I too am a great chief—a great chief of the pale-faces, keen of scent, cunning on the trail. It would be no small glory for you to take my scalp. [*It grows dark.*

SUZANNE.—Well then, to follow out your simile :—In spite of the pleasure I should have in scalping you, oh great chief! a better motive than that has sent me on the warpath. Only be good enough to light your lamp, for really it's getting quite dark.

PROSPER [*rising to take the lamp from the mantel*].—Yes, madame. But, in default of pride, what motive can drive you to this desperate contest?

SUZANNE.—You won't admit that more serious motives may exist?

PROSPER.—I confess that—[*The lamp sputters.*] So! That fool of a servant hasn't put any oil in. [*Rings.*

SUZANNE.—Light a candle—that will be quicker.

PROSPER.—That's so. [*Looks for the matches.*] As I was saying, madame, if it is not the desire—very natural in a woman—especially—Ah! no matches now.

SUZANNE.—A bit of paper!

PROSPER [*bending down and seeing the twisted scrap of paper*]. —This will do. [*Picks it up.*] The very natural desire of a woman not to let herself be outwitted by a man—

[*Holds the paper over the fire. It burns.*

Enter servant, with lighted lamp.

SERVANT.—You rang, sir?

PROSPER [*extinguishing the lighted paper and keeping it in his hand*].—Yes—Good! Thanks! That's what I wanted.

SUZANNE [*aside*].—How vexatious. It was almost done.

[*Exit servant.*

PROSPER.—By a man—(I'll perhaps manage to finish my sentence.) I don't really see what can set you against me.

SUZANNE.—How about the desire to save my friend? You don't take that motive into account?

PROSPER [*still holding the scrap of paper*].—A friend! A friend! Pardon the question, madame. But is it possible for a woman to be so much the friend of another woman as to pull her out of a scrape? [*Aside.*] She's ravishing by lamplight.

SUZANNE.—I might be offended by the question. I prefer to laugh at it.

PROSPER [*picking at the paper*].—Ravishing! [*Aloud.*] Note that I haven't any better opinion of my own sex than of yours. I don't believe in the goodness of either.

[*Suzanne mechanically takes up the envelope and fictitious letter, from the tobacco jar, and plays with it. Prosper starts.*

SUZANNE.—You judge others by yourself.

PROSPER [*laughing to see the letter in her hand*].—If you mean that I am selfish—[*Aside, delightedly.*] Oh! the letter! [*Aloud.*] I confess that I try my best to be so; others only do evil to me, and I don't see what I should gain by doing good to them.

SUZANNE [*throwing the letter back into the jar*].—The pleasure of doing good. If you knew how a kind act brightens the sky, seasons one's food, and softens one's pillow —Ah, Sir Egoist!—you'd be good for your own sake! Of all that you have spent during your life, think what is left to you. The little that you have given——

PROSPER.—Perhaps, yes! [*Aside.*] What a smile—and what a soul!

SUZANNE [*aside*].—If I were to put out the lamp, he'd be forced to light it again.

> [*Starts to turn the wick up and down.*

PROSPER [*springing forward*].—Allow me, madame! Is it smoking?

SUZANNE.—Yes, a little. [*Puts out the lamp.*] Oh, there now!

[*Takes off the chimney and fixes lamp for lighting it again.*

PROSPER [*aside*].—So much the better! [*Aloud.*] Ah! madame, if you believe all you say, if you are really prompted only by goodness of heart—Ah, no, it's not enthusiasm that you inspire in me, it's veneration, idolatry, religion! You're not merely a woman of adorable beauty, charm, wit—but a being come I know not whence, I know not how, to be adored by me without my knowing why—I only know that I must adore you whether I will or no, or be insensate. For of all women you are the only woman that is worth marrying.

SUZANNE.—Talk about a proposal! That's certainly one! But it would be less obscure if you'd light your lamp.

PROSPER [*approaching her*].—No, madame, no. There's nothing so beautiful as the light of an open fire on an autumn evening—or so fitting for what I have to say to you.

SUZANNE.—Light the lamp, or I shall go.

PROSPER.—Command me, I am your slave—But I have no matches!—And I swear to you——

SUZANNE.—Light the lamp!

PROSPER.—Yes, I swear it. I swear that since my return you have hypnotized me—bewitched me——

SUZANNE [*pointing to the lamp*].—Yes, but——

PROSPER.—I'm mad! Or is it reason returning with love?

SUZANNE.—Ah, I'm going.

PROSPER.—You shall not go. No, no! You shall not leave your work unfinished. You've made me believe for an instant that supreme virtue and perfect goodness could exist on this earth. I wish to believe it all my life, and to prove to you that I am worthy of it. See!—here is the letter, madame, the letter—precious talisman—that has drawn you down from heaven to me. I will destroy it—and burn with it, before your eyes—[*Takes*

letter from jar.] my past, and all its errors—which I
here abjure.   [*Throws envelope in fire.*

SUZANNE [*aside*].—I could embrace him for that.

PROSPER [*holding up the envelope with the tongs*].—Look,
madame. It burns! It burns!

SUZANNE [*aside*].—I shall never have the courage to send him
away, now. Bah! I'll take him in my confidence, and
he'll stay.

PROSPER.—Do you want the ashes at your feet?

SUZANNE [*laughing*].—Are you quite sure it's the letter?

PROSPER.—Do you doubt——

SUZANNE.—Your good faith! No, indeed! But give me the
little scrap of paper you had just now.

PROSPER [*searching on the floor*].—The scrap of paper! I
don't understand!

SUZANNE [*laughing*].—There it is.
                    [*Prosper picks it up with astonishment.*

PROSPER.—Well, what then?

SUZANNE [*listening*].—Hush! What's that?

PROSPER.—The barking of dogs. [*Goes to the window.*]
Thirion, Busonier, and Vanhove are coming back this
way.

SUZANNE.—They may come up. Quick! Give it to me!

PROSPER.—Ah, I understand! You're afraid of being surprised
with me in the dark. Don't be alarmed.
                    [*He lights the paper again.*

VANHOVE [*outside, under the window*].—Here, Myrrha, here!

SUZANNE [*watching the paper burn*].—It is fated that he shall
burn it. [*Prosper lights the lamp and throws the burning paper out of the window.*] Ah!

VANHOVE [*without*].—That's the way to set fire to a house,
Monsieur Prosper!

SUZANNE.—Good Heavens!

PROSPER [*turning from the window*].—Fear nothing. It went
out as it fell—and I see some one is picking it up.

SUZANNE [*terrified*].—Vanhove! All is lost!

PROSPER.—What?

SUZANNE.—The letter! It was the letter!

PROSPER.—The letter? What!—that scrap of paper!

SUZANNE.—Yes, yes—that scrap of paper! Quick!—Run!
Run, I tell you!

PROSPER [*rushing to the window*].—But which way?
SUZANNE [*pointing to the door in the rear*].—There!
PROSPER [*going to the other door*].—I run!
SUZANNE.—No—this way!
PROSPER.—This way!   [*Upsets chairs and reaches door.*
SUZANNE.—Meet me at the greenhouse.
PROSPER.—Dead or alive, I'll have it!   [*Exit at rear.*
SUZANNE.—That's what comes of being too clever!   [*Exit.*

ACT THIRD

Scene I.—A conservatory, with dining-room adjoining

Enter Solange, Baptiste, and Henri.

SOLANGE [*takes some fruit from a basket, puts it on a plate
     and hands it to Henri, to prepare for dessert*].—Here!
BAPTISTE.—Hurry, hurry! The gentlemen will come upon us
     hungry as wolves after their hunting and the table isn't
     even set yet.
SOLANGE.—This new-fangled craze for having the dessert on
     the table, together with the soup, instead of keeping it
     for a little surprise, as in my day!
                    [*Noisy shouts and laughter from without.*
HENRI.—There they are!

Enter Thirion, Busonier, and three other hunters, laughing.

THIRION.—I tell you I could have killed him if I had wanted
     to.   [*Redoubled laughter.*
BUSONIER.—A partridge scotched! A growl from Thirion!
ALL [*laughing*].—Long live Thirion!
THIRION.—Long live Thirion! What sorry jesters you are!
     Every one to his taste, I say. Here's Monsieur d'Espars,
     who only cares for one kind of hunting, and that's deer-
     stalking. Busonier prefers to hunt hares. Mr. Tax-
     collector laughing in his corner over there—snipe. Van-
     hove—Oh, he'd hunt elephants if he had his way. But
     I have more modest tastes—I hunt butterflies and young
     ladies.

BUSONIER.—With a gun?

THIRION.—Let me tell you how I came to miss that accursed partridge. I had him at the end of my gun, didn't I! Well!—and I was about to kill him—when, looking down, I spied a tiger trotting along to his nocturnal lair —a tiger——

ALL.—A tiger!

THIRION.—A tiger!—A tiger-beetle!—A gold-winged tiger!— I am carried away by my naturalist instincts. I keep one eye on him—like that. I draw on the partridge while eyeing the beetle. I miss the partridge, but I leap upon the other—and you see I'm not such a bad hunter, since there he is, in this horn.

[*Shows a horn of blue paper stuck in the barrel of his gun.*

BUSONIER.—If that were all we had brought back for dinner!

THIRION.—Dinner! That reminds me—I, for one, could dine——

ALL.—Yes, yes!

HENRI [*aside to Baptiste*].—And the table isn't set.

BAPTISTE.—Would the gentlemen perhaps like to **brush** the dust off first?

BUSONIER.—That's so!—We shouldn't be the worse for an ablution.

BAPTISTE.—The gentlemen's rooms are this way.

[*Exeunt the hunters.*

BUSONIER.—Where's Vanhove?

THIRION.—Can't say! He left us abruptly as we passed my house. [*To Solange.*] Hasn't my wife come yet?

SOLANGE [*entering with a pile of dishes*].—No, sir.

THIRION [*looking at his watch*].—Making her toilet! [*Aside.*] Colomba is always so particular. No décolleté in dress or in language! To think that she's never even called me by my first name. [*Exeunt Thirion and Busonier.*

Enter Claudine.

CLAUDINE.—His wife, good man! Isn't she that thin blond who's always running after Monsieur Paul?

[*She and Henri exchange glances.*

SOLANGE.—Hold your tongue, gossip!

HENRI.—Say, Madame Solange, do they take their coffee here?

SOLANGE.—Yes.   [*Exit Henri to dining-room.*

CLAUDINE.—Then I'll leave you to get the cups ready. I'm going to change my tie—this one's so unbecoming— makes me look like a nurse-maid.   [*Exit.*

SOLANGE.—Oh, indeed. Can't stitch a hem, but she can play on the piano. What are we coming to!   [*Exit.*

Enter Prosper and Suzanne.

PROSPER.—In the conservatory, she said. Here at last!— Thank Heaven!

SUZANNE.—Thank Heaven! Well?

PROSPER.—Well?

SUZANNE.—You have it?

PROSPER.—You haven't it?

SUZANNE.—Not I.

PROSPER.—Nor I.

BOTH.—Ah!

SUZANNE.—Then what did you mean by saying—" Thank Heaven "?

PROSPER.—I meant: I haven't it, but she must have it—thank heaven!

SUZANNE.—But I came in after you!

PROSPER.—Just so! I rush down-stairs, four steps at a time.— I reach the bottom.—No one there—no paper. I say to myself: One of two things must have happened: either Vanhove stamped on the paper to put it out, or picked it up to see that it was extinguished. The paper isn't here, therefore the second hypothesis is the correct one. He has picked it up, then thrown it away. Dogs have a mania for chasing everything. His dog, seeing the paper, must have seized it, then dropped it a few steps further on. Follow the trail, and I'll find it. I followed the trail——

SUZANNE.—And you found nothing?

PROSPER.—But my reasoning was good!

SUZANNE.—It was the wind that chased it.

PROSPER.—There is no wind.

SUZANNE.—Then the first hypothesis was the correct one.

PROSPER.—Just what I said to myself: Vanhove trod on the paper. I didn't look carefully! But fortunately Mademoiselle Suzanne is more clever than I—She has found it.

SUZANNE.—But I didn't look for it. I came down—you weren't there—so I said to myself: He's got it—run! And so—I ran!

PROSPER.—By a thousand crocodiles! Then I've got to begin over again to-morrow, at daybreak?

SUZANNE.—To-morrow?—right away!

PROSPER.—Without an overcoat!

SUZANNE.—What's an overcoat got to do with it?

PROSPER.—But mademoiselle, consider!

SUZANNE.—Would you have the first passer-by pick it up?

PROSPER.—No.

SUZANNE.—And take it to Vanhove?

PROSPER.—I'd blow out what brains I have left.

SUZANNE.—Well, march then!

PROSPER [*buttoning his coat and shivering*].—Yes, mademoi- selle!—Br-r-r r.

SUZANNE [*throwing Clarisse's shawl over him*].—You're cold. There, take my shawl.

PROSPER.—No, no, mademoiselle.

SUZANNE.—Yes, yes!

PROSPER [*letting himself be wrapped in the shawl*].—She daz- zles me, fascinates me, intoxicates me! I am disarmed, subdued—[*the shawl stops his mouth*] muzzled.

SUZANNE.—Quick—march!

PROSPER.—Yes, mademoiselle! Muzzled! [*Exit.*

SUZANNE.—Here I've been running about like a squirrel in its cage, ever since morning, all for a wicked little scrap of paper—and on account of that—Poor boy! He's tak- ing trouble enough to undo the mischief he's done— I won't speak ill of him. But cursed be all scribbling, scribblings and scribblers! Anything goes in conver- sation. "I love you," is a pretty phrase to speak, but to write it! It freezes on the way. I might send a world of kisses by letter to—well, this man, for instance! A lot of satisfaction he'd get! He wouldn't even blush. [*Rising.*] Strange!—It's I who am blushing. How absurd! Surely I wouldn't play such a trick on myself as to hide any after-thought on his account? Come, come! Let's see!—what does this mean? Ah, Mademoiselle Suzanne, I'm going to keep my eye on you.

Enter Marthe.

MARTHE.—Ah! It's godmother! Have you seen Monsieur Paul?

SUZANNE [*aside*].—Here's one who doesn't mince matters. [*Aloud.*] No, I haven't seen him; but have you seen Monsieur Vanhove?

MARTHE.—No. He's walking up and down in his room.

SUZANNE.—Walking up and down! We're lost!

Enter Busonier.

BUSONIER.—Who's this walking up and down at half-past six o'clock? Don't people dine here?

MARTHE.—I'll go and find out. [*Exit.*

SUZANNE.—Busonier, my good friend, answer me quickly!

BUSONIER.—What is it?

SUZANNE.—You were with Vanhove when Monsieur Prosper threw that burning paper from the window?

BUSONIER.—What? You know——

SUZANNE.—Who picked it up?

BUSONIER.—The paper?

SUZANNE.—Was it Vanhove?

BUSONIER.—Vanhove?

SUZANNE.—Answer me! You kill me with suspense!

BUSONIER.—But give me time, my dear friend. What strange interest!—

SUZANNE [*impatiently*].—Well?

BUSONIER.—Ah! I recollect. It was I who picked it up.

SUZANNE.—You?

BUSONIER.—I'm sure of it.

SUZANNE.—And then?

BUSONIER.—Then?

SUZANNE.—What did you do with it?

BUSONIER.—What did I—? What strange interest!

SUZANNE.—Oh, what a man!

BUSONIER.—Heavens, I believe I threw it—no, no, I didn't throw it away.

SUZANNE [*eagerly*].—You have it?

BUSONIER.—No, I gave it to Thirion.

SUZANNE.—To Thirion?

> [*Paul appears at the rear and disappears quickly.*]

BUSONIER.—Or rather he took it out of my hands. I'm sure of it. That was it!

SUZANNE.—Thirion!—a fool!—Unlucky chance! Tell me at least where he is—I want to speak to him.

BUSONIER.—He was here with me just now. [*Calls.*] Thirion!

SUZANNE [*stopping him*].—No, no! Don't call him!

BUSONIER.—I must not call him?

SUZANNE.—Let us look for him—find him.—Come!

BUSONIER.—But—What strange int——

SUZANNE [*dragging him*].—Come, come!   [*Exeunt.*

Enter Paul, in travelling-dress.

PAUL.—Nobody! I'll venture.   [*Coming down.*

Enter Paul, in travelling dress.

SOLANGE.—Monsieur Paul! you here?

PAUL.—Hush!

SOLANGE [*lowers her voice*].—And Madame Thirion told me to take away your plate!

PAUL.—I believe you, Solange. She drives me away! She sends me to Chinon to study for my degree!

SOLANGE.—But at least you'll take dinner before you start?

PAUL.—Oh, I started some time ago. Under the pretext that my place had been engaged in advance, she made me take the five o'clock stage-coach, in front of the door, putting me under the driver's special care. I've been *en route* an hour already.

SOLANGE.—How's that?

PAUL.—You see: I was alone in the coach. We had reached the outskirts of the village, near the little hill—I opened the door softly, jumped to the ground without being seen—and came across the fields.

SOLANGE.—What for?

PAUL.—What for, Solange? Why, to see her—you know

who I mean—to tell her that I love her—that I love
her much more than this morning—a thousand times
more—and that I don't wish to leave her—and that I
want to marry her—and that I needn't be a Bachelor of
Arts for that!

SOLANGE.—If Mademoiselle Marthe should hear you! What a
lecture!

PAUL.—Marthe! Not she!

SOLANGE.—My stars! He has lost his senses!

PAUL.—She'd be only too glad to see me!

SOLANGE.—To see you! You count on seeing her?

PAUL.—I should think so—during dinner.

SOLANGE.—And where, if you please?

PAUL.—Here! The conservatory will be awfully convenient.
—Very comfortable here.—I can hide here all winter.
And I shall see her—and I'll talk to her all day—and
I'll be free, like the savage in his native forests, with-
out guardian or preceptress! No more Colomba!
Down with Colomba!

SOLANGE.—What a dare-devil!

PAUL.—And to begin, I'll write a little note to Mademoiselle
Marthe. [*Hunts through his pockets.*] Well, my note-
book will do! Ah! I must have dropped it when I
jumped from the coach! Here's a piece of a pencil, at
any rate. Give me some paper, quickly. Paper!

SOLANGE.—I? Oh, I dare say.

PAUL.—You refuse?

SOLANGE.—You'll want me to deliver your letter, too, very
likely.

PAUL.—Of course.

SOLANGE.—Well, just wait a minute. Did you ever hear the
like? [*Aside.*] I must go, or he'll end by coaxing me.

PAUL.—Solange, my dear Solange.

SOLANGE.—None of that! Go away, you saucy boy.   [*Exit.*

PAUL.—And I counted on her. What shall I do? [*Feels in
his pockets.*] There's the pencil all right—but the
paper? Ah! [*Falls upon a bench and finds himself
facing Thirion's horn of paper.*] Oh, Providence! This
horn! [*Takes it up and shakes it.*] What's that?—a
little bell? [*Opens and looks in.*] A beetle!—Some of

my guardian's game. Bah! One more or less in his collection! He'll think he lost it on the way. [*Shakes out the beetle.*] That animal should offer up a candle to love—he's saved from the camphor-bottle. [*He tears off the burnt edge.*] So! That looks better! It's written on, but there's one side blank. What luck! [*Writes.*] "I have returned. They want to make me study for my bachelor's degree, but I don't want to be a bachelor, I want to be your husband. I am hidden in the conservatory. Yours for life "—

THIRION [*outside*].—The paper?

PAUL [*rising*].—Somebody—my guardian!

[*Disappears among the plants.*

Enter Suzanne, Busonier, and Thirion.

THIRION.—But what paper?—But which paper? I don't understand a word of what you're saying.

SUZANNE.—Don't scream so loud.

THIRION [*lowering his voice*].—What paper?

SUZANNE.—That Prosper—

THIRION.—Lighted!

SUZANNE.—Threw from the window—

THIRION.—That I picked up!—

SUZANNE.—That you took from his hands.

THIRION.—Ah! The bit of burnt paper. Speak!—Was that it?

SUZANNE.—At last!

THIRION [*without heeding her*].—Now, just put yourself in my place. You say, "the paper." What paper? There are so many pa—

SUZANNE [*impatiently to Busonier*].—Oh! He's even more provoking than you.

THIRION.—If you had said at once the scrap of paper—

SUZANNE.—Well then, the scrap of paper. So! The scrap of paper. Where is—the scrap of paper?

THIRION.—Strange! You want that paltry fragment——

SUZANNE.—Yes!

THIRION.—But you know it was burnt.

SUZANNE AND BUSONIER [*exasperated, accenting every syllable*].—What—did—you—do—with—it?

THIRION.—Why, I made a little horn of it.

SUZANNE.—A little horn?

THIRION.—Yes, to hold my coleoptera, which was tickling the palm of my hand most abominably!

SUZANNE.—Where is this horn?

THIRION.—Why, there! In the barrel of my gun.

BUSONIER.—At last!

THIRION [*grumblingly*].—At last!

SUZANNE.—At last I have it!

THIRION [*looking into his gun*].—Gone!

SUZANNE.—Lost!

THIRION.—Oh, that rascal of a beetle. He must have worked about until he tumbled to the ground—cage and all.

SUZANNE.—Then he can't be far. Let us look for him.

[*All hunt on the floor.*

THIRION [*searching among the plants*].—Remarkable!—The intelligence of these animals! What an interesting paper I can write about it for the entomological society of Chinon. [*Uttering a cry.*] Ah! [*Suzanne and Busonier run up, thinking he has found the horn.*] I will call it—" A Prisoner's Escape "—or, " A Coleoptera in the Bastille "—or——

SUZANNE.—Nothing!

THIRION AND BUSONIER.—Nothing!

SUZANNE.—Oh, there's no use saying: " We must find it." Look for it—Look! [*Perceiving Vanhove.*] No!— Don't look!

BUSONIER AND THIRION [*stupefied*].—Ah!

Enter Vanhove, Clarisse, Marthe, Colomba, the hunters, Baptiste, and Henri.

VANHOVE.—Well, aren't we going to dine to-day?

MARTHE.—Yes—dinner is ready.

BAPTISTE.—Dinner is on the table, madame.

ALL.—Ah!

BUSONIER.—Welcome news!

CLARISSE [*aside to Suzanne*].—He's gone?

SUZANNE [*still searching with her eyes*].—The beetle? Yes, he's gone.

CLARISSE.—The beetle?

SUZANNE.—Oh no! Him!—Prosper! Yes, yes, my friend. [*Aside.*] Poor boy, searching out there.

CLARISSE.—He's gone!—and the letter burned! Ah, Suzanne, at last I breathe again.

SUZANNE [*aside*].—I—suffocate.

VANHOVE [*aside*].—She is worried. She cannot have succeeded with that man. Now I must take the affair upon myself. [*Offers his arm to Suzanne.*] Suzanne!

SUZANNE [*with a last look on the ground, takes his arm mechanically*].—Thanks, my friend.

MARTHE.—Have you lost anything?

SUZANNE.—Yes, a little brooch.

VANHOVE.—There?

SUZANNE.—Oh, don't stop to look for it. It's not worth the trouble. [*To Marthe.*] Tell Solange to come here a minute.

MARTHE.—All right. [*Aside.*] To think that Paul hasn't come! [*Exeunt to dining-room.*

Enter Paul.

PAUL [*coming out from the foliage, on all fours, letter in hand*]. —At last! There I've been listening to the buzzing of words for a quarter of an hour. [*Rubbing his hands and legs.*] Anything but comfortable in there!—with plants pricking my arms, plants pricking my legs—I say, who's going to carry my letter?

Enter Claudine.

CLAUDINE [*admiring lace collar she is wearing*].—There! Now I look like somebody! [*Seeing Paul.*] Hello! The little dark-eyed fellow! The tall blonde's young man.

PAUL [*turning away in alarm*].—Oh!

CLAUDINE.—The gentleman is perhaps looking for the dining-room?

PAUL.—Oh, mademoiselle—Don't tell anybody you saw me. Not a word!

CLAUDINE.—Make your mind easy. It's my business to be discreet.

PAUL [*aside*].—Discreet! In fact—my letter! I've read of such things in novels. If I were to try! [*Aloud.*] Mademoiselle!

CLAUDINE.—Sir?

PAUL [*embarrassed*].—You are very pretty.

CLAUDINE.—So I've been told, sir.

PAUL [*looking down*].—And with good reason. Only—there's one thing lacking——

CLAUDINE [*looking at him*].—What's that? Eyes?

PAUL.—Oh, no. They're all right. [*Timidly.*] I meant, a pair of pretty ear-rings.

CLAUDINE [*aside*].—Oho! Bribery and corruption.

PAUL [*aside*].—I hope she won't be offended. [*Aloud.*] If I dared. [*Slips his purse into her hand.*

CLAUDINE.—Anything you please, sir.

PAUL [*delighted*].—May I? Then take this little note, will you?

CLAUDINE.—I needn't ask who it's for.

PAUL.—You'll give it—

CLAUDINE.—While I'm changing the plates.

PAUL.—Ah! Marton or Lisette! Wait! I must kiss you!

CLAUDINE.—That one's for me. I'll keep it.

[*Exit to dining-room.*

PAUL.—I'm coming on! A runaway! Clandestine *billet-doux!* Conquest of a soubrette!—Again somebody! The devil take him! [*Hides.*

Enter Prosper, wrapped in his shawl.

PROSPER.—Nothing, nothing, nothing!—Nothing but a beastly cold and the appetite of a wolf. They're dining without me. This is the last straw. I enter panting and blowing, in an absurd costume, with the appetite of a drover—absolutely ridiculous! Ah, Prosper!—After three years of voyaging, to be wrecked by a woman's breath—blush at thine own disgrace!—And if there's any pride left in thee, behold thyself in this shawl. What grotesque monster dost thou resemble? Hercules in the shirt of Nessus. It devours thee, it eats into thy flesh, it burns thy bones, and thou hast not the wit to take it off. Thou wearest it for the sake of its owner, whom thou lovest. Speak out, miserable wretch! Thou lovest her—thou lovest her so that with the appetite of a wolf thou'lt stand reciting thy monologue, instead of going to dinner. Go eat, buffoon!—go eat!

Enter Solange.

SOLANGE.—Monsieur!

PROSPER.—Don't stop me—I'm hungry. [*Solange tries to hold him by his shawl.*] Don't touch my shawl!

SOLANGE.—But are you not Monsieur Prosper?

PROSPER.—Yes—Prosper Block, who's half famished! But don't touch my shawl.

SOLANGE.—But Mademoiselle Suzanne——

PROSPER [*turning quickly*].—Mademoiselle Suzanne?

SOLANGE.—She said I was to watch for monsieur on his return——

PROSPER.—Speak!

SOLANGE.—And to say to monsieur that she'd lost a little horn——

PROSPER.—A horn?

SOLANGE.—Of paper, with a little bug in it.

PROSPER.—A little beast? A horn of paper with a little bug? Well, what's that to me?

SOLANGE.—She said to beg you to look for it immediately.

PROSPER.—Look for it? Immediately? And my dinner?

SOLANGE.—She didn't say anything about dinner.—Only she said I was to ask you for her shawl.

PROSPER [*gives up the shawl*].—Her shawl! The last straw! [*Falls upon a bench.*] I am dead.

SOLANGE.—Sir!

PROSPER.—Go! Go!—[*Exit Solange.*]—If I search, I don't dine. If I don't search, but enter, I don't dine; for her threatening eyes will destroy my appetite. I am her slave, her negro slave. [*Rises.*] She wants her horn —immediately!—and her little bug. Some ridiculous whim—Absurd! No matter, I enter upon my duties. Bridled, muzzled! I would have it so. Come, search, Bow-wow.—Search for thy mistress' horn, and the little bug. Search!

[*Begins to hunt about, and disappears in the shrubbery for a moment.*

PAUL [*coming out*].—I hear nothing. He must be at dinner. [*Looking towards the dining-room.*] Ah, the door is open—I see them all. They're going to change the plates. [*Prosper comes down, hunting to right and left.*] There's Claudine making a sign to me. Yes, yes! Now she's taking a plate.—Now she's going—where is she going then? Oh, the stupid, it is not—She's given the letter to Colomba. [*Cries out.*] Oh!

PROSPER.—What's that?

PAUL.—Somebody!—I'm lost. [*Vanishes in the shrubbery.*

PROSPER.—I heard a cry. I must have stepped on the beast. [*Looks around and picks up the fragment of burnt paper.*] It can't be that! [*He opens it.*] A fragment of burnt paper! Blue paper! [*Reads.*] The ends of words—" My mother—hove—hove—" Vanhove! It's the letter. Here! Torn! How?——

Enter Vanhove.

[*Turns and sees Vanhove.*] Ah, good. That's how!

VANHOVE.—I thought I heard a cry.

PROSPER [*aside*].—We're to cut each other's throats here, it seems! Very good! But after dinner!

VANHOVE [*perceiving him*].—Ah, it's you.

PROSPER.—I beg your pardon, sir, I'm afraid I've kept you waiting. [*Starts to enter the dining-room.*

VANHOVE.—Two words, sir, if you please.

PROSPER [*aside*].—It's decreed I shall fight on an empty stomach.

VANHOVE.—Do you still persist in the request you made me this morning, sir? [*Clatter of plates.*

PROSPER [*with a regretful glance at the dining-room*].—Yes —and no. [*Aside.*] Confound it, I'd forgotten all about that. [*Aloud.*] Yes, on principle—but, in reality, no, no!

VANHOVE.—Explain yourself!

PROSPER.—I will explain.—Madame Vanhove showed such a great repugnance to this union——

VANHOVE.—For good reasons.

PROSPER.—Reasons! [*Aside.*] I'm spoiling everything. A

little assurance. [*Aloud.*] What reasons, sir? For what reasons?

VANHOVE [*quietly*].—Possibly your forgetfulness of an old love which it would pain her to see sacrificed to a new one.

PROSPER.—Indeed! [*Aside.*] He's come to the point at once. So much the better. [*Aloud.*] I see you know all, sir.

VANHOVE.—All!

PROSPER [*rising*].—Then perhaps you'll be willing to defer our conversation until after dinner.

VANHOVE.—No, sir! The matter is too serious to admit of any delay.

PROSPER.—Oh, not so serious as you imagine. I loved the lady—whom, you know; we exchanged a few confidences, a few letters, it's true. But permit me to say that I confined myself to the most respectful homage —the purest kind of love—and that her virtue——

VANHOVE.—No, sir!

PROSPER.—No, sir? What do you mean?

VANHOVE.—No, sir! No!

PROSPER.—Thunder and lightning, this is a most unfortunate misapprehension, and I give you my word of honor——

VANHOVE.—Don't swear. She is guilty. She has confessed it to me.

PROSPER.—She has confessed?

VANHOVE.—All.

PROSPER.—But what? All what? There wasn't the half, nor the quarter——

VANHOVE.—All.

PROSPER.—She can't have accused herself of what didn't exist. Woman's slander doesn't go that far.

VANHOVE.—All, I tell you. Your desertion, for an imagined betrayal; your voyages; your return, and the light way in which you treat the love which she still feels for you.

PROSPER [*aside*].—The love—Well! Her choice of a confidant is what tickles me. [*Aloud.*] Then she told you? Quite simply, like that?

VANHOVE.—No matter how—she told me.

PROSPER.—Charming! And you have come?

VANHOVE.—Yes.

PROSPER.—To offer me?

VANHOVE.—Yes.

PROSPER.—A duel?

VANHOVE.—No—a reconciliation with her.

PROSPER.—What? Beg pardon?

VANHOVE.—I said—a reconciliation with her.

PROSPER.—You! To reconcile me!

VANHOVE.—The honor of my house demands it.

PROSPER.—Oh, it's your honor.—[*Aside.*] He understands it as they do in the Marquesas Islands.

VANHOVE [*offering his hand*].—And so, sir, I offer you my hand as a friend.

PROSPER.—Ah, you are very kind! Very kind, indeed! [*Aside.*] Too kind!

VANHOVE.—Make her happy——

PROSPER.—Yes, sir. Yes, sir.

VANHOVE.—And me too.

PROSPER [*aside*].—And him too! He says that with an air of dignity!—[*Aloud.*] Thunder and lightning, sir, have you thought over what you are proposing to me? If I should refuse, sir?

VANHOVE.—If you should refuse! Ah! I would kill you.

PROSPER.—Ah!

VANHOVE.—Without fail! For it shall not be said that a gentle and good woman trusted to your love and that you refused her the satisfaction which she has a right to expect.

PROSPER.—The satisfaction—I refuse her—

VANHOVE.—That's what I said.

PROSPER [*aside*].—Satisfaction! What high-sounding words!

VANHOVE.—Your choice, sir?

PROSPER.—It's all up. I prefer to fight. But, thunder and lightning, surely this will be the first time that ever a husband fought in order that his wife might——

VANHOVE.—Sir, I beg you not to mix my wife's name up in this.

PROSPER.—Sir, it's necessary.

VANHOVE.—No, sir, it's not necessary. Your weapons?

PROSPER.—Are those you choose.

Enter Suzanne and Clarisse.

SUZANNE [*aside*].—Just what I feared!

CLARISSE [*aside*].—A challenge?

SUZANNE [*throwing herself between them*].—Ah, Prosper! Have Vanhove's arguments been of no more avail than my tears?

PROSPER [*surprised*].—Hey?

SUZANNE.—Must I then throw myself at your feet while I appeal to your honor?

VANHOVE [*restraining her*].—Isn't that what you want?

PROSPER.—What under the sun does all this mean?

SUZANNE.—No, my friend! No! Your Suzanne has never been guilty. [*Softly to Prosper.*] Bear me out in all I say. [*Aloud.*] No, I have never betrayed my vows. You know it well. [*Softly.*] Talk as I do.

PROSPER.—But!——

SUZANNE.—But never was truer love repaid with such ingratitude.

PROSPER.—Me?

SUZANNE.—Stupid! [*Aloud.*] And if you refuse to retrieve my honor——

PROSPER [*softly*].—I—

SUZANNE.—I will kill myself. Yes!—And it's you—you who will have dealt the fatal blow. Speak, sir, speak! Speak!

PROSPER.—Ah! I must then—[*Aside.*] I don't understand a word, but I have her now. [*To Vanhove.*] Ah, I must then——

VANHOVE. Yes!

PROSPER. —Very well, very well! I understand, I understand.

VANHOVE.—What is your answer?

PROSPER.—Well, my answer, my answer—[*Resolutely.*] Is all that quite true, madame?

SUZANNE [*effusively*].—Ah! [*Apart to him.*] Bravo! Well done!

PROSPER [*aside*].—Bravo! Well done! Oh, just wait a bit. [*Aloud.*] You swear that you have been faithful to me?

SUZANNE.—Ah! Do you ask that?

VANHOVE.—Do you ask that?

PROSPER.—No, sir, no! I no longer ask it.

SUZANNE [*aside to Prosper*].—Good! Courage!

PROSPER.—You love me?

SUZANNE [*with ardor*].—Ah! [*Aside to Prosper.*] Make-believe.

PROSPER [*aside*].—Ah! Of course! Make-believe. [*Aloud.*] And I too, madame, I love you.

SUZANNE [*aside*].—Make-believe.

PROSPER [*apart*].—Ah! Of course! Make-believe! [*Aloud.*] And I call monsieur to witness this mutual affection.

SUZANNE [*aside*].—Enough! Enough!

PROSPER.—And I will marry you, madame, on my word of honor—I will marry you when you will.

VANHOVE.—At last!

SUZANNE [*aside*].—Always in make-believe.

PROSPER [*aside*].—Ah! Of course! Make-believe in good earnest. In good earnest! [*Aloud.*] Come to my arms, Suzanne, come to my arms.

SUZANNE [*drawing back*].—Oh! But——

VANHOVE [*pushing her into Prosper's arms*].—Never mind us, Suzanne. It's all in the family.

PROSPER [*embracing her*].—Ah! My dear Suzanne!

SUZANNE.—Ah! Prosper! [*Aside.*] Ah! Traitor!

PROSPER.—Get out of this if you can!

Enter Thirion, Busonier, Colomba, Marthe, the three hunters, Baptiste, and Henri.

VANHOVE.—Gentlemen, I have the honor of announcing the marriage of my cousin, Suzanne, with Monsieur Prosper Block.

ALL.—Ah!

SUZANNE.—What!—Already?

[*All surround them and congratulate them.*

THIRION [*in the foreground, holding the scrap of blue paper in his hand. He is slightly intoxicated*].—A letter to Colomba! A letter that I seized without being seen, at the moment when the waitress was slipping it under her plate. Ah! The emotion!—the champagne! I am suffocated. Let me read. [*Reads.*] "I leave to-night, but far or near, my love—" He calls Colomba his love. Ah, wretch!—If I knew! And no signature!

[*Folds the paper.*

VANHOVE [*coming down with a cup of coffee*].—Don't you take coffee, Thirion? [*Thirion tries to put on a good face.*] What a face! [*To Prosper.*] Just look!

THIRION.—An idea! The master of the house! He must know the handwriting of everybody here. [*To Vanhove, giving him the folded paper.*] Who wrote that?

VANHOVE.—That? [*Reads.*] "I have returned——

THIRION.—"I have returned!" He says that he is leaving.

VANHOVE.—" They want me to study for my bachelor's degree "——

THIRION.—His bachelor's degree? No, no—it reads "My love "——

VANHOVE.—"My bachelor's degree "—It's written in lead pencil.

THIRION.—No, no! [*Takes the folded paper and hands it back opened.*] There! There!

PROSPER [*recognizing the letter*].—The letter!
[*Snatches it from Vanhove.*

VANHOVE [*laughing*].—Come, let's see it.

PROSPER.—No, you shall not see it.

VANHOVE [*still laughing at Thirion*].—Hey?

THIRION.—What does this mean?

PROSPER.—It means that I admit nobody here into my confidence.

THIRION.—It's he! He wrote it.

VANHOVE.—This letter—

PROSPER.—Well, yes—I wrote it! What of it?

THIRION.—You! My friend! Under my roof! To declare his passion for Colomba——

VANHOVE [*jumping*].—Eh?

PROSPER [*shrugging his shoulders*].—What nonsense!

VANHOVE.—But, sir, this is monstrous! This morning you ask for the hand of Marthe; this evening you promise to marry Suzanne; and you still find time to love——

THIRION.—Colomba!

COLOMBA [*coming forward*].—Yes, dear?

PROSPER.—What nonsense! Who's thinking of loving Colomba?

THIRION.—You, wretch!

PROSPER.—Do keep still!

THIRION.—You call her " my love! "

PROSPER.—It's a lie!

VANHOVE.—Your proof, sir.

PROSPER [*embarrassed*].—My proof!

[*Showing the letter to Suzanne.*

SUZANNE.—The letter!

CLARISSE.—The letter!

PROSPER.—My proof?—is that I call upon Mademoiselle Suzanne, my future wife, gentlemen, to take cognizance at once.   [*Offers the letter to Suzanne.*

VANHOVE [*snatching the letter*].—So be it! Suzanne!

SUZANNE [*laughing*].—Quite unnecessary, my friend. I know what it is.

VANHOVE.—You know?

SUZANNE.—A mere bit of nonsense. Burn it.

VANHOVE.—Take care, Suzanne. Your happiness is at stake.

SUZANNE [*picking up a lighted candle from the table*].—Burn! Burn!

VANHOVE.—You wish it? [*To Prosper.*] You are a happy man to marry a woman—

[*Lights the paper and throws it on the ground.*

PROSPER [*watching the paper burn*].—Ah, you rogue! You've given us enough trouble.

THIRION.—All the same it was written " my love! "

COLOMBA.—What's that?

SUZANNE.—Good news. We're going to marry Marthe and Paul!

PAUL [*rushing from his hiding place*].—What joy!

COLOMBA.—He was there all the time!

PAUL [*kissing Marthe's hand*].—Ah, how happy I am.

PROSPER [*to Suzanne*].—And I!

SUZANNE.—You! You're going to start for Honolulu!

PROSPER.—With my wife, yes.

SUZANNE.—Never!

CLARISSE.—Ah! My dear Suzanne!

PROSPER.—Ah! My dear Suzanne!

SUZANNE.—I see it's decreed I am to sacrifice myself for everybody—and all on account of a letter——

PROSPER.—Ah, dear little scrap of paper—don't scold it!

SUZANNE.—A pretty chase it has led us.